ADULT
Contemporary

BY

BENDIK KALTENBORN

DRAWN & QUARTERLY

Published by arrangement with No Comprendo Press A/S, Oslo. 2013. nocomprendopress.com

Translated and edited by Bendik Kaltenborn and Tom Devlin.

This translation has been published with the financial support of NORLA.

ISBN 978-1-77046-175-8. First edition: August 2015. Printed in China. 10 9 8 7 6 5 4 3 2 1

drawnandquarterly.com

Library and Archives Canada Cataloguing in Publication

Kaltbenborn, Bendik, 1981-

[Liker stilen. English]

Adult contemporary / Bendik Kaltbenborn.

Translation of: Liker stilen.

Liker Stilen was originally published in Oslo in 2013 by No Comprendo Press.

ISBN 978-1-77046-175-8 (pbk.)

1. Graphic novels. I. Title. II. Title: Liker stilen. English.

PN6790.N674L5413 2014 741.5'9481 C2014-903570-5

Published in the USA by Drawn & Quarterly, a client publisher of Farrar, Straus and Giroux

Orders: 888.330.8477

Published in Canada by Drawn & Quarterly, a client publisher of Raincoast Books

Orders: 800.663.5714

Published in the UK by Drawn & Quarterly, a client publisher of Publishers Group UK

Orders: info@pguk.co.uk

Special thanks to Dongery, Yokoland, Aslak Gurholt Rønsen, Espen Friberg, Espen Holtestaul, Cis-Doris Andreassen, Kristoffer Kjølberg, Gerd Elise Mørland, Todd Terje Olsen, Anne Schäffer, Matthias Wivel, Xue Ting Yang, Snorre Bryne, Gabriel Vossgraf Moro, Lars Fiske, Sindre Goksøyr, Flu Hartberg, Martin Lundell, Håvard «Lillezmurf», Daniel Herskedal, Jim Woodring, Joost Swarte, Marc Bell, Martin Asbjørnsen, Tronsmo, my family, my friends, and Blaffen.

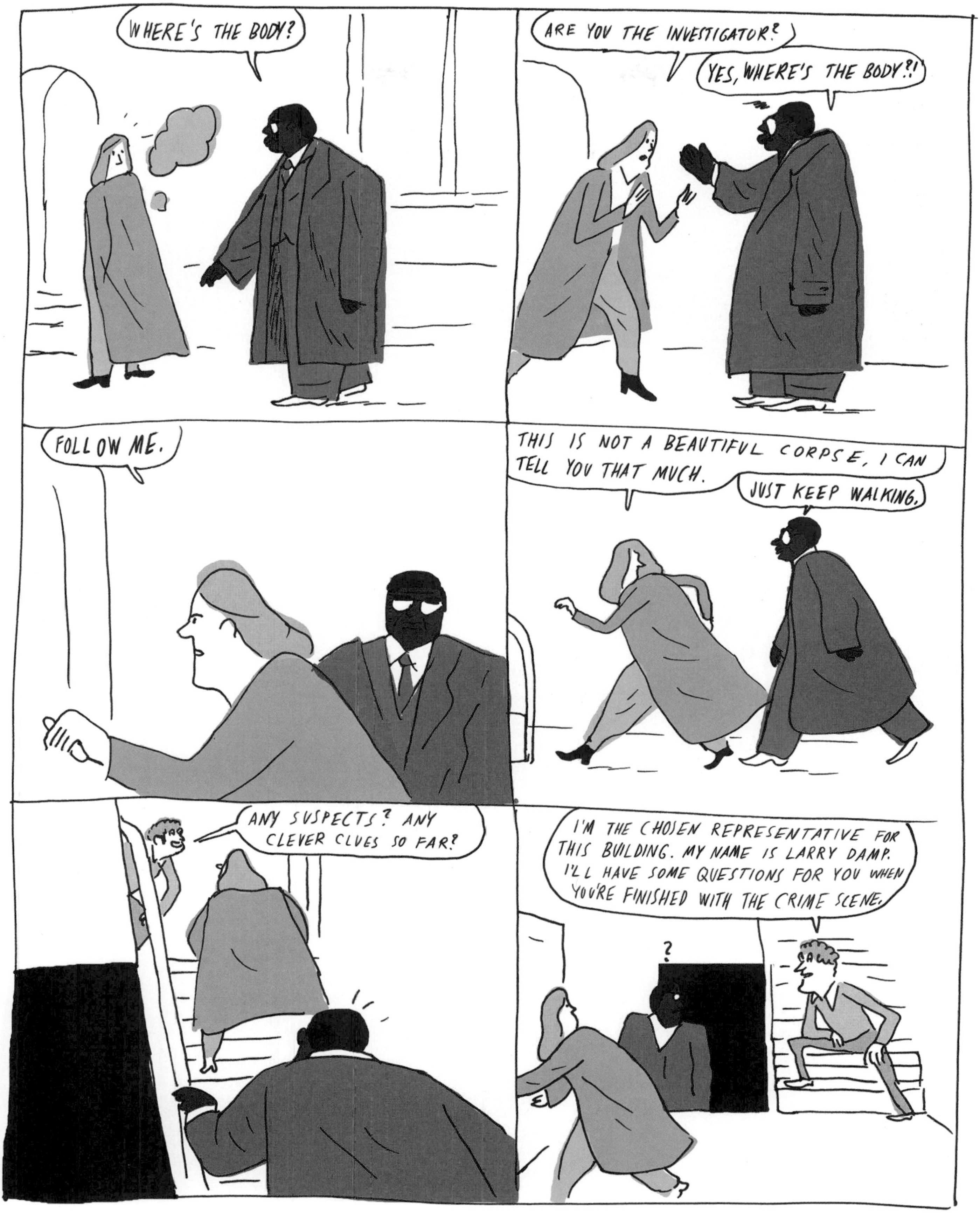
WHERE'S THE BODY?
ARE YOU THE INVESTIGATOR?
YES, WHERE'S THE BODY?!
FOLLOW ME.
THIS IS NOT A BEAUTIFUL CORPSE, I CAN TELL YOU THAT MUCH.
JUST KEEP WALKING.
ANY SUSPECTS? ANY CLEVER CLUES SO FAR?
?
I'M THE CHOSEN REPRESENTATIVE FOR THIS BUILDING. MY NAME IS LARRY DAMP. I'LL HAVE SOME QUESTIONS FOR YOU WHEN YOU'RE FINISHED WITH THE CRIME SCENE.

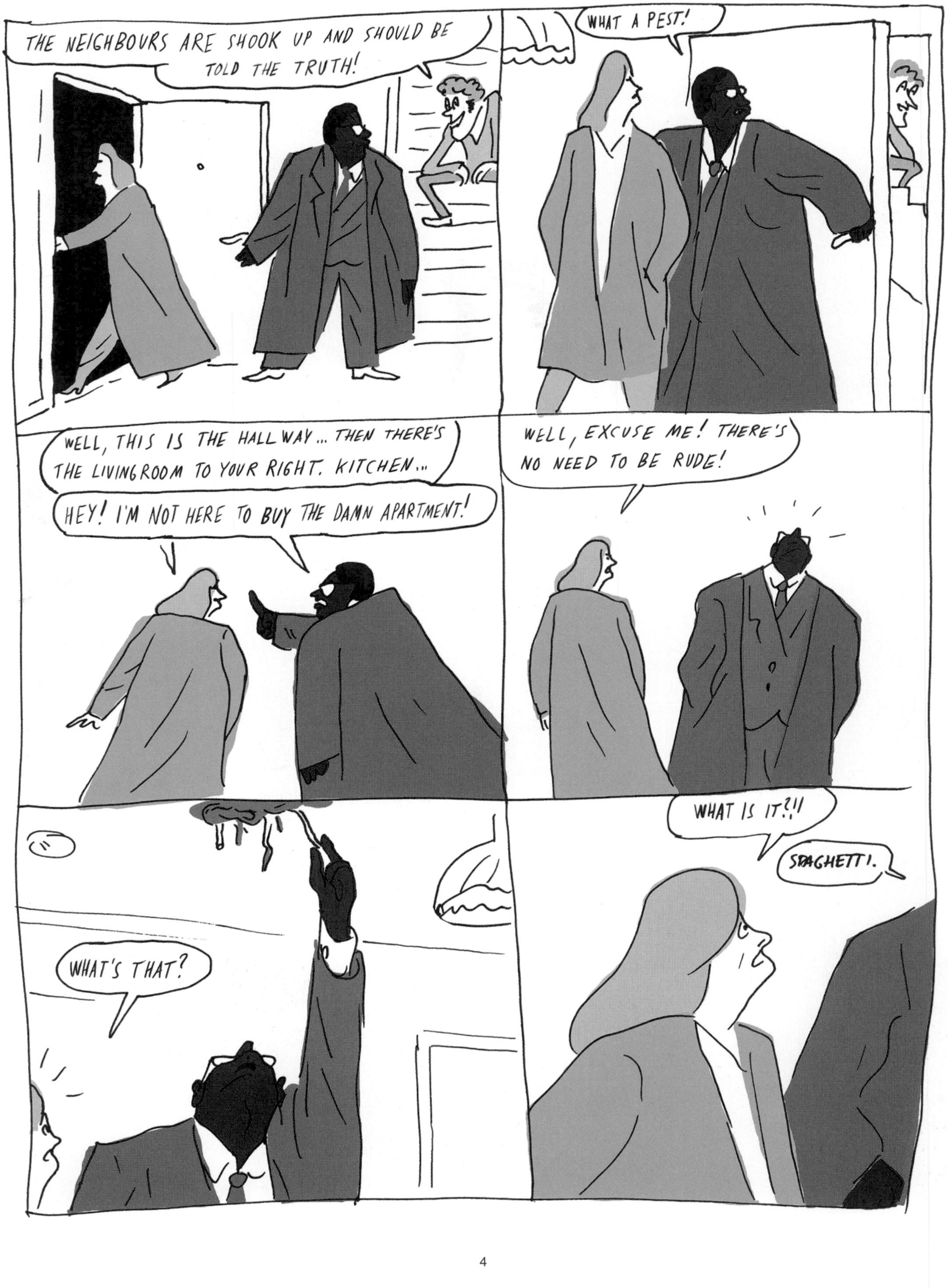
THE NEIGHBOURS ARE SHOOK UP AND SHOULD BE TOLD THE TRUTH!
WHAT A PEST!
WELL, THIS IS THE HALLWAY... THEN THERE'S THE LIVINGROOM TO YOUR RIGHT. KITCHEN...
HEY! I'M NOT HERE TO BUY THE DAMN APARTMENT!
WELL, EXCUSE ME! THERE'S NO NEED TO BE RUDE!
WHAT'S THAT?
WHAT IS IT?!!
SPAGHETTI.

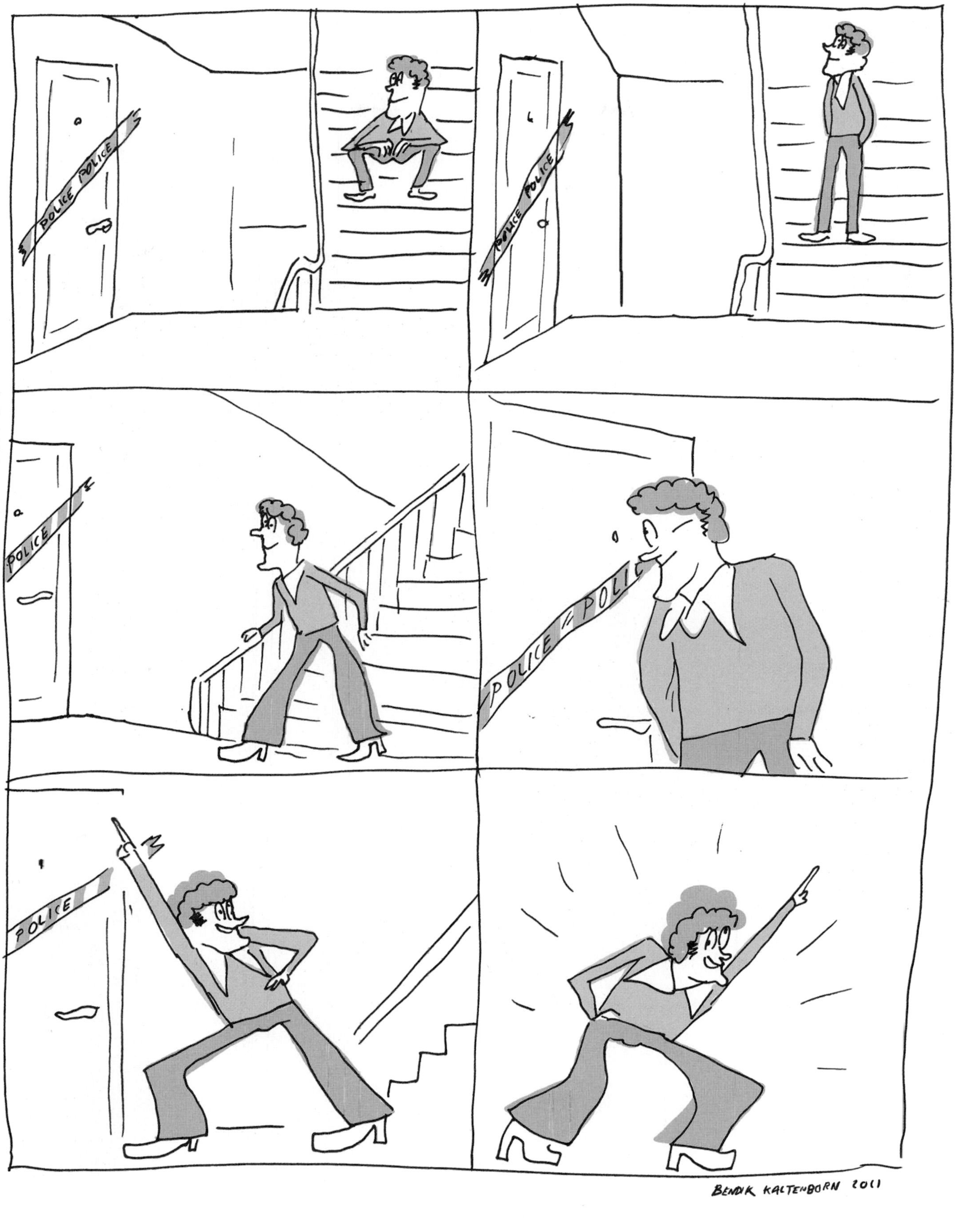
POLICE POLICE
POLICE POLICE
POLICE
POLICE POLI
POLICE
BENDIK KALTENBORN 2011

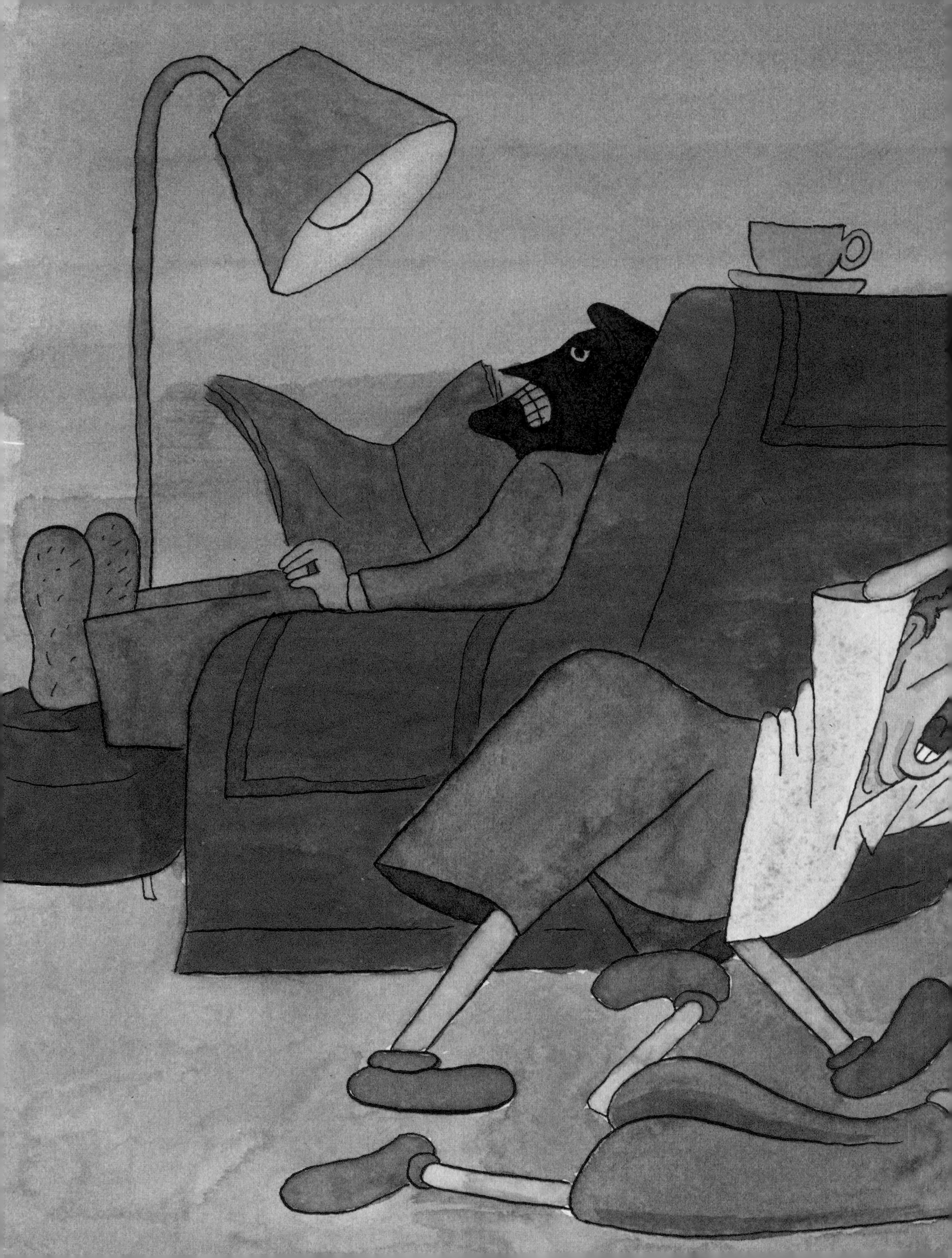

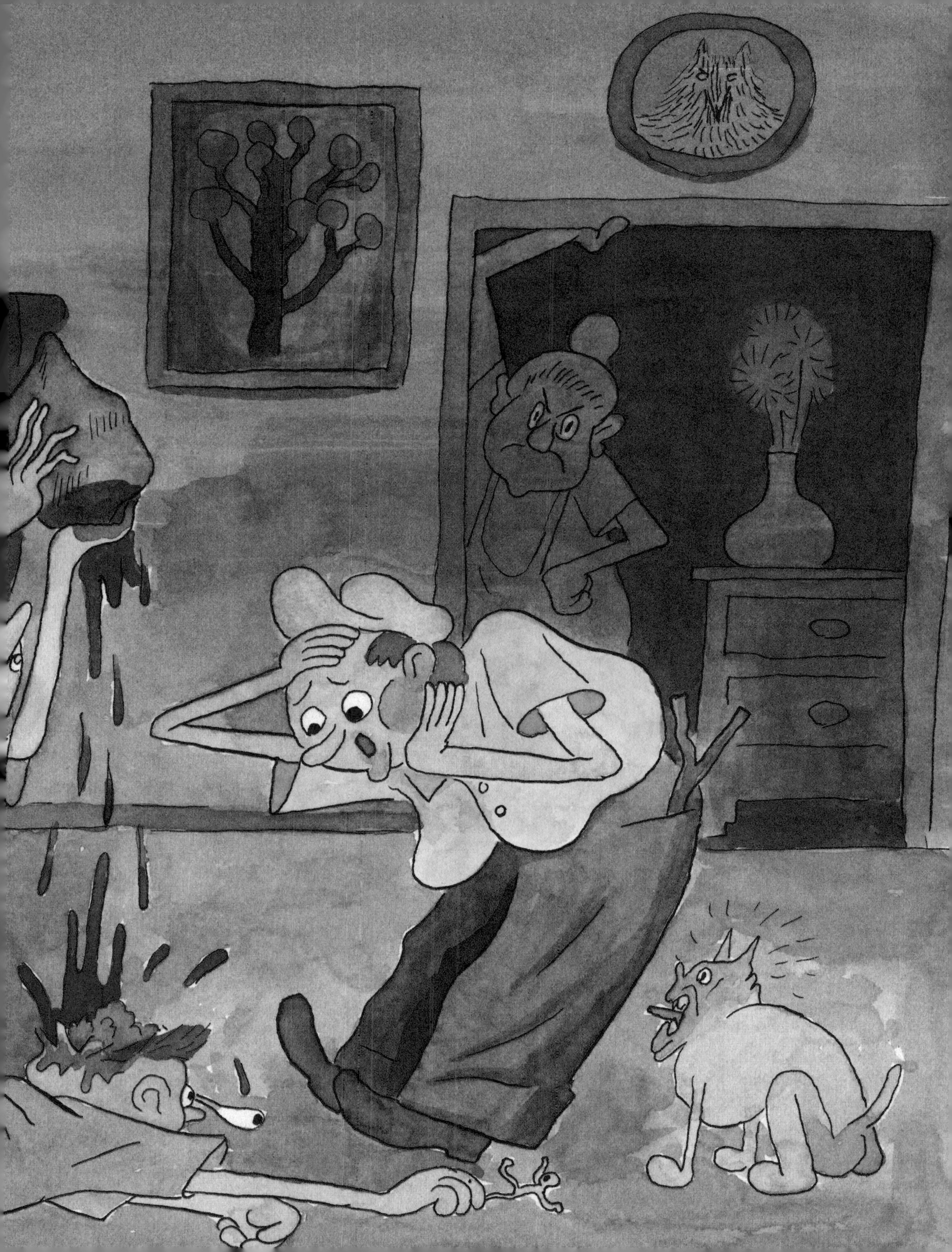

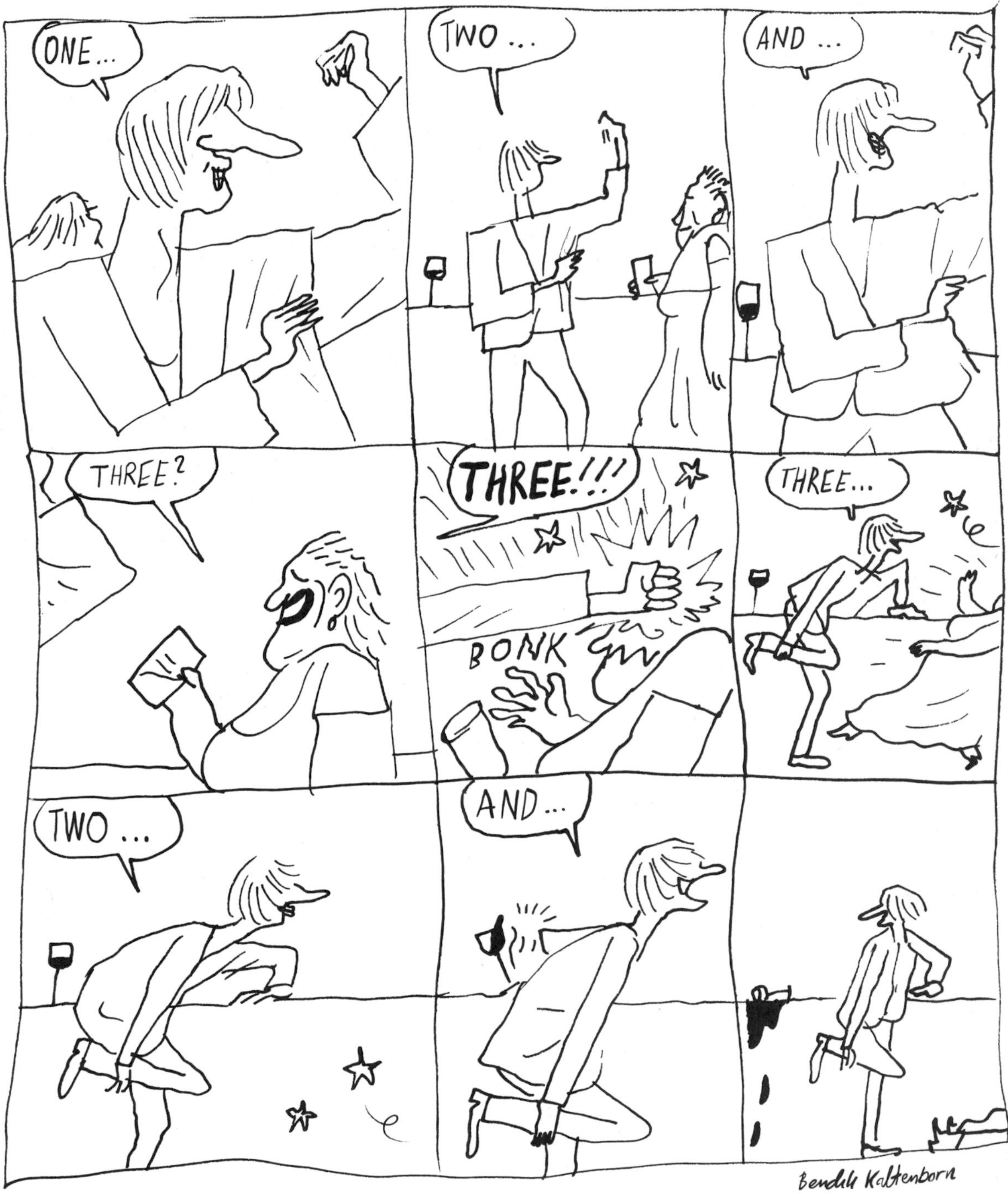

ONE...
TWO ...
AND ...
THREE?
THREE!!!!
BONK
THREE...
TWO ...
AND...
Bendik Kaltenborn

DADDY-O

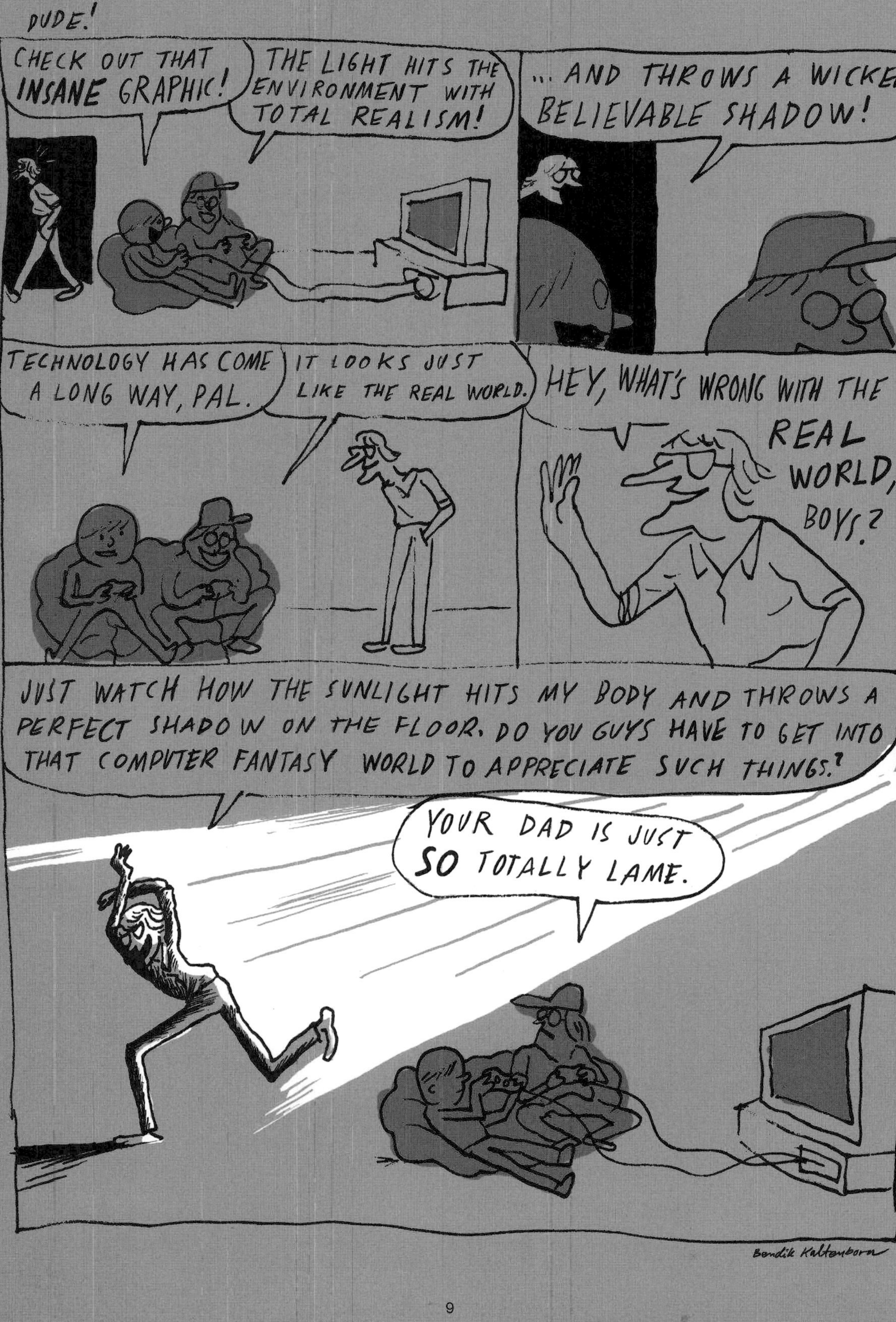
DUDE!
CHECK OUT THAT INSANE GRAPHIC!
THE LIGHT HITS THE ENVIRONMENT WITH TOTAL REALISM!
... AND THROWS A WICKED BELIEVABLE SHADOW!
TECHNOLOGY HAS COME A LONG WAY, PAL.
IT LOOKS JUST LIKE THE REAL WORLD.
HEY, WHAT'S WRONG WITH THE REAL WORLD, BOYS?
JUST WATCH HOW THE SUNLIGHT HITS MY BODY AND THROWS A PERFECT SHADOW ON THE FLOOR. DO YOU GUYS HAVE TO GET INTO THAT COMPUTER FANTASY WORLD TO APPRECIATE SUCH THINGS?
YOUR DAD IS JUST SO TOTALLY LAME.
Bendik Kaltenborn

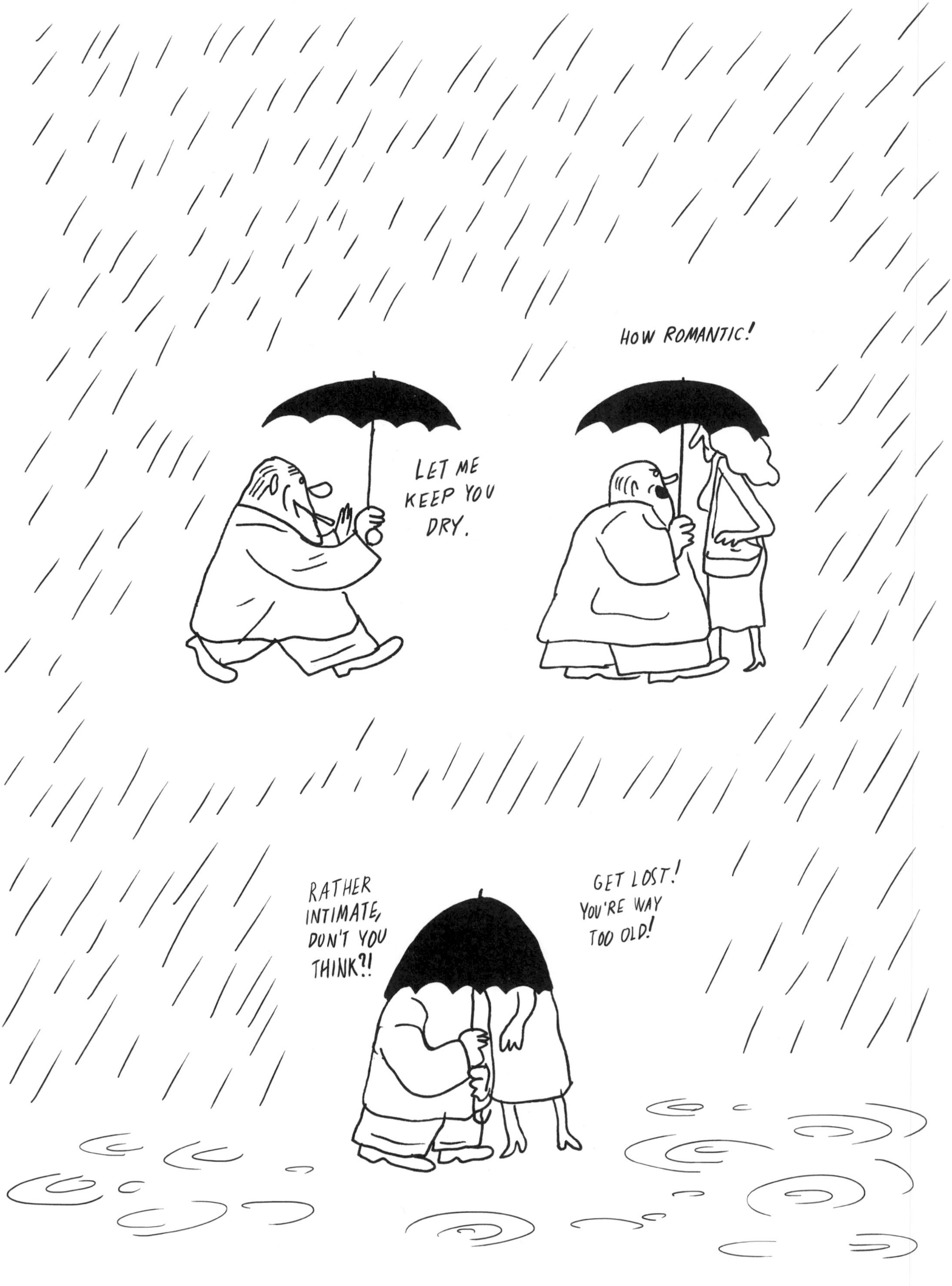
LET ME KEEP YOU DRY.
HOW ROMANTIC!
RATHER INTIMATE, DON'T YOU THINK?!
GET LOST! YOU'RE WAY TOO OLD!

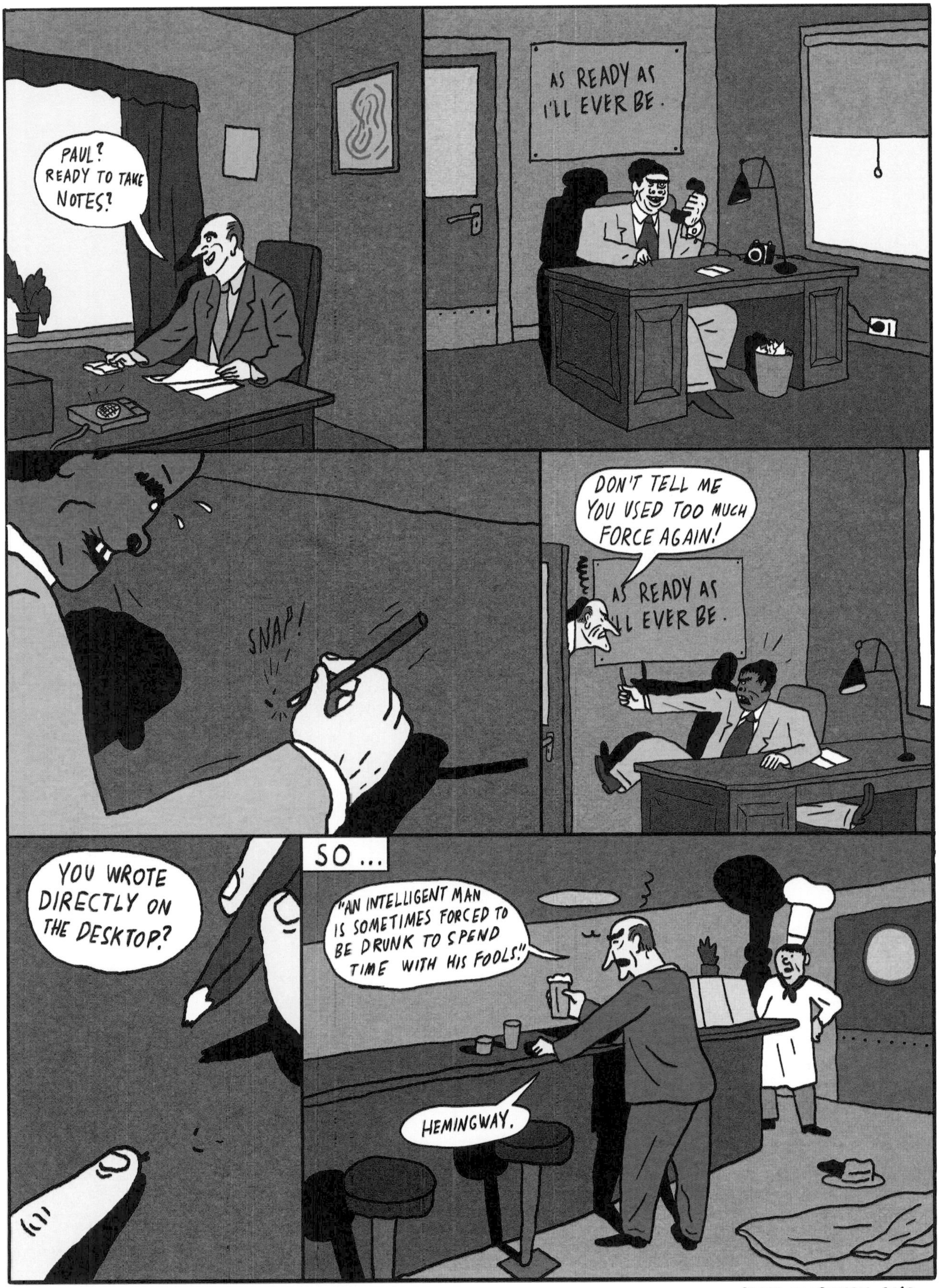
PAUL? READY TO TAKE NOTES?
AS READY AS I'LL EVER BE.
SNAP!
DON'T TELL ME YOU USED TOO MUCH FORCE AGAIN!
AS READY AS I'LL EVER BE.
YOU WROTE DIRECTLY ON THE DESKTOP?
SO...
"AN INTELLIGENT MAN IS SOMETIMES FORCED TO BE DRUNK TO SPEND TIME WITH HIS FOOLS."
HEMINGWAY.

BENDIK KALTENBORN · 2010

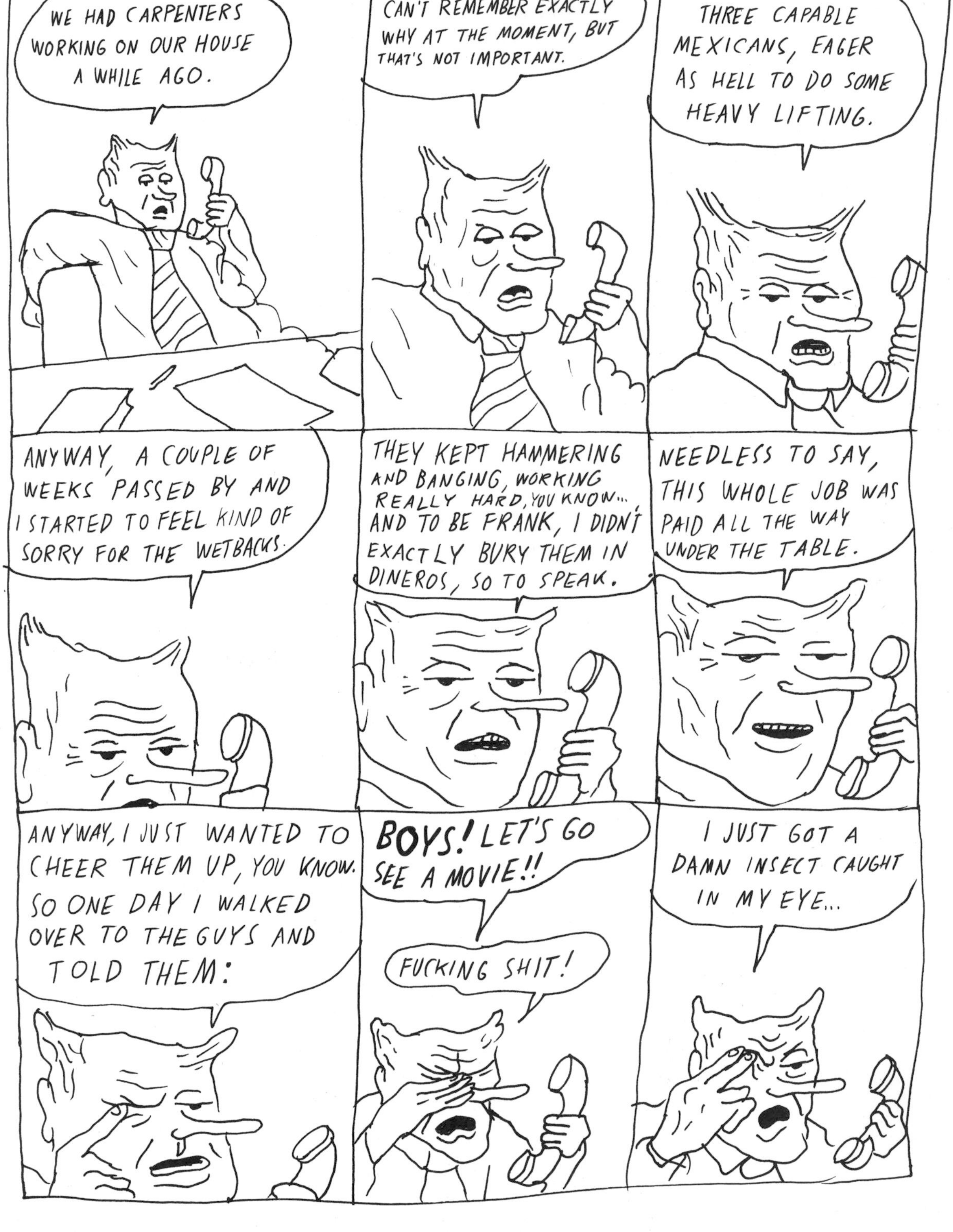
WE HAD CARPENTERS WORKING ON OUR HOUSE A WHILE AGO.
CAN'T REMEMBER EXACTLY WHY AT THE MOMENT, BUT THAT'S NOT IMPORTANT.
THREE CAPABLE MEXICANS, EAGER AS HELL TO DO SOME HEAVY LIFTING.
ANYWAY, A COUPLE OF WEEKS PASSED BY AND I STARTED TO FEEL KIND OF SORRY FOR THE WETBACKS.
THEY KEPT HAMMERING AND BANGING, WORKING REALLY HARD, YOU KNOW... AND TO BE FRANK, I DIDN'T EXACTLY BURY THEM IN DINEROS, SO TO SPEAK.
NEEDLESS TO SAY, THIS WHOLE JOB WAS PAID ALL THE WAY UNDER THE TABLE.
ANYWAY, I JUST WANTED TO CHEER THEM UP, YOU KNOW. SO ONE DAY I WALKED OVER TO THE GUYS AND TOLD THEM:
BOYS! LET'S GO SEE A MOVIE!!
FUCKING SHIT!
I JUST GOT A DAMN INSECT CAUGHT IN MY EYE...

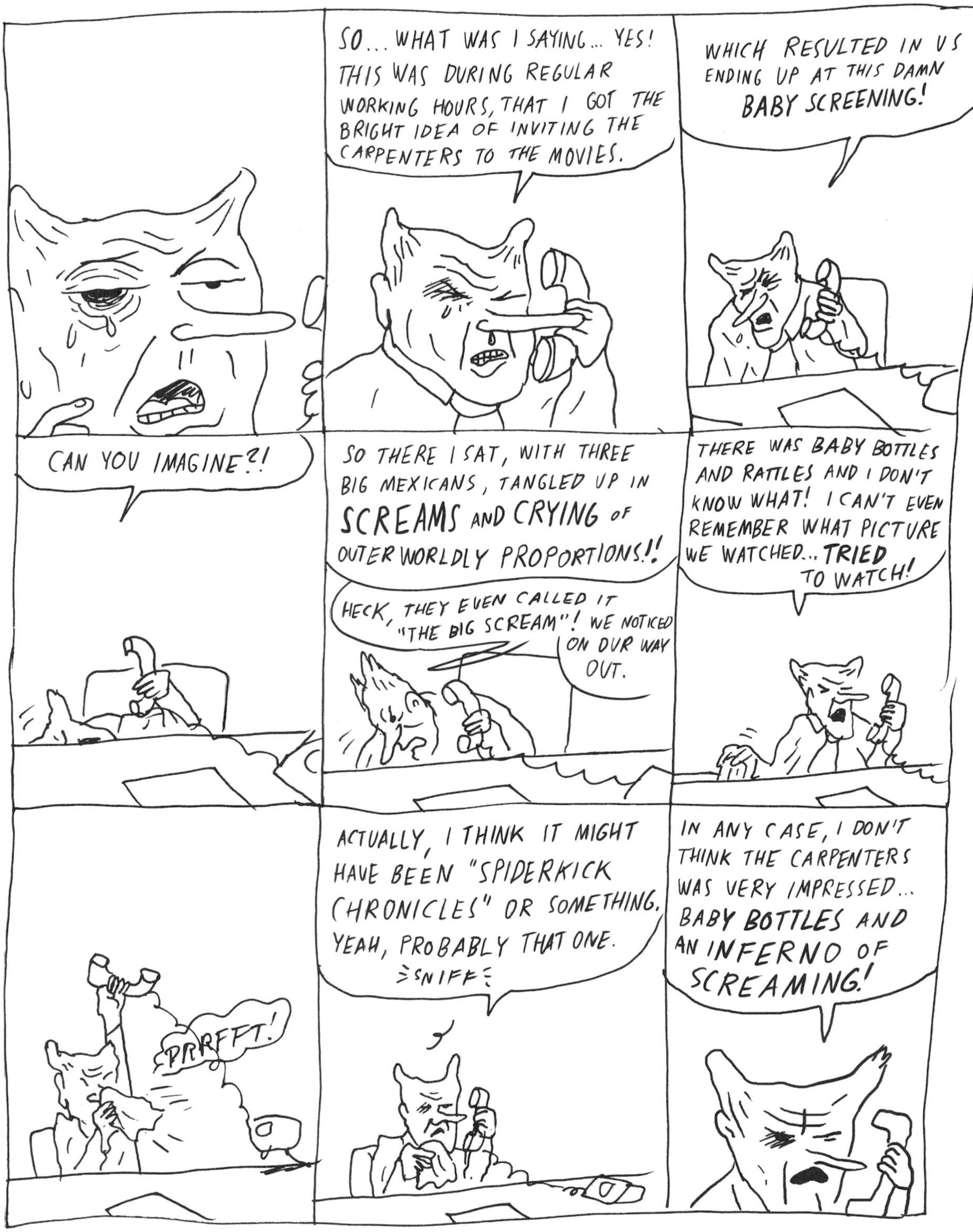
SO... WHAT WAS I SAYING... YES! THIS WAS DURING REGULAR WORKING HOURS, THAT I GOT THE BRIGHT IDEA OF INVITING THE CARPENTERS TO THE MOVIES.
WHICH RESULTED IN US ENDING UP AT THIS DAMN BABY SCREENING!
CAN YOU IMAGINE?!
SO THERE I SAT, WITH THREE BIG MEXICANS, TANGLED UP IN SCREAMS AND CRYING OF OUTER WORLDLY PROPORTIONS!!
HECK, THEY EVEN CALLED IT "THE BIG SCREAM"! WE NOTICED ON OUR WAY OUT.
THERE WAS BABY BOTTLES AND RATTLES AND I DON'T KNOW WHAT! I CAN'T EVEN REMEMBER WHAT PICTURE WE WATCHED... TRIED TO WATCH!
PRRFFT!
ACTUALLY, I THINK IT MIGHT HAVE BEEN "SPIDERKICK CHRONICLES" OR SOMETHING. YEAH, PROBABLY THAT ONE.
SNIFF
IN ANY CASE, I DON'T THINK THE CARPENTERS WAS VERY IMPRESSED... BABY BOTTLES AND AN INFERNO OF SCREAMING!

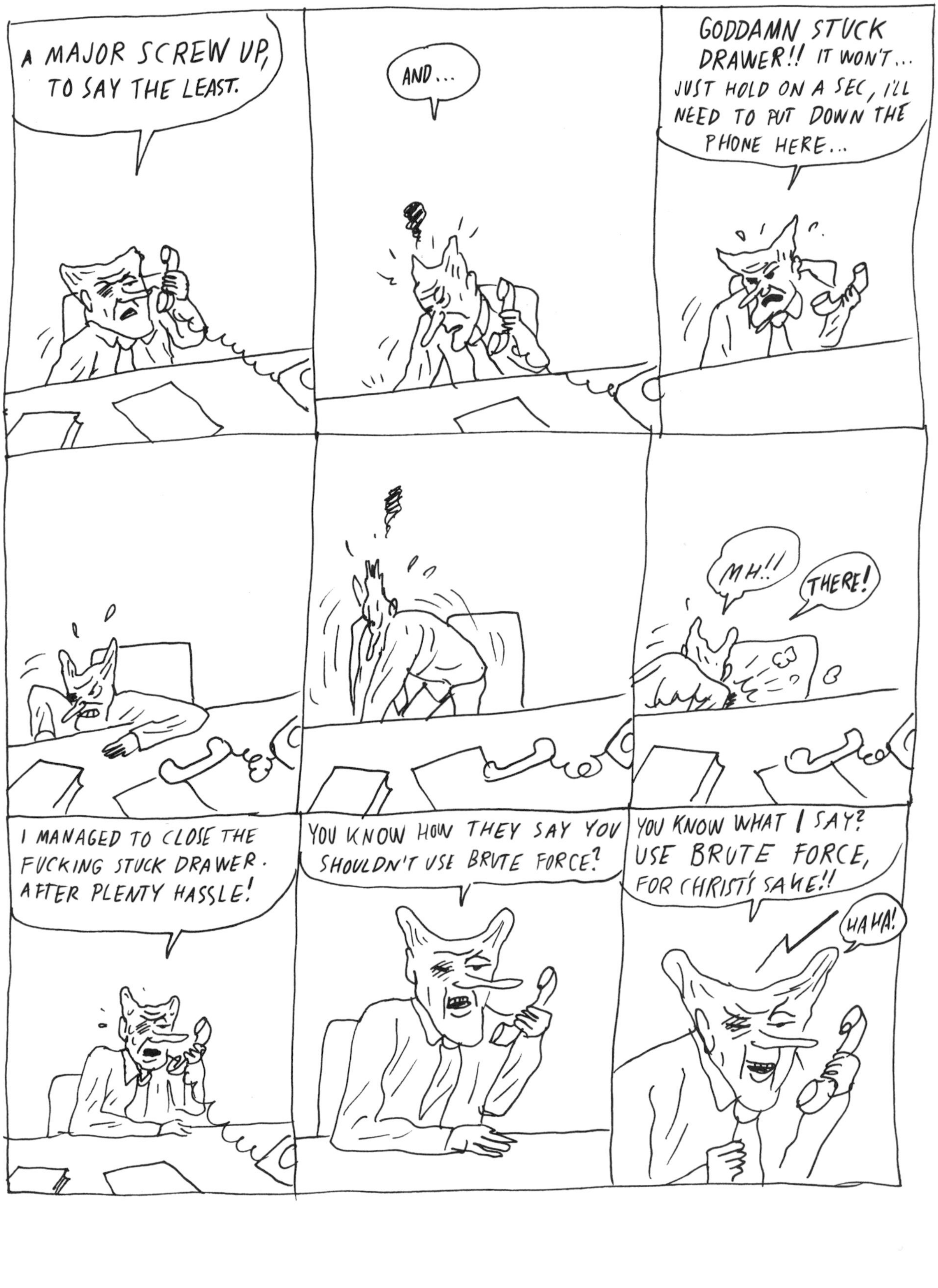
A MAJOR SCREW UP, TO SAY THE LEAST.
AND...
GODDAMN STUCK DRAWER!! IT WON'T... JUST HOLD ON A SEC, I'LL NEED TO PUT DOWN THE PHONE HERE...
MH!!
THERE!
I MANAGED TO CLOSE THE FUCKING STUCK DRAWER. AFTER PLENTY HASSLE!
YOU KNOW HOW THEY SAY YOU SHOULDN'T USE BRUTE FORCE?
YOU KNOW WHAT I SAY? USE BRUTE FORCE, FOR CHRIST'S SAKE!!
HAHA!

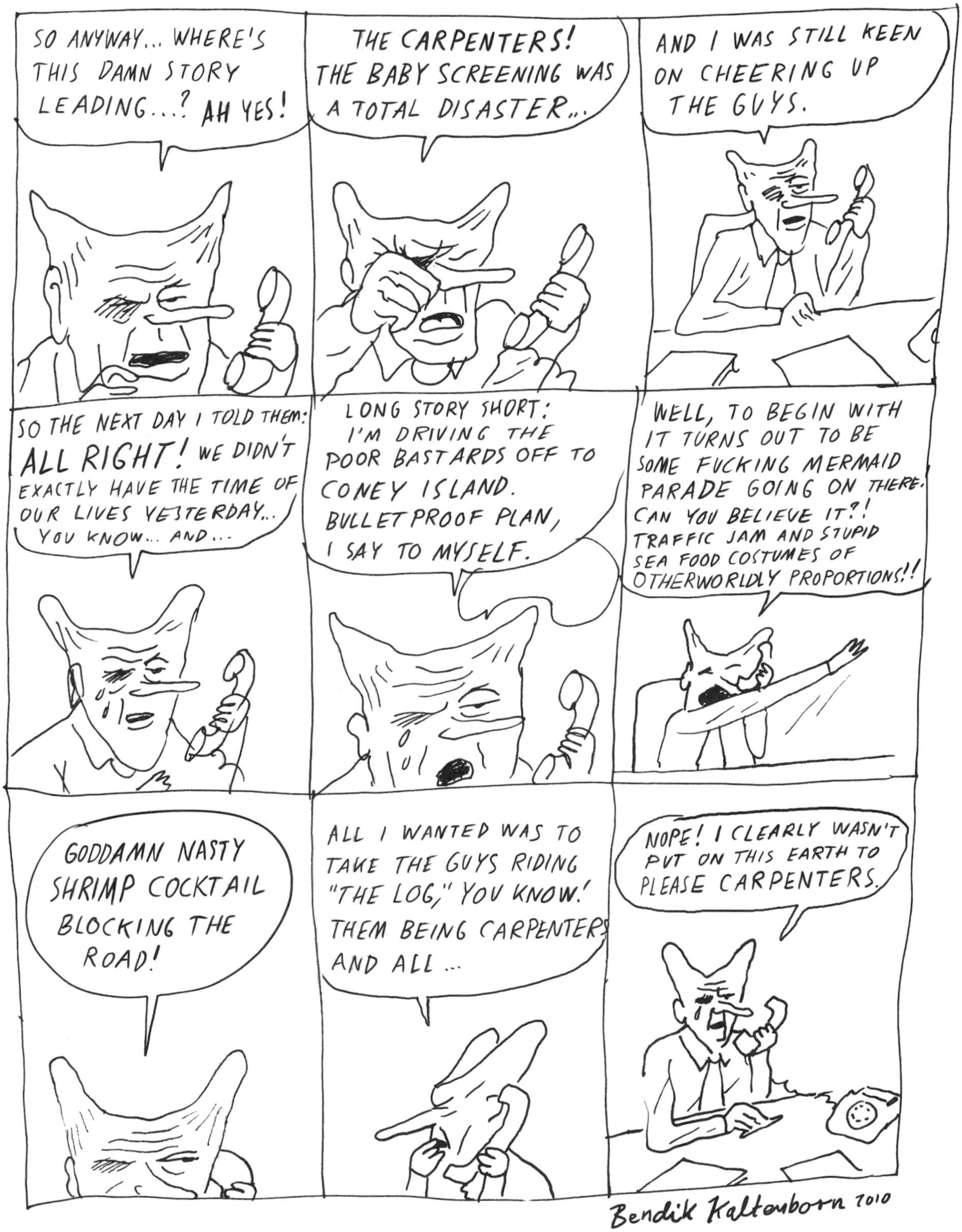
SO ANYWAY... WHERE'S THIS DAMN STORY LEADING...? AH YES!
THE CARPENTERS! THE BABY SCREENING WAS A TOTAL DISASTER...
AND I WAS STILL KEEN ON CHEERING UP THE GUYS.
SO THE NEXT DAY I TOLD THEM: ALL RIGHT! WE DIDN'T EXACTLY HAVE THE TIME OF OUR LIVES YESTERDAY... YOU KNOW... AND...
LONG STORY SHORT: I'M DRIVING THE POOR BASTARDS OFF TO CONEY ISLAND. BULLETPROOF PLAN, I SAY TO MYSELF.
WELL, TO BEGIN WITH IT TURNS OUT TO BE SOME FUCKING MERMAID PARADE GOING ON THERE. CAN YOU BELIEVE IT?! TRAFFIC JAM AND STUPID SEA FOOD COSTUMES OF OTHERWORLDLY PROPORTIONS!!
GODDAMN NASTY SHRIMP COCKTAIL BLOCKING THE ROAD!
ALL I WANTED WAS TO TAKE THE GUYS RIDING "THE LOG," YOU KNOW! THEM BEING CARPENTERS AND ALL...
NOPE! I CLEARLY WASN'T PUT ON THIS EARTH TO PLEASE CARPENTERS.
Bendik Kaltenborn 2010

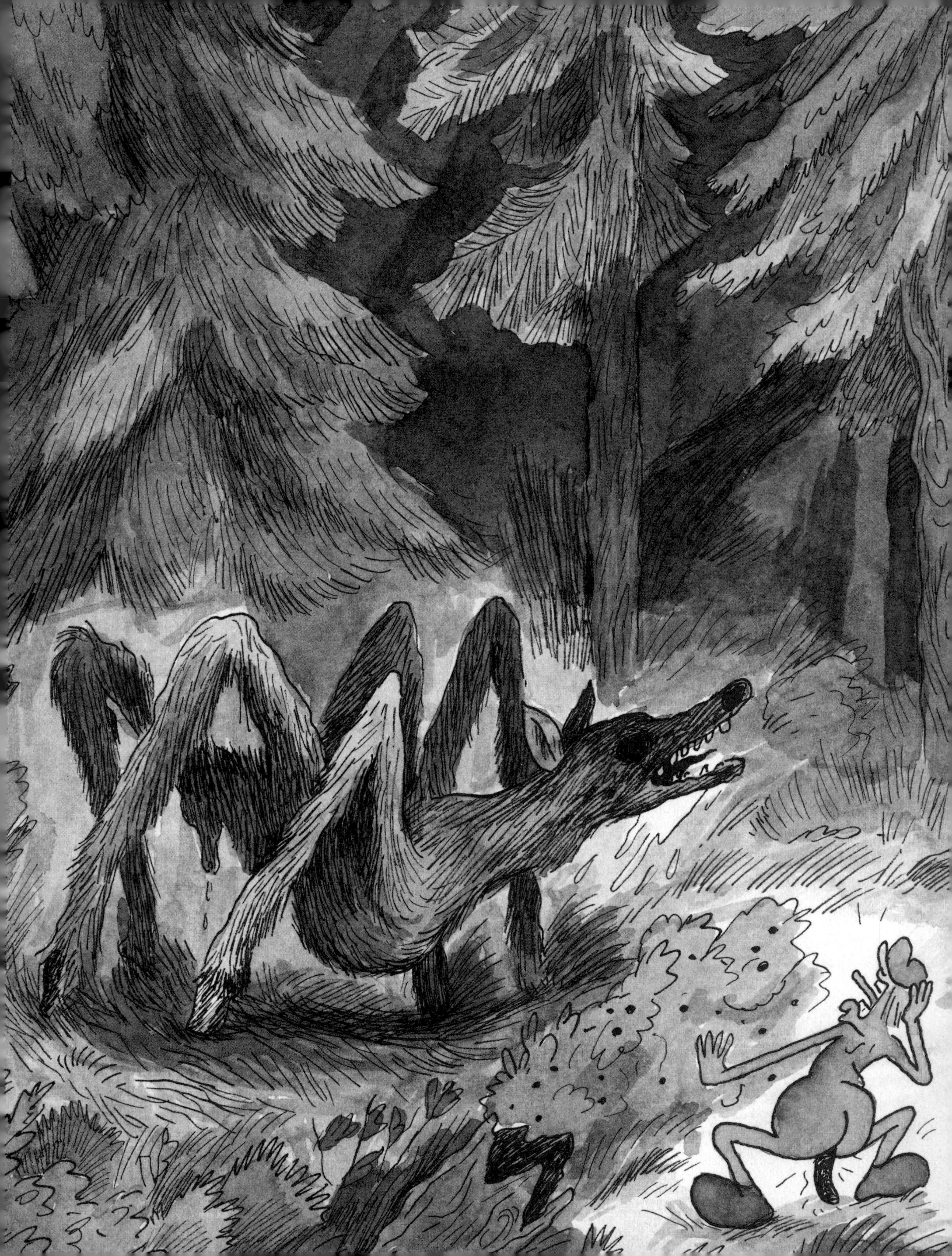

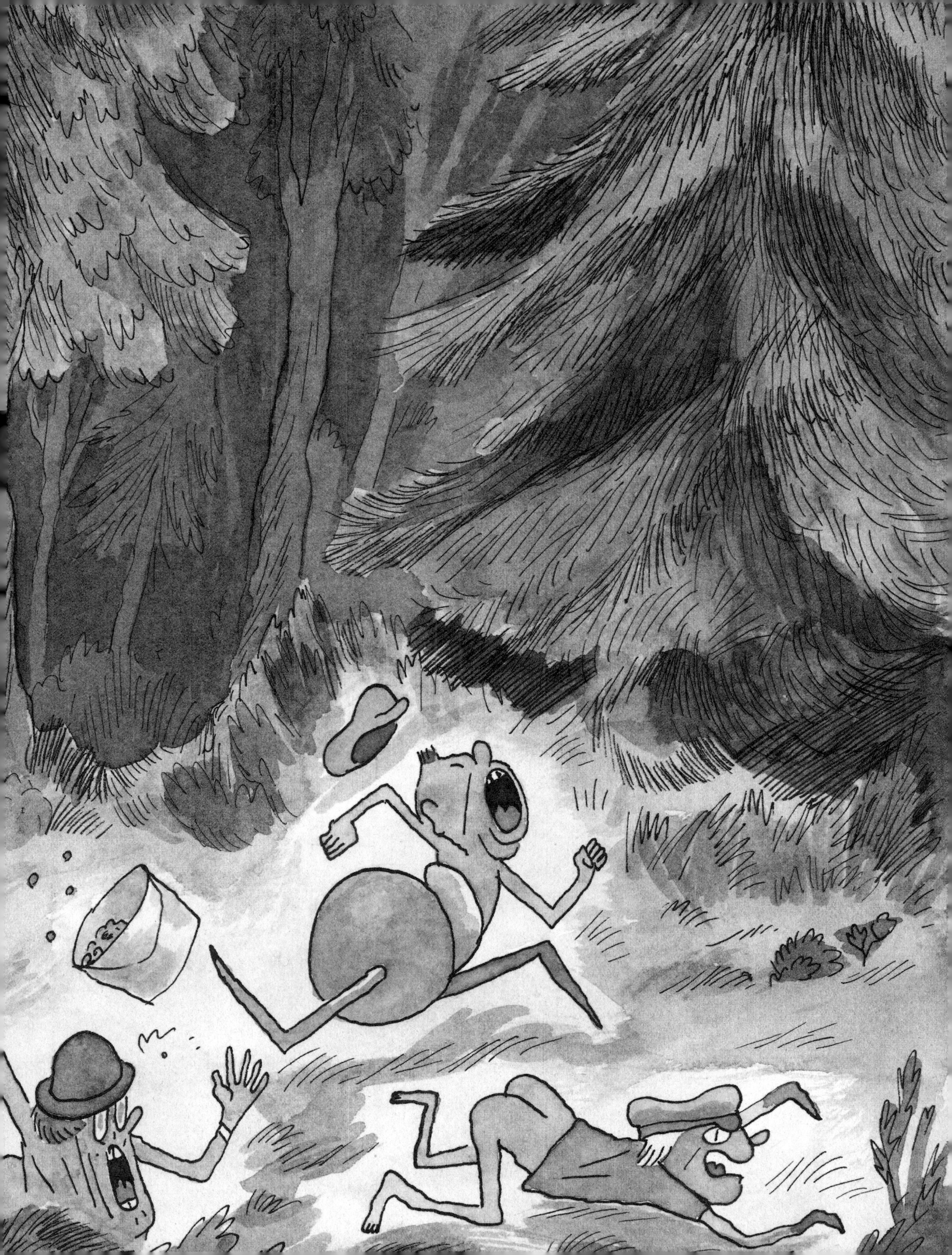

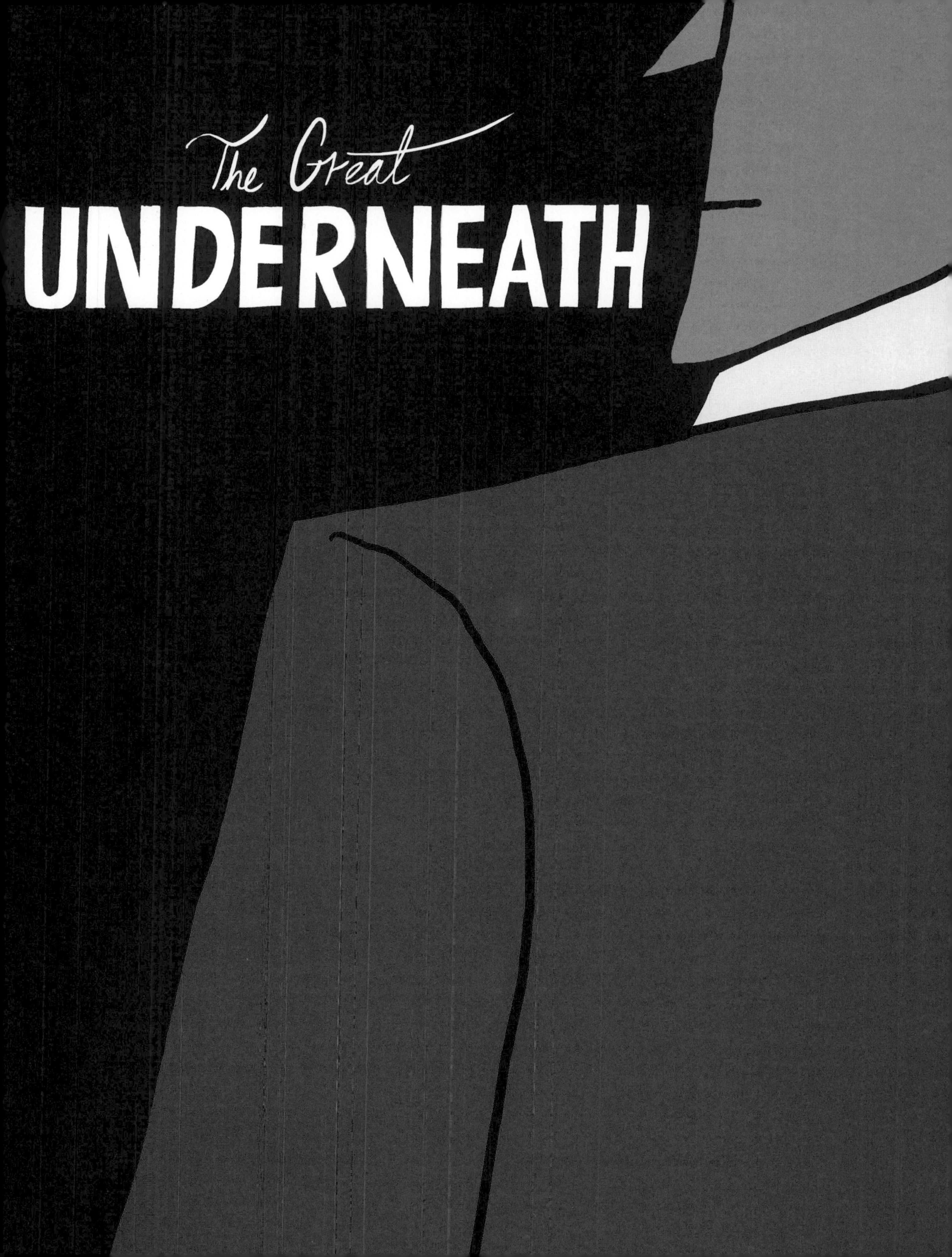
The Great
UNDERNEATH

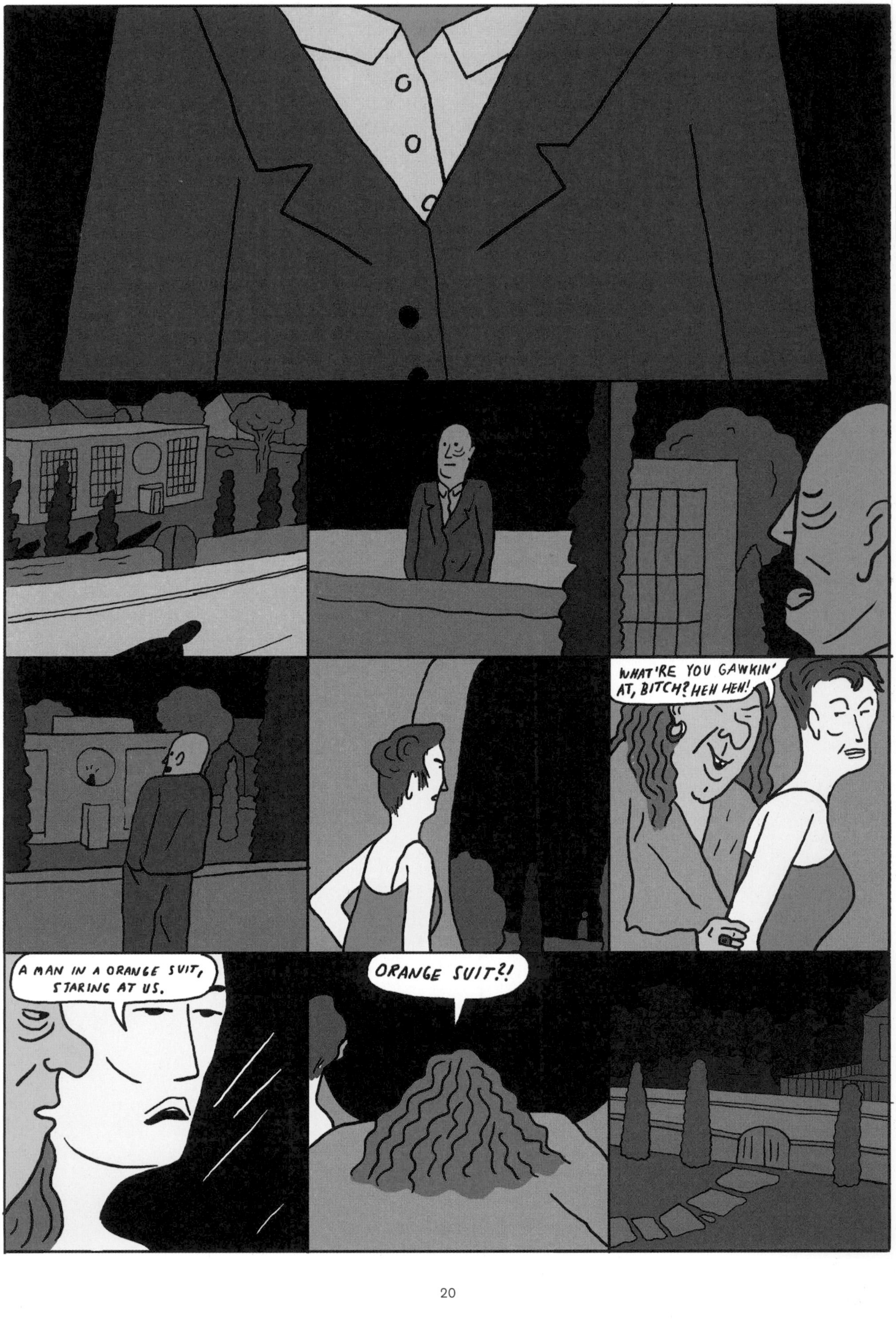
WHAT'RE YOU GAWKIN' AT, BITCH? HEH HEH!
A MAN IN A ORANGE SUIT, STARING AT US.
ORANGE SUIT?!

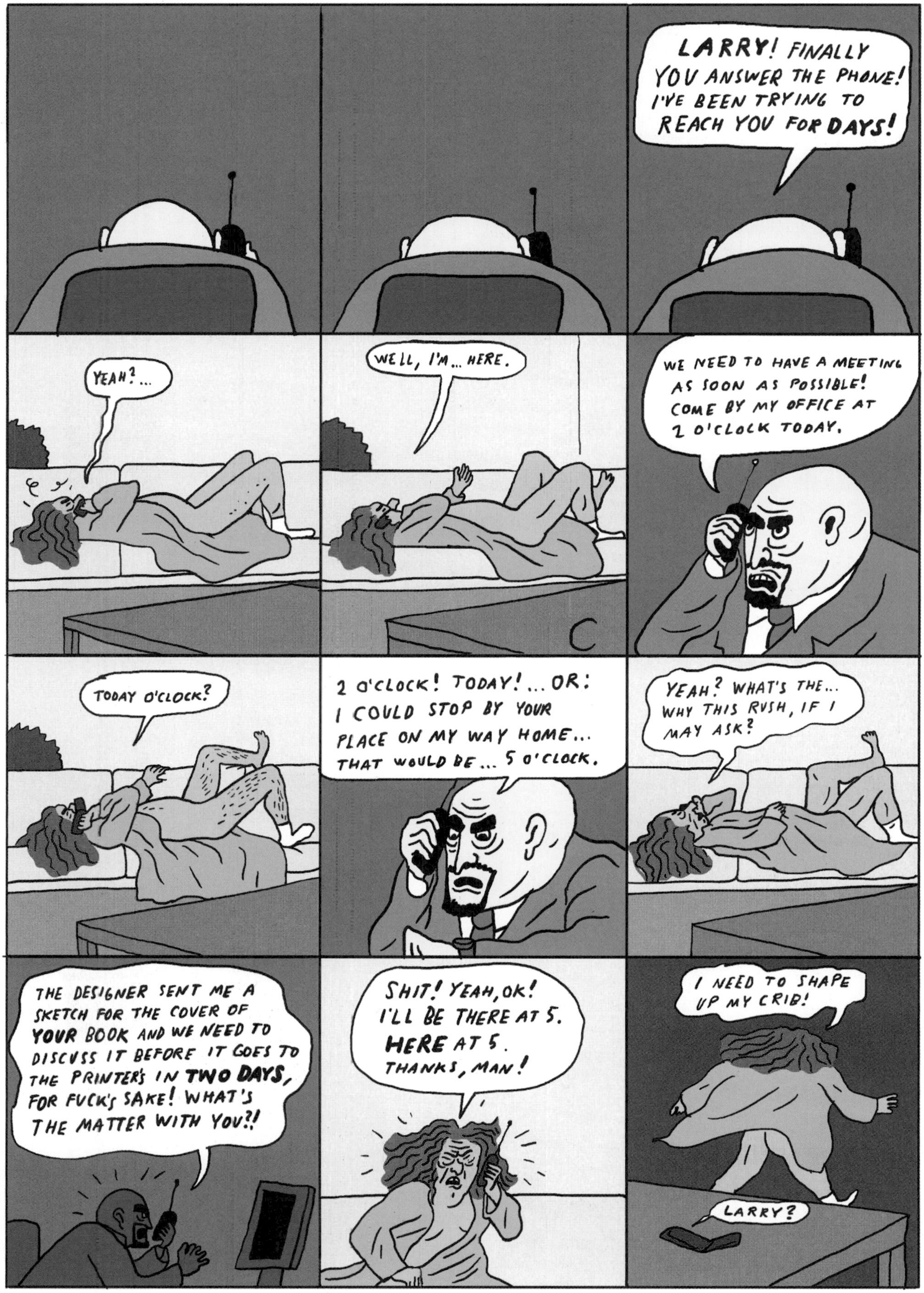
LARRY! FINALLY YOU ANSWER THE PHONE! I'VE BEEN TRYING TO REACH YOU FOR DAYS!
YEAH?...
WELL, I'M... HERE.
WE NEED TO HAVE A MEETING AS SOON AS POSSIBLE! COME BY MY OFFICE AT 2 O'CLOCK TODAY.
TODAY O'CLOCK?
2 O'CLOCK! TODAY! ... OR: I COULD STOP BY YOUR PLACE ON MY WAY HOME... THAT WOULD BE... 5 O'CLOCK.
YEAH? WHAT'S THE... WHY THIS RUSH, IF I MAY ASK?
THE DESIGNER SENT ME A SKETCH FOR THE COVER OF YOUR BOOK AND WE NEED TO DISCUSS IT BEFORE IT GOES TO THE PRINTER'S IN TWO DAYS, FOR FUCK'S SAKE! WHAT'S THE MATTER WITH YOU?!
SHIT! YEAH, OK! I'LL BE THERE AT 5. HERE AT 5. THANKS, MAN!
I NEED TO SHAPE UP MY CRIB!
LARRY?

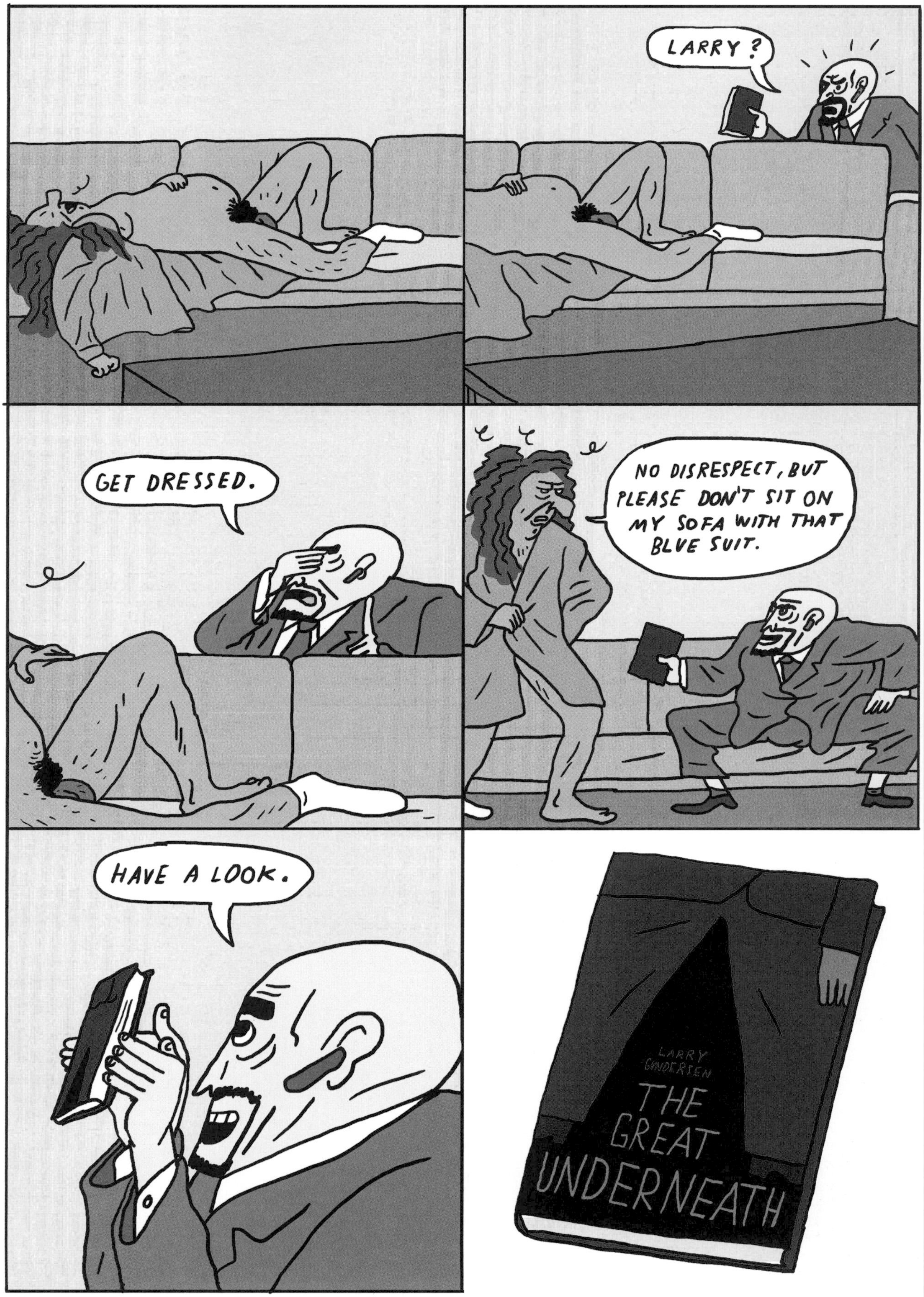
LARRY?
GET DRESSED.
NO DISRESPECT, BUT PLEASE DON'T SIT ON MY SOFA WITH THAT BLUE SUIT.
HAVE A LOOK.
LARRY GUNDERSEN
THE GREAT UNDERNEATH

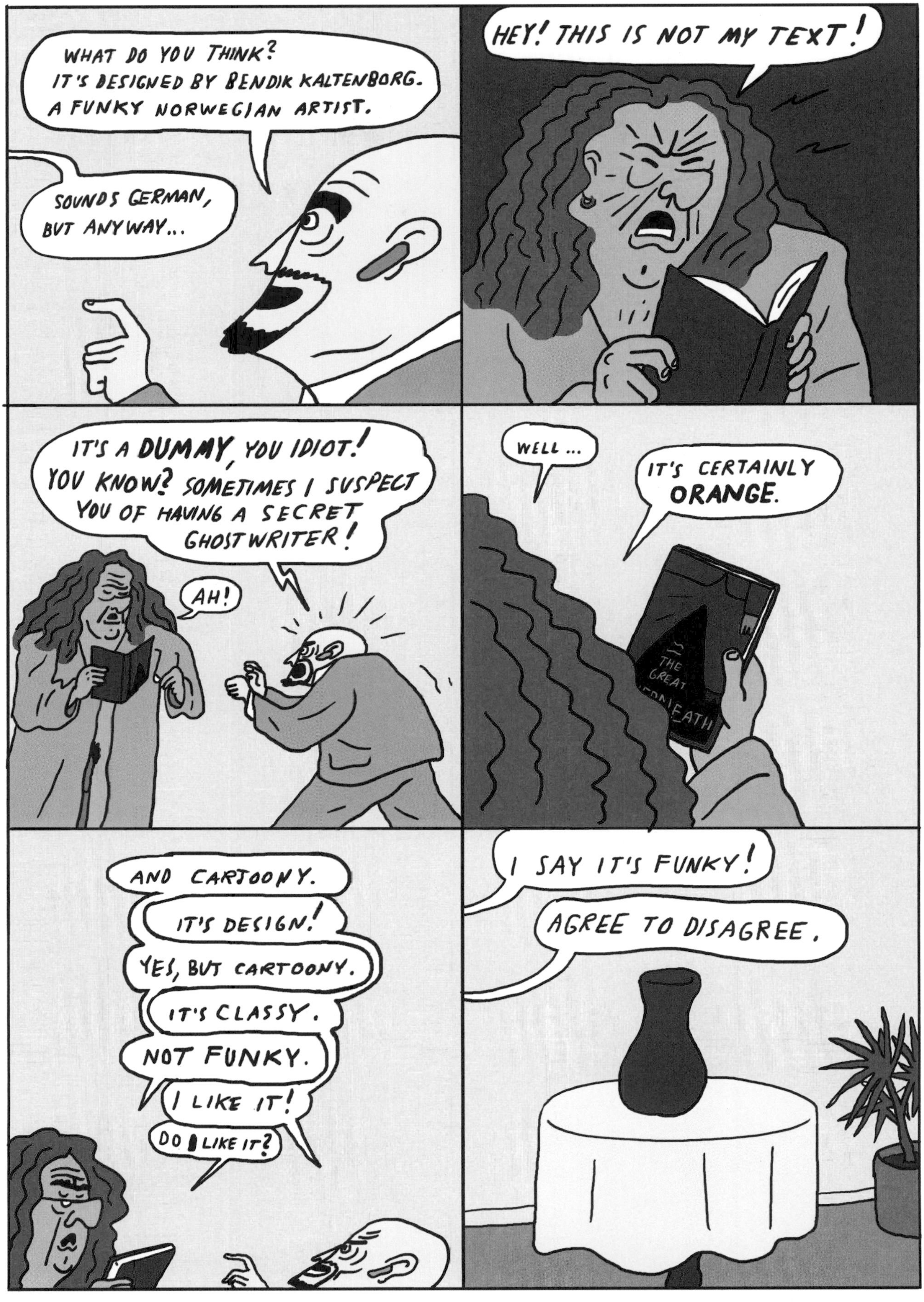

WHAT DO YOU THINK? IT'S DESIGNED BY BENDIK KALTENBORG. A FUNKY NORWEGIAN ARTIST.
SOUNDS GERMAN, BUT ANYWAY...
HEY! THIS IS NOT MY TEXT!
IT'S A DUMMY, YOU IDIOT! YOU KNOW? SOMETIMES I SUSPECT YOU OF HAVING A SECRET GHOSTWRITER!
AH!
WELL ...
IT'S CERTAINLY ORANGE.
THE GREAT
AND CARTOONY.
IT'S DESIGN!
YES, BUT CARTOONY.
IT'S CLASSY.
NOT FUNKY.
I LIKE IT!
DO I LIKE IT?
I SAY IT'S FUNKY!
AGREE TO DISAGREE.

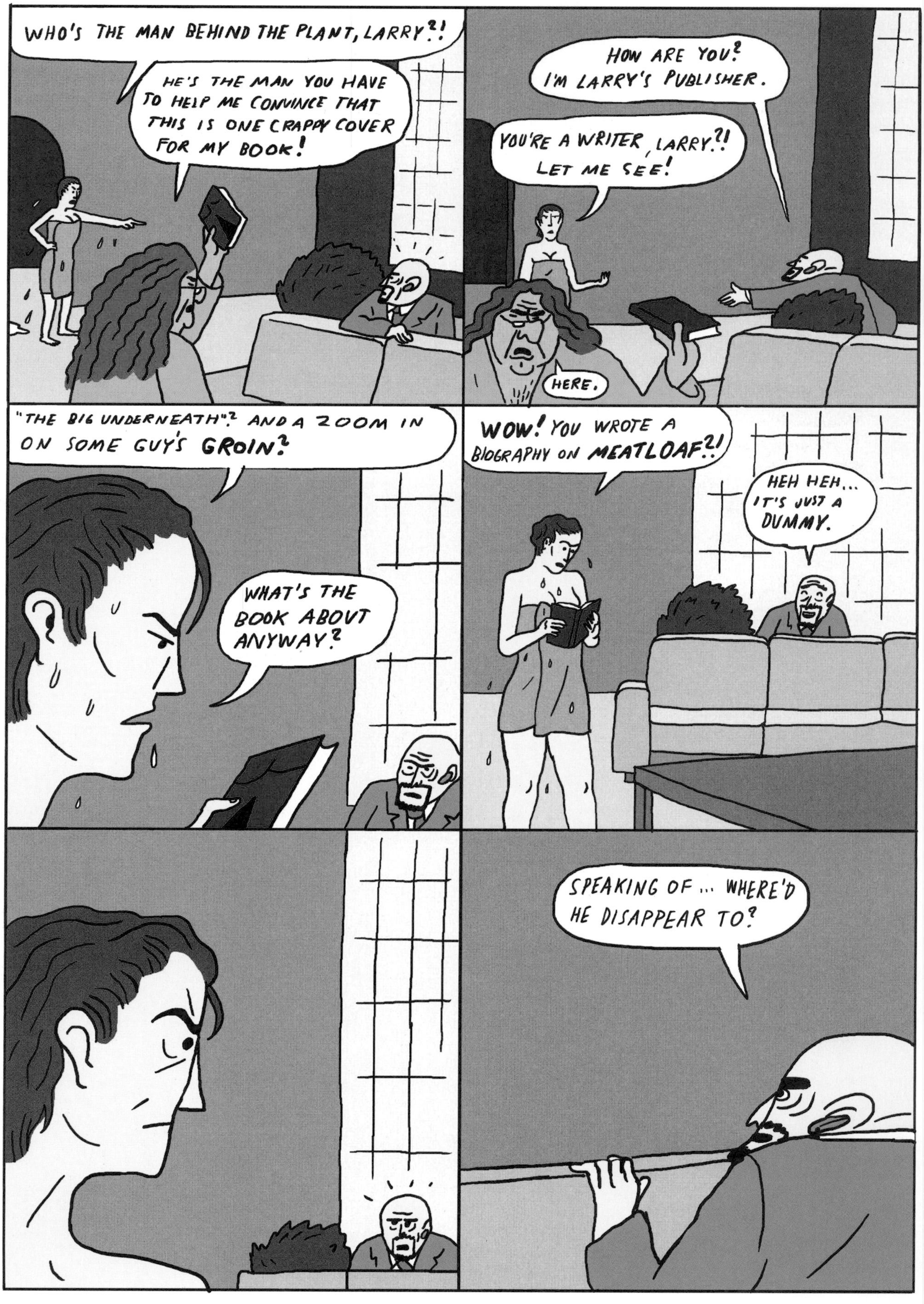
WHO'S THE MAN BEHIND THE PLANT, LARRY?!
HE'S THE MAN YOU HAVE TO HELP ME CONVINCE THAT THIS IS ONE CRAPPY COVER FOR MY BOOK!
HOW ARE YOU? I'M LARRY'S PUBLISHER.
YOU'RE A WRITER, LARRY?! LET ME SEE!
HERE.
"THE BIG UNDERNEATH"? AND A ZOOM IN ON SOME GUY'S GROIN?
WHAT'S THE BOOK ABOUT ANYWAY?
WOW! YOU WROTE A BIOGRAPHY ON MEATLOAF?!
HEH HEH... IT'S JUST A DUMMY.
SPEAKING OF... WHERE'D HE DISAPPEAR TO?

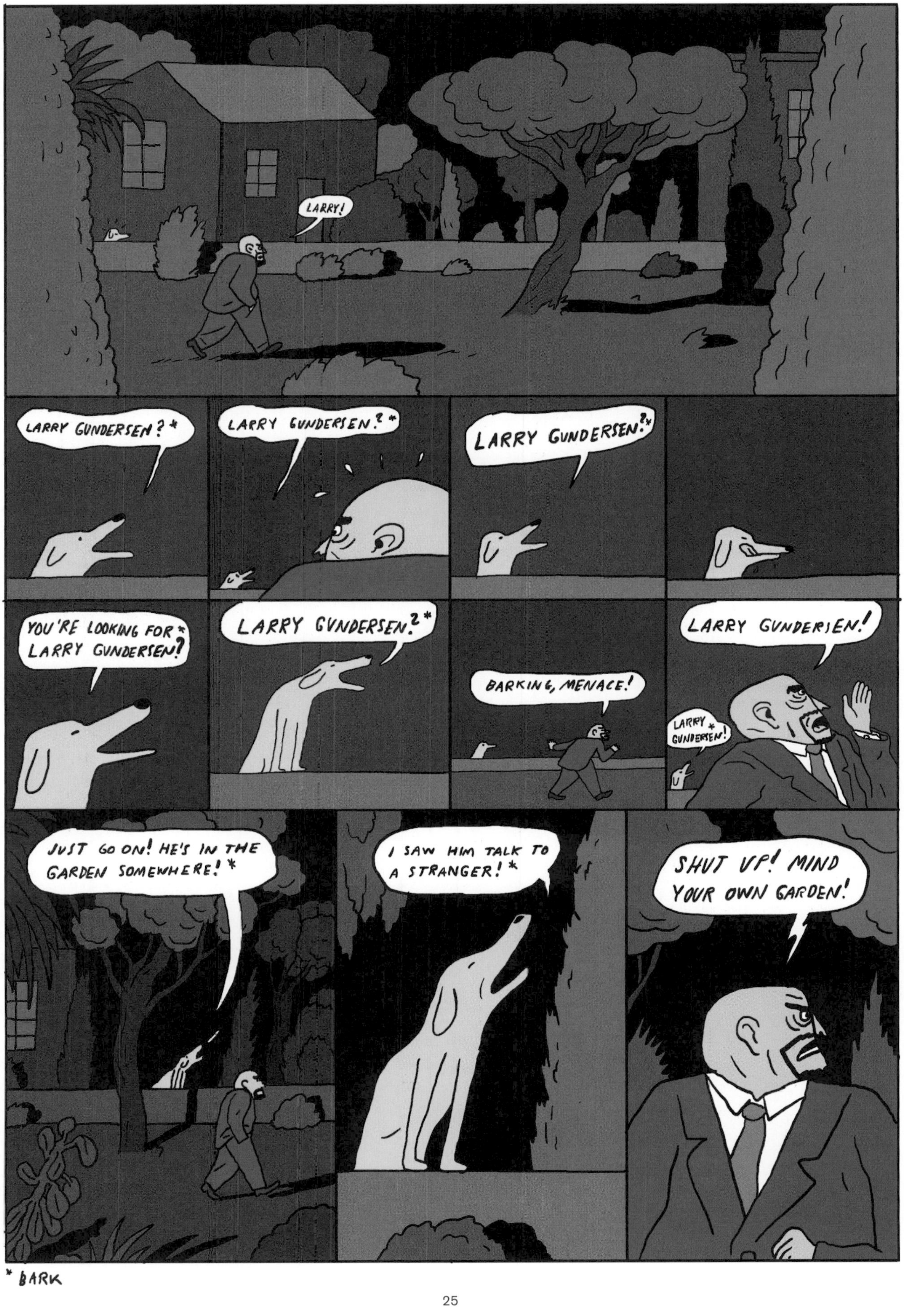
LARRY!
LARRY GUNDERSEN? *
LARRY GUNDERSEN? *
LARRY GUNDERSEN? *
YOU'RE LOOKING FOR * LARRY GUNDERSEN?
LARRY GUNDERSEN? *
BARKING MENACE!
LARRY GUNDERSEN!
LARRY * GUNDERSEN!
JUST GO ON! HE'S IN THE GARDEN SOMEWHERE! *
I SAW HIM TALK TO A STRANGER! *
SHUT UP! MIND YOUR OWN GARDEN!

* BARK

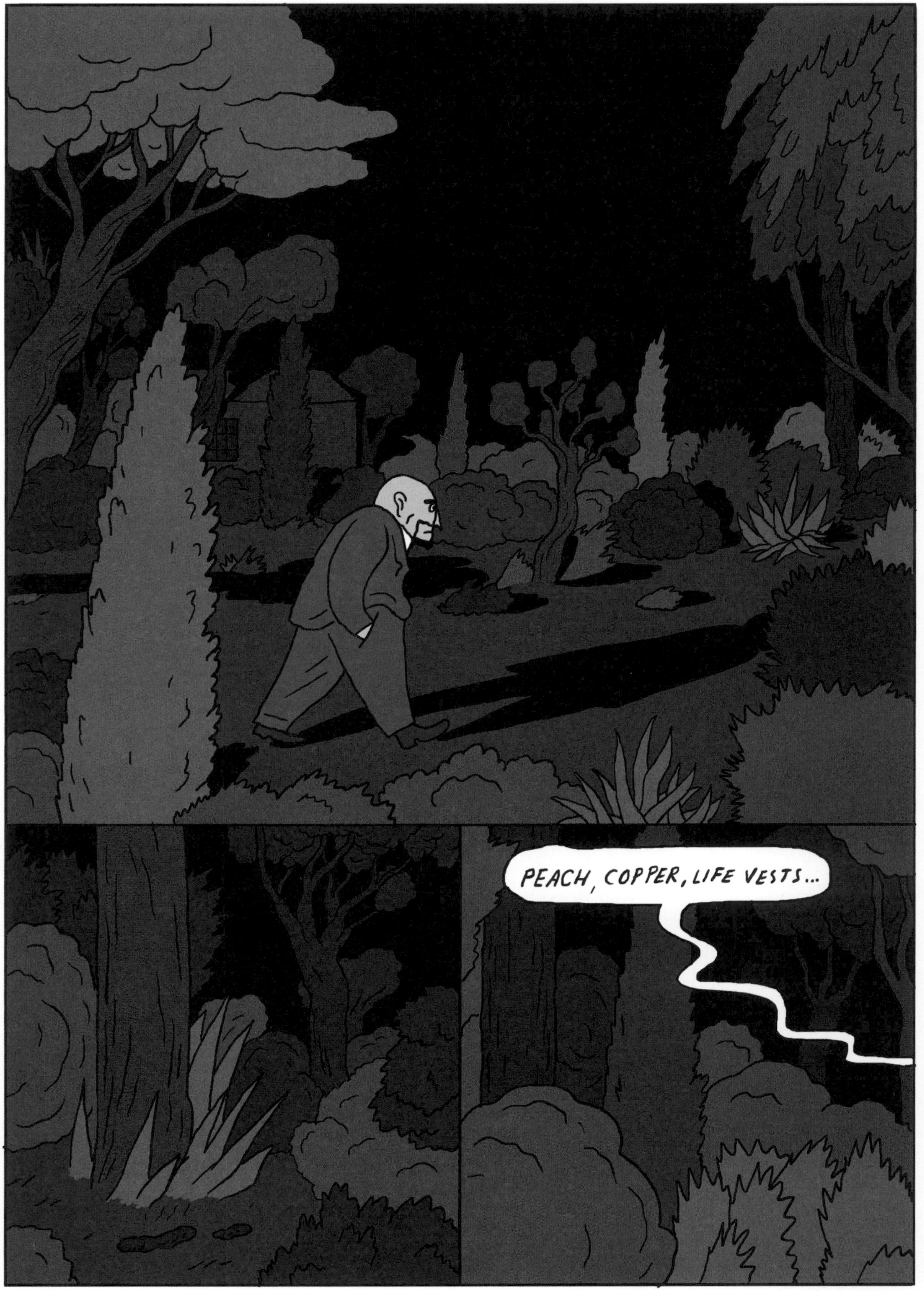
PEACH, COPPER, LIFE VESTS...

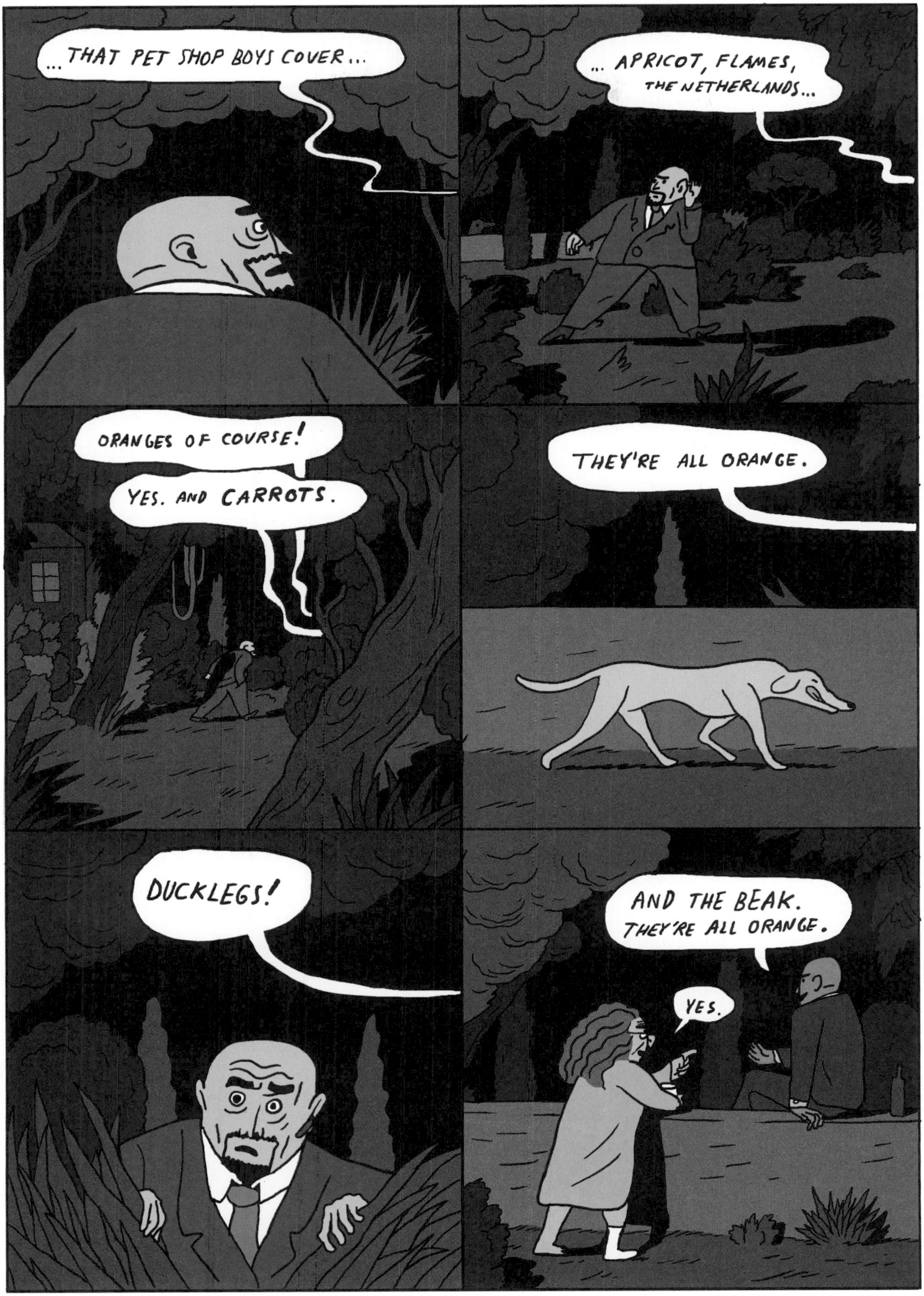
...THAT PET SHOP BOYS COVER...
... APRICOT, FLAMES, THE NETHERLANDS...
ORANGES OF COURSE!
YES. AND CARROTS.
THEY'RE ALL ORANGE.
DUCKLEGS!
AND THE BEAK. THEY'RE ALL ORANGE.
YES.

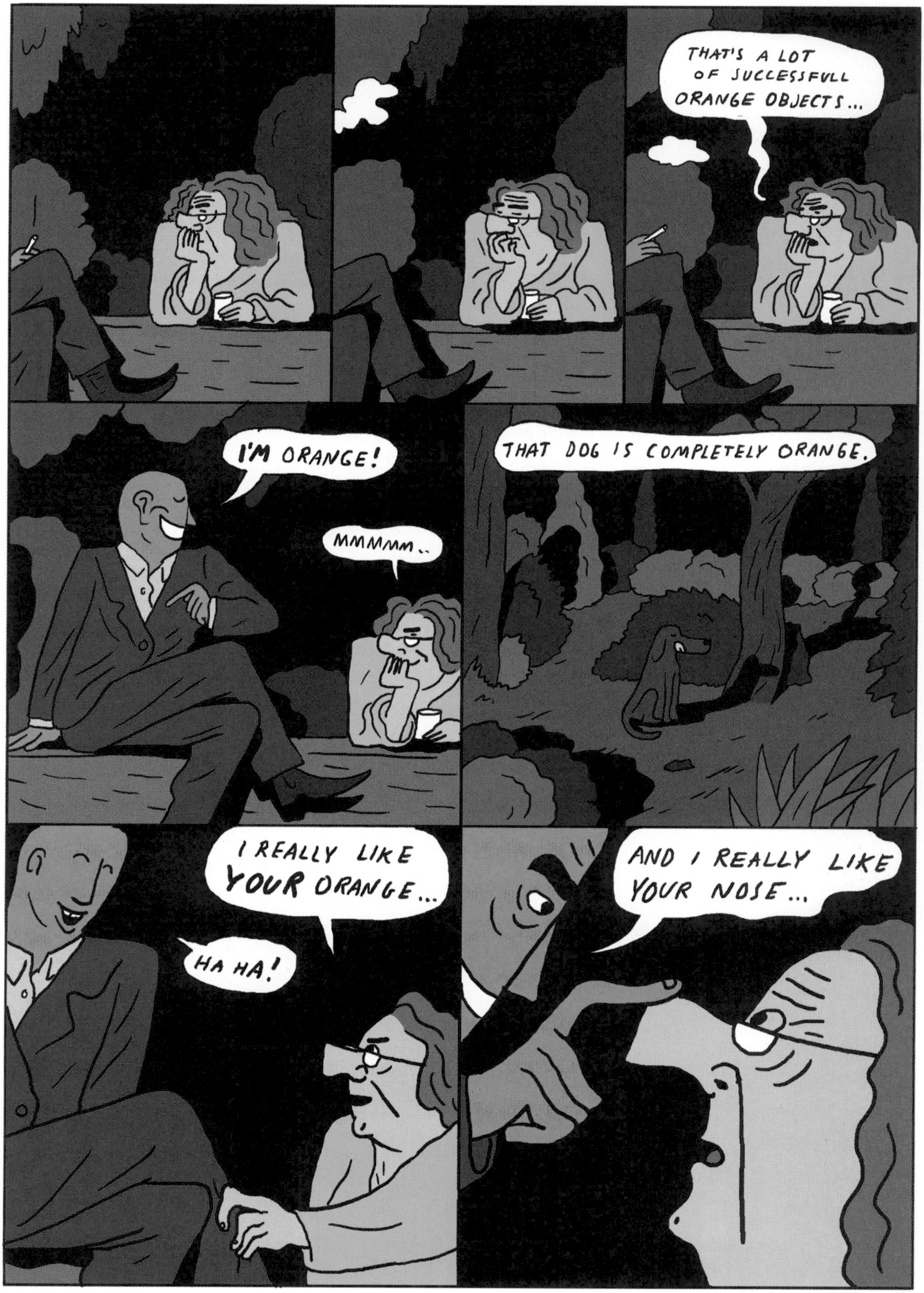

THAT'S A LOT OF SUCCESSFULL ORANGE OBJECTS...
I'M ORANGE!
MMMMM..
THAT DOG IS COMPLETELY ORANGE.
I REALLY LIKE YOUR ORANGE...
HA HA!
AND I REALLY LIKE YOUR NOSE...

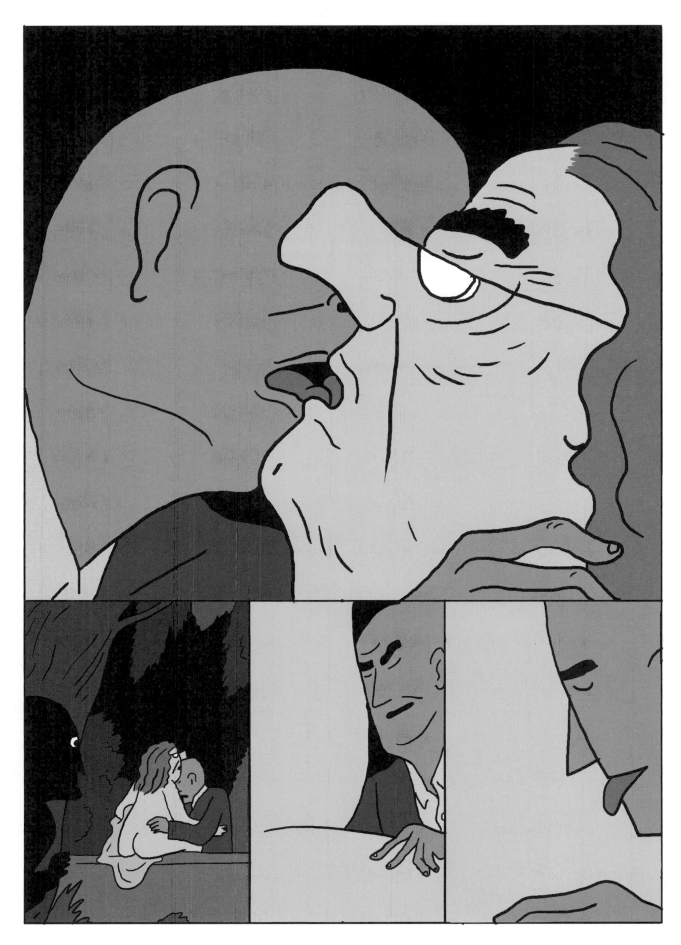

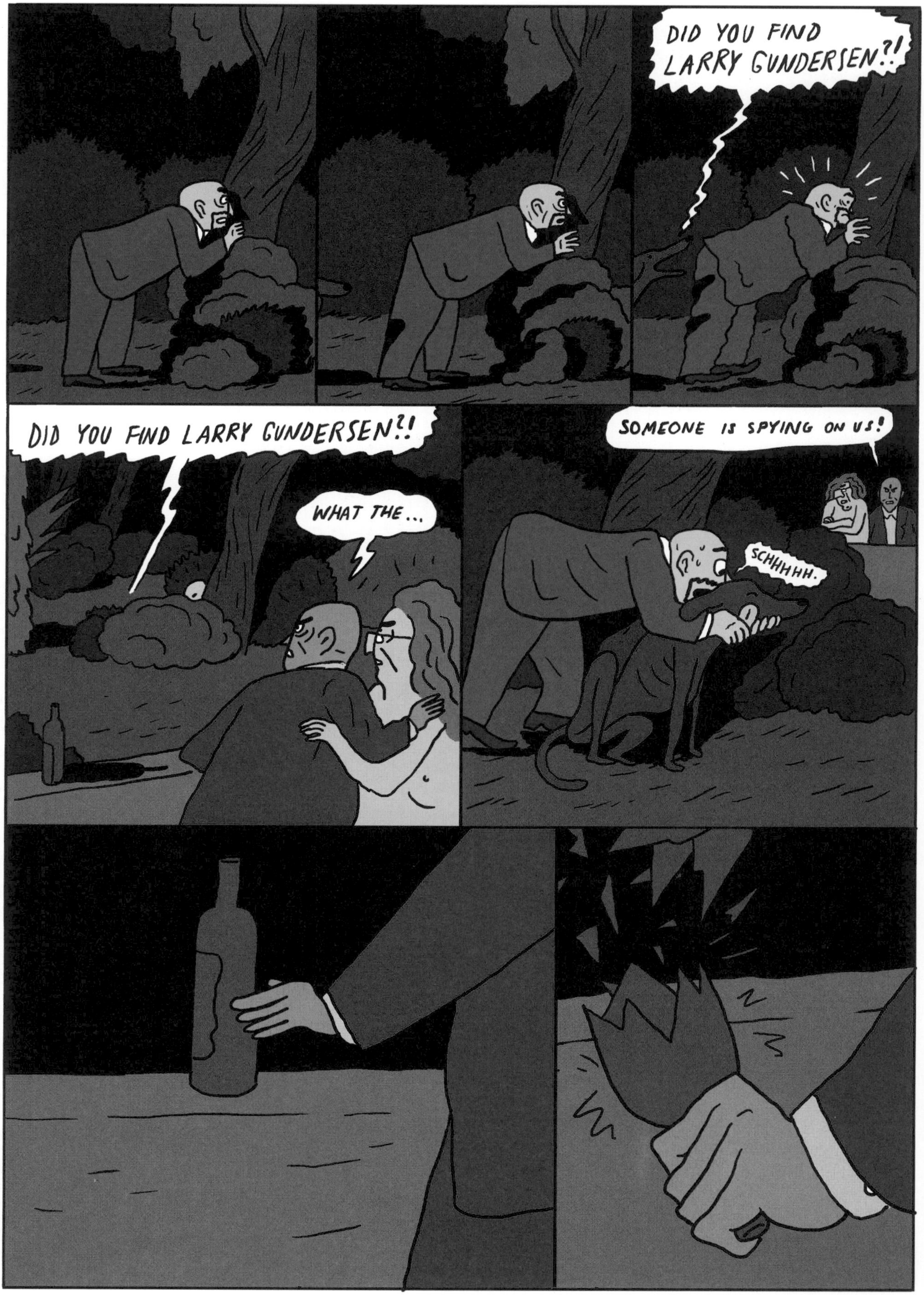
DID YOU FIND LARRY GUNDERSEN?!
DID YOU FIND LARRY GUNDERSEN?!
WHAT THE...
SOMEONE IS SPYING ON US!
SCHHHHH.

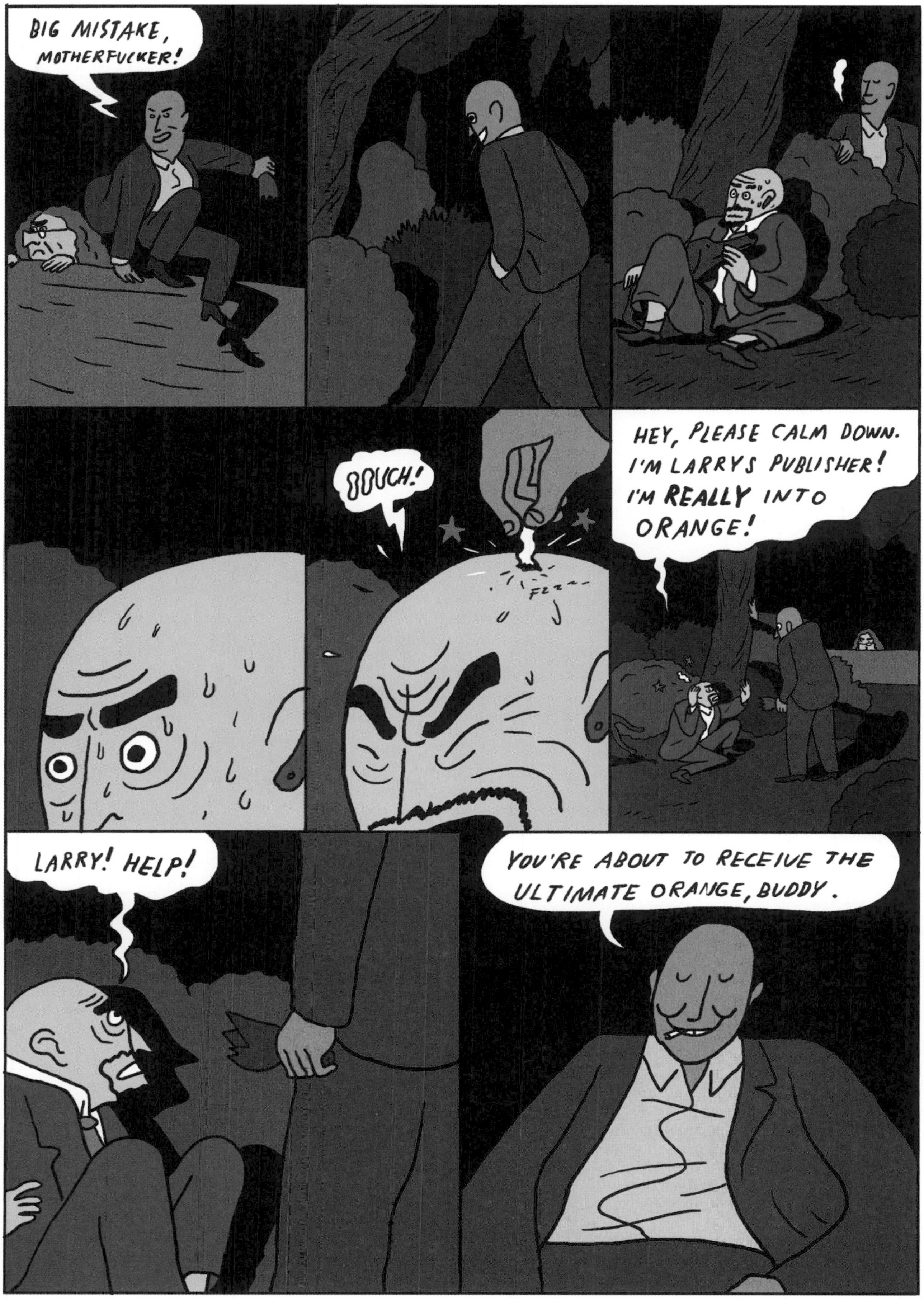
BIG MISTAKE, MOTHERFUCKER!
OOUCH!
FZZ...
HEY, PLEASE CALM DOWN. I'M LARRYS PUBLISHER! I'M **REALLY** INTO ORANGE!
LARRY! HELP!
YOU'RE ABOUT TO RECEIVE THE ULTIMATE ORANGE, BUDDY.

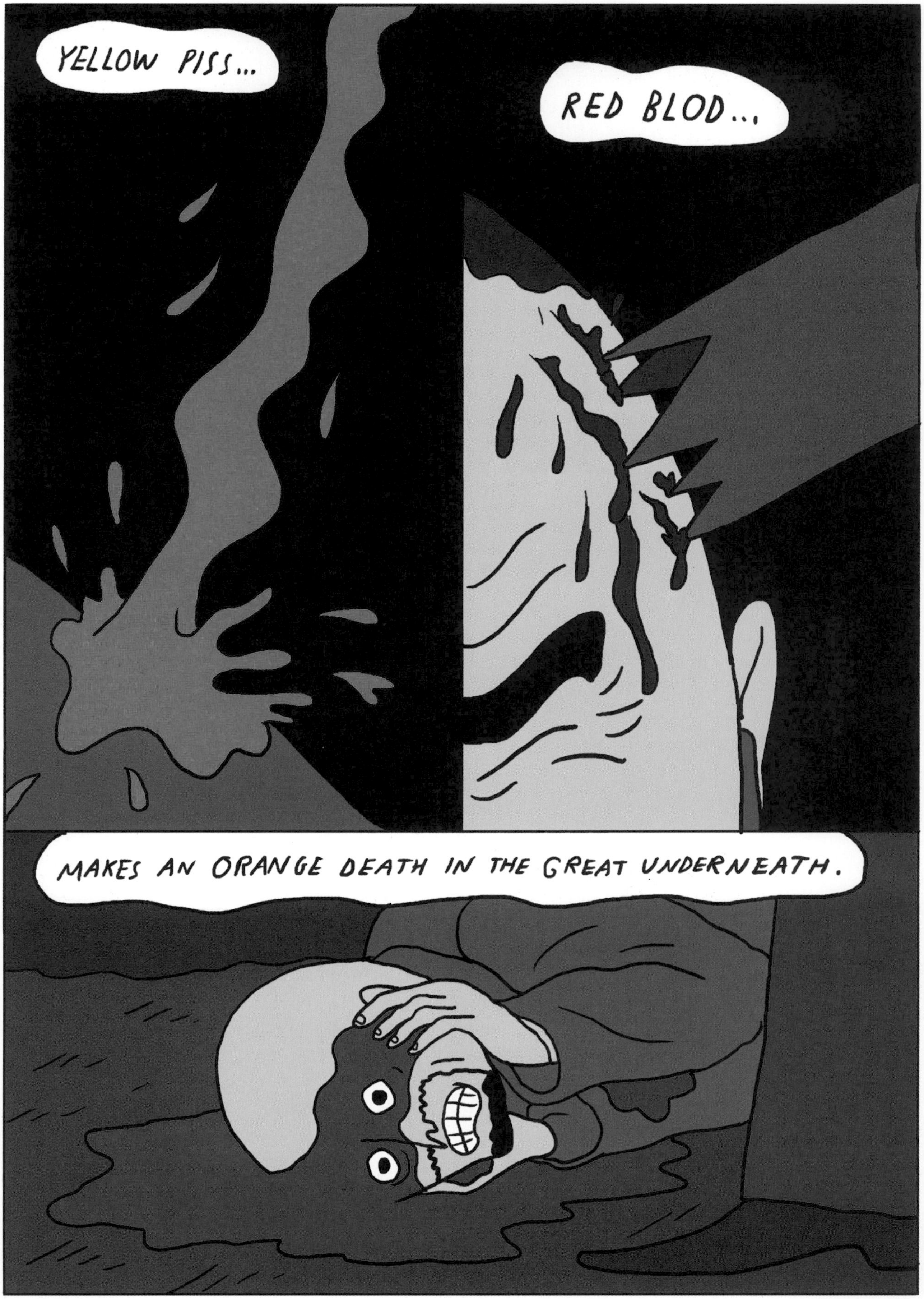
YELLOW PISS...
RED BLOD...
MAKES AN ORANGE DEATH IN THE GREAT UNDERNEATH.

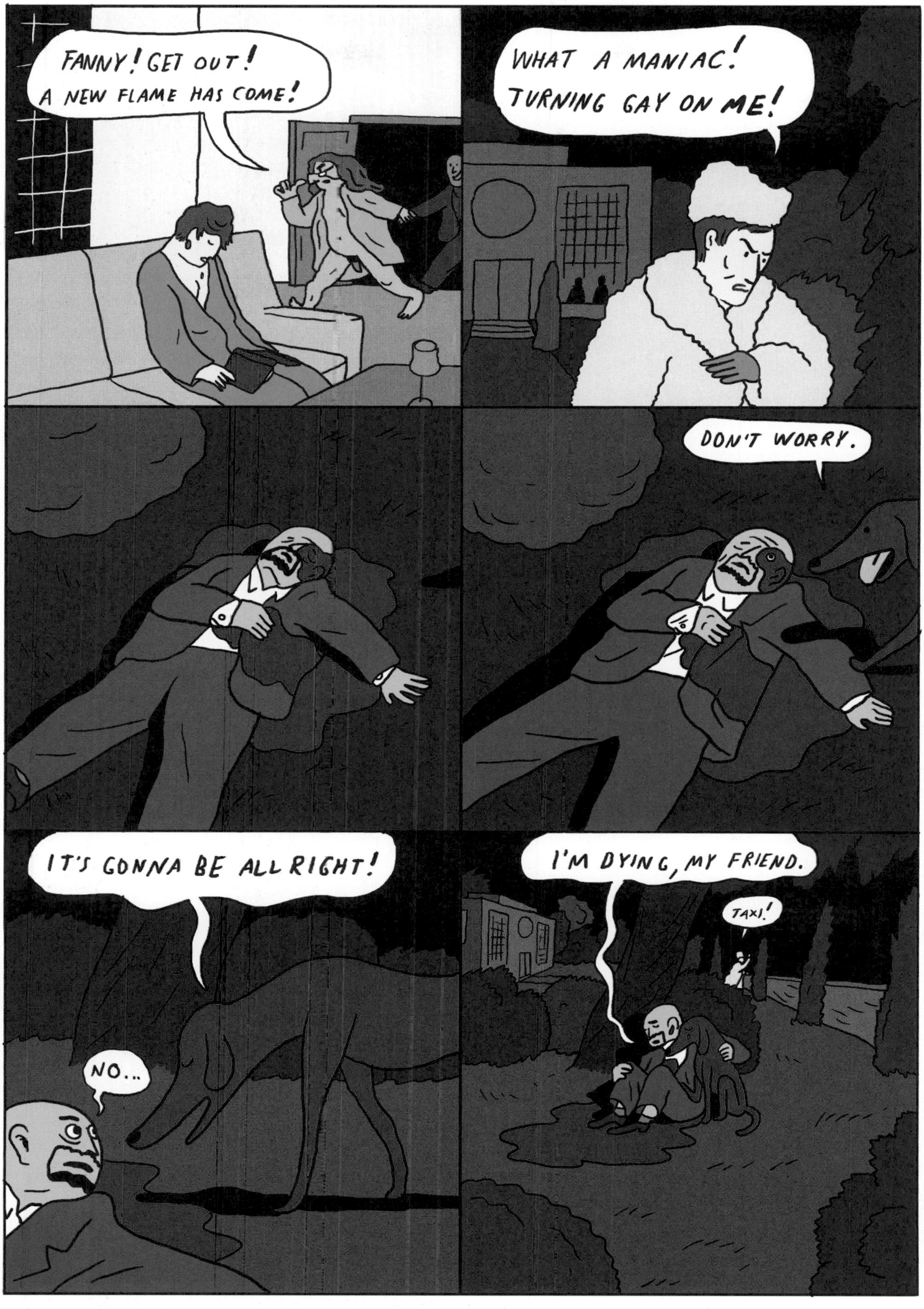
FANNY! GET OUT! A NEW FLAME HAS COME!
WHAT A MANIAC! TURNING GAY ON ME!
DON'T WORRY.
IT'S GONNA BE ALL RIGHT!
NO...
I'M DYING, MY FRIEND.
TAXI!

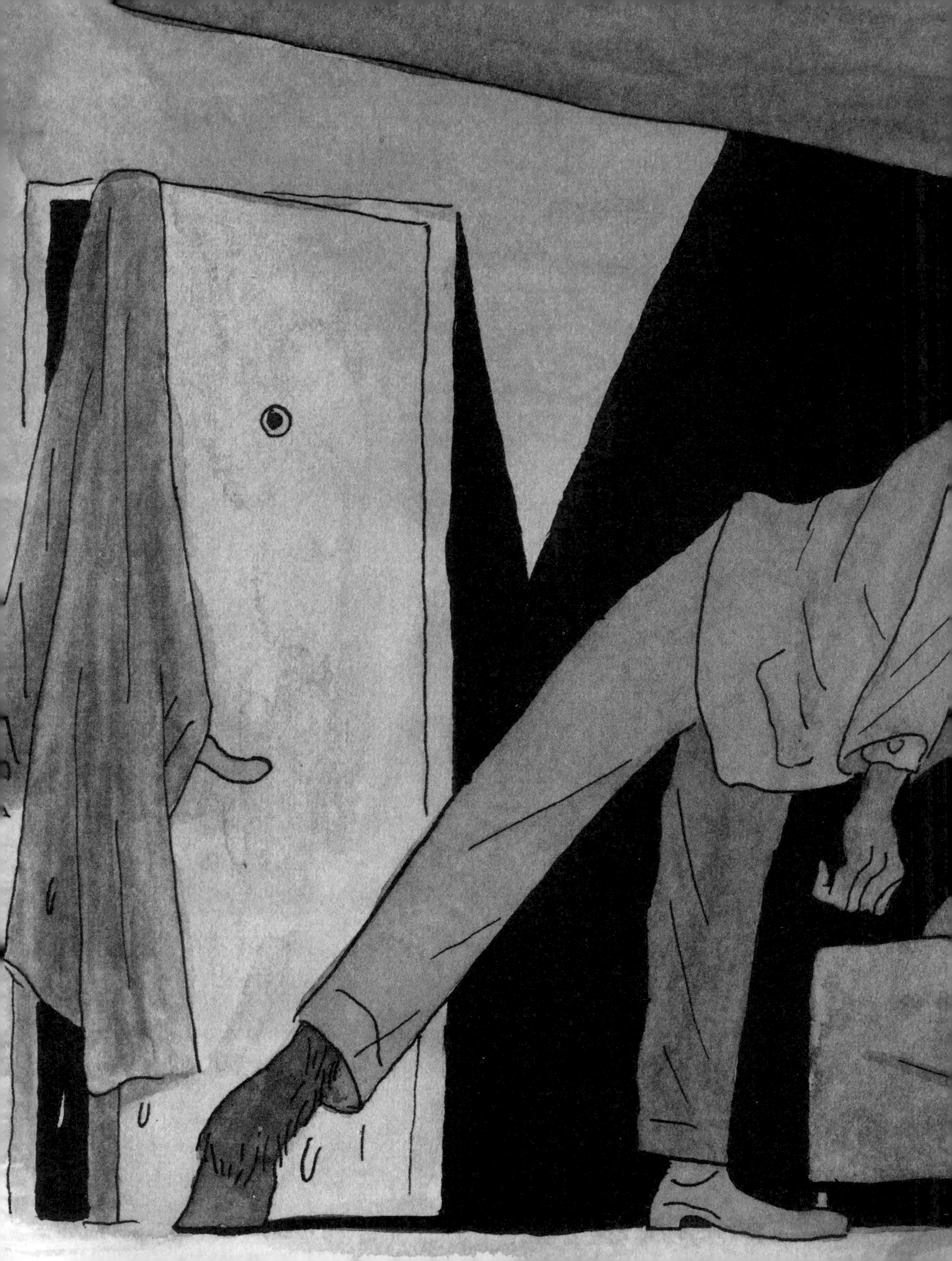

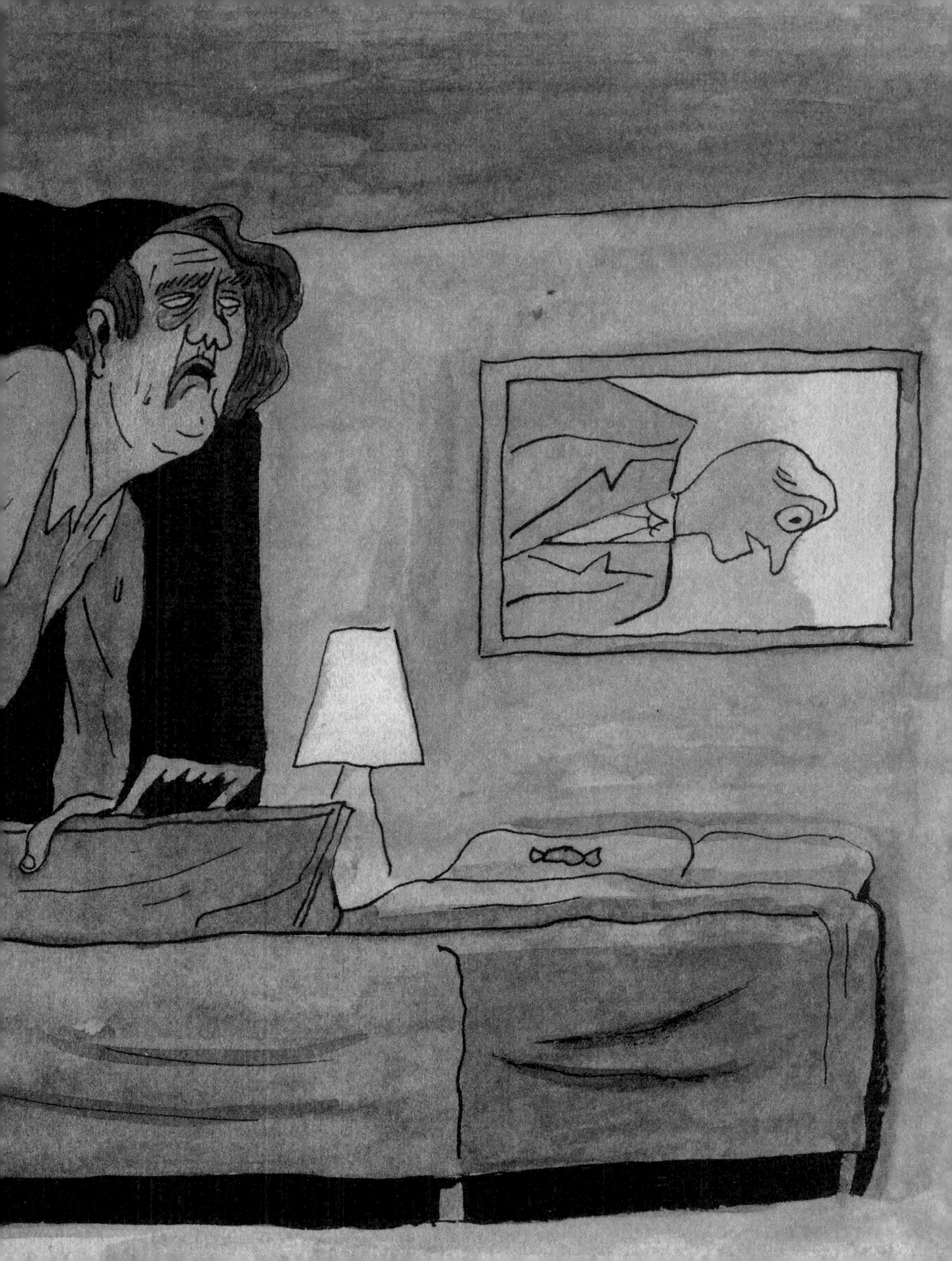

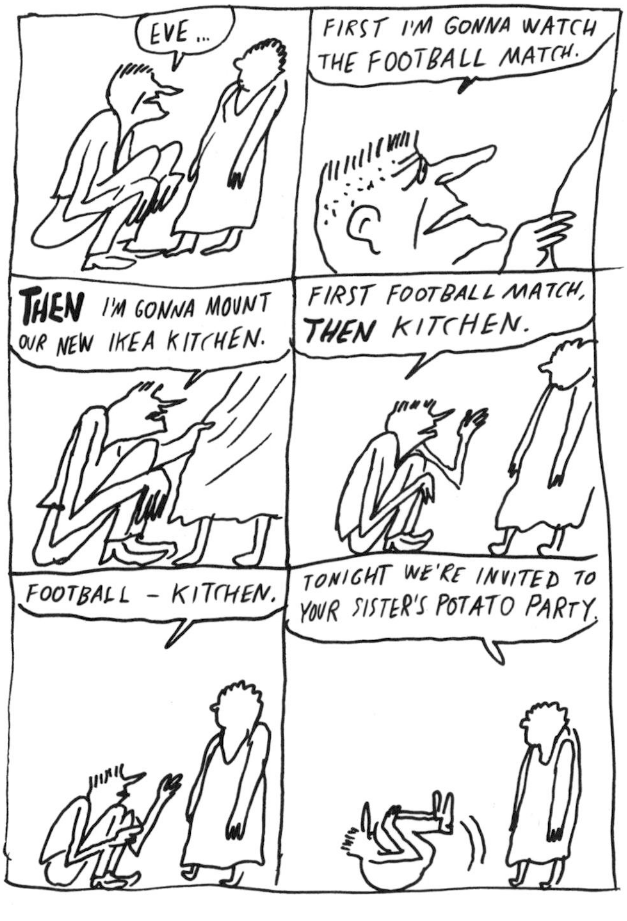
EVE ...
FIRST I'M GONNA WATCH THE FOOTBALL MATCH.
THEN I'M GONNA MOUNT OUR NEW IKEA KITCHEN.
FIRST FOOTBALL MATCH, THEN KITCHEN.
FOOTBALL - KITCHEN.
TONIGHT WE'RE INVITED TO YOUR SISTER'S POTATO PARTY.

SERIOUSLY?

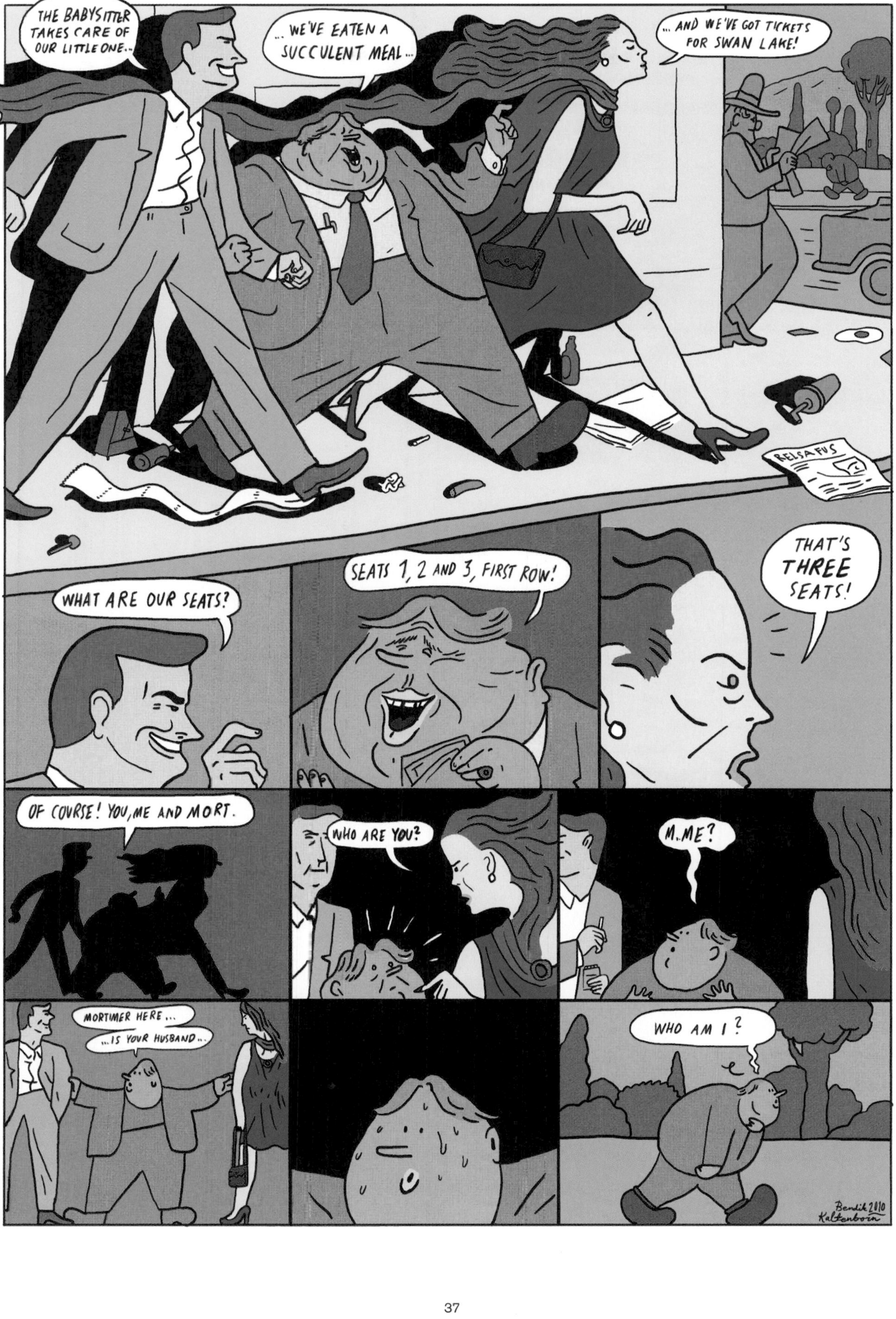
THE BABYSITTER TAKES CARE OF OUR LITTLE ONE...
... WE'VE EATEN A SUCCULENT MEAL...
... AND WE'VE GOT TICKETS FOR SWAN LAKE!
WHAT ARE OUR SEATS?
SEATS 1, 2 AND 3, FIRST ROW!
THAT'S THREE SEATS!
OF COURSE! YOU, ME AND MORT.
WHO ARE YOU?
M..ME?
MORTIMER HERE...
...IS YOUR HUSBAND...
WHO AM I?
Bendik 2010 Kaltenborn

ROYAL

KALTENBORN, BENDIK 2011

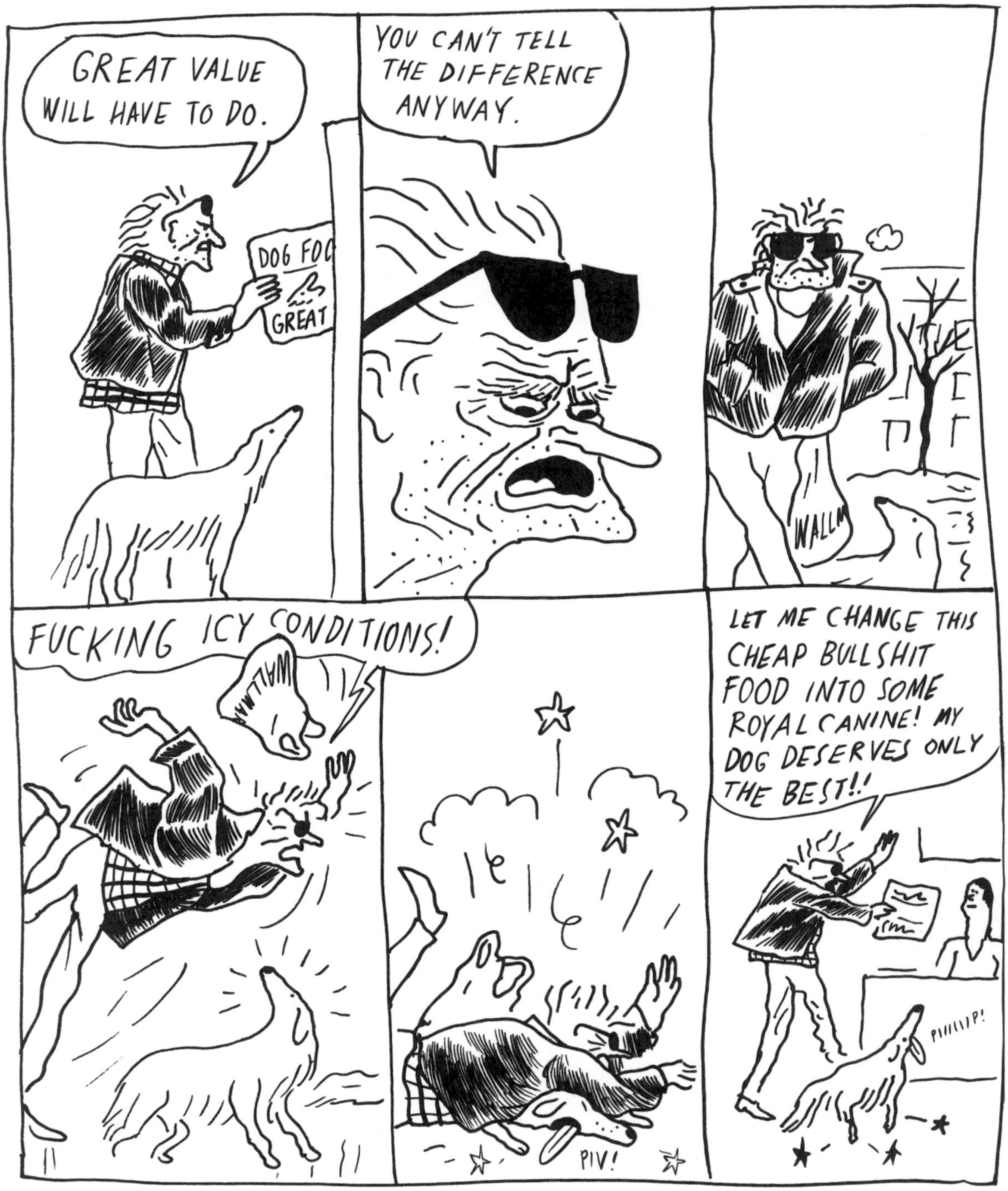

GREAT VALUE WILL HAVE TO DO.
DOG FOO
GREAT
YOU CAN'T TELL THE DIFFERENCE ANYWAY.
WALLM
FUCKING ICY CONDITIONS!
WALLMA
PIV!
LET ME CHANGE THIS CHEAP BULLSHIT FOOD INTO SOME ROYAL CANINE! MY DOG DESERVES ONLY THE BEST!!
PIIIIIIP!

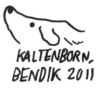

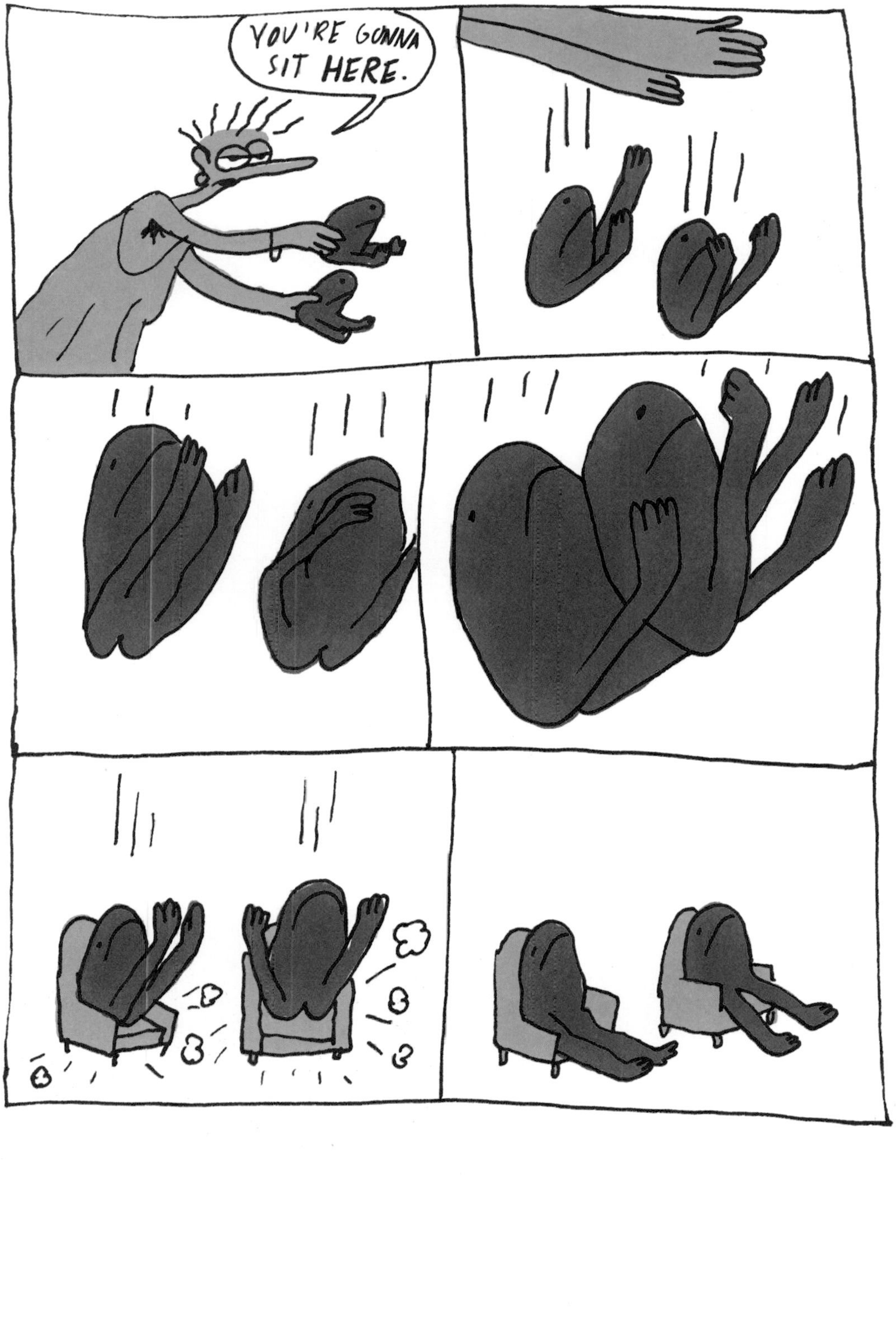
YOU'RE GONNA SIT HERE.

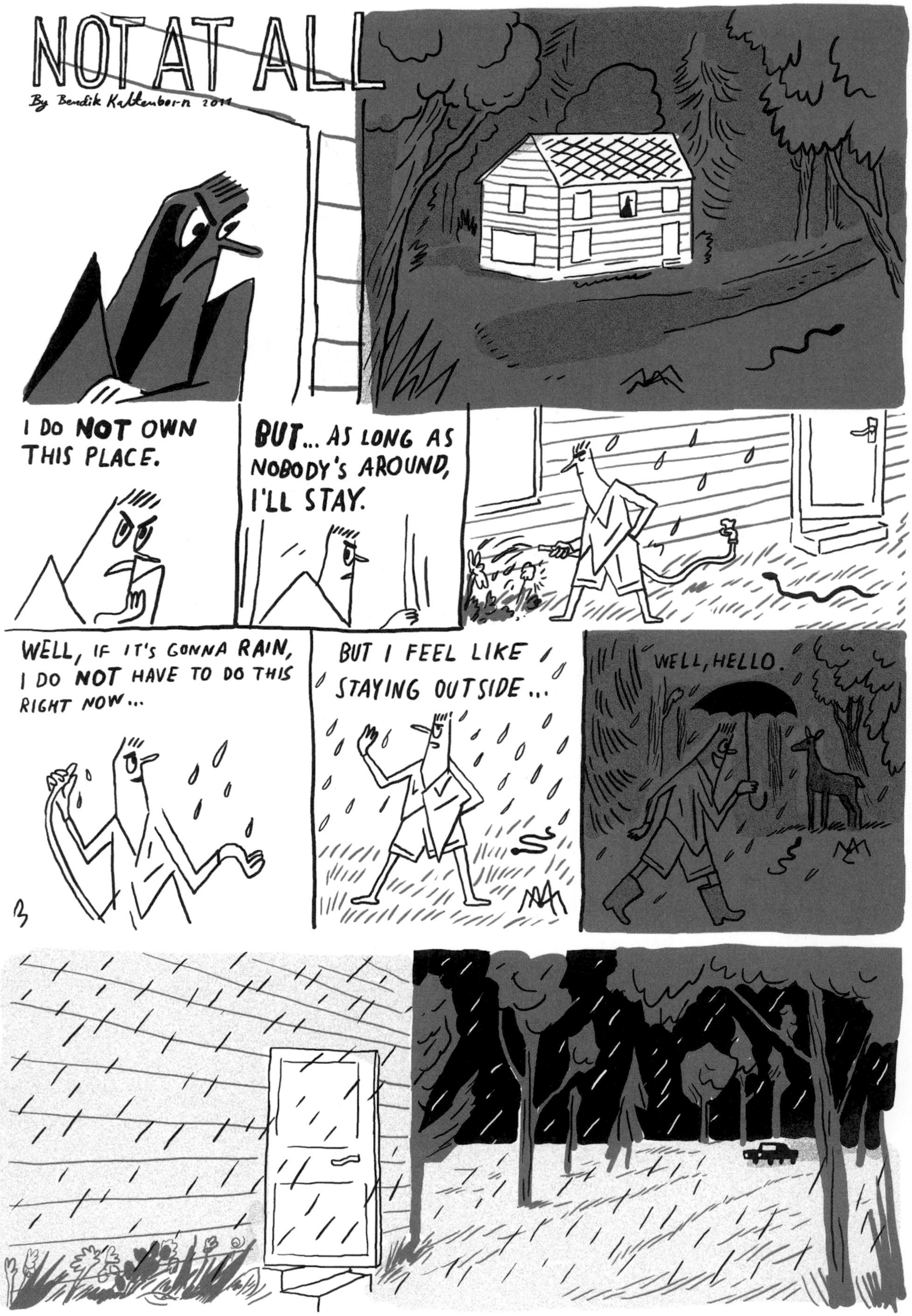

NOT AT ALL
By Bendik Kaltenborn 2011
I DO NOT OWN THIS PLACE.
BUT... AS LONG AS NOBODY'S AROUND, I'LL STAY.
WELL, IF IT'S GONNA RAIN, I DO NOT HAVE TO DO THIS RIGHT NOW...
BUT I FEEL LIKE STAYING OUTSIDE...
WELL, HELLO.

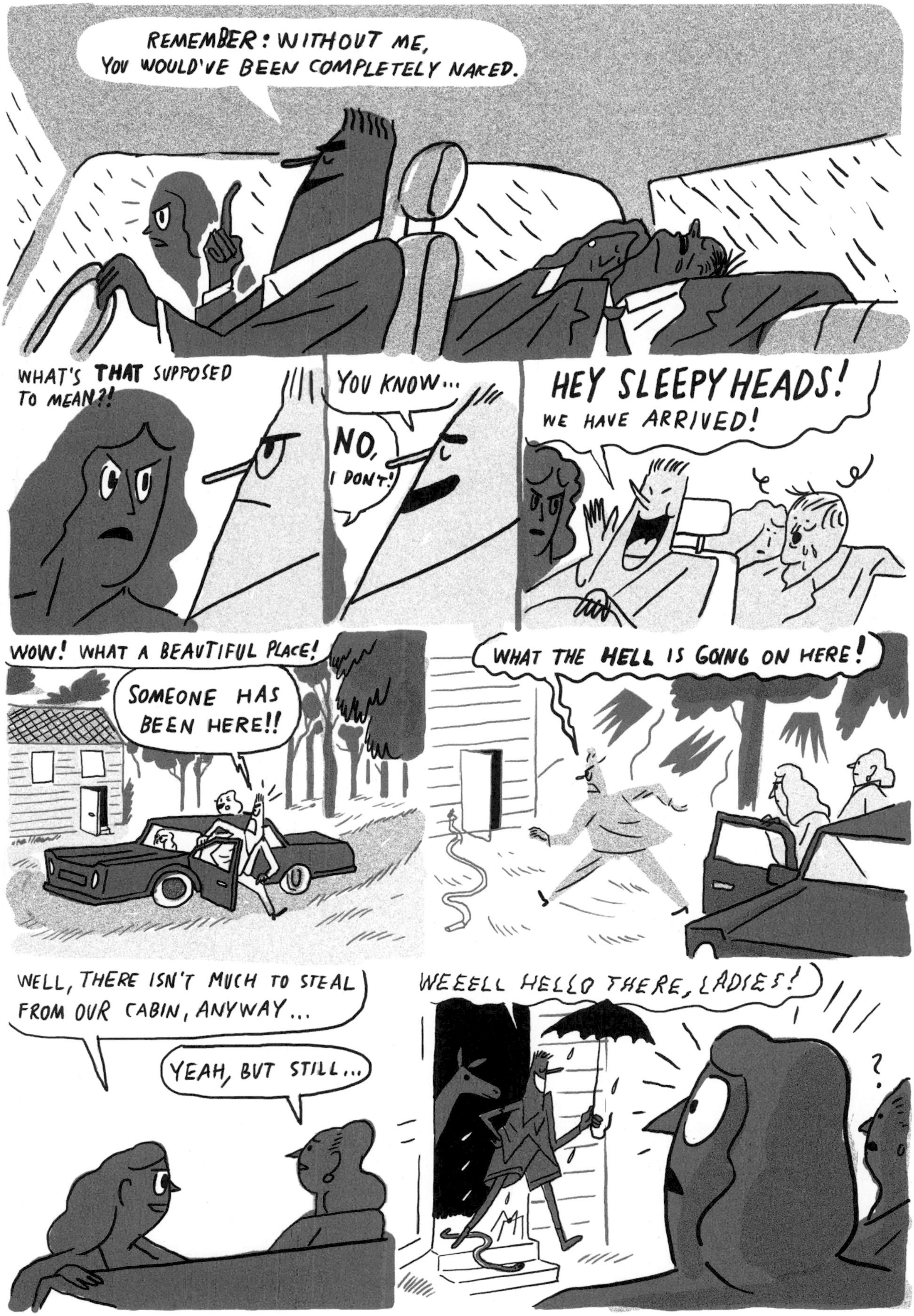
REMEMBER: WITHOUT ME, YOU WOULD'VE BEEN COMPLETELY NAKED.
WHAT'S THAT SUPPOSED TO MEAN?!
YOU KNOW...
NO, I DON'T!
HEY SLEEPY HEADS! WE HAVE ARRIVED!
WOW! WHAT A BEAUTIFUL PLACE!
SOMEONE HAS BEEN HERE!!
WHAT THE HELL IS GOING ON HERE!
WELL, THERE ISN'T MUCH TO STEAL FROM OUR CABIN, ANYWAY...
YEAH, BUT STILL...
WEEELL HELLO THERE, LADIES!
?

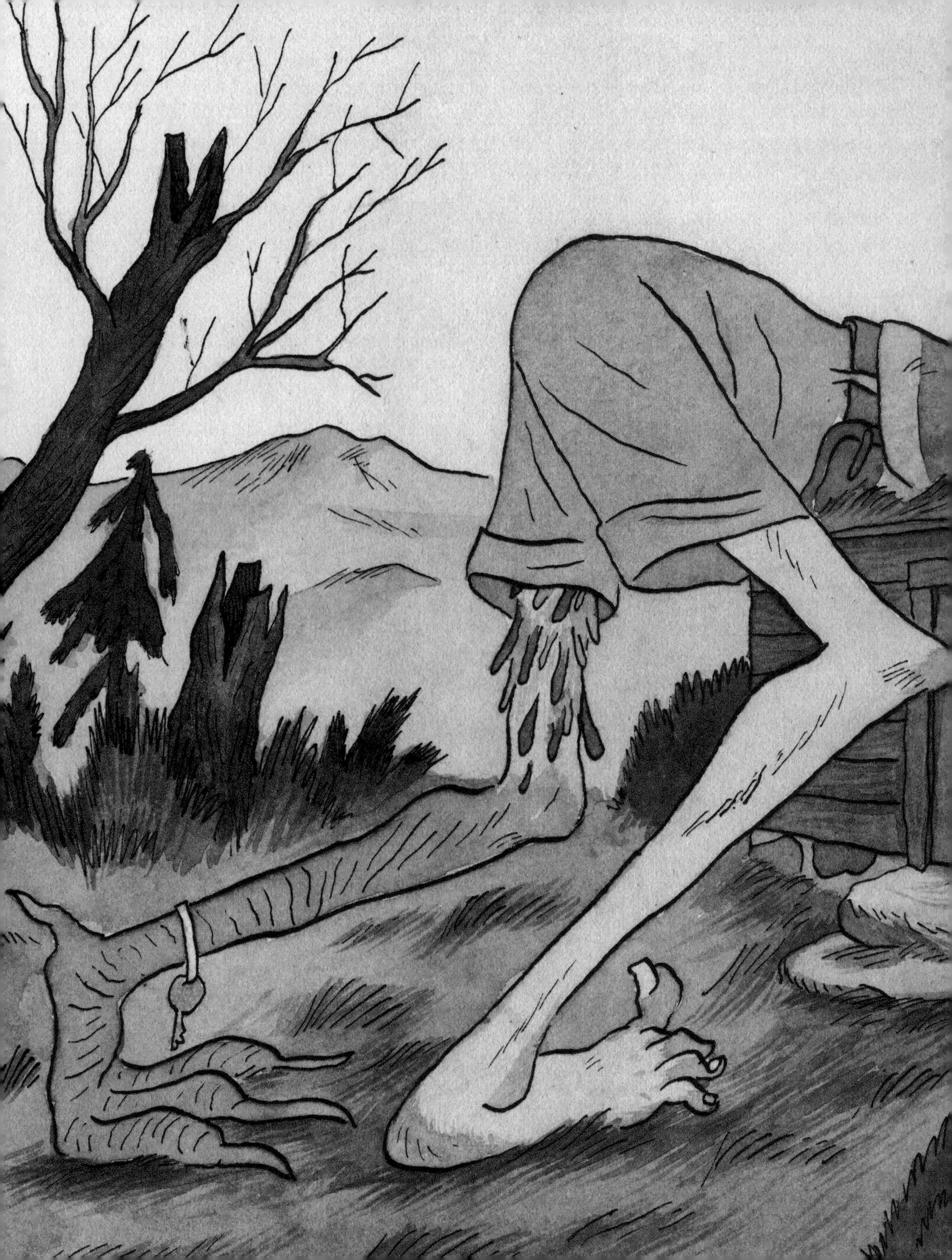

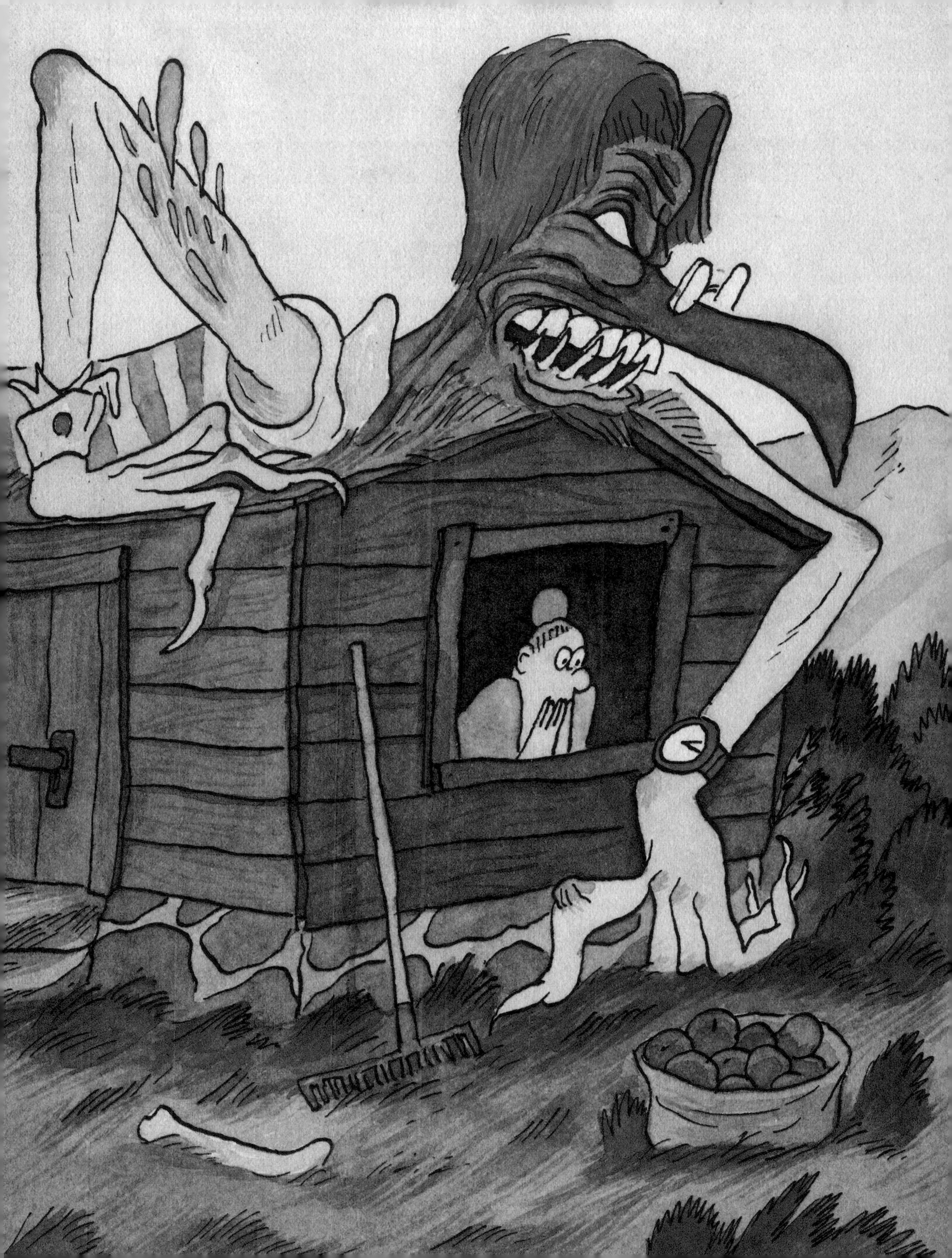

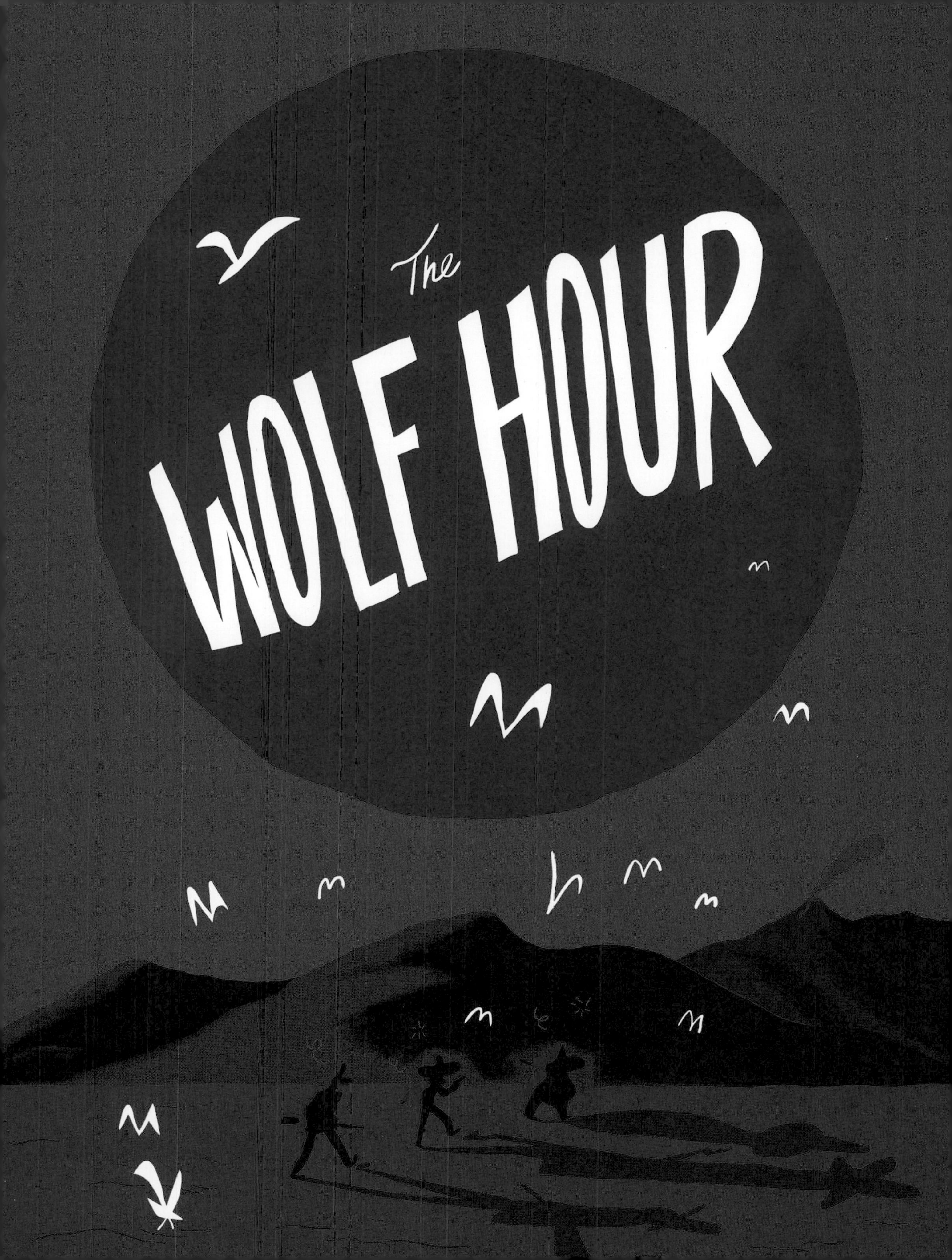
The
WOLF HOUR

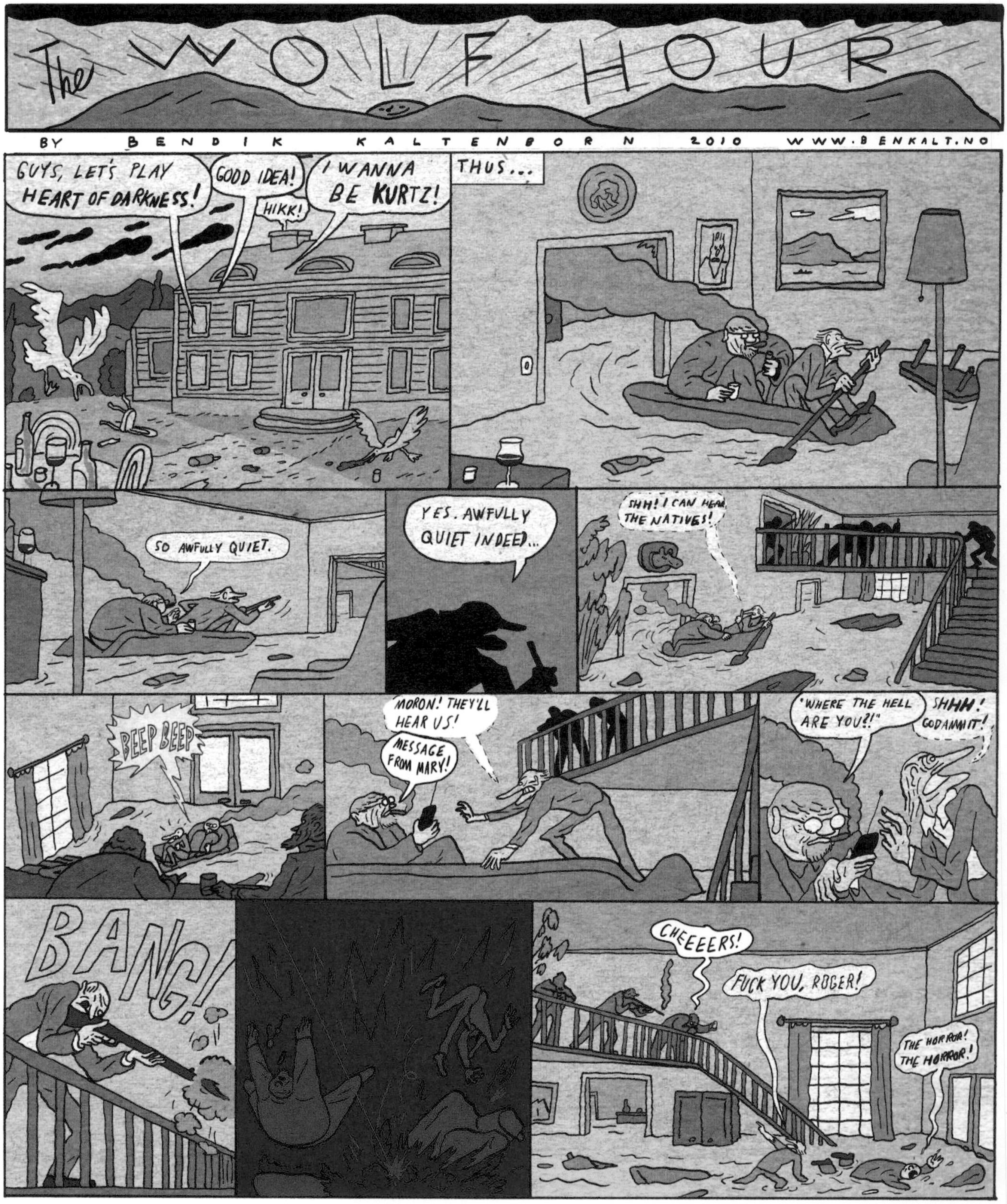
The WOLF HOUR
BY BENDIK KALTENBORN 2010 WWW.BENKALT.NO
GUYS, LET'S PLAY HEART OF DARKNESS!
GOOD IDEA!
HIKK!
I WANNA BE KURTZ!
THUS...
SO AWFULLY QUIET.
YES. AWFULLY QUIET INDEED...
SHH! I CAN HEAR THE NATIVES!
BEEP BEEP
MORON! THEY'LL HEAR US!
MESSAGE FROM MARY!
"WHERE THE HELL ARE YOU?!"
SHHH! GODAMMIT!
BANG!
CHEEEERS!
FUCK YOU, ROGER!
THE HORROR! THE HORROR!

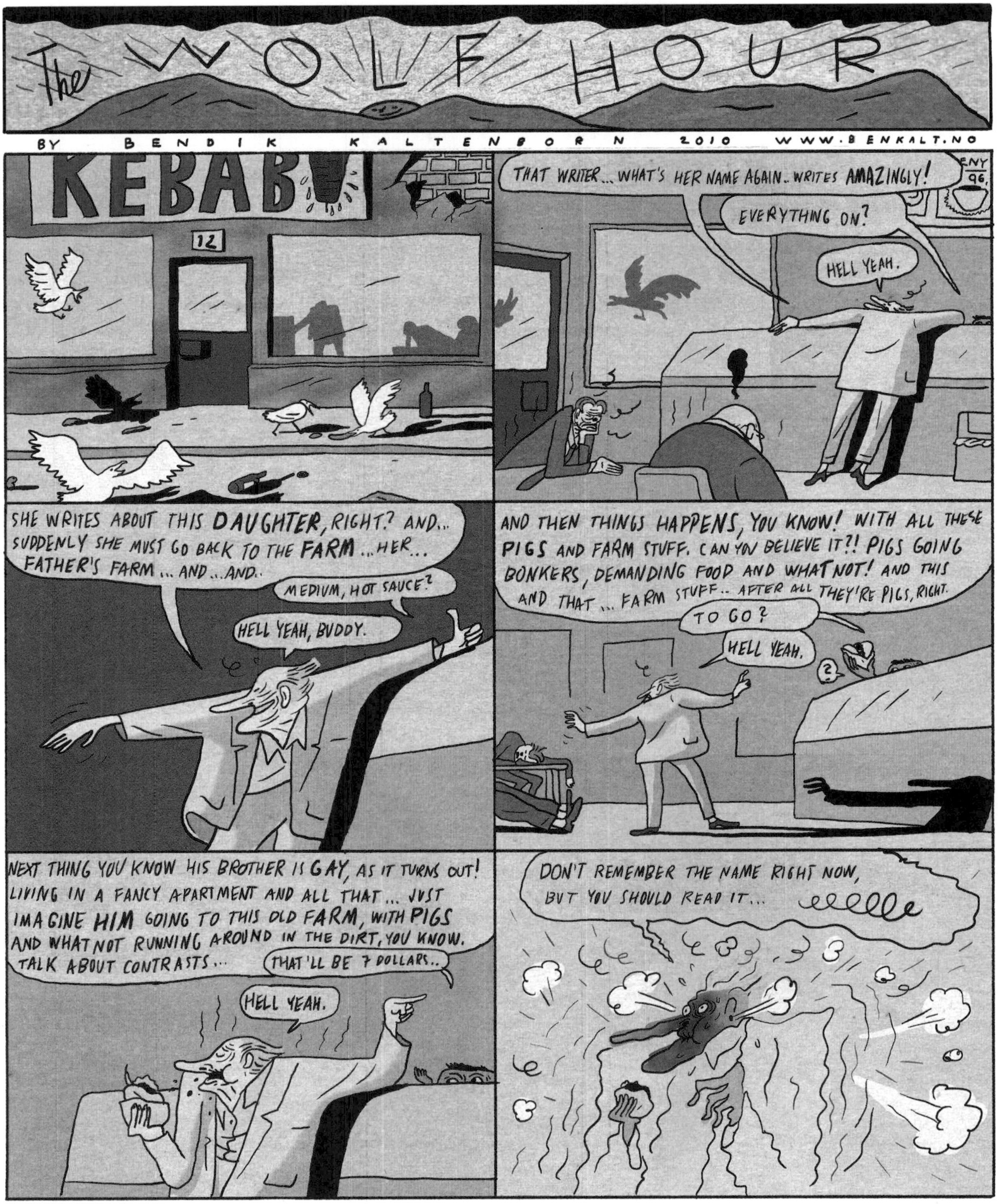

The WOLF HOUR
BY BENDIK KALTENBORN 2010 WWW.BENKALT.NO
KEBAB
12
THAT WRITER... WHAT'S HER NAME AGAIN.. WRITES AMAZINGLY!
EVERYTHING ON?
HELL YEAH.
SHE WRITES ABOUT THIS DAUGHTER, RIGHT? AND... SUDDENLY SHE MUST GO BACK TO THE FARM ... HER... FATHER'S FARM ... AND ... AND.
MEDIUM, HOT SAUCE?
HELL YEAH, BUDDY.
AND THEN THINGS HAPPENS, YOU KNOW! WITH ALL THESE PIGS AND FARM STUFF. CAN YOU BELIEVE IT?! PIGS GOING BONKERS, DEMANDING FOOD AND WHATNOT! AND THIS AND THAT ... FARM STUFF.. AFTER ALL THEY'RE PIGS, RIGHT.
TO GO?
HELL YEAH.
NEXT THING YOU KNOW HIS BROTHER IS GAY, AS IT TURNS OUT! LIVING IN A FANCY APARTMENT AND ALL THAT ... JUST IMAGINE HIM GOING TO THIS OLD FARM, WITH PIGS AND WHATNOT RUNNING AROUND IN THE DIRT, YOU KNOW. TALK ABOUT CONTRASTS...
THAT'LL BE 7 DOLLARS...
HELL YEAH.
DON'T REMEMBER THE NAME RIGHT NOW, BUT YOU SHOULD READ IT...

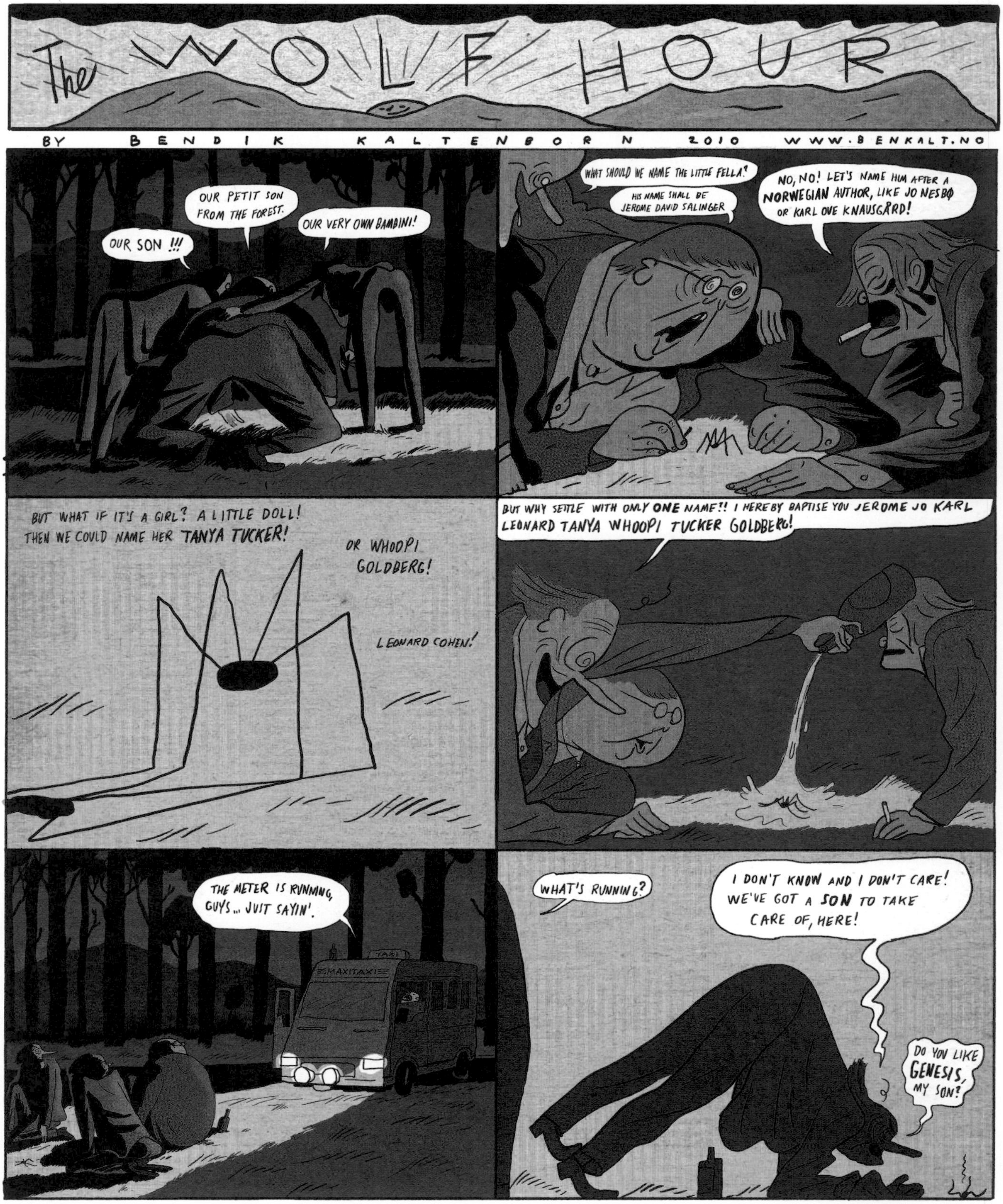
The WOLF HOUR
BY BENDIK KALTENBORN 2010 WWW.BENKALT.NO
OUR SON !!!
OUR PETIT SON FROM THE FOREST.
OUR VERY OWN BAMBINI!
WHAT SHOULD WE NAME THE LITTLE FELLA?
HIS NAME SHALL BE JEROME DAVID SALINGER
NO, NO! LET'S NAME HIM AFTER A NORWEGIAN AUTHOR, LIKE JO NESBØ OR KARL OVE KNAUSGÅRD!
BUT WHAT IF IT'S A GIRL? A LITTLE DOLL! THEN WE COULD NAME HER TANYA TUCKER!
OR WHOOPI GOLDBERG!
LEONARD COHEN!
BUT WHY SETTLE WITH ONLY ONE NAME!! I HEREBY BAPTISE YOU JEROME JO KARL LEONARD TANYA WHOOPI TUCKER GOLDBERG!
THE METER IS RUNNING, GUYS... JUST SAYIN'.
MAXITAXI
WHAT'S RUNNING?
I DON'T KNOW AND I DON'T CARE! WE'VE GOT A SON TO TAKE CARE OF, HERE!
DO YOU LIKE GENESIS, MY SON?

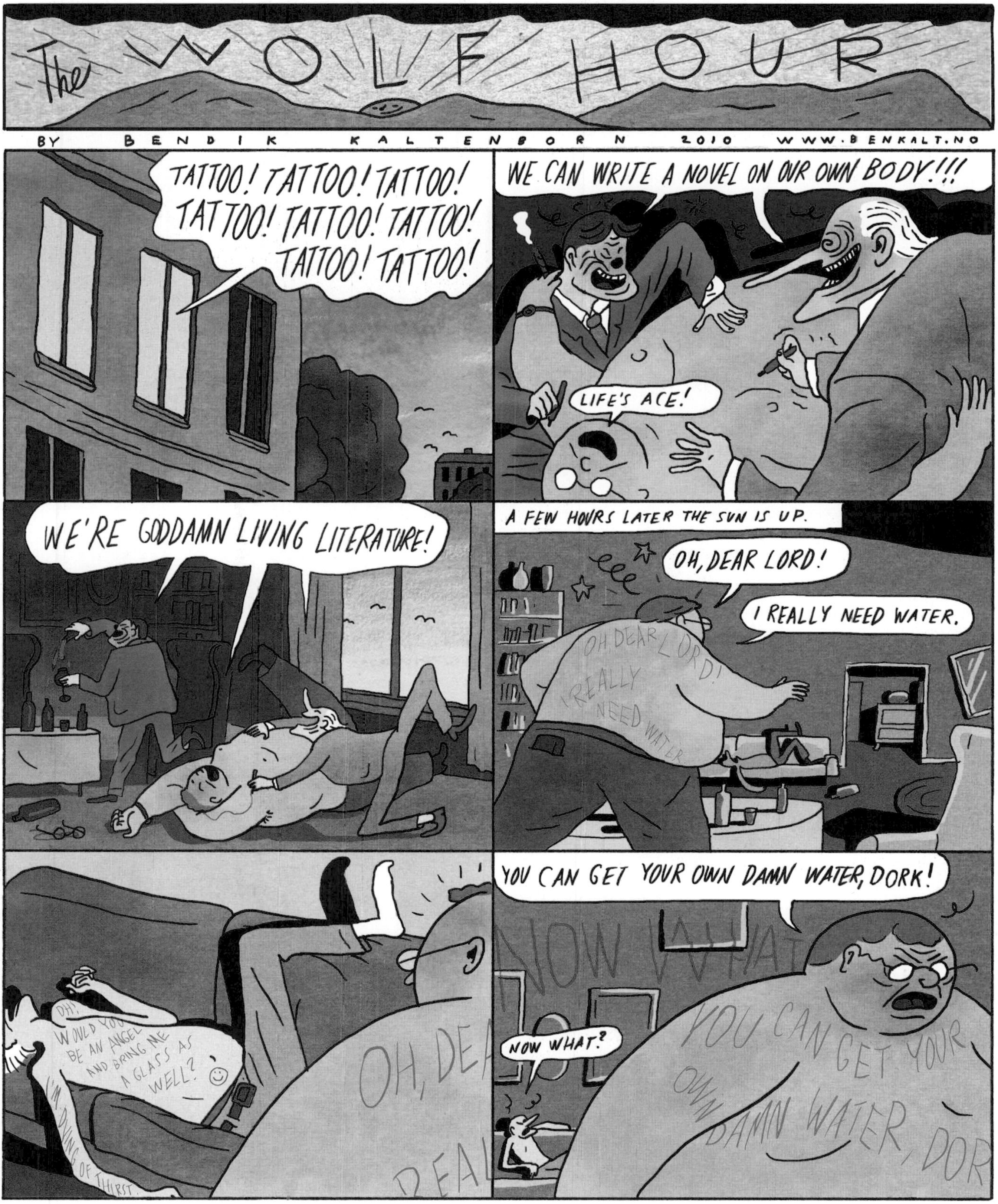

The WOLF HOUR
BY BENDIK KALTENBORN 2010 WWW.BENKALT.NO
TATTOO! TATTOO! TATTOO! TATTOO! TATTOO! TATTOO! TATTOO! TATTOO!
WE CAN WRITE A NOVEL ON OUR OWN BODY!!!
LIFE'S ACE!
WE'RE GODDAMN LIVING LITERATURE!
A FEW HOURS LATER THE SUN IS UP.
OH, DEAR LORD!
I REALLY NEED WATER.
OH, DEAR LORD! I REALLY NEED WATER
OH! WOULD YOU BE AN ANGEL AND BRING ME A GLASS AS WELL? I'M DYING OF THIRST.
YOU CAN GET YOUR OWN DAMN WATER, DORK!
NOW WHAT
NOW WHAT?
YOU CAN GET YOUR OWN DAMN WATER, DOR

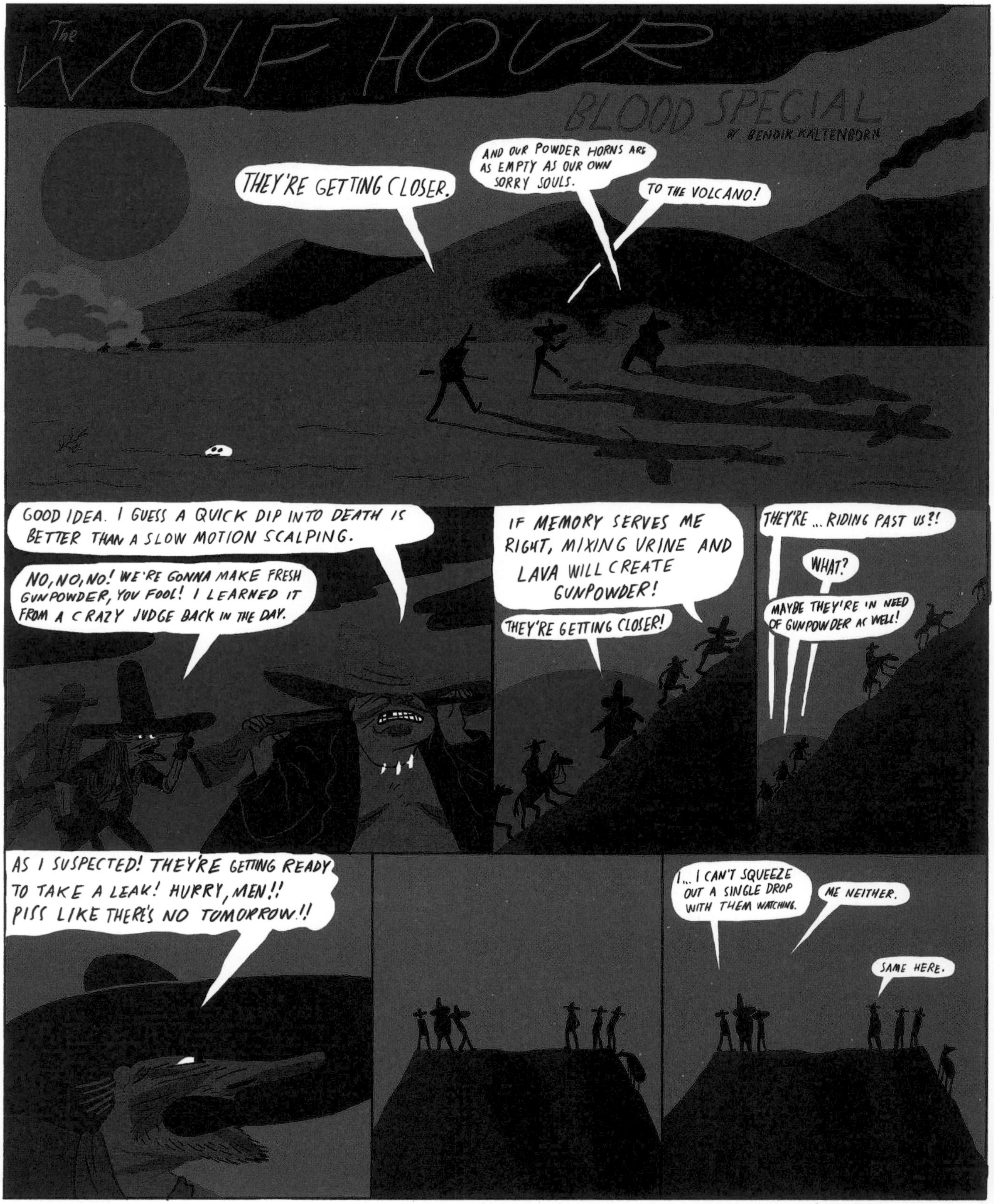
The WOLF HOUR
BLOOD SPECIAL
BY BENDIK KALTENBORN
THEY'RE GETTING CLOSER.
AND OUR POWDER HORNS ARE AS EMPTY AS OUR OWN SORRY SOULS.
TO THE VOLCANO!
GOOD IDEA. I GUESS A QUICK DIP INTO DEATH IS BETTER THAN A SLOW MOTION SCALPING.
NO, NO, NO! WE'RE GONNA MAKE FRESH GUNPOWDER, YOU FOOL! I LEARNED IT FROM A CRAZY JUDGE BACK IN THE DAY.
IF MEMORY SERVES ME RIGHT, MIXING URINE AND LAVA WILL CREATE GUNPOWDER!
THEY'RE GETTING CLOSER!
THEY'RE ... RIDING PAST US?!
WHAT?
MAYBE THEY'RE IN NEED OF GUNPOWDER AS WELL!
AS I SUSPECTED! THEY'RE GETTING READY TO TAKE A LEAK! HURRY, MEN!! PISS LIKE THERE'S NO TOMORROW!!
I... I CAN'T SQUEEZE OUT A SINGLE DROP WITH THEM WATCHING.
ME NEITHER.
SAME HERE.

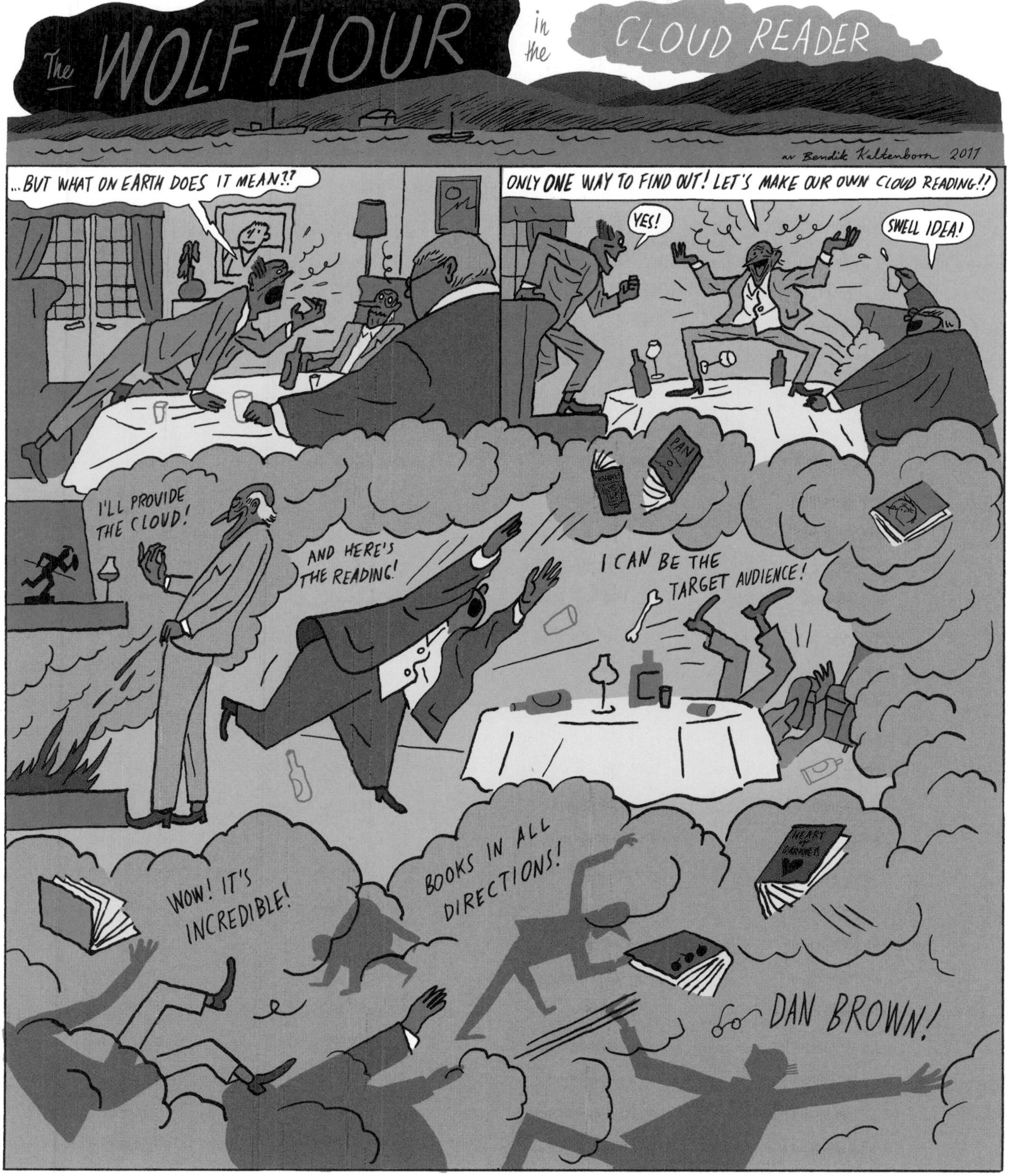

The WOLF HOUR in the CLOUD READER
av Bendik Kaltenborn 2011
...BUT WHAT ON EARTH DOES IT MEAN?!?
ONLY ONE WAY TO FIND OUT! LET'S MAKE OUR OWN CLOUD READING!!
YES!
SWELL IDEA!
PAN
I'LL PROVIDE THE CLOUD!
AND HERE'S THE READING!
I CAN BE THE TARGET AUDIENCE!
WOW! IT'S INCREDIBLE!
BOOKS IN ALL DIRECTIONS!
HEART OF DARKNESS
DAN BROWN!

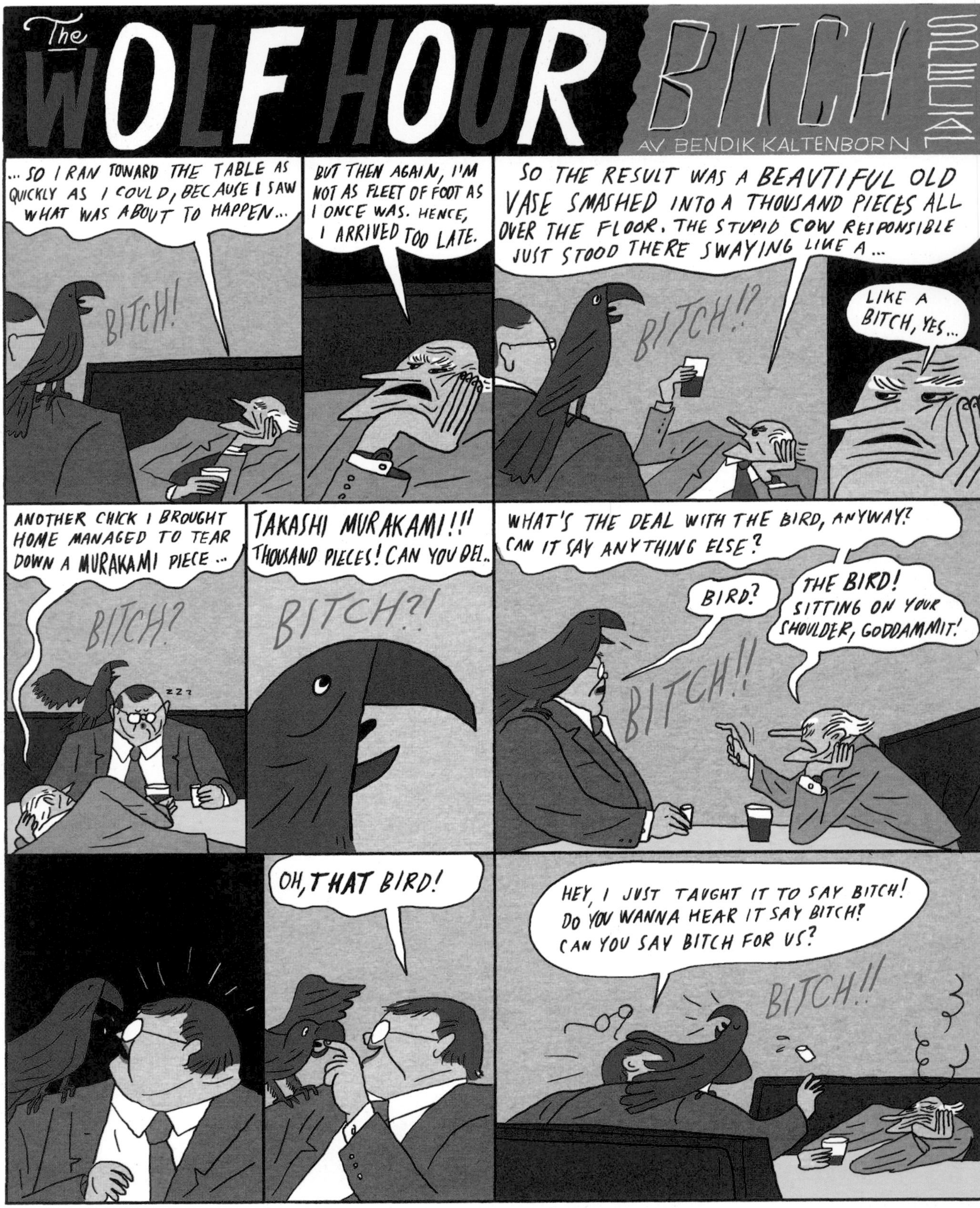
The WOLF HOUR
BITCH SPECIAL
AV BENDIK KALTENBORN
... SO I RAN TOWARD THE TABLE AS QUICKLY AS I COULD, BECAUSE I SAW WHAT WAS ABOUT TO HAPPEN...
BITCH!
BUT THEN AGAIN, I'M NOT AS FLEET OF FOOT AS I ONCE WAS. HENCE, I ARRIVED TOO LATE.
SO THE RESULT WAS A BEAUTIFUL OLD VASE SMASHED INTO A THOUSAND PIECES ALL OVER THE FLOOR. THE STUPID COW RESPONSIBLE JUST STOOD THERE SWAYING LIKE A...
BITCH!?
LIKE A BITCH, YES...
ANOTHER CHICK I BROUGHT HOME MANAGED TO TEAR DOWN A MURAKAMI PIECE...
BITCH?
TAKASHI MURAKAMI!!! THOUSAND PIECES! CAN YOU BEL..
BITCH?!
WHAT'S THE DEAL WITH THE BIRD, ANYWAY? CAN IT SAY ANYTHING ELSE?
BIRD?
THE BIRD! SITTING ON YOUR SHOULDER, GODDAMMIT!
BITCH!!
OH, THAT BIRD!
HEY, I JUST TAUGHT IT TO SAY BITCH! DO YOU WANNA HEAR IT SAY BITCH? CAN YOU SAY BITCH FOR US?
BITCH!!

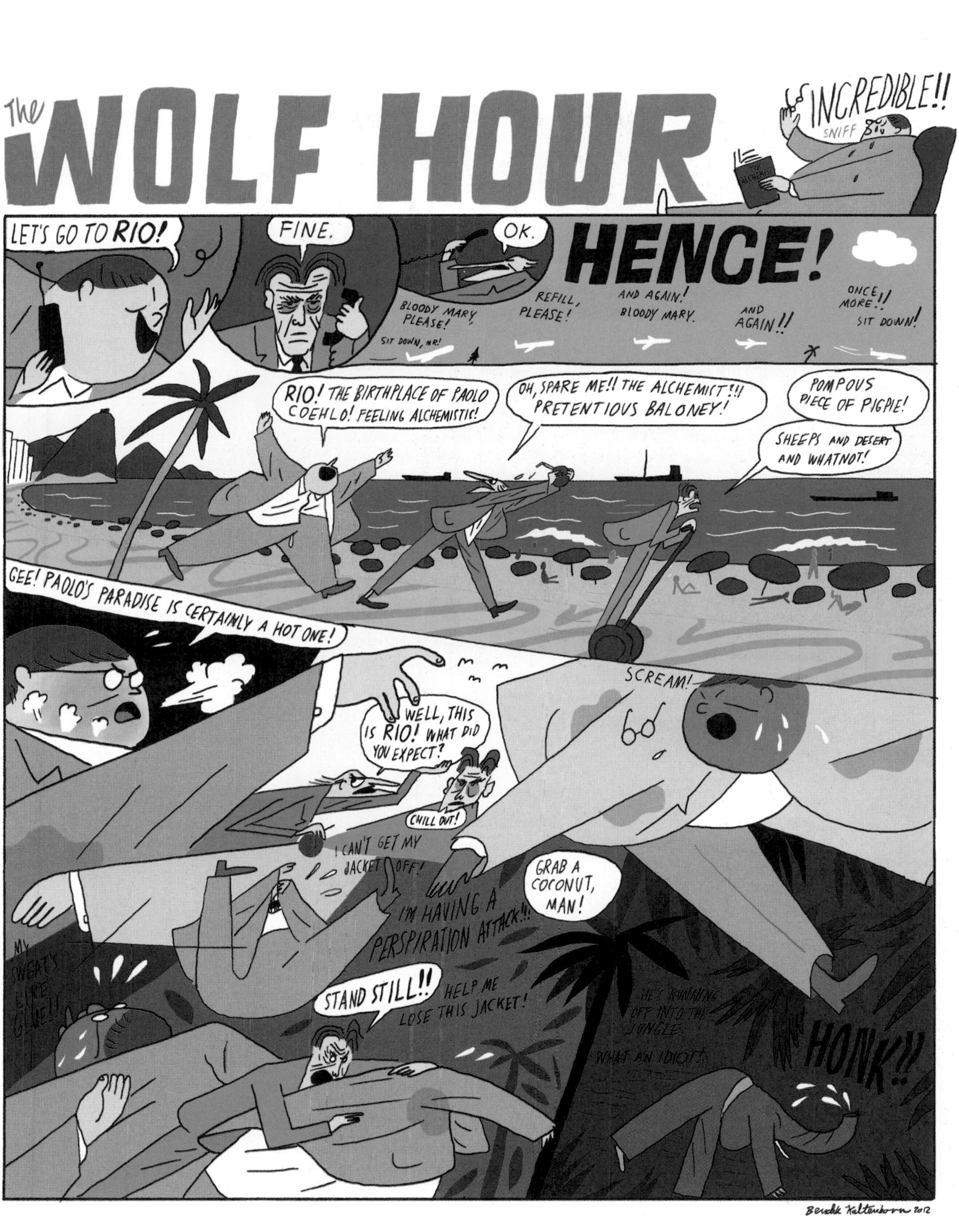
The WOLF HOUR
INCREDIBLE!!
SNIFF
THE ALCHEMIST
LET'S GO TO RIO!
FINE.
OK.
HENCE!
BLOODY MARY PLEASE!
SIT DOWN, MR!
REFILL, PLEASE!
AND AGAIN! BLOODY MARY.
AND AGAIN!!
ONCE MORE!!
SIT DOWN!
RIO! THE BIRTHPLACE OF PAOLO COEHLO! FEELING ALCHEMISTIC!
OH, SPARE ME!! THE ALCHEMIST!!! PRETENTIOUS BALONEY!
POMPOUS PIECE OF PIGPIE!
SHEEPS AND DESERT AND WHATNOT!
GEE! PAOLO'S PARADISE IS CERTAINLY A HOT ONE!
SCREAM!
WELL, THIS IS RIO! WHAT DID YOU EXPECT?
CHILL OUT!
I CAN'T GET MY JACKET OFF!
I'M HAVING A PERSPIRATION ATTACK!!
GRAB A COCONUT, MAN!
MY SWEAT'S LIKE GLUE!!
STAND STILL!!
HELP ME LOSE THIS JACKET!
HE'S RUNNING OFF INTO THE JUNGLE.
WHAT AN IDIOT!
HONK!!
Bendik Kaltenborn 2012

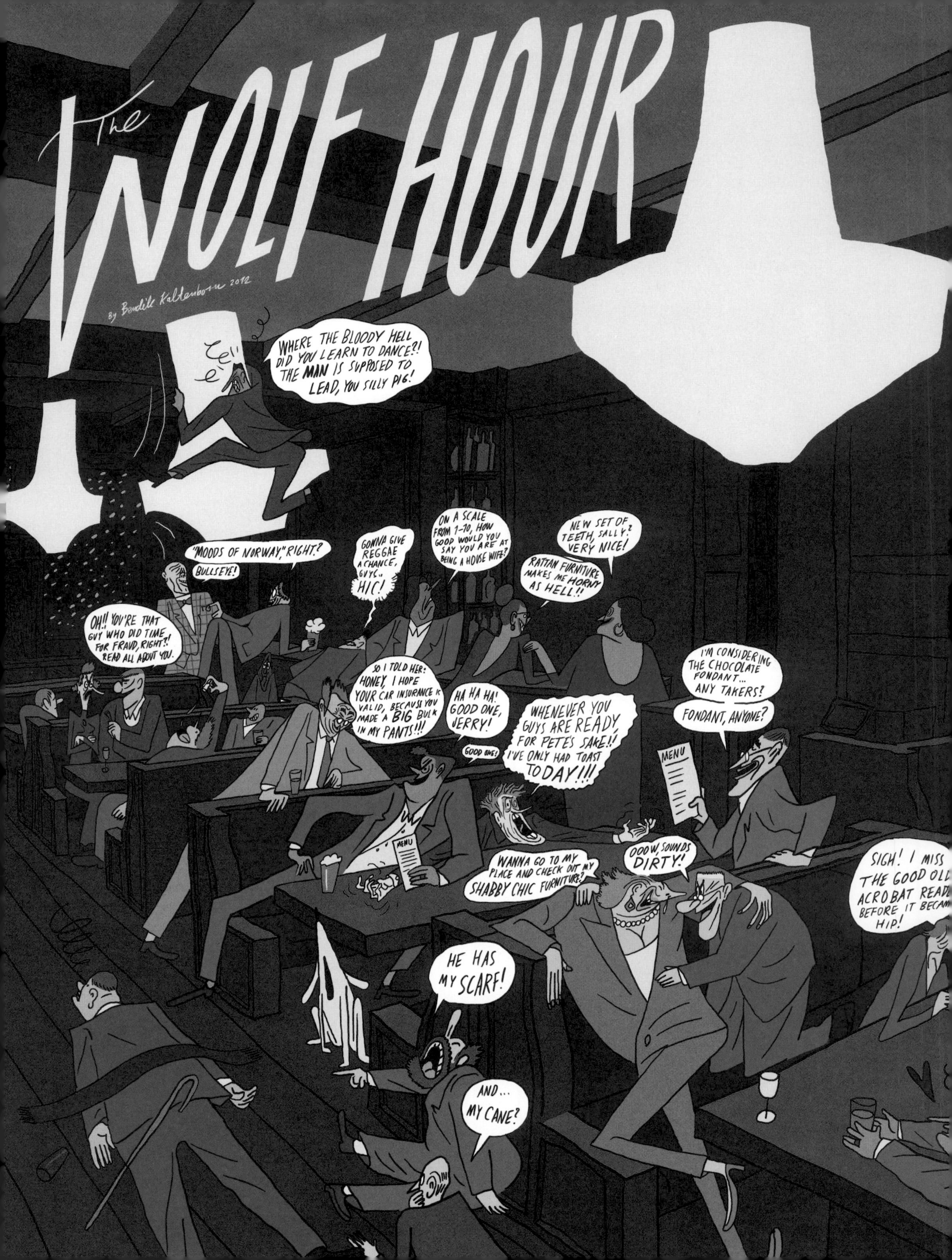
The WOLF HOUR
By Bendik Kaltenborn 2012
WHERE THE BLOODY HELL DID YOU LEARN TO DANCE?! THE MAN IS SUPPOSED TO LEAD, YOU SILLY PIG!
"MOODS OF NORWAY," RIGHT?
BULLSEYE!
GONNA GIVE REGGAE A CHANCE, GUYS.. HIC!
ON A SCALE FROM 1-10, HOW GOOD WOULD YOU SAY YOU ARE AT BEING A HOUSE WIFE?
NEW SET OF TEETH, SALLY? VERY NICE!
RATTAN FURNITURE MAKES ME HORNY AS HELL!!
OH!! YOU'RE THAT GUY WHO DID TIME FOR FRAUD, RIGHT?! READ ALL ABOUT YOU.
SO I TOLD HER: HONEY, I HOPE YOUR CAR INSURANCE IS VALID, BECAUSE YOU MADE A BIG BULK IN MY PANTS!!!
HA HA HA! GOOD ONE, JERRY!
GOOD ONE!
WHENEVER YOU GUYS ARE READY, FOR PETE'S SAKE!! I'VE ONLY HAD TOAST TODAY!!!
I'M CONSIDERING THE CHOCOLATE FONDANT... ANY TAKERS?
FONDANT, ANYONE?
MENU
MENU
WANNA GO TO MY PLACE AND CHECK OUT MY SHABBY CHIC FURNITURE?
OOOW, SOUNDS DIRTY!
SIGH! I MISS THE GOOD OLD ACROBAT READ BEFORE IT BECAM HIP!
HE HAS MY SCARF!
AND... MY CANE?

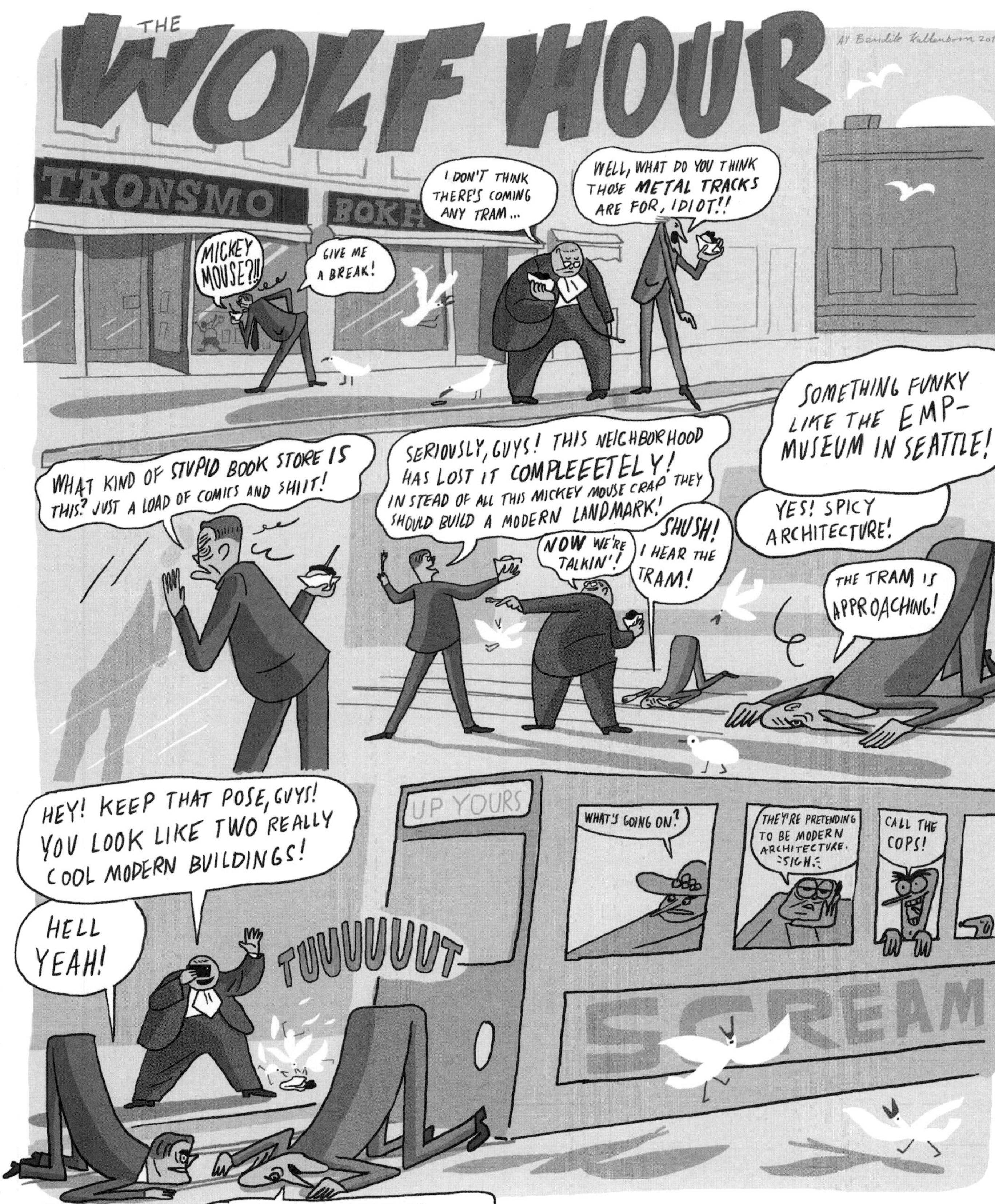
THE WOLF HOUR
AV Bendik Kaltenborn 2012
TRONSMO
BOKH
MICKEY MOUSE?!!
GIVE ME A BREAK!
I DON'T THINK THERE'S COMING ANY TRAM...
WELL, WHAT DO YOU THINK THOSE METAL TRACKS ARE FOR, IDIOT?!
WHAT KIND OF STUPID BOOK STORE IS THIS? JUST A LOAD OF COMICS AND SHIIT!
SERIOUSLY, GUYS! THIS NEIGHBORHOOD HAS LOST IT COMPLEEETELY! INSTEAD OF ALL THIS MICKEY MOUSE CRAP THEY SHOULD BUILD A MODERN LANDMARK!
SOMETHING FUNKY LIKE THE EMP-MUSEUM IN SEATTLE!
YES! SPICY ARCHITECTURE!
NOW WE'RE TALKIN'!
SHUSH! I HEAR THE TRAM!
THE TRAM IS APPROACHING!
HEY! KEEP THAT POSE, GUYS! YOU LOOK LIKE TWO REALLY COOL MODERN BUILDINGS!
UP YOURS
WHAT'S GOING ON?
THEY'RE PRETENDING TO BE MODERN ARCHITECTURE. SIGH.
CALL THE COPS!
HELL YEAH!
TUUUUUUT
SCREAM
DAMN! NOW IT STOPPED.

The WOLF HOUR URINAL WISDOM

BENDIK KALTENBORN 2012

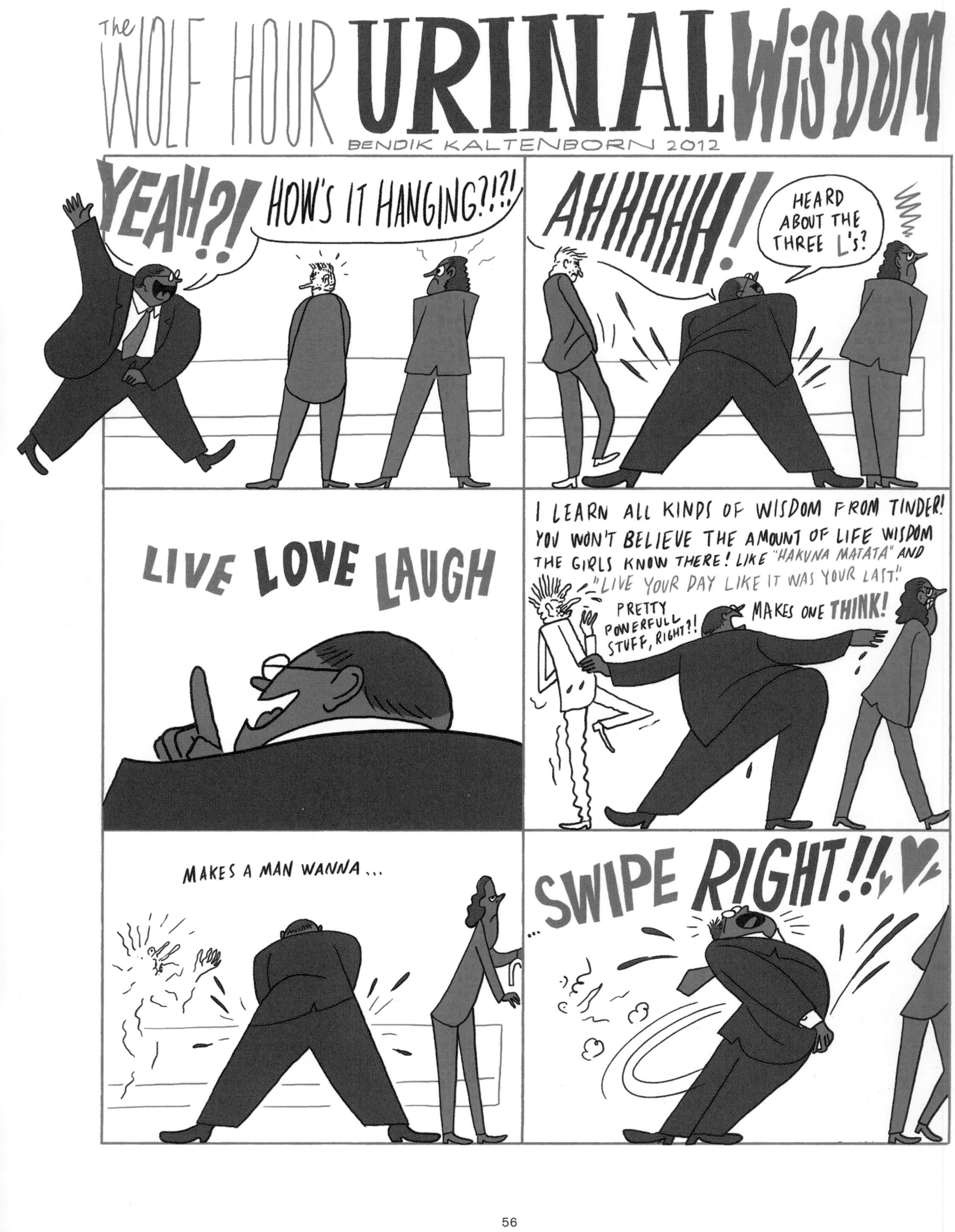
YEAH?!
HOW'S IT HANGING?!?!
AHHHHH!
HEARD ABOUT THE THREE L's?
LIVE LOVE LAUGH
I LEARN ALL KINDS OF WISDOM FROM TINDER! YOU WON'T BELIEVE THE AMOUNT OF LIFE WISDOM THE GIRLS KNOW THERE! LIKE "HAKUNA MATATA" AND "LIVE YOUR DAY LIKE IT WAS YOUR LAST."
PRETTY POWERFULL STUFF, RIGHT?!
MAKES ONE THINK!
MAKES A MAN WANNA ...
... SWIPE RIGHT!!!

The WOLF HOUR CRIME TIME

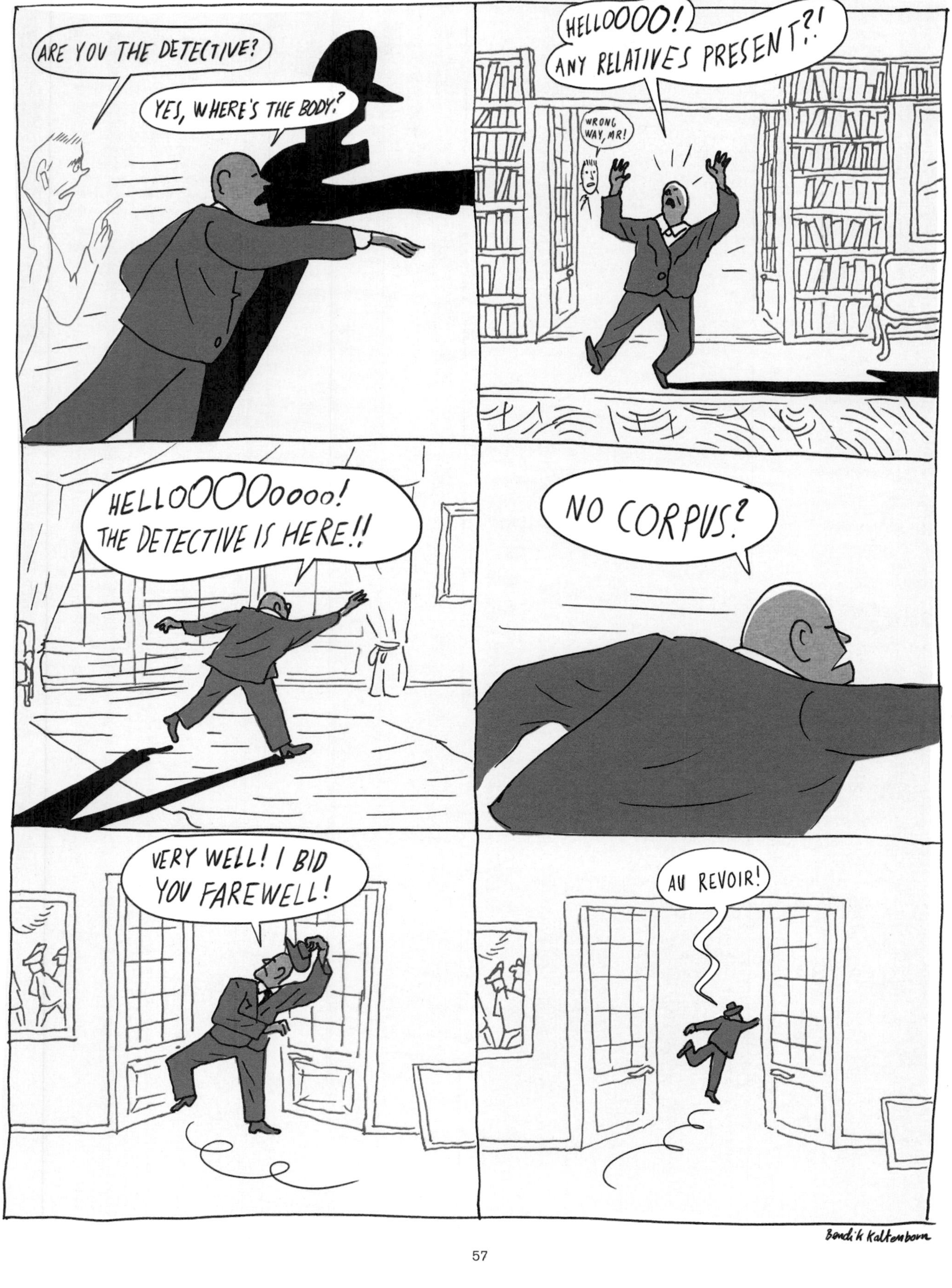
ARE YOU THE DETECTIVE?
YES, WHERE'S THE BODY?
HELLOOOO! ANY RELATIVES PRESENT?!
WRONG WAY, MR!
HELLOOOOoooo! THE DETECTIVE IS HERE!!
NO CORPUS?
VERY WELL! I BID YOU FAREWELL!
AU REVOIR!
Bendik Kaltenborn

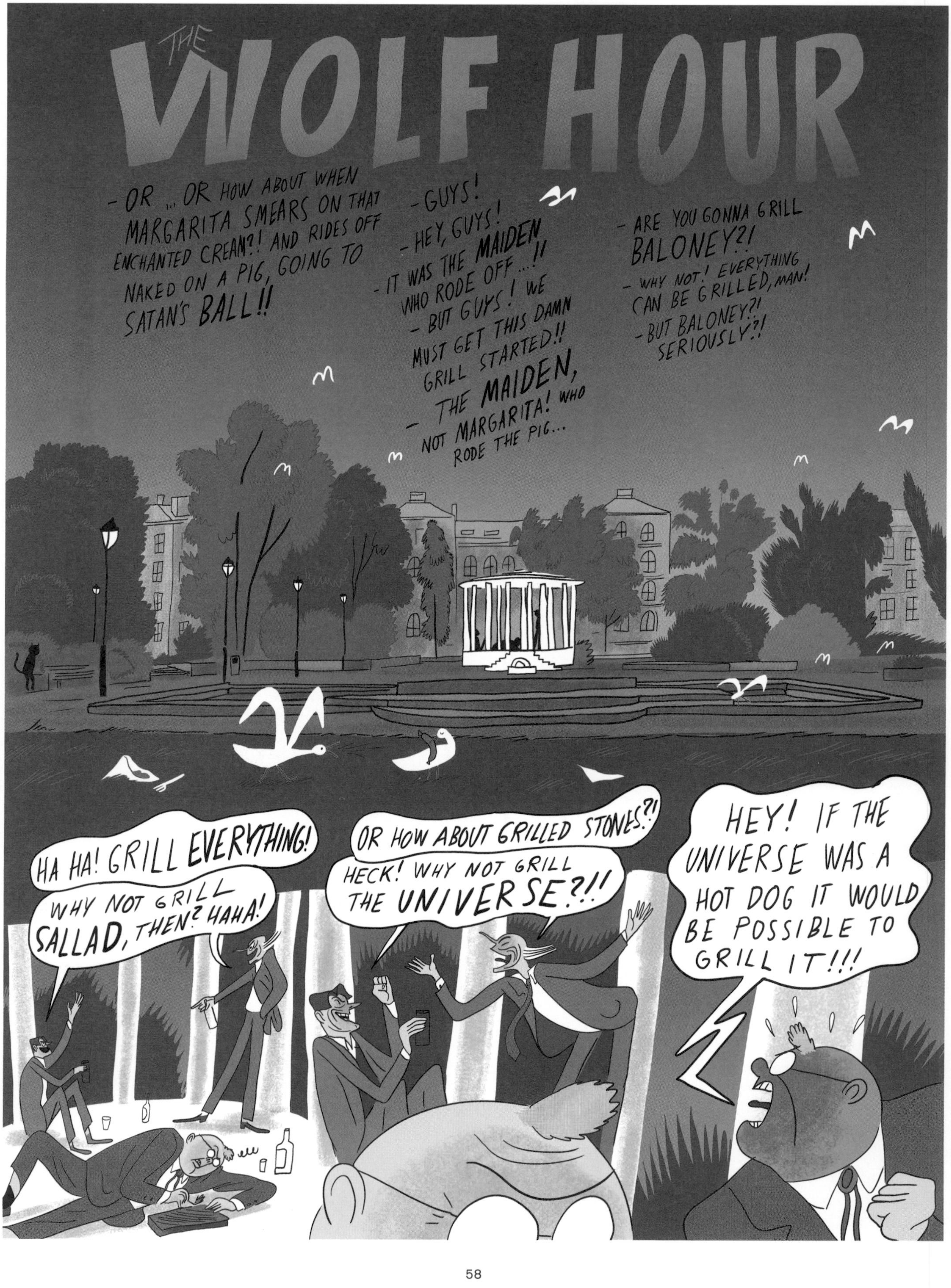
THE WOLF HOUR
- OR ... OR HOW ABOUT WHEN MARGARITA SMEARS ON THAT ENCHANTED CREAM?! AND RIDES OFF NAKED ON A PIG, GOING TO SATAN'S BALL!!
- GUYS!
- HEY, GUYS!
- IT WAS THE MAIDEN WHO RODE OFF...!!
- BUT GUYS! WE MUST GET THIS DAMN GRILL STARTED!!
- THE MAIDEN, NOT MARGARITA! WHO RODE THE PIG...
- ARE YOU GONNA GRILL BALONEY?!
- WHY NOT! EVERYTHING CAN BE GRILLED, MAN!
- BUT BALONEY?! SERIOUSLY?!
HA HA! GRILL EVERYTHING!
WHY NOT GRILL SALLAD, THEN? HAHA!
OR HOW ABOUT GRILLED STONES?!
HECK! WHY NOT GRILL THE UNIVERSE?!!
HEY! IF THE UNIVERSE WAS A HOT DOG IT WOULD BE POSSIBLE TO GRILL IT!!!

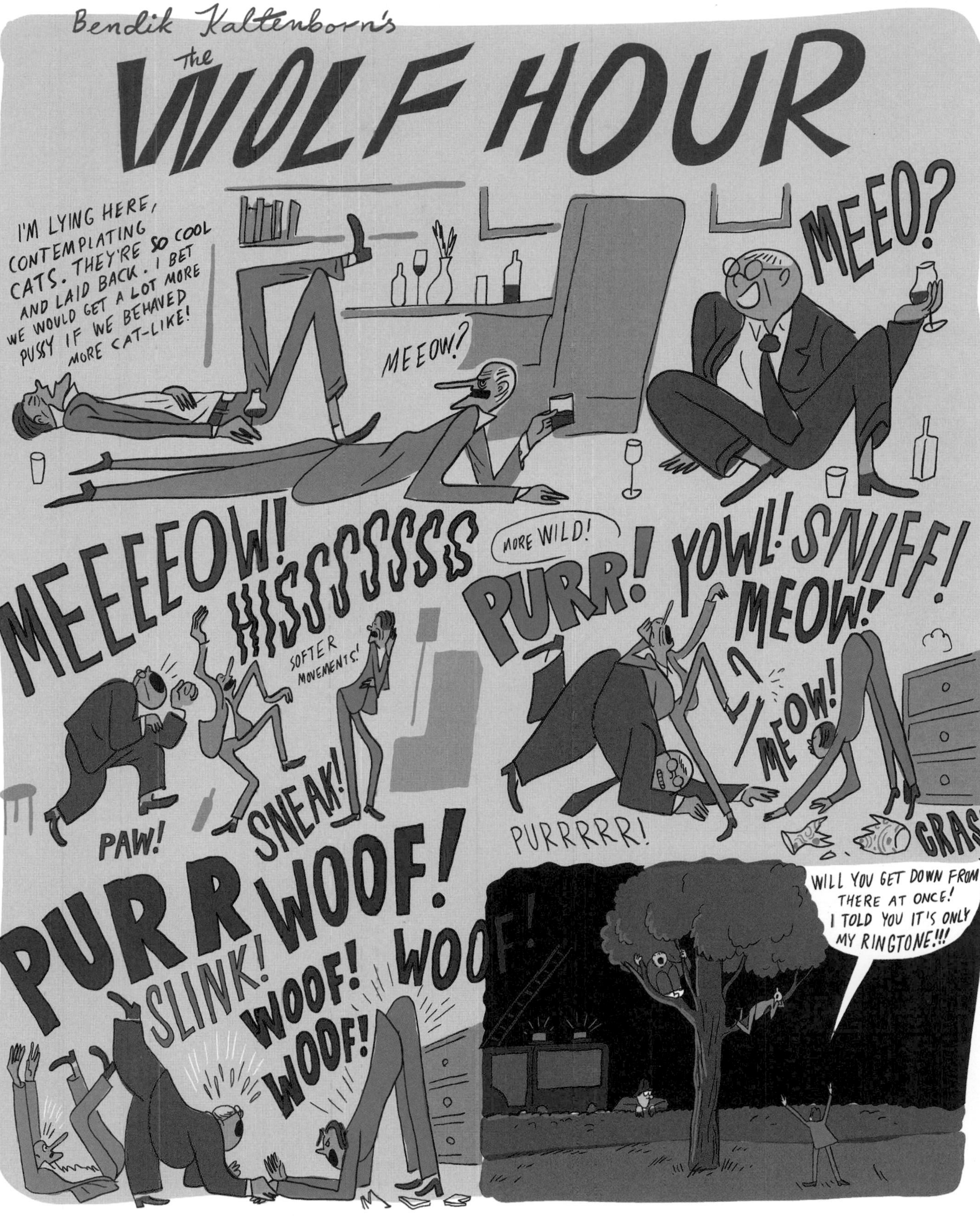
Bendik Kaltenborn's
the WOLF HOUR
I'M LYING HERE, CONTEMPLATING CATS. THEY'RE SO COOL AND LAID BACK. I BET WE WOULD GET A LOT MORE PUSSY IF WE BEHAVED MORE CAT-LIKE!
MEEOW?
MEEO?
MEEEEEOW!
HISSSSSSS
SOFTER MOVEMENTS!
MORE WILD!
PURR!
YOWL!
SNIFF!
MEOW!
MEOW!
PAW!
SNEAK!
PURRRRR!
CRASH!
PURR
WOOF!
SLINK!
WOOF!
WOOF!
WOOF!
WILL YOU GET DOWN FROM THERE AT ONCE! I TOLD YOU IT'S ONLY MY RINGTONE!!!

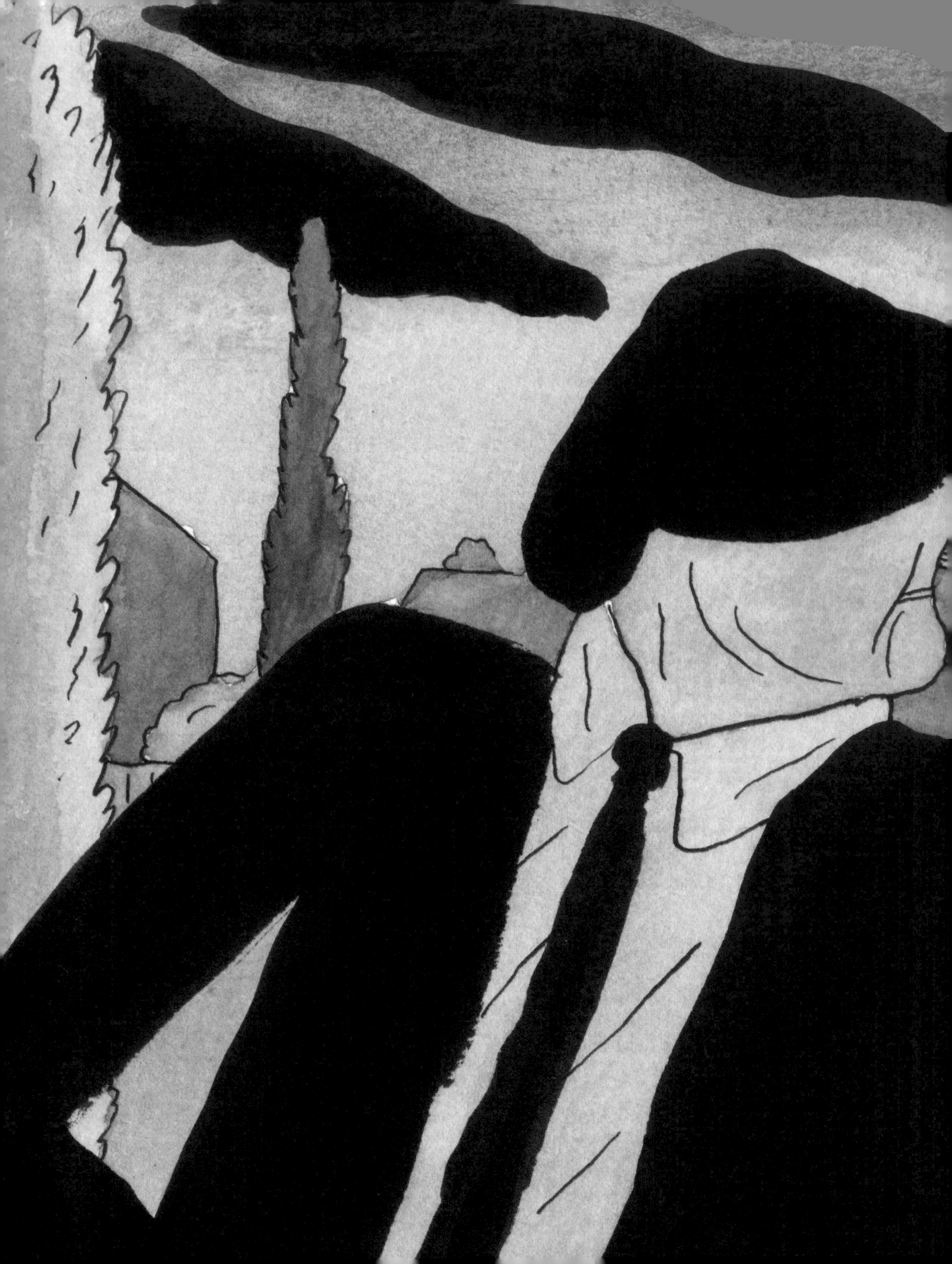

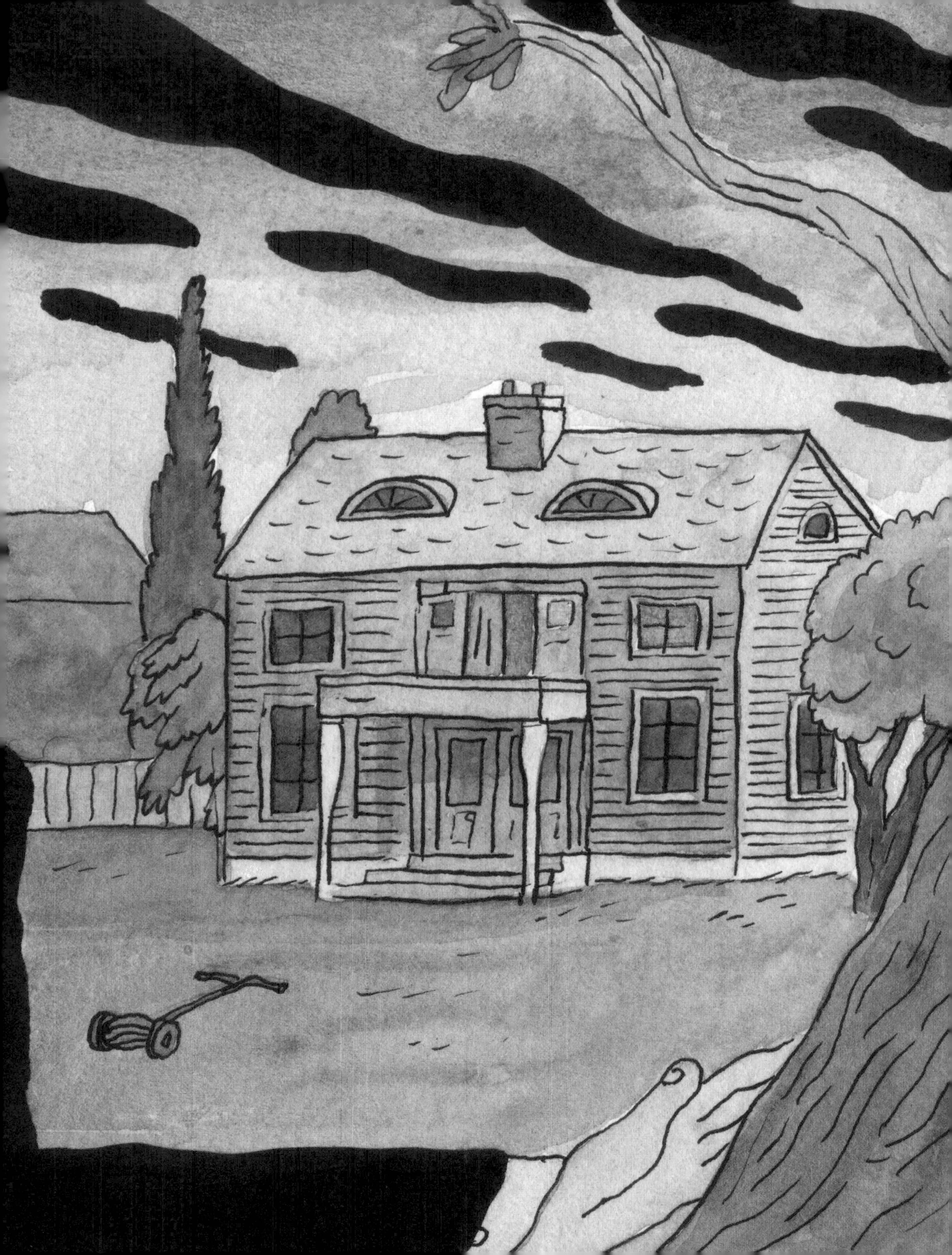

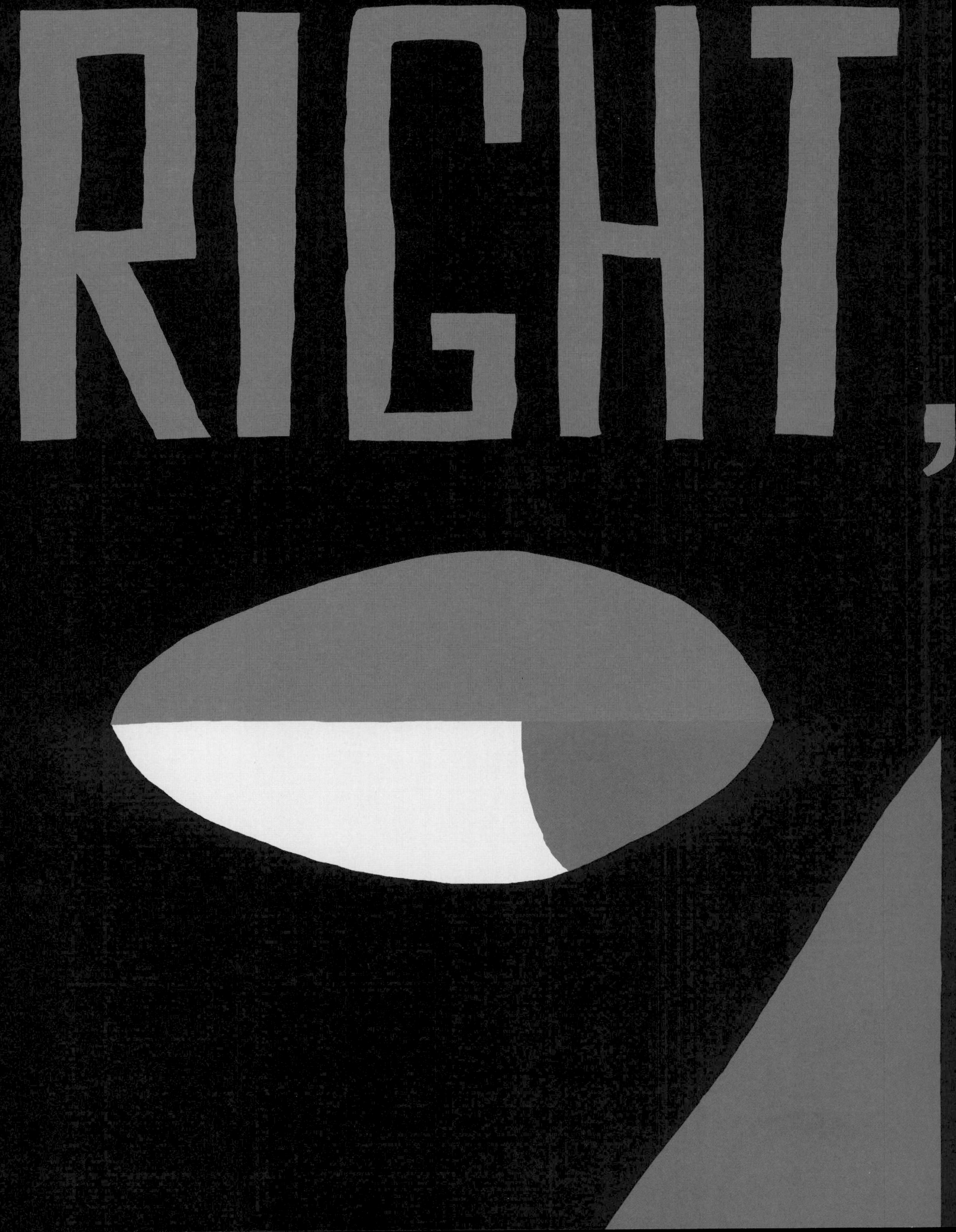
RIGHT,

RIGHT

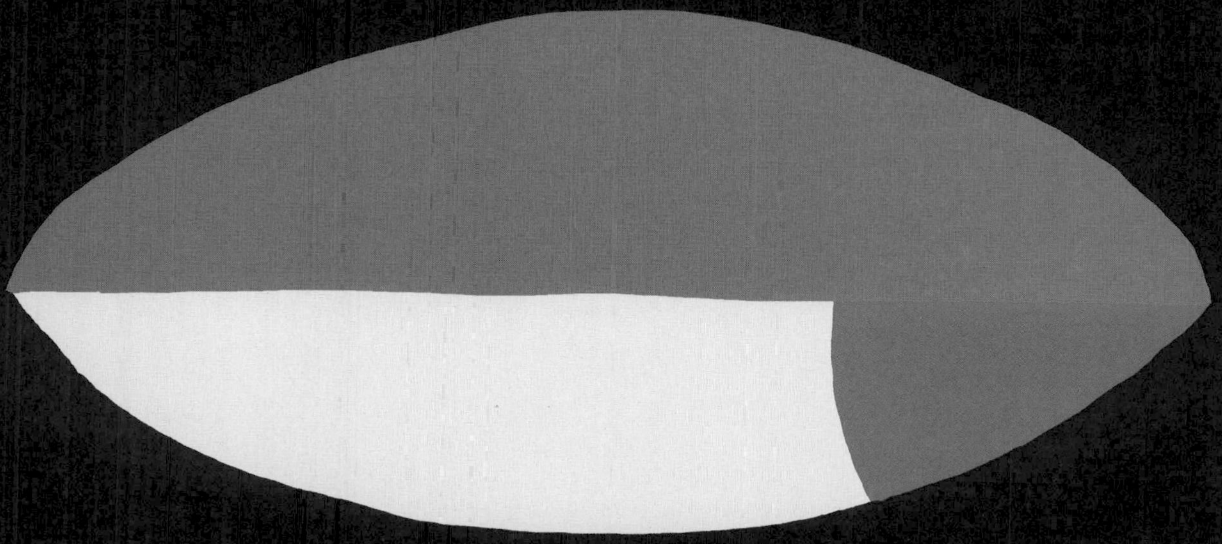

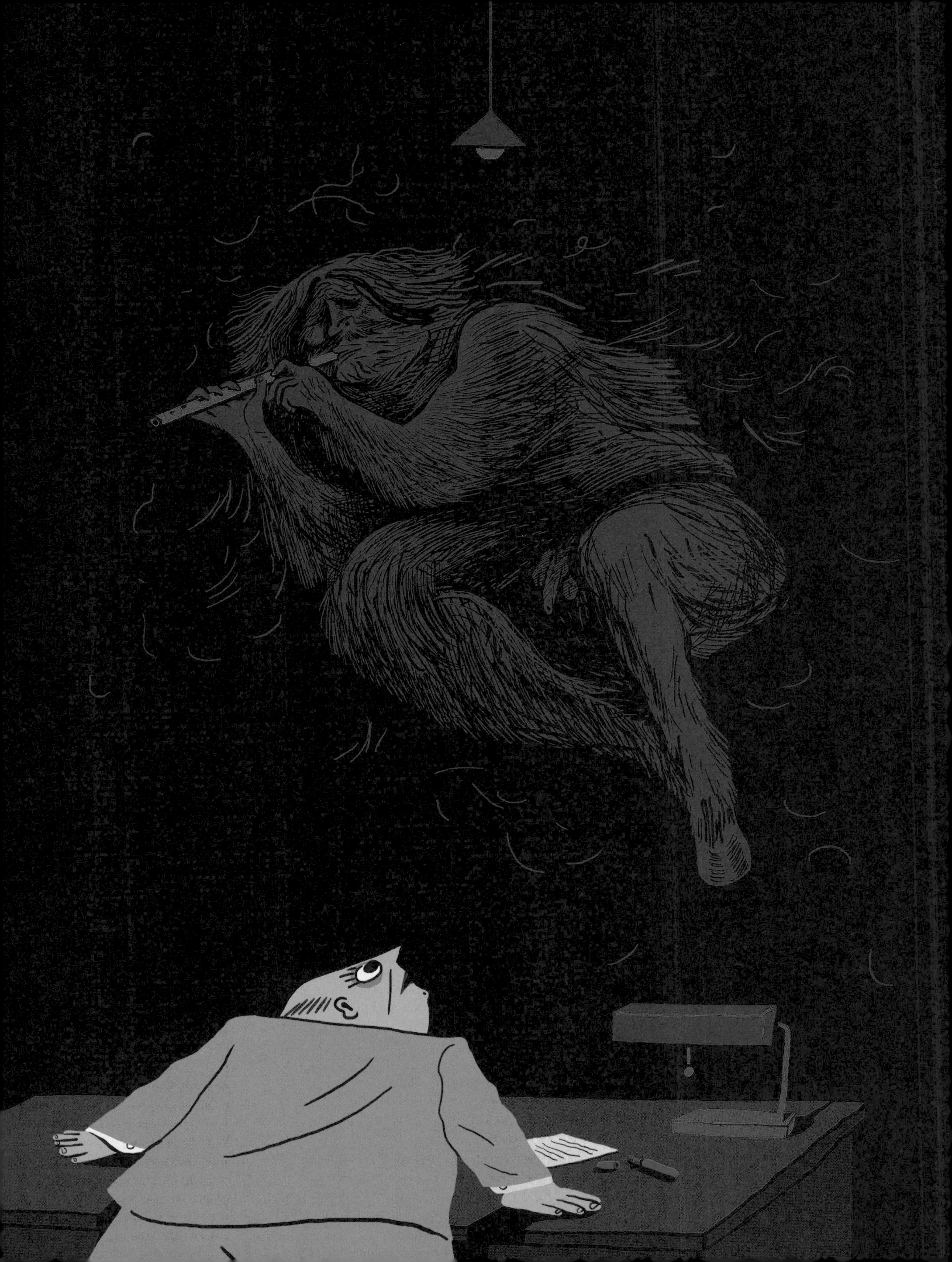

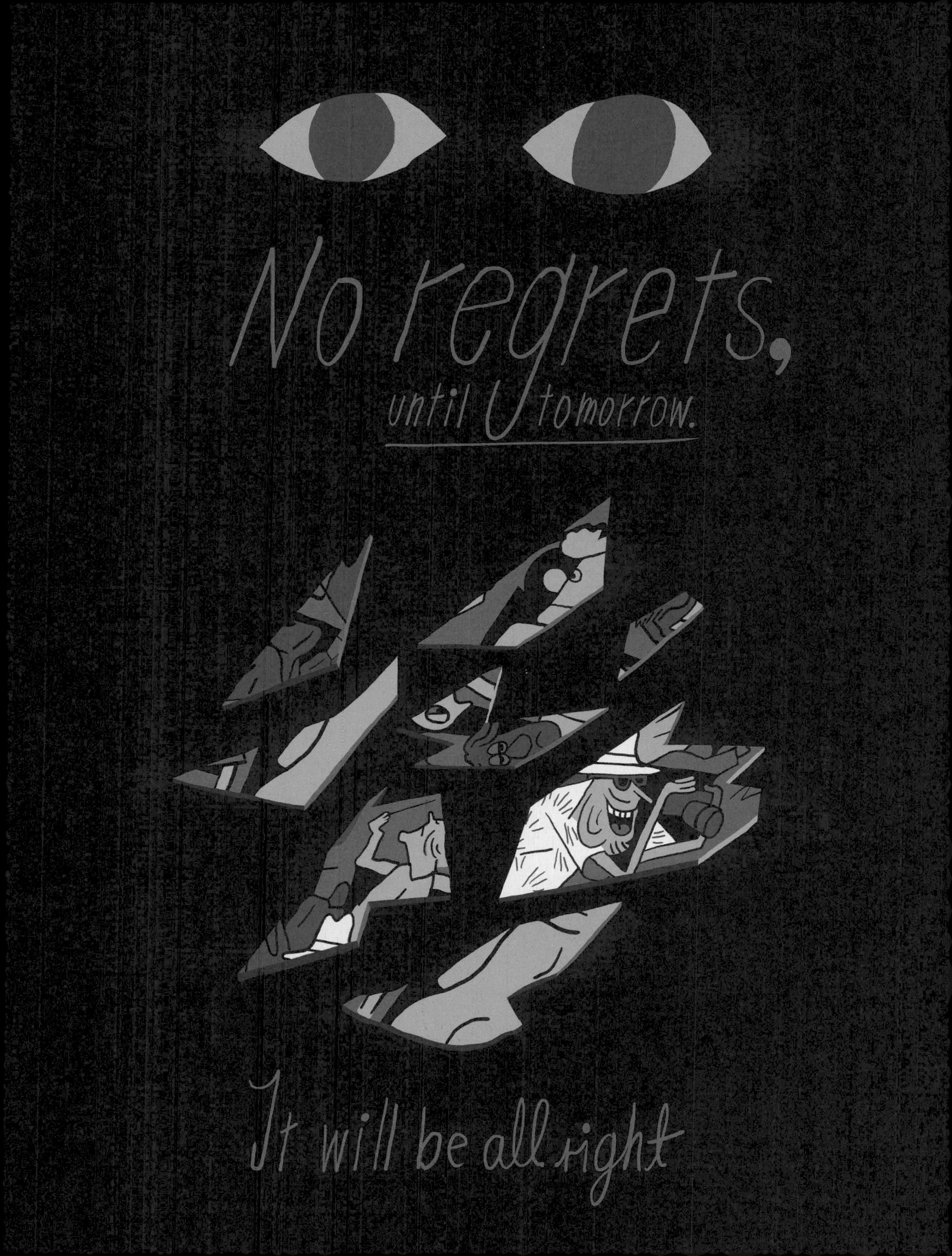
No regrets,
until tomorrow.
It will be all right

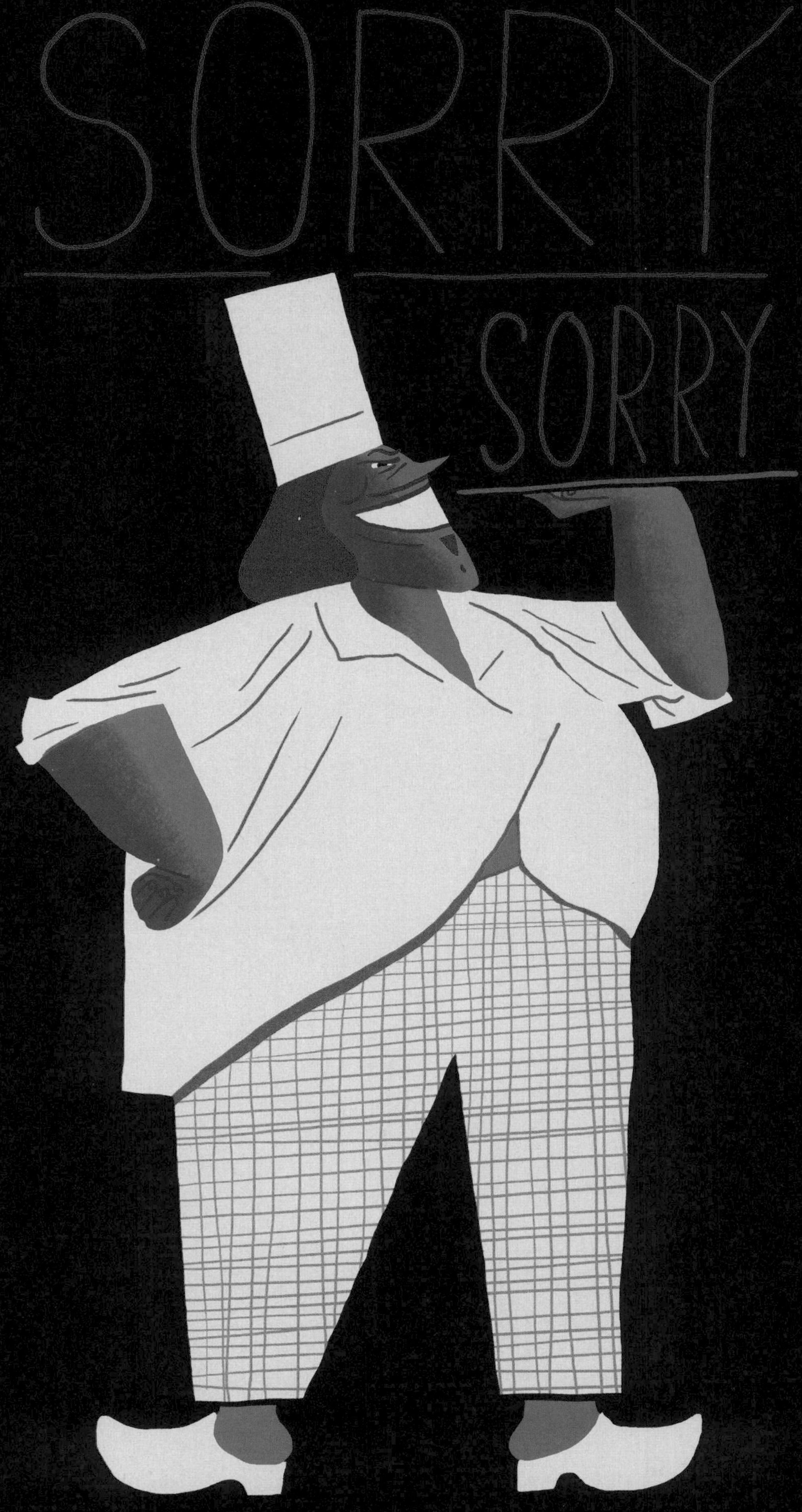
SORRY
SORRY

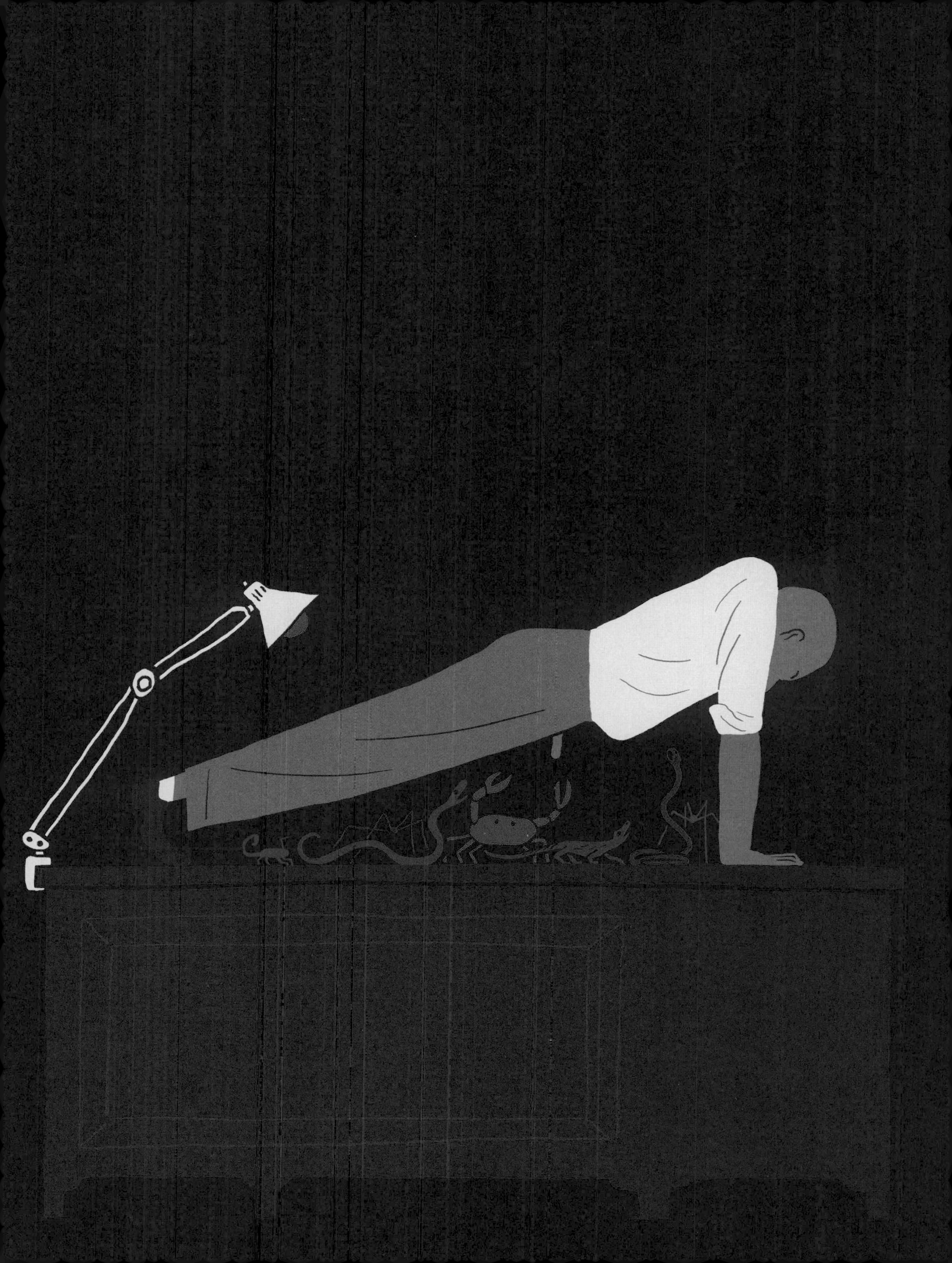

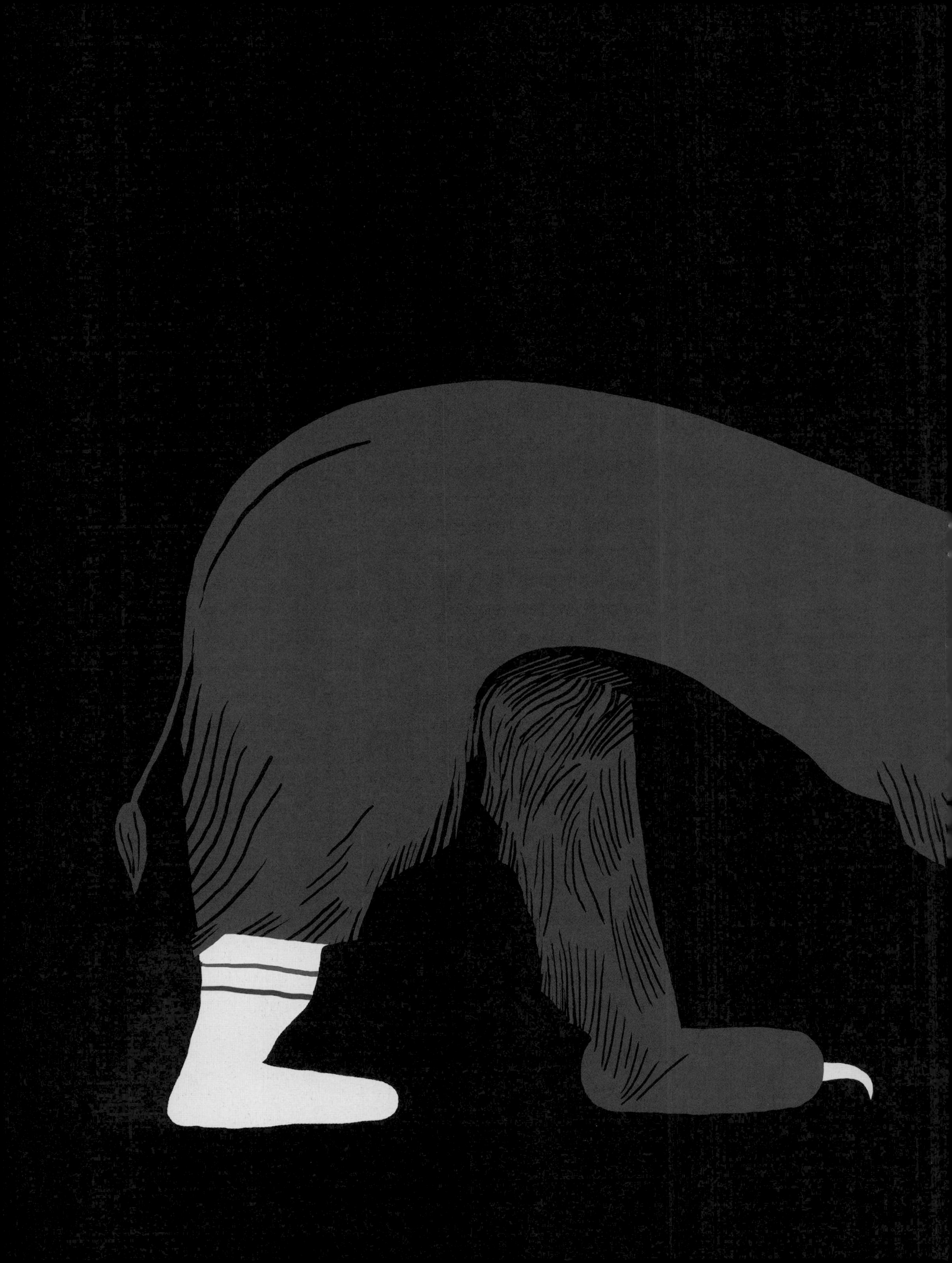

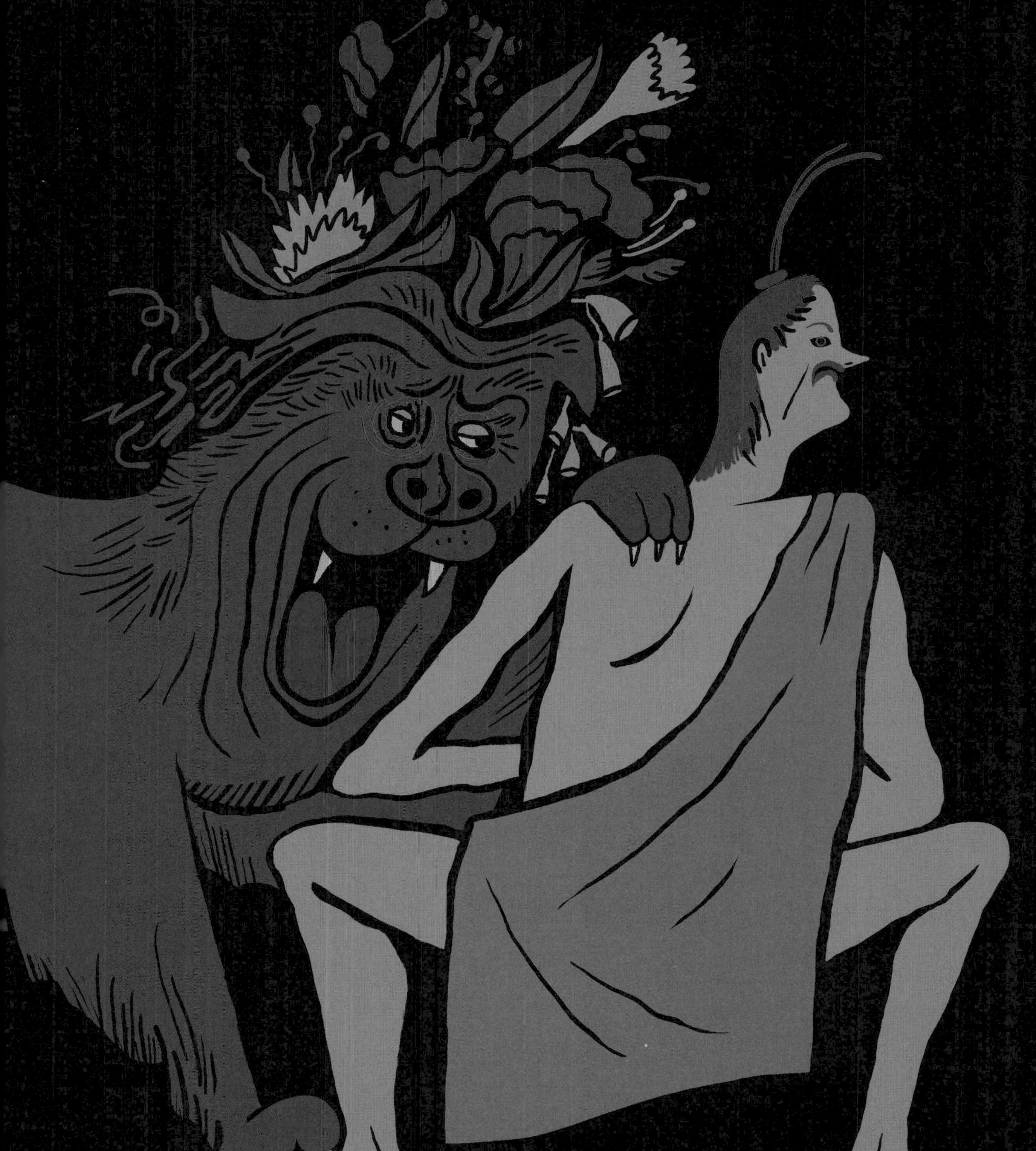

UNCLE BLUEBALLS

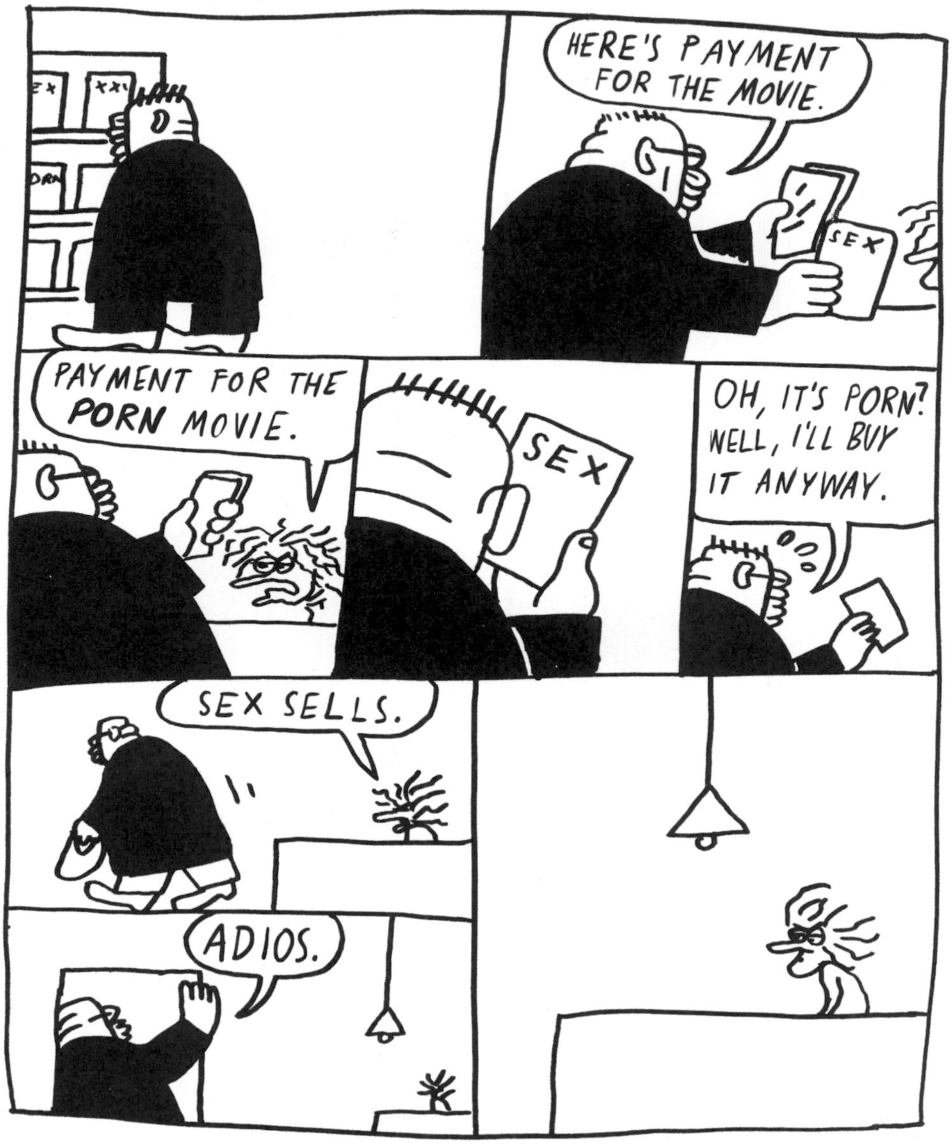
HERE'S PAYMENT FOR THE MOVIE.
SEX
PAYMENT FOR THE PORN MOVIE.
SEX
OH, IT'S PORN? WELL, I'LL BUY IT ANYWAY.
SEX SELLS.
ADIOS.

UNCLE BLUEBALLS

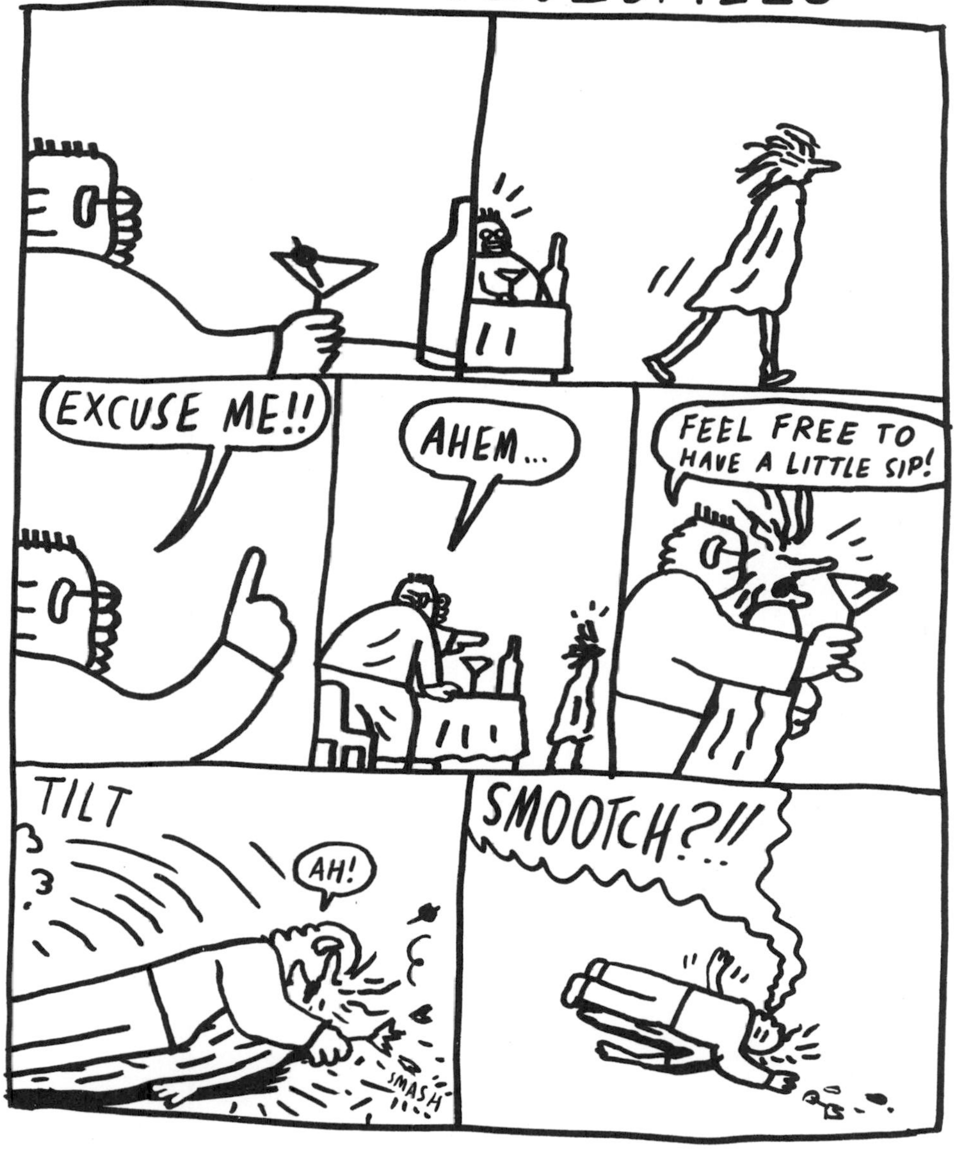

EXCUSE ME!!
AHEM...
FEEL FREE TO HAVE A LITTLE SIP!
TILT
AH!
SMASH
SMOOTCH?!!

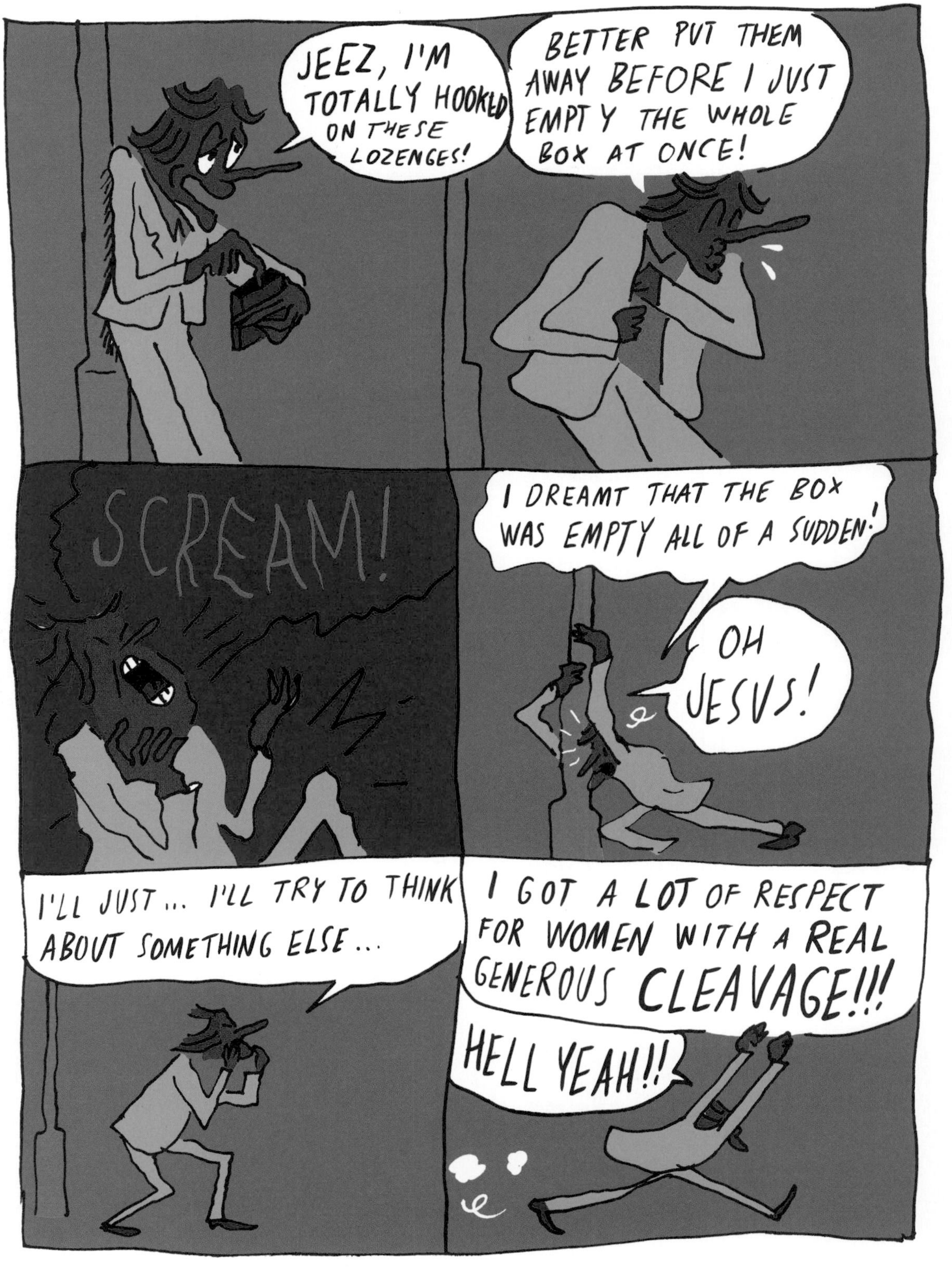
JEEZ, I'M TOTALLY HOOKED ON THESE LOZENGES!
BETTER PUT THEM AWAY BEFORE I JUST EMPTY THE WHOLE BOX AT ONCE!
SCREAM!
I DREAMT THAT THE BOX WAS EMPTY ALL OF A SUDDEN!
OH JESUS!
I'LL JUST... I'LL TRY TO THINK ABOUT SOMETHING ELSE...
I GOT A LOT OF RESPECT FOR WOMEN WITH A REAL GENEROUS CLEAVAGE!!!
HELL YEAH!!

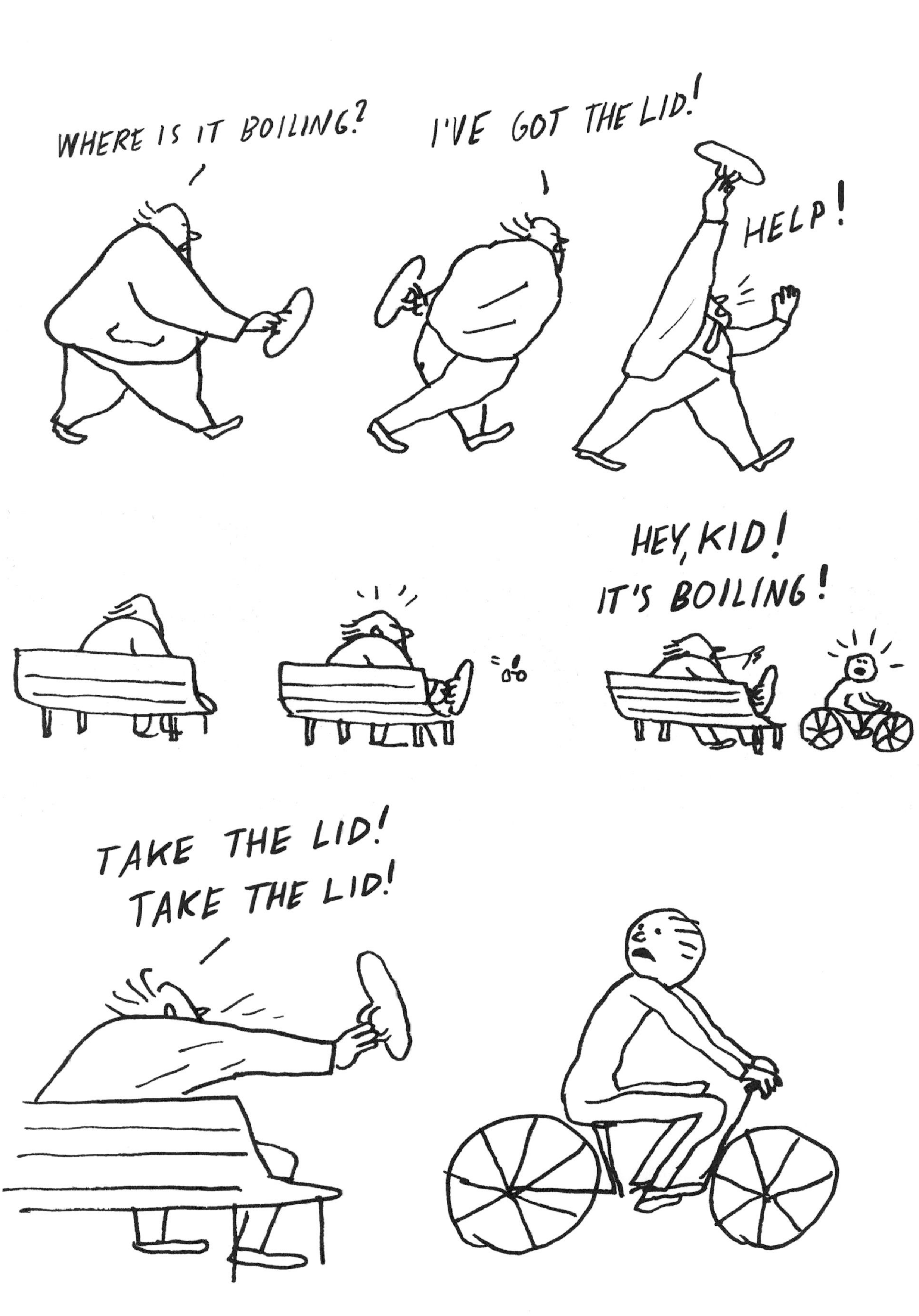
WHERE IS IT BOILING?
I'VE GOT THE LID!
HELP!
HEY, KID!
IT'S BOILING!
TAKE THE LID!
TAKE THE LID!

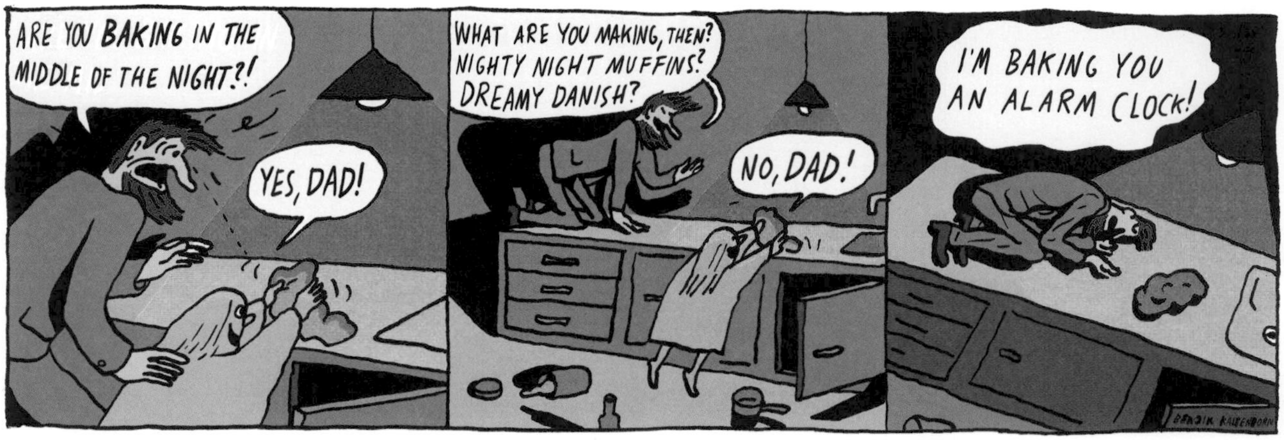
ARE YOU BAKING IN THE MIDDLE OF THE NIGHT?!
YES, DAD!
WHAT ARE YOU MAKING, THEN? NIGHTY NIGHT MUFFINS? DREAMY DANISH?
NO, DAD!
I'M BAKING YOU AN ALARM CLOCK!

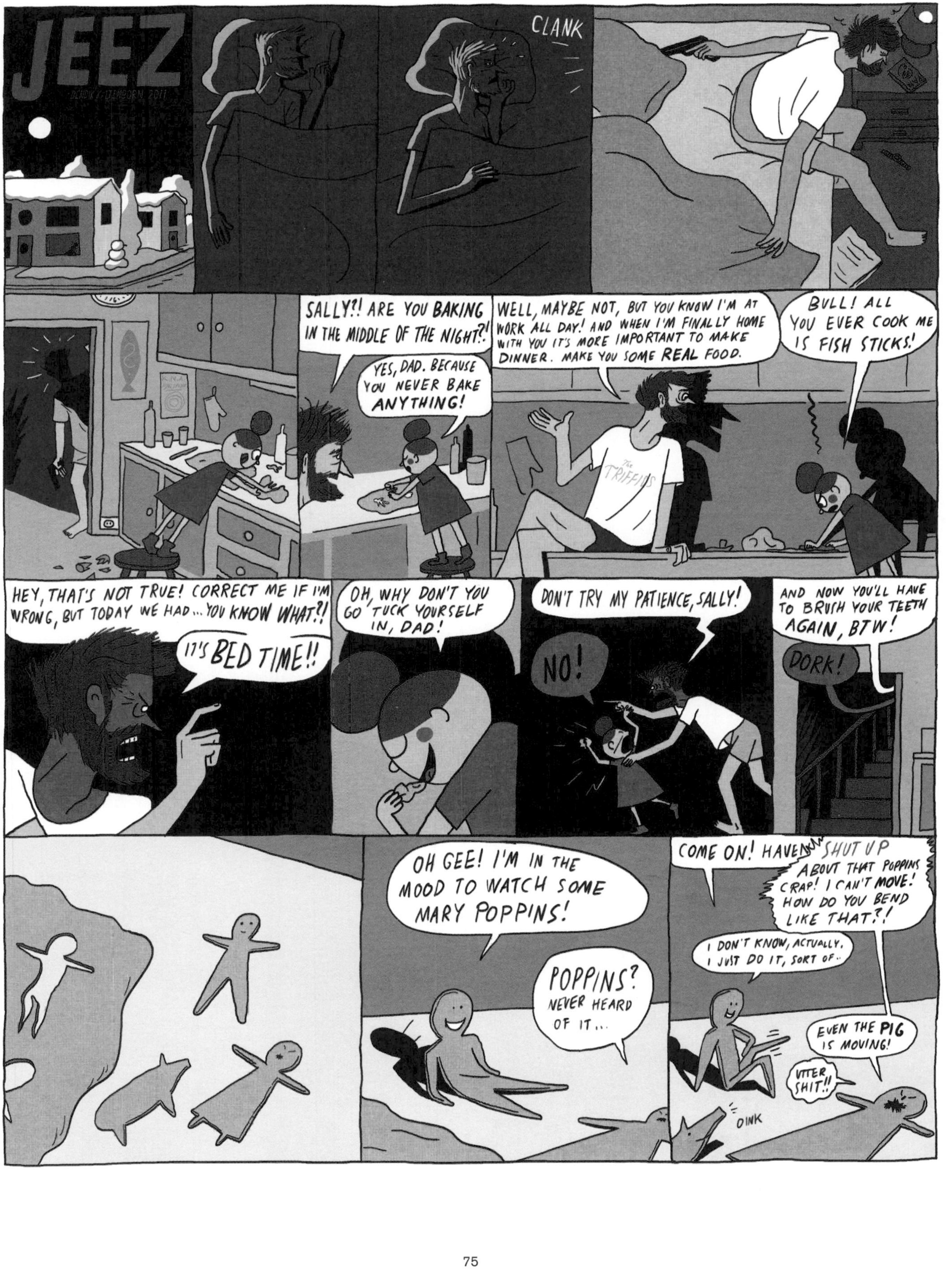
JEEZ
CLANK
SALLY?! ARE YOU BAKING IN THE MIDDLE OF THE NIGHT?!
YES, DAD. BECAUSE YOU NEVER BAKE ANYTHING!
WELL, MAYBE NOT, BUT YOU KNOW I'M AT WORK ALL DAY! AND WHEN I'M FINALLY HOME WITH YOU IT'S MORE IMPORTANT TO MAKE DINNER. MAKE YOU SOME REAL FOOD.
BULL! ALL YOU EVER COOK ME IS FISH STICKS!
HEY, THAT'S NOT TRUE! CORRECT ME IF I'M WRONG, BUT TODAY WE HAD... YOU KNOW WHAT?!
IT'S BED TIME!!
OH, WHY DON'T YOU GO TUCK YOURSELF IN, DAD!
DON'T TRY MY PATIENCE, SALLY!
NO!
AND NOW YOU'LL HAVE TO BRUSH YOUR TEETH AGAIN, BTW!
DORK!
OH GEE! I'M IN THE MOOD TO WATCH SOME MARY POPPINS!
POPPINS? NEVER HEARD OF IT...
COME ON! HAVEN
SHUT UP ABOUT THAT POPPINS CRAP! I CAN'T MOVE! HOW DO YOU BEND LIKE THAT?!
I DON'T KNOW, ACTUALLY. I JUST DO IT, SORT OF..
EVEN THE PIG IS MOVING!
UTTER SHIT!!
OINK

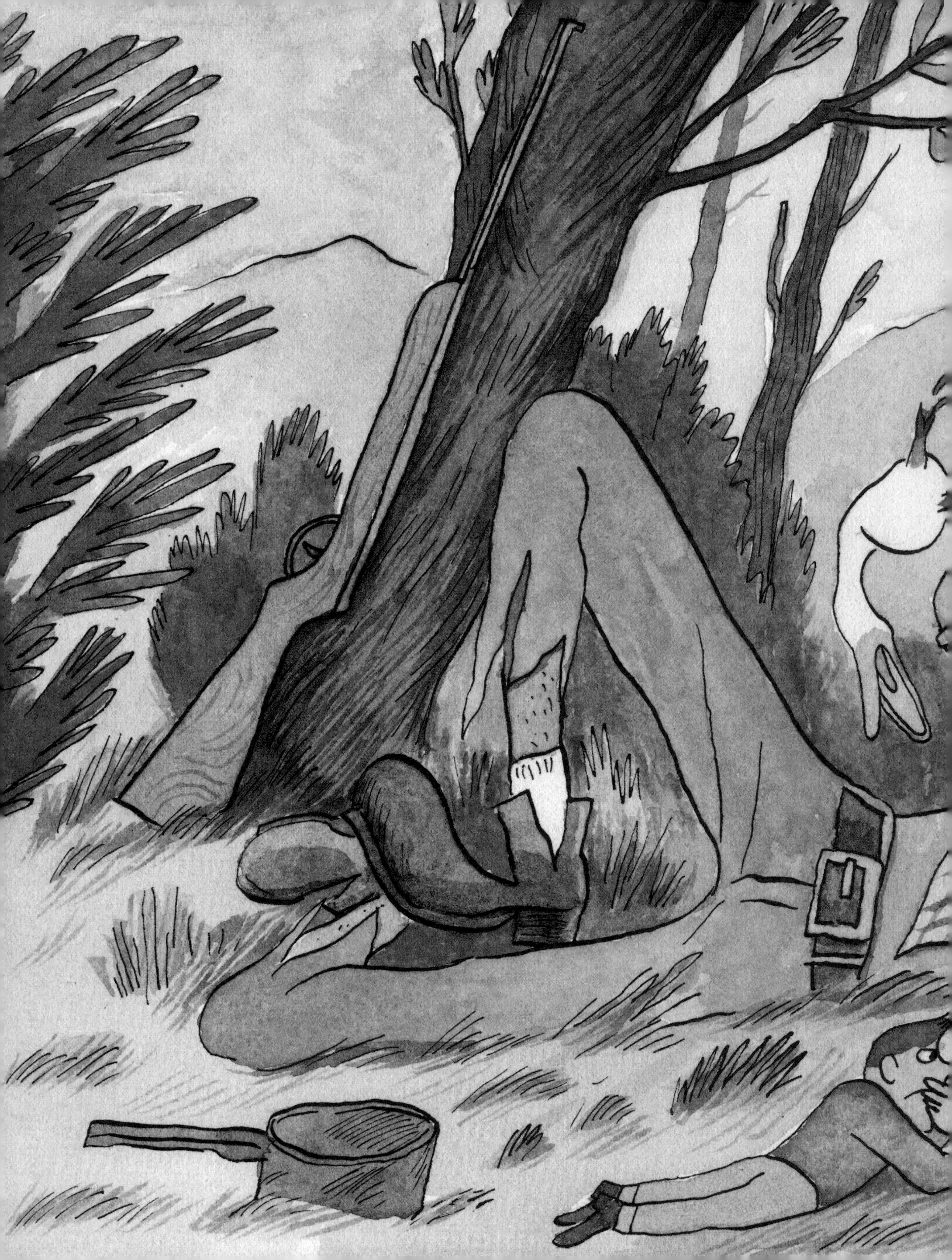

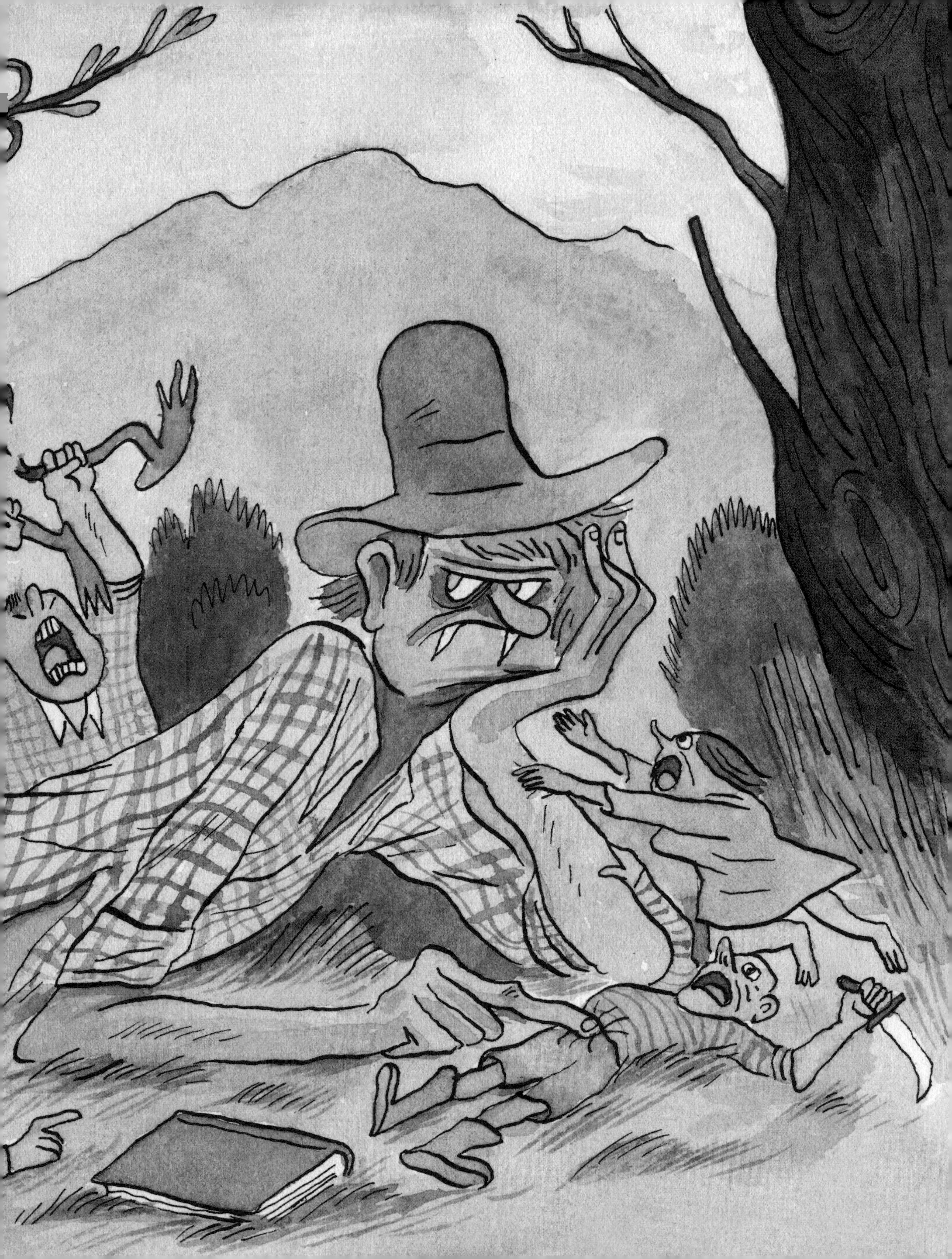

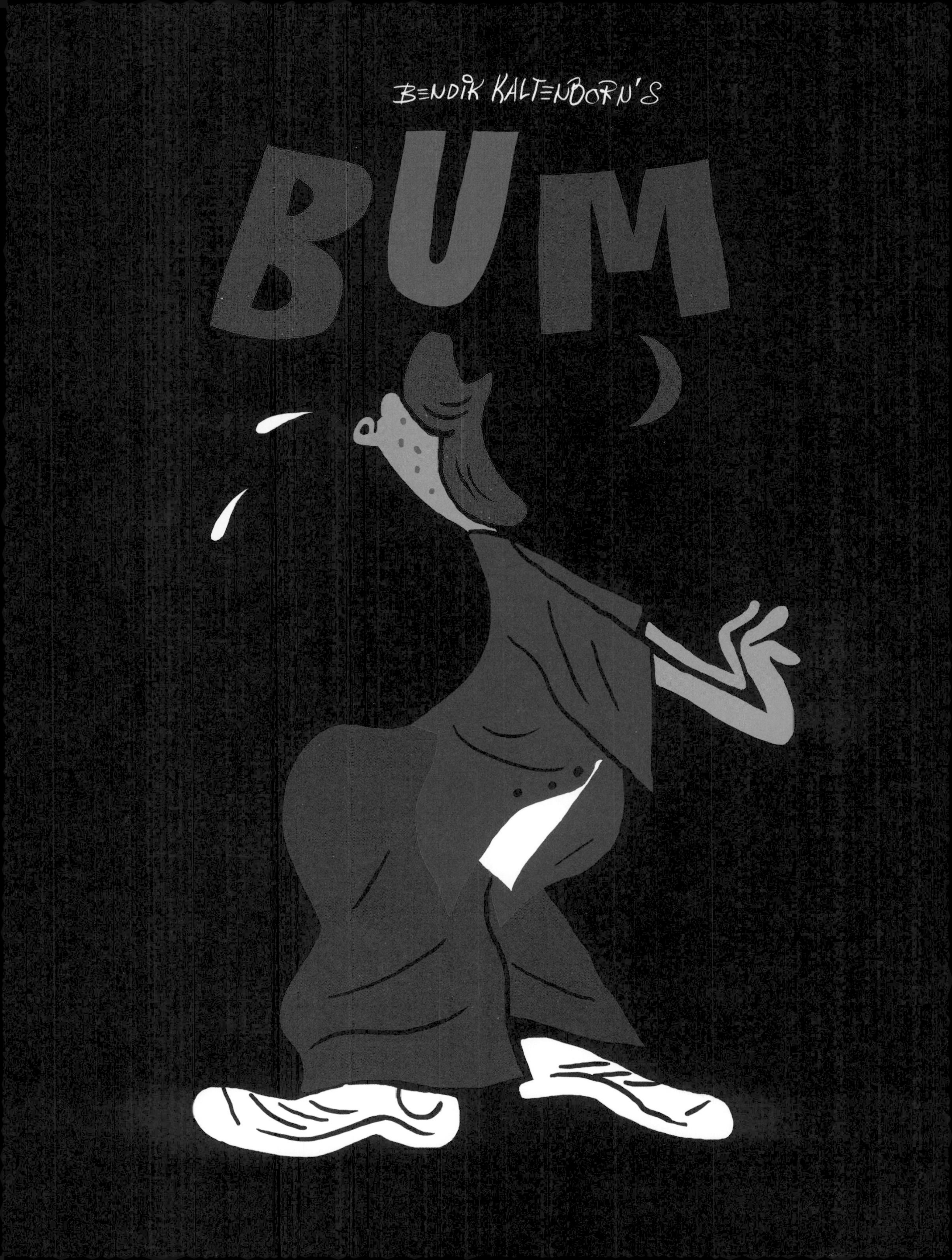
BENDIK KALTENBORN'S
BUM

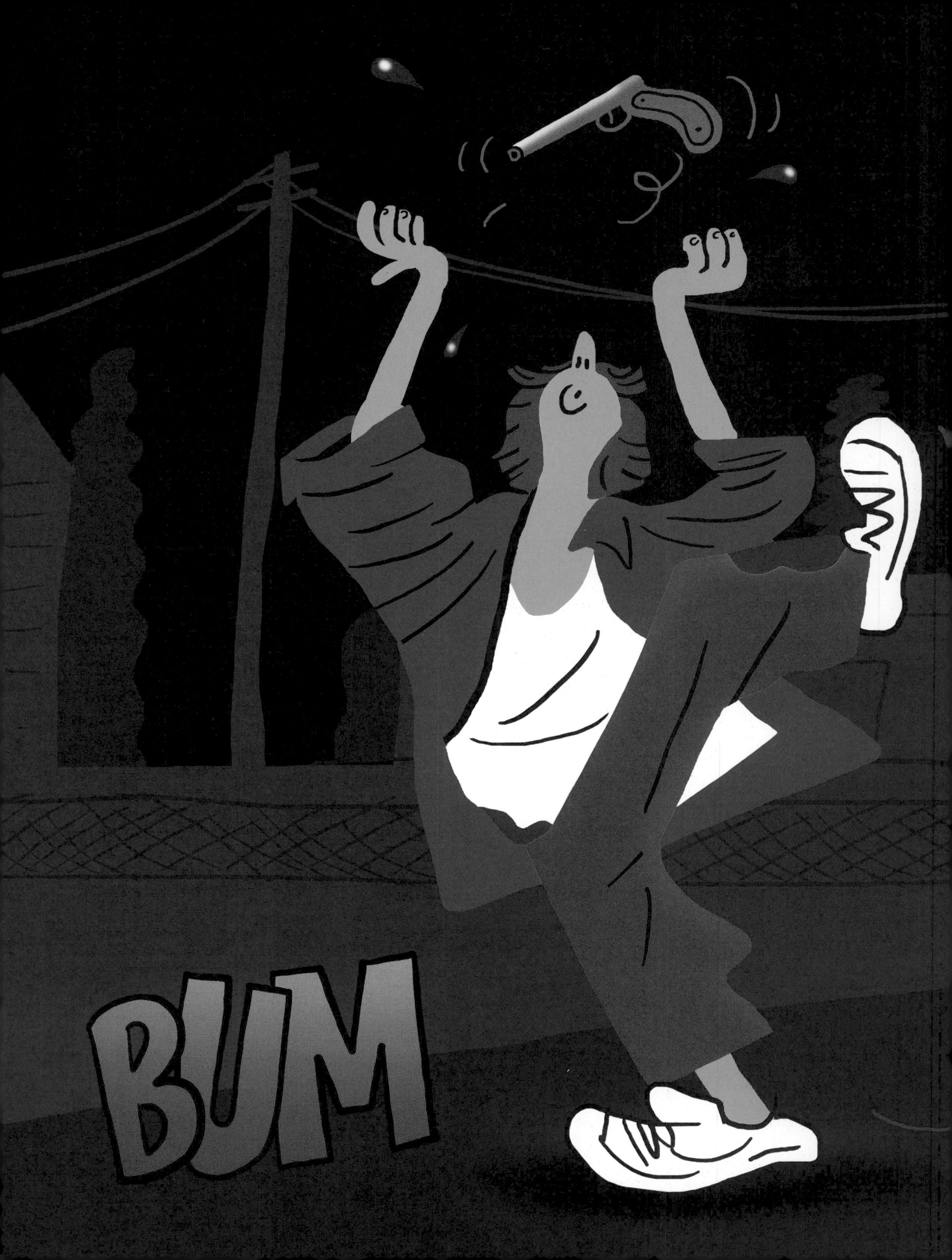
BUM

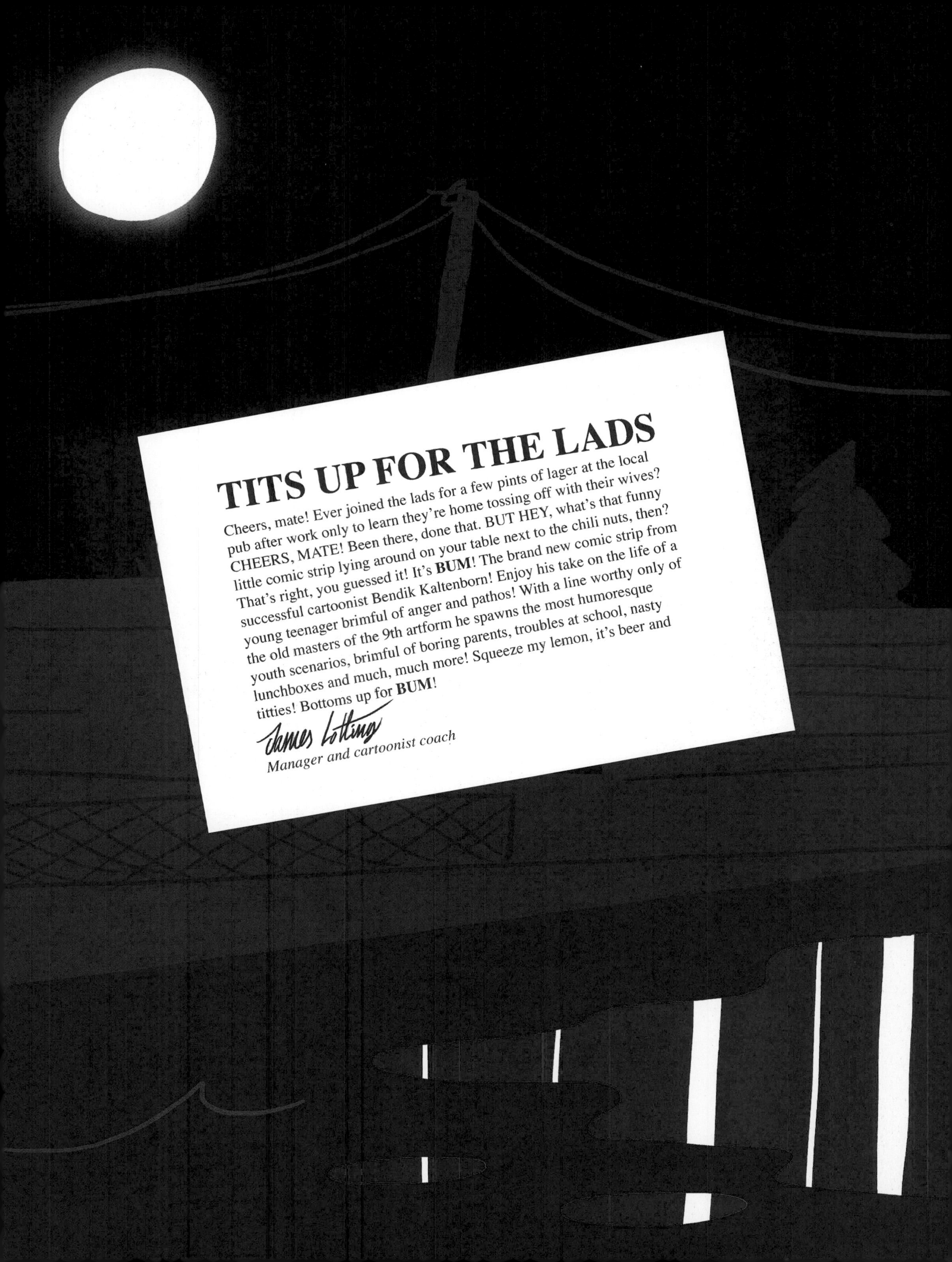
TITS UP FOR THE LADS
Cheers, mate! Ever joined the lads for a few pints of lager at the local pub after work only to learn they're home tossing off with their wives? CHEERS, MATE! Been there, done that. BUT HEY, what's that funny little comic strip lying around on your table next to the chili nuts, then? That's right, you guessed it! It's BUM! The brand new comic strip from successful cartoonist Bendik Kaltenborn! Enjoy his take on the life of a young teenager brimful of anger and pathos! With a line worthy only of the old masters of the 9th artform he spawns the most humoresque youth scenarios, brimful of boring parents, troubles at school, nasty lunchboxes and much, much more! Squeeze my lemon, it's beer and titties! Bottoms up for BUM!
James Lotting
Manager and cartoonist coach

BENDIK KALTENBORN'S
BUM

[redacted] May 28
HAHAHAHAh condom on his head. Well I never ....
pfffffffthahahahah
Message

[redacted] May 23
cooooooooooolio
Message

[redacted] May 23
haha today's youth, man.
Message

[redacted] May 20
Happy to get rid of that previous guest strip, but this is way worse ....
Message

BENDIK KALTENBORN'S
BUM

[redacted] May 25
This is the only comic that's actually worse than that other one, but not by much.
Message

[redacted] May 25
uhm.. and what was tha point??? not funny
Message

[redacted] May 25
What is this???
Message

[redacted] May 25
This comic rules.
Message

[redacted] May 25
I guess the title says it all ... not even close to being any good, actually the worst I've seen in a while.
Message

[redacted] May 25
Why is this running? =O
Message

[redacted] May 25
agree with the first comment. this is some of the worst crap... I can't find the words ...
Message

[redacted] May 25
Never seen a more striking title for a comic strip ever.
Message

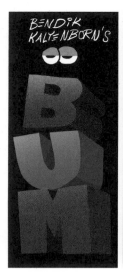

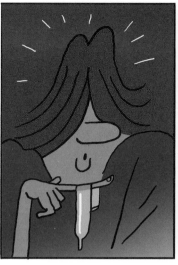

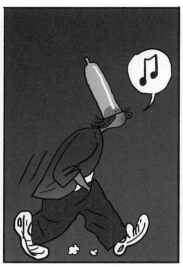

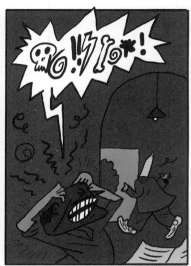

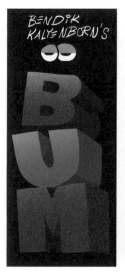

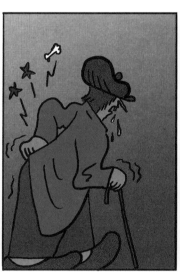

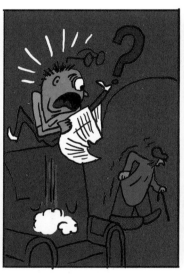

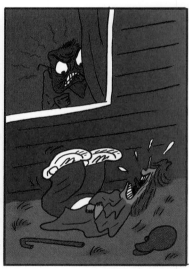

BENDIK KALTENBORN'S
BUM
Feeling down?
Yup. Foreskin problems ...
Dude, that sucks. What happened?
Foreskin problems, dude!!!

[redacted] May 30
Is the point of this strip to have a baby paint on a canvas and then get it exhibited at an art gallery?
Message

[redacted] May 30
This whole comic is seriously crappy. I can't understand how this was chosen by the Dagbladet.no ....
Message

[redacted] May 30
Still not funny, but I guess that's what's funny. This didn't go as planned, or is that actually what it did? :p
Message

BENDIK KALTENBORN'S
BUM
I WISH I WAS A LITTLE BIT TALLER
I WISH I WAS A BALLER

[redacted] May 27
This is really the worst try to make a comic I've ever seen.
Message

[redacted] May 27
The previous guest strip was a load of teenage crap.
This is far worse.
Message

[redacted] May 27
And what is the point?
Message

[redacted] May 27
Ditto!
Message

[redacted] May 27
What the hell is this, then? You just got rid of that previous bullshit comic, and then you managed to find something even worse? :S
Message

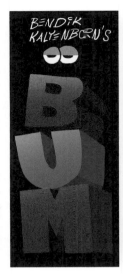

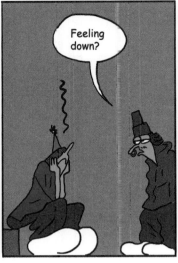

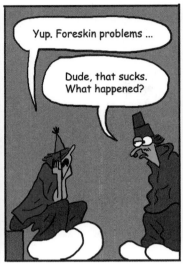

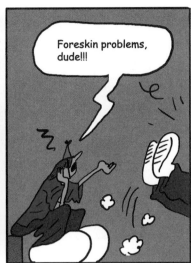

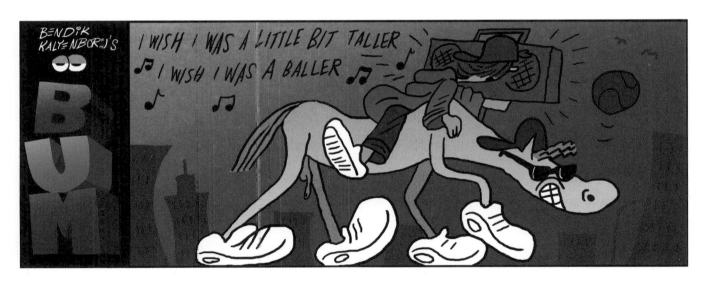

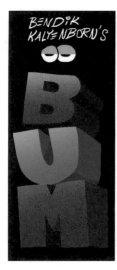

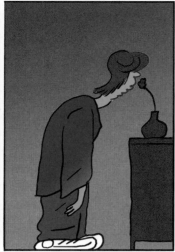

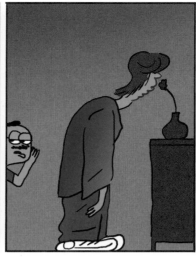

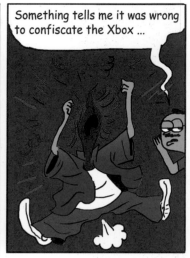

BENDIK KALTENBORN'S
BUM
Something tells me it was wrong to confiscate the Xbox ...

[redacted] May 28
Yeah, 10 points! The best and most interesting guest strip in the history, get lost suckers! If you can't see the satire and humor here (even Comic Sans) you're not even worth the pixels on you screen. More Kaltenborn everywhere!
Message

[redacted] May 28
Move over Pondus! Next stop own magazine?
Message

[redacted] May 28
The fact that someone actually bother to defend this bullshit comic from behind an anonymus account tells me two things.
Either you're the creater of this comic trying desperately to find the meaning of it.
Or you're a troll pouring gasoline on the fire.
Either way, go team retard.
Message

[redacted] May 28
I agree with Thor Ivar. This is the most boring strip ever to appear in the world of comics, so the title is very fitting.
Message

[redacted] May 28
This comic is a parody of the comic strip format, pointing out how meaningless many of today's guest strips appear. The character is probably inspired by Jeremy from Zits by Jerry Scott/Jim Borgman.This is one of the most interesting guest strips I've seen. It manages to kick hard without really saying anything, while the previous one tried too hard ending up saying very little. Look at that dog, it's in pain, it's sad. A big part of the charm of this comic is all the angry readers it gets writing here.
Respect to dagbladet for including new voices and for being innovative.
Message

[redacted] May 28
Interpreter wanted... No matter how hard I tried I can't find either humor or charm in these strips. Is it just me?
Message

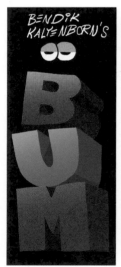

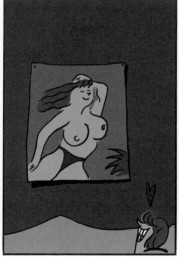

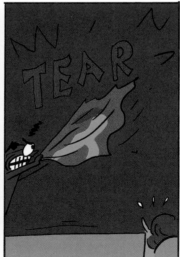

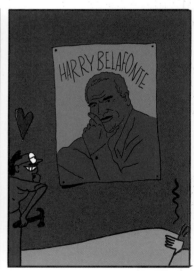

BENDIK KALTENBORN'S
BUM
TEAR
HARRY BELAFONTE

[redacted] May 26
@Ronny: Haha! Was thinking the same.
Message

[redacted] May 26
I follow this strip just to read all the negative feedback
Message

[redacted] May 26
Why do I read this at all? :S
Message

[redacted] May 26
meh
Message

BENDIK KALTENBORN'S
BUM

[redacted] May 25
Where's Veslemøy? I MISS IT!
THIS is SHIT!!
Message

[redacted] May 24
....
Message

[redacted] May 24
This comic was actually really bad ...!!! Better luck next time with choosing a guest strip..
Message

[redacted] May 24
Guest strips are running for two weeks, that's why Veslemøy disapeared, and this one will disapear next week.
Message

[redacted] May 24
I sincerely hope that the ones wanting Veslemøy back just want's the least of two evils.
Message

[redacted] May 24
Crap
Message

[redacted] May 24
Veslemøy!
Message

[redacted] May 24
I don't understand this comic, wondering what the people recommending it see. Must be a prank from dagbladet to run this baloney, seems like that's the point. Get back Veslemøy, I say!!
Message

[redacted] May 24
don't understand this one either
Message

[redacted] May 24
since I don't understand this one (either), I'm wondering wether it's funny or not .....
Message

[redacted] May 24
Get Veslemøy back!
Message

[redacted] May 24
Just....stop -_-
Message

[redacted] May 24
Sorry, nothing personal Bendik, but I want Veslemøy back!!!
Message

BENDIK KALTENBORN'S
BUM
French test tomorrow ...
OOOOUI!
French test tomorrow?
Yup.
CROC MONSIEUR!

[redacted] May 23
Stupid comic, hope it won't last long...
Message

[redacted] May 23
So, is this irony or could someone explain what's the deal here?
Message

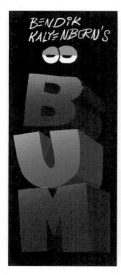

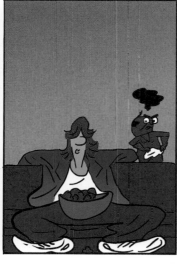

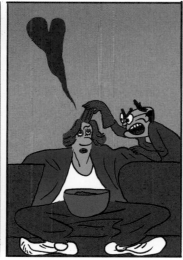

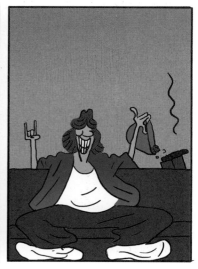

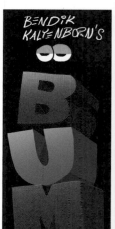

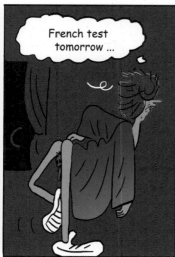

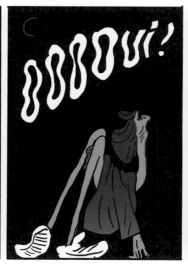

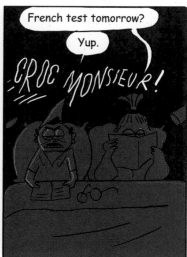

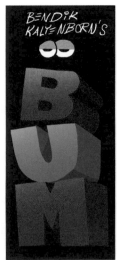

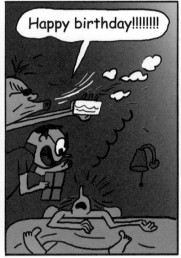

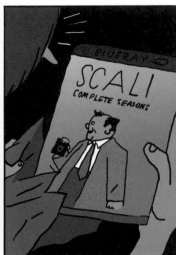

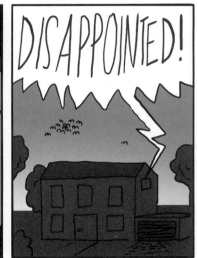

BENDIK KALTENBORN'S
BUM
Happy birthday!!!!!!!!
BLUERAY
SCALI
COMPLETE SEASONS
DISAPPOINTED!

[redacted] May 21
http://www.epguides.com/commish/
Message

[redacted] May 19
I want Veslemøy
Message

[redacted] May 19
VESLEMØY!!!!!!!!!!!!!!!
Message

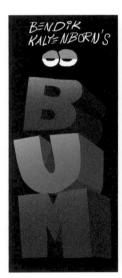

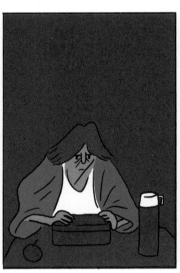

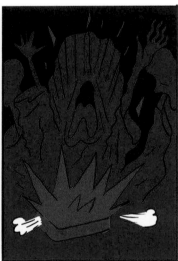

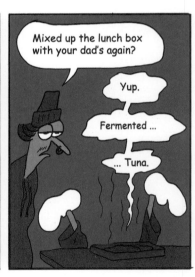

BENDIK KALTENBORN'S
BUM
Mixed up the lunch box with your dad's again?
Yup.
Fermented ...
... Tuna.

[redacted] May 23
I think both this and Veslemøy sucks, but at least veslemøy was involuntarily funny
Message

[redacted] May 23
Eivind, get a grip.
I'm sitting here thinking Veslemøy is a lot better.
But this is another kind of comic, and you must respect that there are things that you maybe not like/understand.
That's a unnecessary mentality, to think that since you like other things this is crap.
I say think before you comment.
And let Veslemøy run regularly on DB.no ;)
Message

[redacted] May 21
should be unlegal to print such shit in one of the biggest newspapers
Message

[redacted] May 21
WHERE'S VESLEMØY????
Message

BENDIK KALYENBORN'S
BUM

[redacted] May 27
Lord..
Message

[redacted] May 23
I think he's trying to do a trick...?
Message

[redacted] May 18
Looks just like that 7Up-dude!
Message

[redacted] May 18
I am too stupid to understand this one.
Message

[redacted] May 18
Boring, boring, boring
Message

[redacted] May 18
Can't we have both Veslemøy and Bånn!
Message

[redacted] May 18
Let's give bånn a chance, but unfortunately it looks bånn ...
Message

[redacted] May 18
WHERE IS VESLEMØY?????????????????????????????
Message

[redacted] May 18
huh
Message

[redacted] May 18
don't understand...
Message

[redacted] May 18
Don't wanna be rude, but I miss veslemøy.
Message

BENDIK KALYENBORN'S
BUM
10

[redacted] May 20
I agree with Kim André. But bad drawings can be saved by a good punchline. But when both these are missing... then we're not exactly left with very much....
Message

[redacted] May 20
Well. If you ask me it's interesting and has an artistic style of a primary pupil.
Message

[redacted] May 20
Kaltenborn has more than average drawing skills; check his website-- lot's of good stuff there. But I think he masters longer and more experimental stories better. When it comes to interesting and artistic style he is- if you ask me - one of the nations greatest comic artists.
Message

[redacted] May 20
Readig this comic makes me want to never move back to Norway. Is it f....... possible!! Get Veslemoy back!
Message

[redacted] May 20
I think the whole point of this comic is that it's SUPPOSED to be crap. Some kind of artistic irony or something, I don't know. That's the only explanation I can find, since every single strip so far has been totaly without any meaning. If the goal of this comic is to suck monkeys trough a garden hose it deserves standing ovations.
Message

[redacted] May 20
Bring back Veslemøy...
Message

[redacted] May 20
What is this? There's no entertainment in this crap. I get the fact that they're chaning guest strips now and then, but even the most pretentious from Veslemøy was unbelievably better than this. No, humor, no meaning, no point. Total waste.
Message

[redacted] May 20
WTF??? Dear Bendik Kalyeborn.... if you're gonna make a funny comic there's two specific things you should master: Above average drawing skills and something called HUMOR!
Message

[redacted] May 20
Enough, ENOUGH, ENOUGH!!! I get more joy from staring at a black piece of paper. I'm starting to doubt there's anything in this comic I don't get. I join the chorus: get veslemøy back. Nuf said!
Message

[redacted] May 20
What a delightfull comic!! fun, charming, full of energy, imaginative, nice drawings, nice style, etc etc etc!!! This comic really deserves a permanent spot in Dagbladet!!
kidding...
Message

[redacted] May 20
What the hell?
Message

[redacted] May 20
I can't with my strongest will understand how this can be better than Veslemøy. This isn't even worthy of a unknowingly teenagers scribbles. The other comics got something to say, hidden behind more or less good drawing skills. But this one doesn't even have a little bit of charm. Total miss from the editor.
Message

[redacted] May 20
...wtf?
Message

[redacted] May 20
I thought is was impossible to produce worse crap than Veslemøy. I was wrong. But now we've definetily reached the bottom.
Message

[redacted] May 20
Huh?
Message

[redacted] May 20
Bring back Veslemøy!!!!
Message

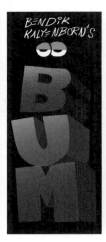

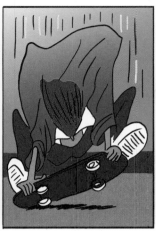

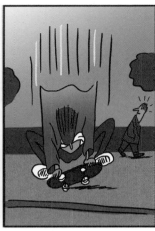

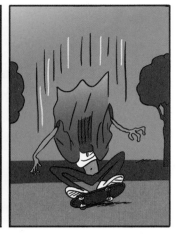

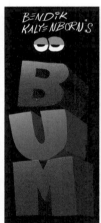

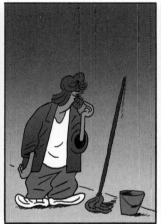

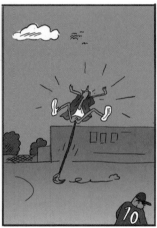

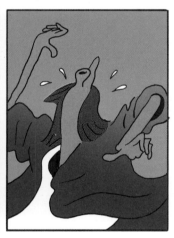

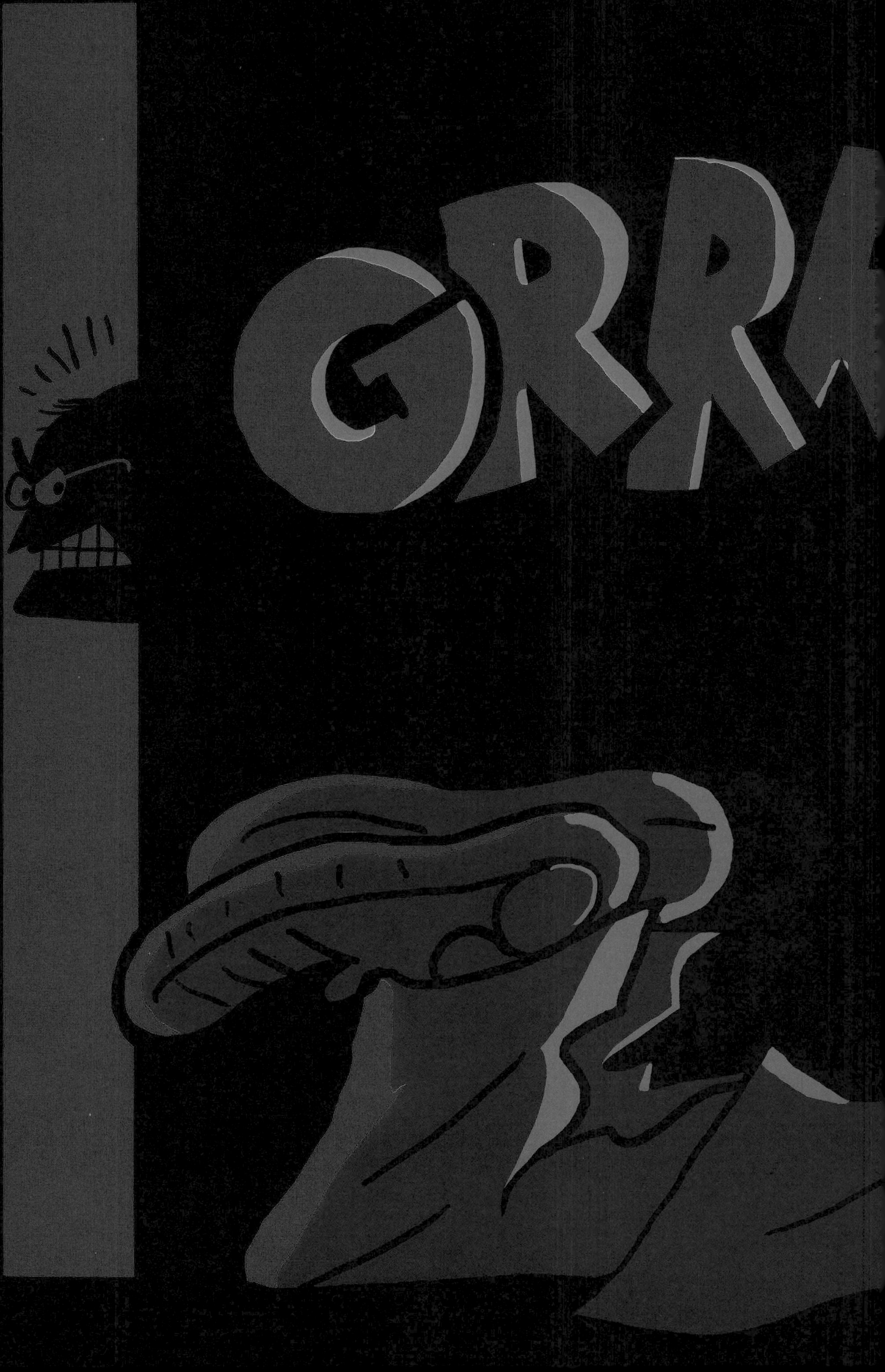
GRR

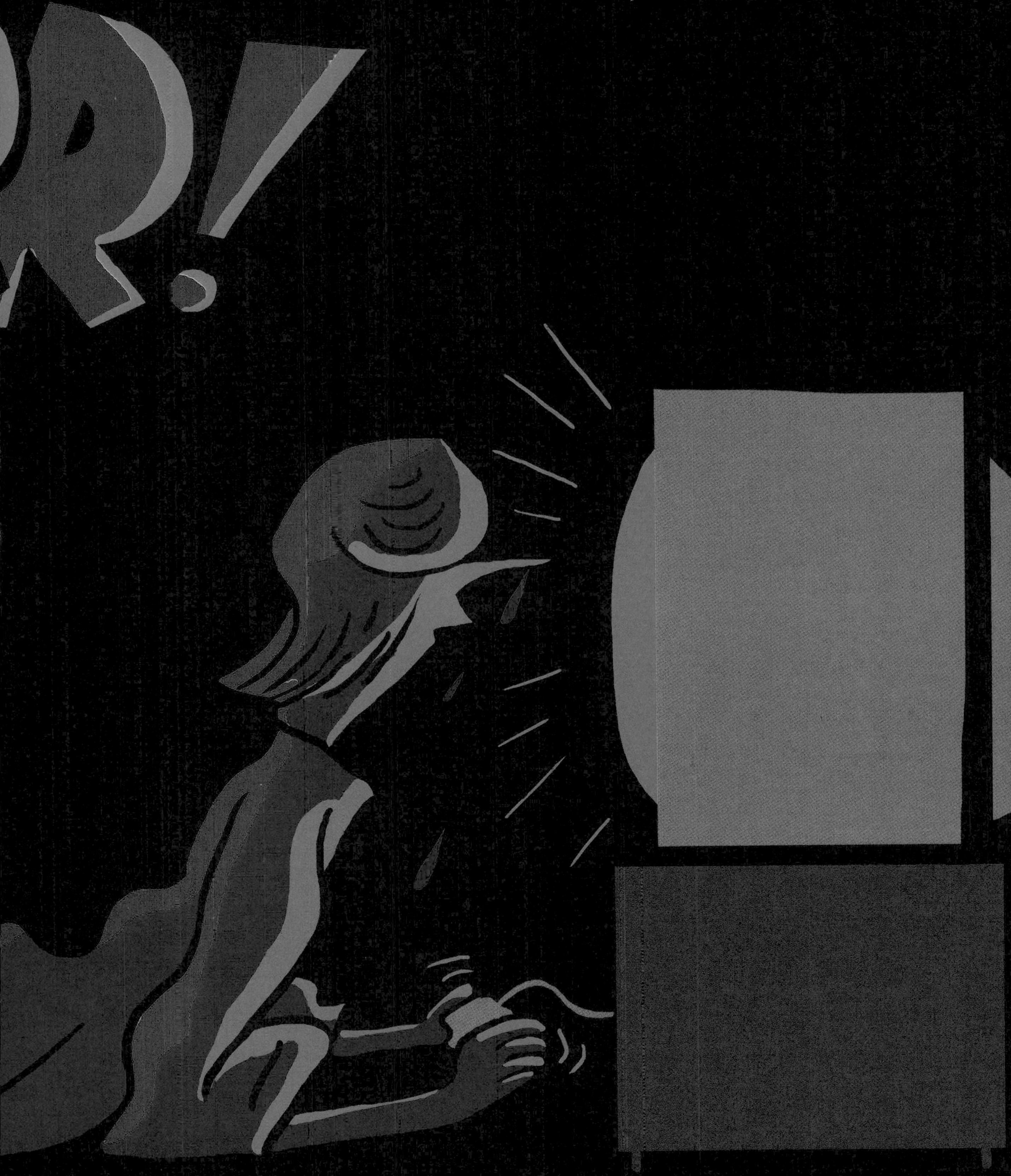

— Dear God. Thank you for making a hole in my garden.
Do you have a plan or any instructions for it?

— In any case, you did a great job!

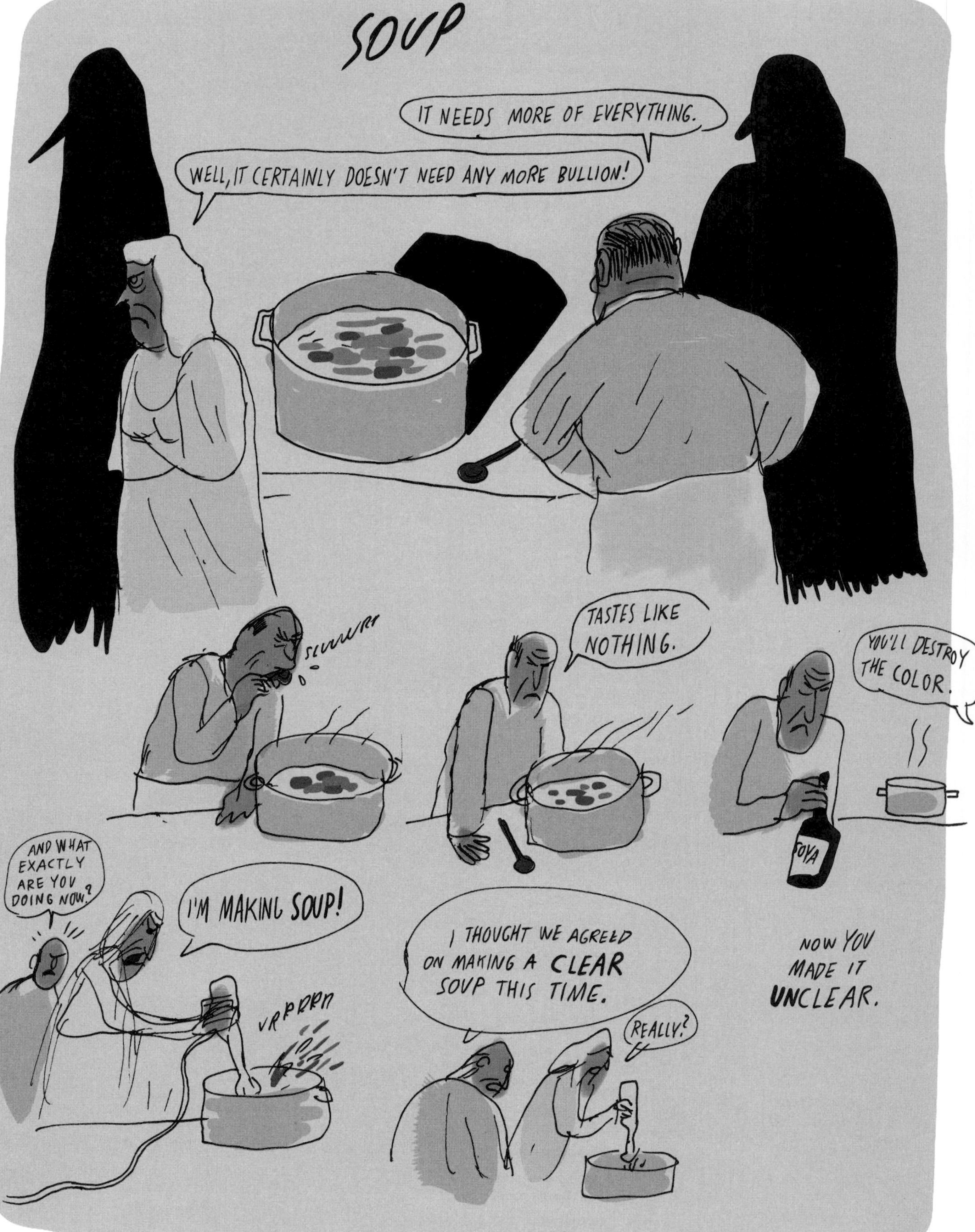
SOUP
IT NEEDS MORE OF EVERYTHING.
WELL, IT CERTAINLY DOESN'T NEED ANY MORE BULLION!
SLUUURP
TASTES LIKE NOTHING.
YOU'LL DESTROY THE COLOR.
SOYA
AND WHAT EXACTLY ARE YOU DOING NOW?
I'M MAKING SOUP!
VRRRRN
I THOUGHT WE AGREED ON MAKING A CLEAR SOUP THIS TIME.
REALLY?
NOW YOU MADE IT UNCLEAR.

The CONCERT

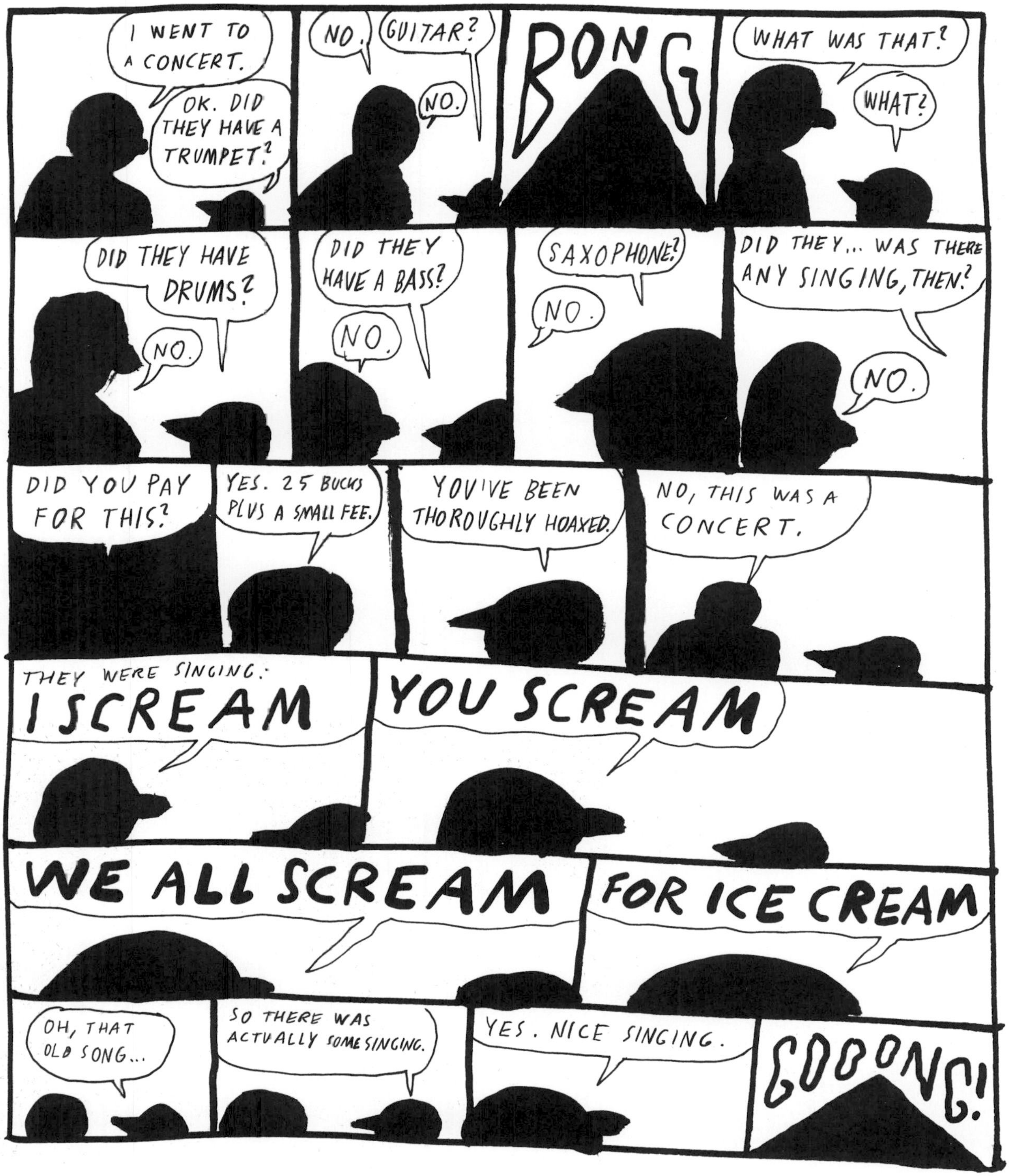
I WENT TO A CONCERT.
OK. DID THEY HAVE A TRUMPET?
NO.
GUITAR?
NO.
BONG
WHAT WAS THAT?
WHAT?
DID THEY HAVE DRUMS?
NO.
DID THEY HAVE A BASS?
NO.
SAXOPHONE?
NO.
DID THEY... WAS THERE ANY SINGING, THEN?
NO.
DID YOU PAY FOR THIS?
YES. 25 BUCKS PLUS A SMALL FEE.
YOU'VE BEEN THOROUGHLY HOAXED.
NO, THIS WAS A CONCERT.
THEY WERE SINGING: I SCREAM
YOU SCREAM
WE ALL SCREAM
FOR ICE CREAM
OH, THAT OLD SONG...
SO THERE WAS ACTUALLY SOME SINGING.
YES. NICE SINGING.
GOOONG!

BENDIK KALTENBORN 2009

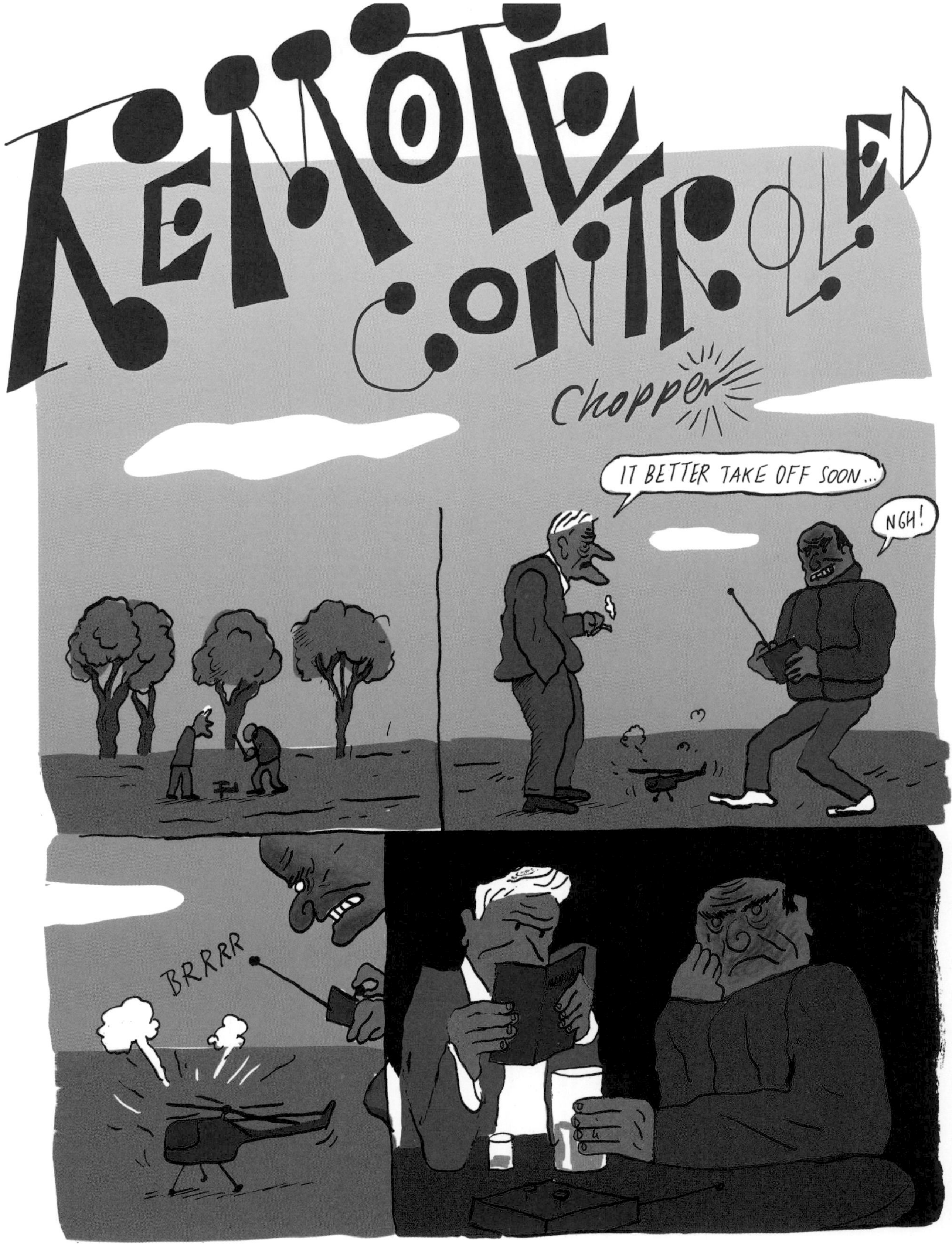
REMOTE CONTROLLED
Chopper
IT BETTER TAKE OFF SOON...
NGH!
BRRRR

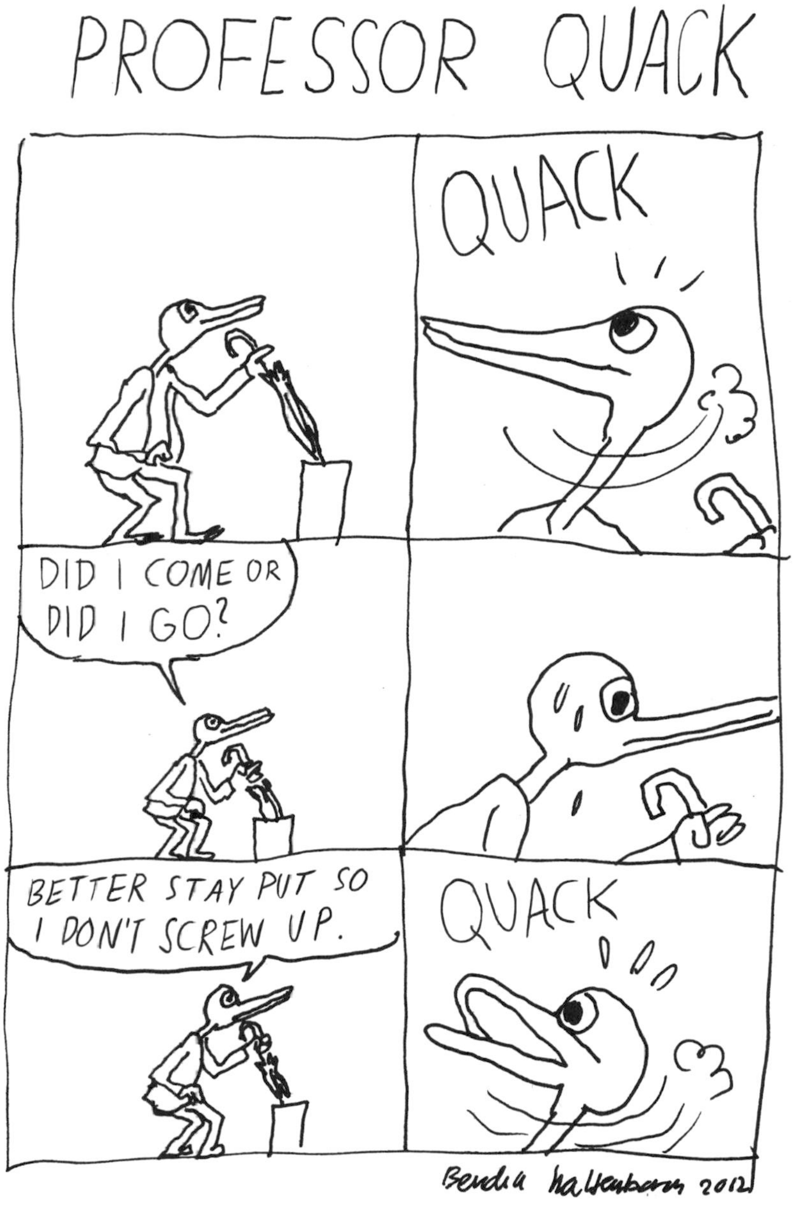
PROFESSOR QUACK
QUACK
DID I COME OR DID I GO?
BETTER STAY PUT SO I DON'T SCREW UP.
QUACK

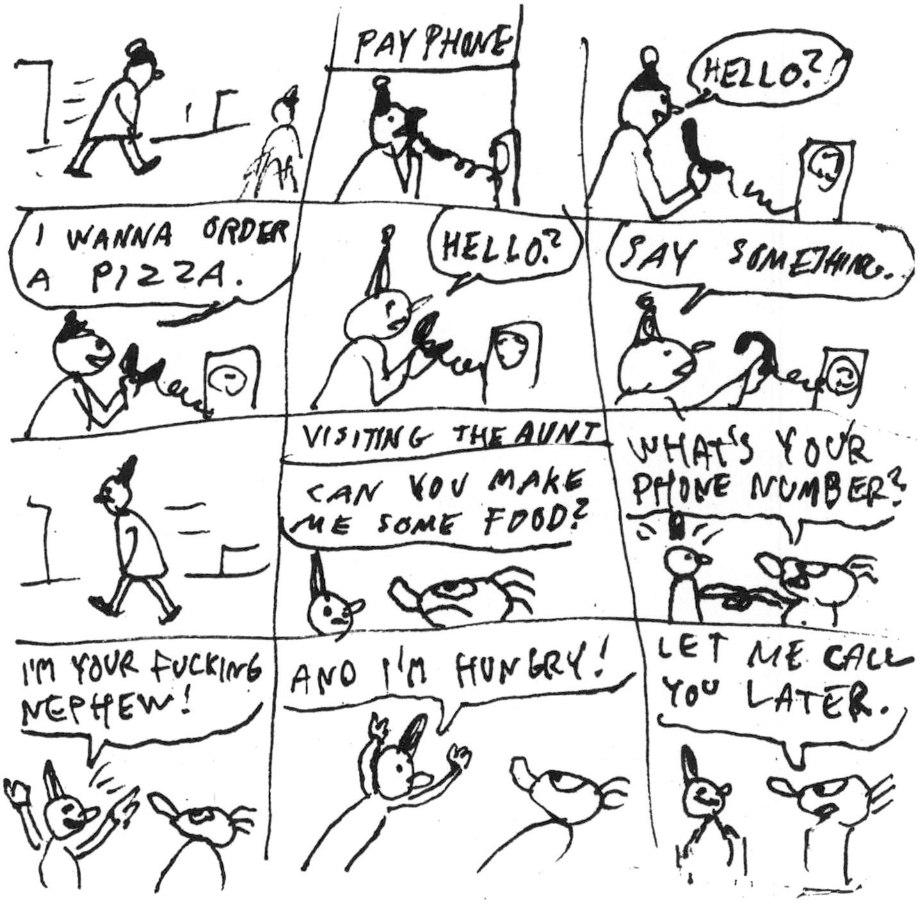
PAY PHONE
HELLO?
I WANNA ORDER A PIZZA.
HELLO?
SAY SOMETHING.
VISITING THE AUNT
CAN YOU MAKE ME SOME FOOD?
WHAT'S YOUR PHONE NUMBER?
I'M YOUR FUCKING NEPHEW!
AND I'M HUNGRY!
LET ME CALL YOU LATER.

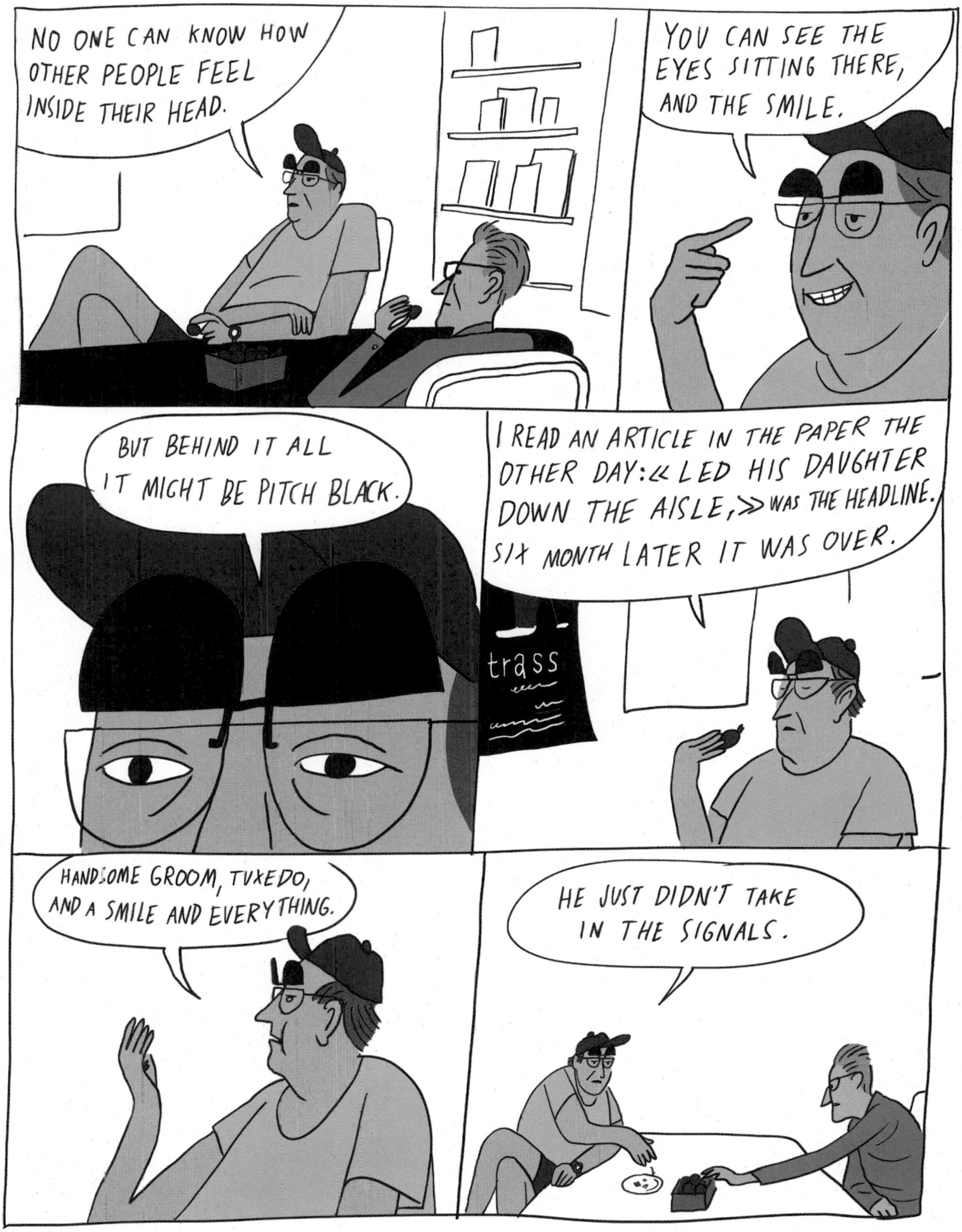
NO ONE CAN KNOW HOW OTHER PEOPLE FEEL INSIDE THEIR HEAD.
YOU CAN SEE THE EYES SITTING THERE, AND THE SMILE.
BUT BEHIND IT ALL IT MIGHT BE PITCH BLACK.
trass
I READ AN ARTICLE IN THE PAPER THE OTHER DAY: «LED HIS DAUGHTER DOWN THE AISLE,» WAS THE HEADLINE. SIX MONTH LATER IT WAS OVER.
HANDSOME GROOM, TUXEDO, AND A SMILE AND EVERYTHING.
HE JUST DIDN'T TAKE IN THE SIGNALS.

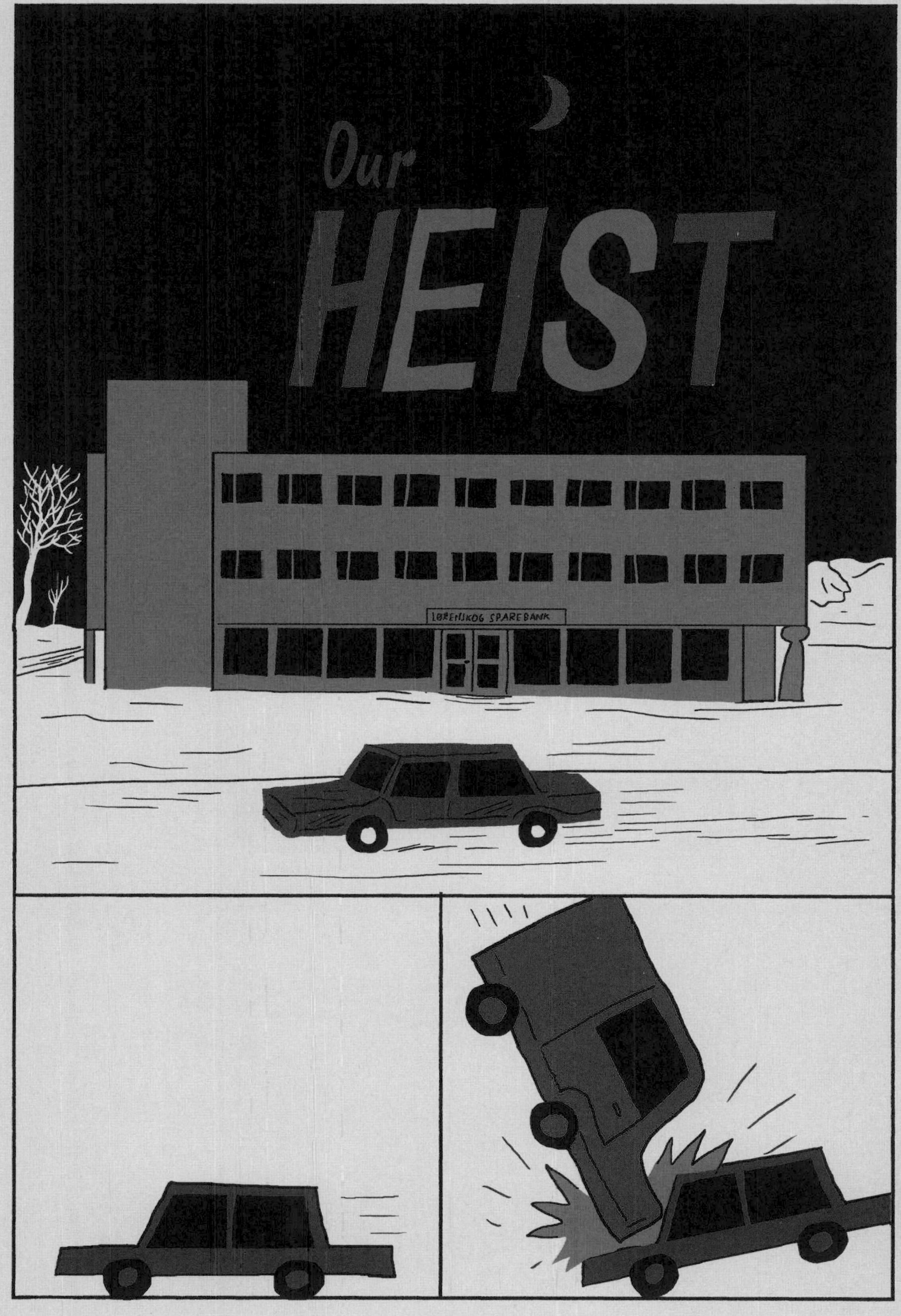
Our
HEIST
LØRENSKOG SPAREBANK

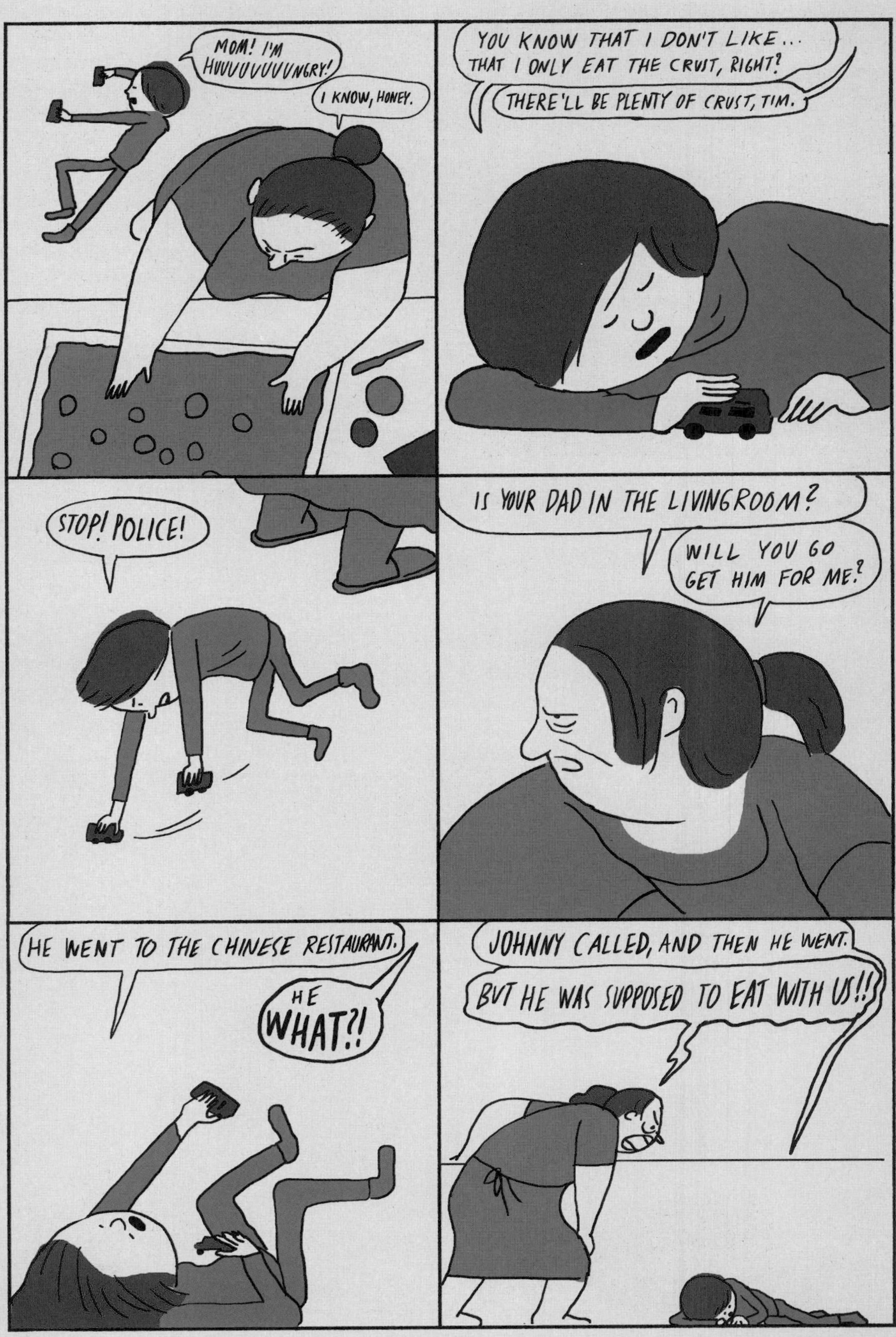
MOM! I'M HUUUUUUUUNGRY!
I KNOW, HONEY.
YOU KNOW THAT I DON'T LIKE... THAT I ONLY EAT THE CRUST, RIGHT?
THERE'LL BE PLENTY OF CRUST, TIM.
STOP! POLICE!
IS YOUR DAD IN THE LIVINGROOM?
WILL YOU GO GET HIM FOR ME?
HE WENT TO THE CHINESE RESTAURANT.
HE WHAT?!
JOHNNY CALLED, AND THEN HE WENT.
BUT HE WAS SUPPOSED TO EAT WITH US!!

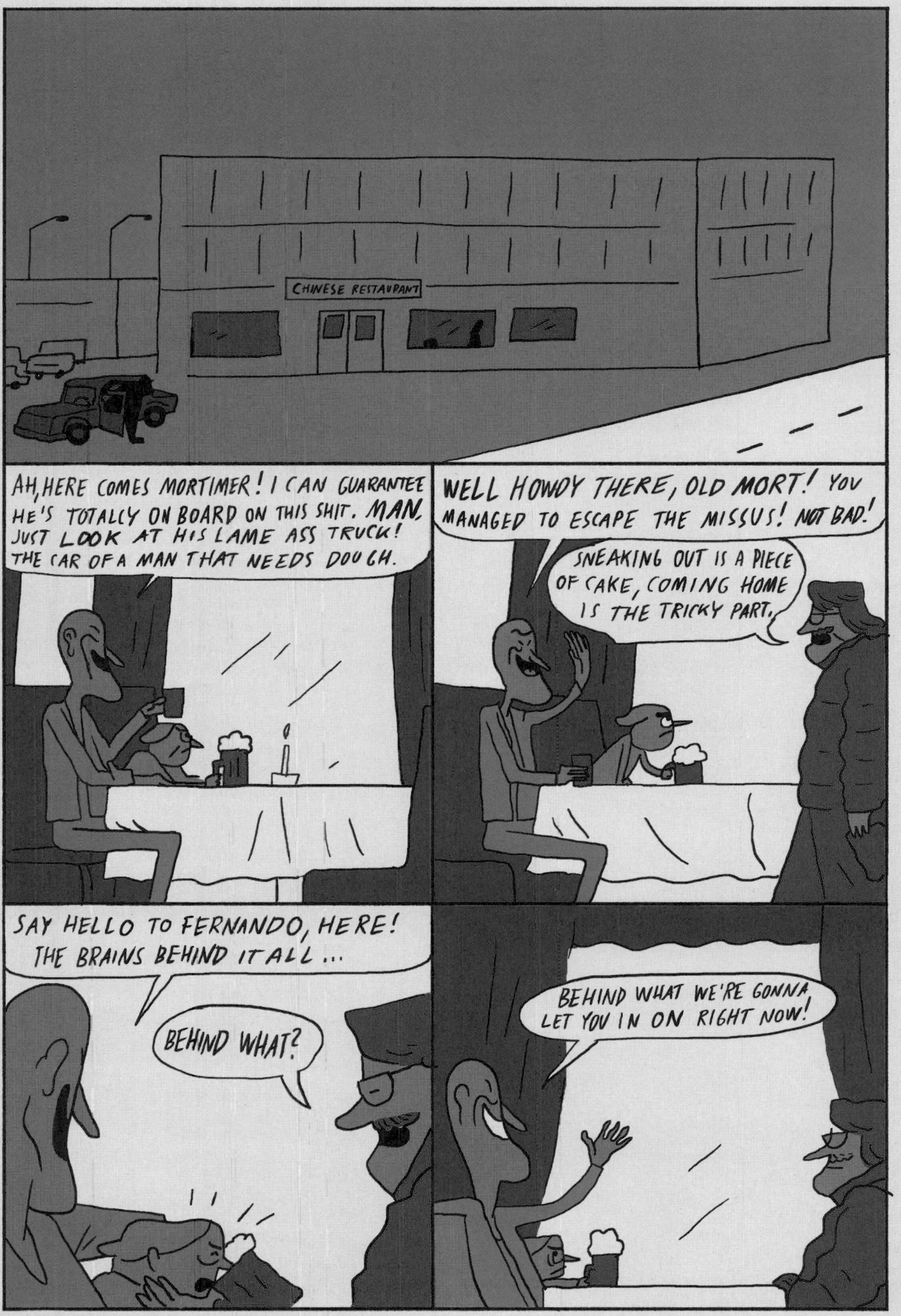
CHINESE RESTAURANT
AH, HERE COMES MORTIMER! I CAN GUARANTEE HE'S TOTALLY ON BOARD ON THIS SHIT. MAN, JUST LOOK AT HIS LAME ASS TRUCK! THE CAR OF A MAN THAT NEEDS DOUGH.
WELL HOWDY THERE, OLD MORT! YOU MANAGED TO ESCAPE THE MISSUS! NOT BAD!
SNEAKING OUT IS A PIECE OF CAKE, COMING HOME IS THE TRICKY PART.
SAY HELLO TO FERNANDO, HERE! THE BRAINS BEHIND IT ALL...
BEHIND WHAT?
BEHIND WHAT WE'RE GONNA LET YOU IN ON RIGHT NOW!

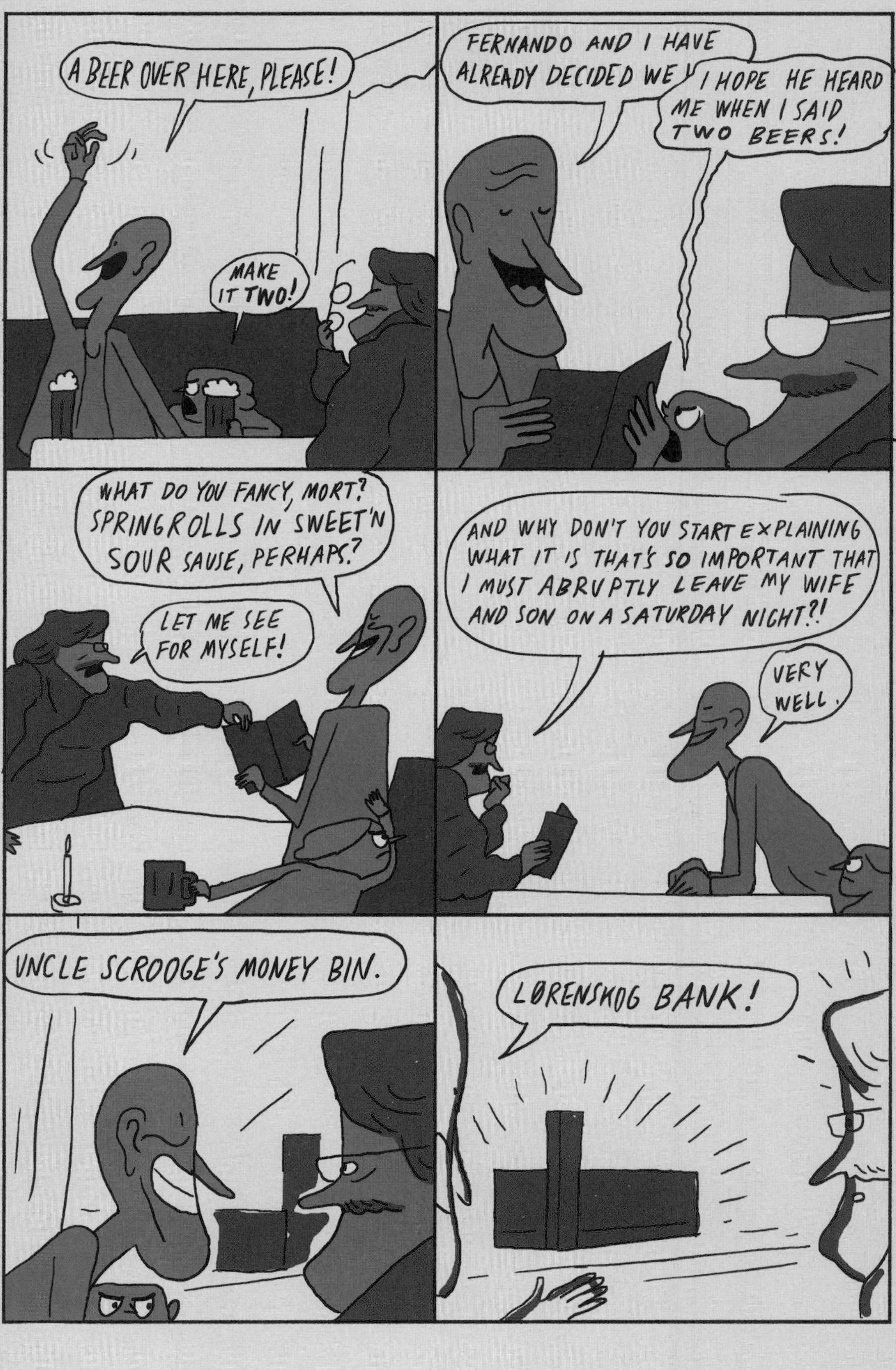
A BEER OVER HERE, PLEASE!
MAKE IT TWO!
FERNANDO AND I HAVE ALREADY DECIDED WE
I HOPE HE HEARD ME WHEN I SAID TWO BEERS!
WHAT DO YOU FANCY, MORT? SPRINGROLLS IN SWEET'N SOUR SAUSE, PERHAPS?
LET ME SEE FOR MYSELF!
AND WHY DON'T YOU START EXPLAINING WHAT IT IS THAT'S SO IMPORTANT THAT I MUST ABRUPTLY LEAVE MY WIFE AND SON ON A SATURDAY NIGHT?!
VERY WELL.
UNCLE SCROOGE'S MONEY BIN.
LØRENSKOG BANK!

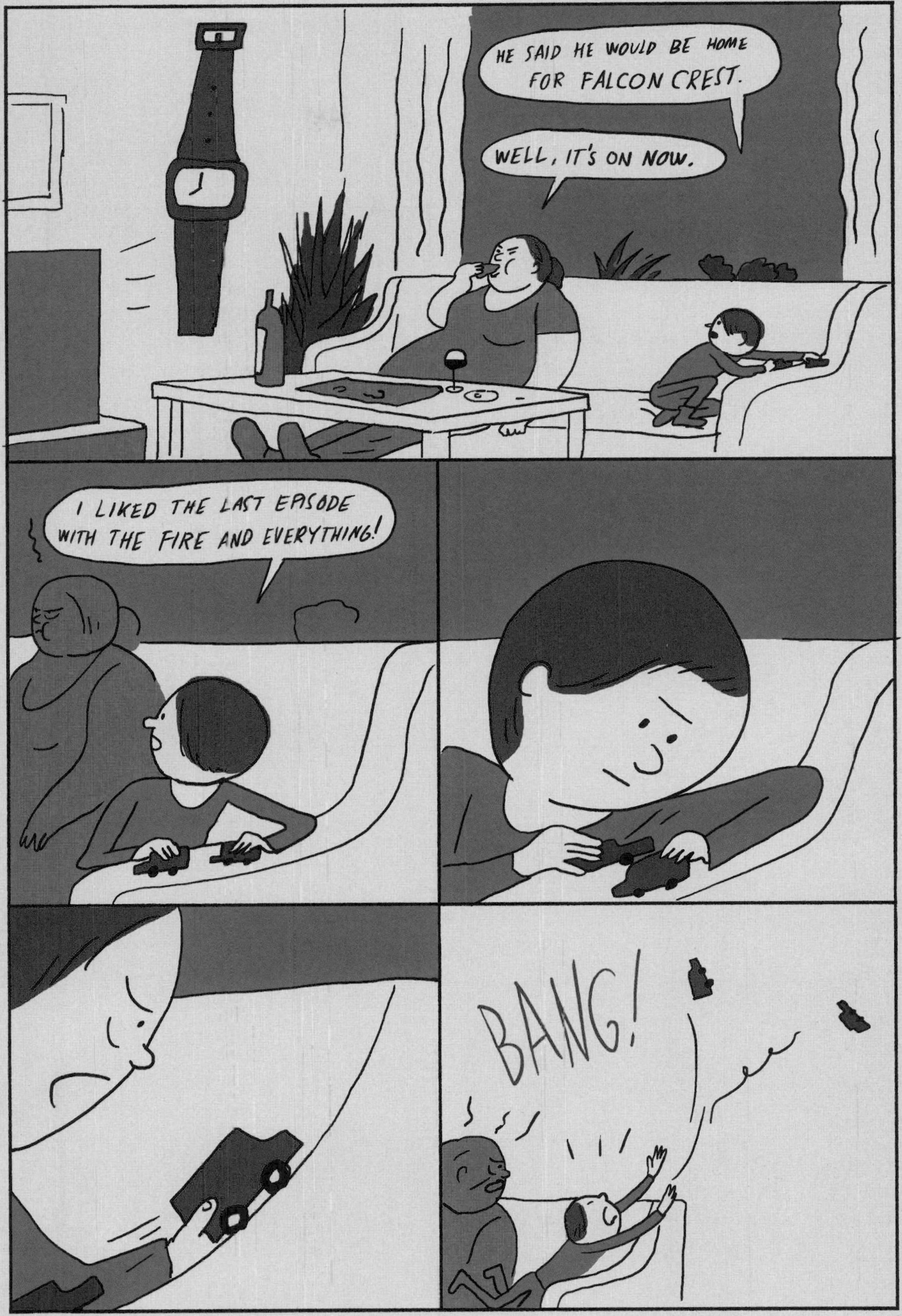
HE SAID HE WOULD BE HOME FOR FALCON CREST.
WELL, IT'S ON NOW.
I LIKED THE LAST EPISODE WITH THE FIRE AND EVERYTHING!
BANG!

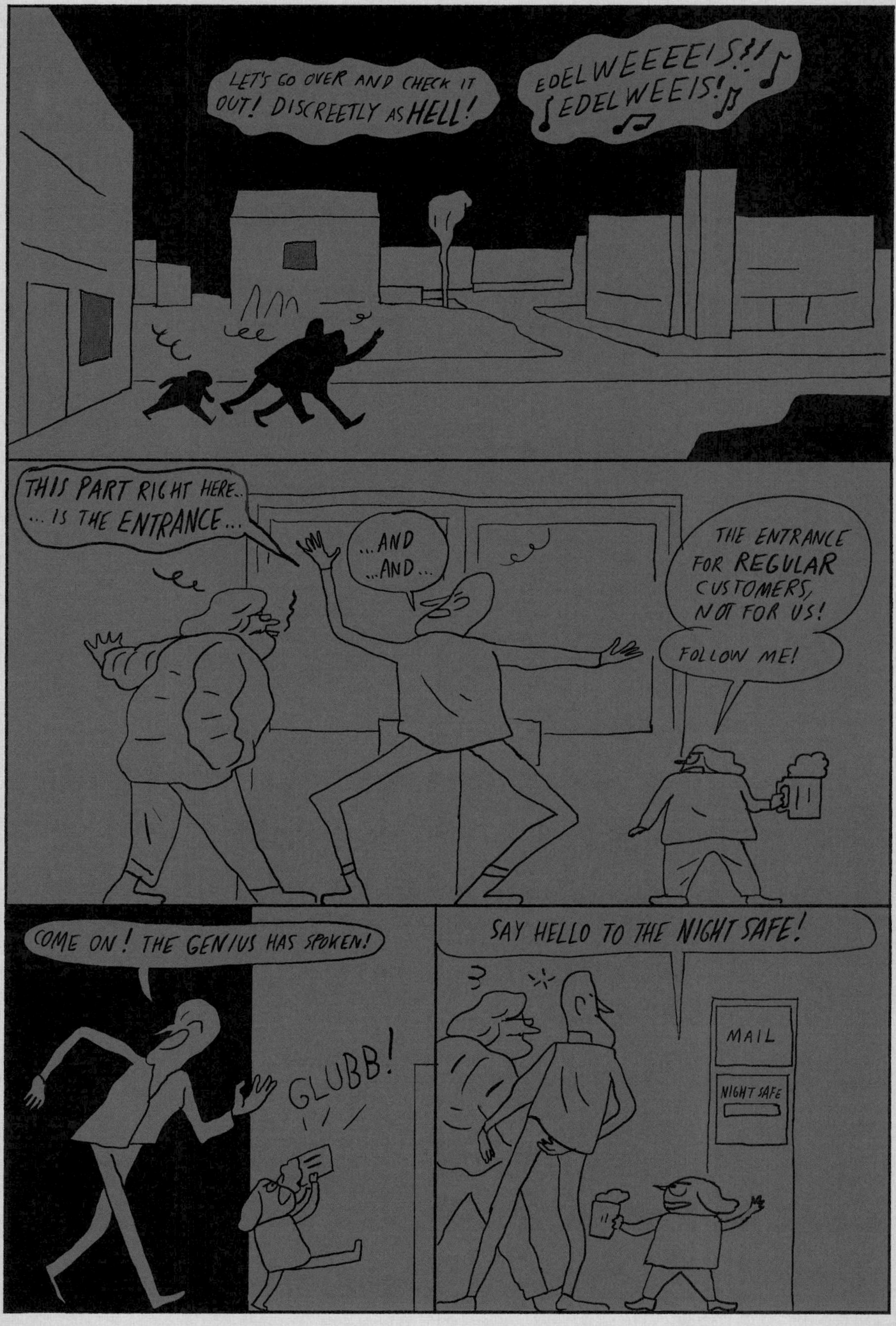
LET'S GO OVER AND CHECK IT OUT! DISCREETLY AS HELL!
EDELWEEEEIS!! EDELWEEIS!
THIS PART RIGHT HERE.. ... IS THE ENTRANCE...
...AND ...AND...
THE ENTRANCE FOR REGULAR CUSTOMERS, NOT FOR US!
FOLLOW ME!
COME ON! THE GENIUS HAS SPOKEN!
GLUBB!
SAY HELLO TO THE NIGHT SAFE!
MAIL
NIGHT SAFE

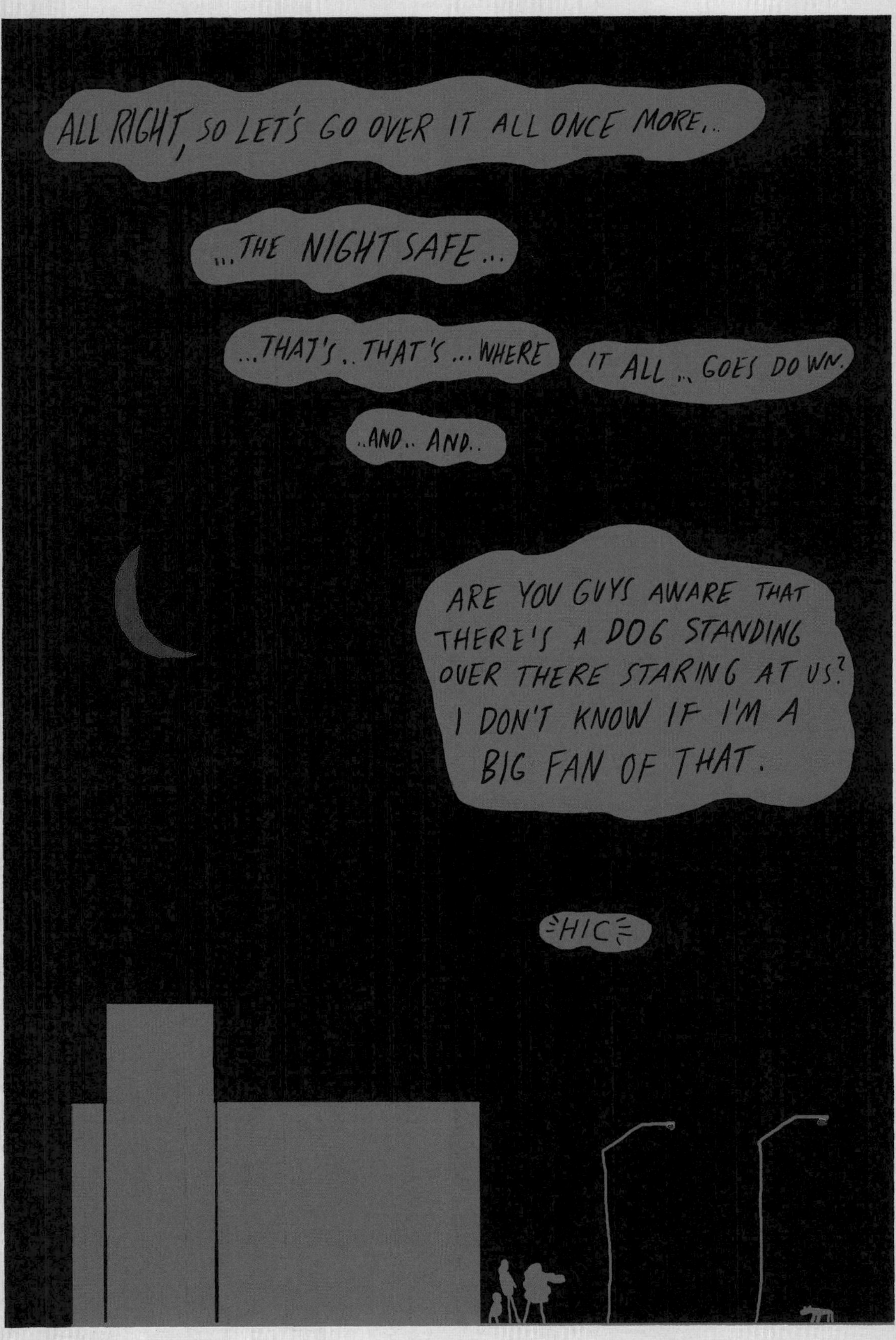
ALL RIGHT, SO LET'S GO OVER IT ALL ONCE MORE...
...THE NIGHT SAFE...
...THAT'S.. THAT'S ...WHERE
IT ALL .. GOES DOWN.
..AND.. AND..
ARE YOU GUYS AWARE THAT THERE'S A DOG STANDING OVER THERE STARING AT US? I DON'T KNOW IF I'M A BIG FAN OF THAT.
HIC

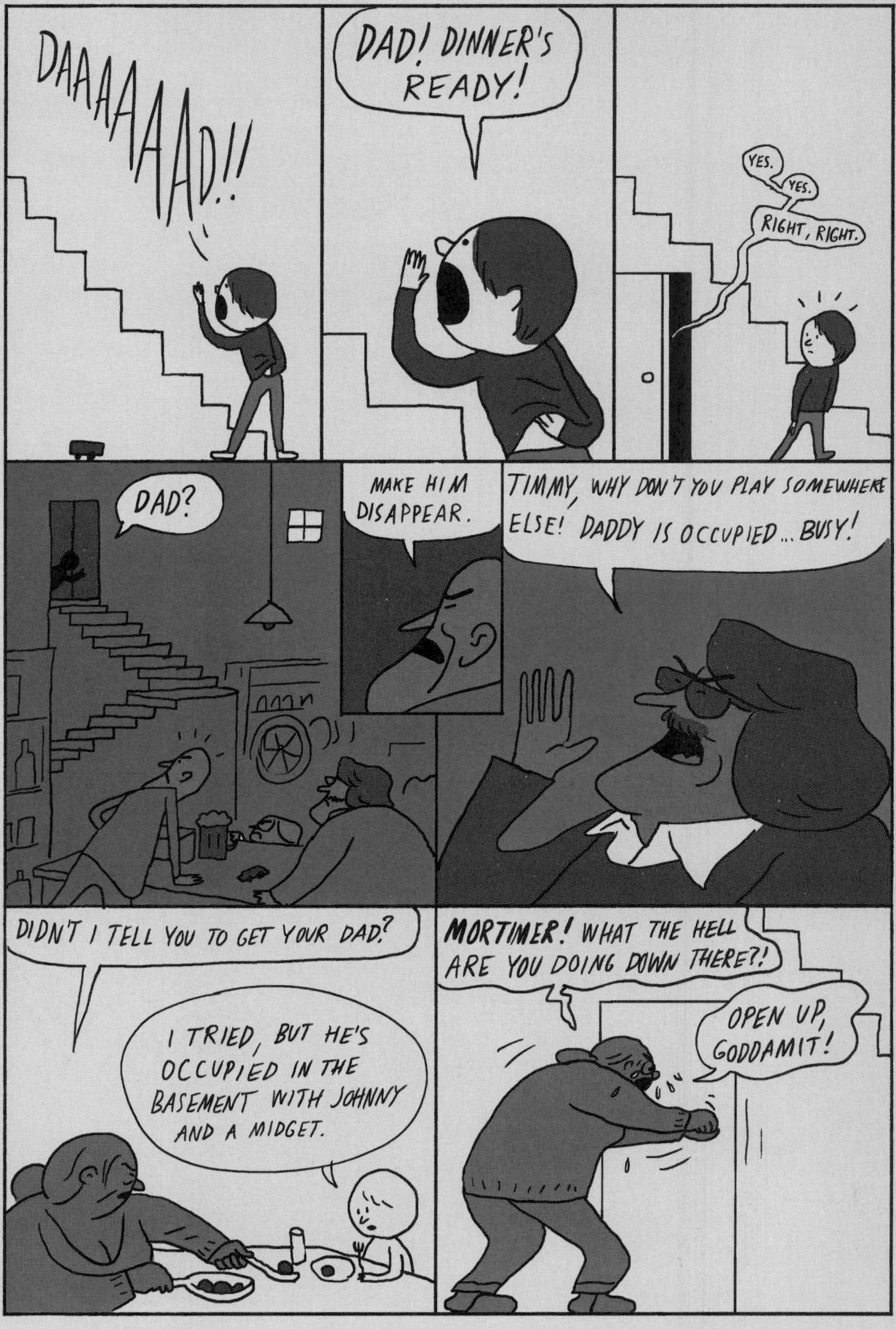

DAAAAAAAD!!
DAD! DINNER'S READY!
YES.
YES.
RIGHT, RIGHT.
DAD?
MAKE HIM DISAPPEAR.
TIMMY, WHY DON'T YOU PLAY SOMEWHERE ELSE! DADDY IS OCCUPIED... BUSY!
DIDN'T I TELL YOU TO GET YOUR DAD?
I TRIED, BUT HE'S OCCUPIED IN THE BASEMENT WITH JOHNNY AND A MIDGET.
MORTIMER! WHAT THE HELL ARE YOU DOING DOWN THERE?!
OPEN UP, GODDAMIT!

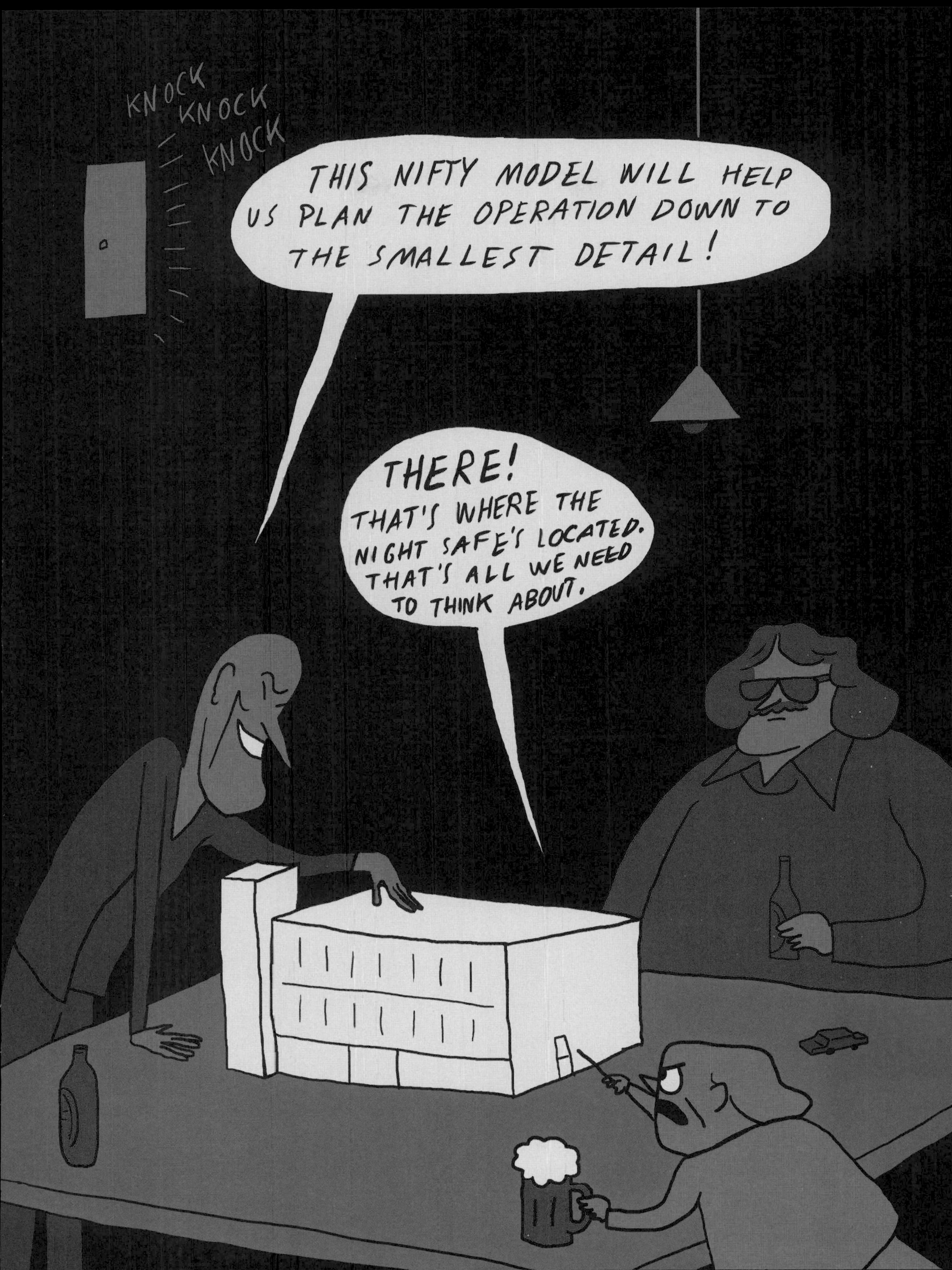
KNOCK
KNOCK
KNOCK
THIS NIFTY MODEL WILL HELP US PLAN THE OPERATION DOWN TO THE SMALLEST DETAIL!
THERE! THAT'S WHERE THE NIGHT SAFE'S LOCATED. THAT'S ALL WE NEED TO THINK ABOUT.

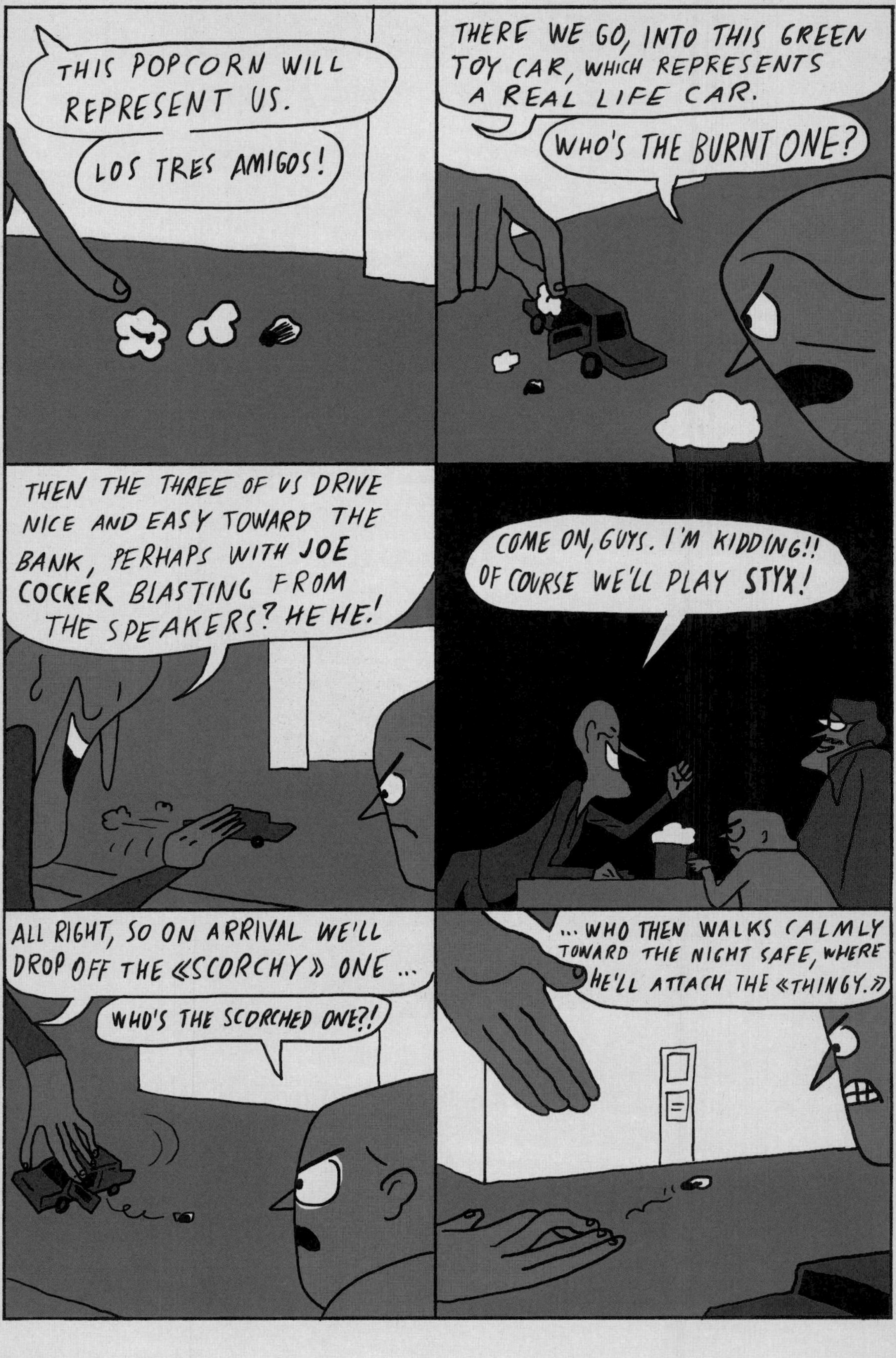

THIS POPCORN WILL REPRESENT US.
LOS TRES AMIGOS!
THERE WE GO, INTO THIS GREEN TOY CAR, WHICH REPRESENTS A REAL LIFE CAR.
WHO'S THE BURNT ONE?
THEN THE THREE OF US DRIVE NICE AND EASY TOWARD THE BANK, PERHAPS WITH JOE COCKER BLASTING FROM THE SPEAKERS? HE HE!
COME ON, GUYS. I'M KIDDING!! OF COURSE WE'LL PLAY STYX!
ALL RIGHT, SO ON ARRIVAL WE'LL DROP OFF THE «SCORCHY» ONE ...
WHO'S THE SCORCHED ONE?!
... WHO THEN WALKS CALMLY TOWARD THE NIGHT SAFE, WHERE HE'LL ATTACH THE «THINGY.»

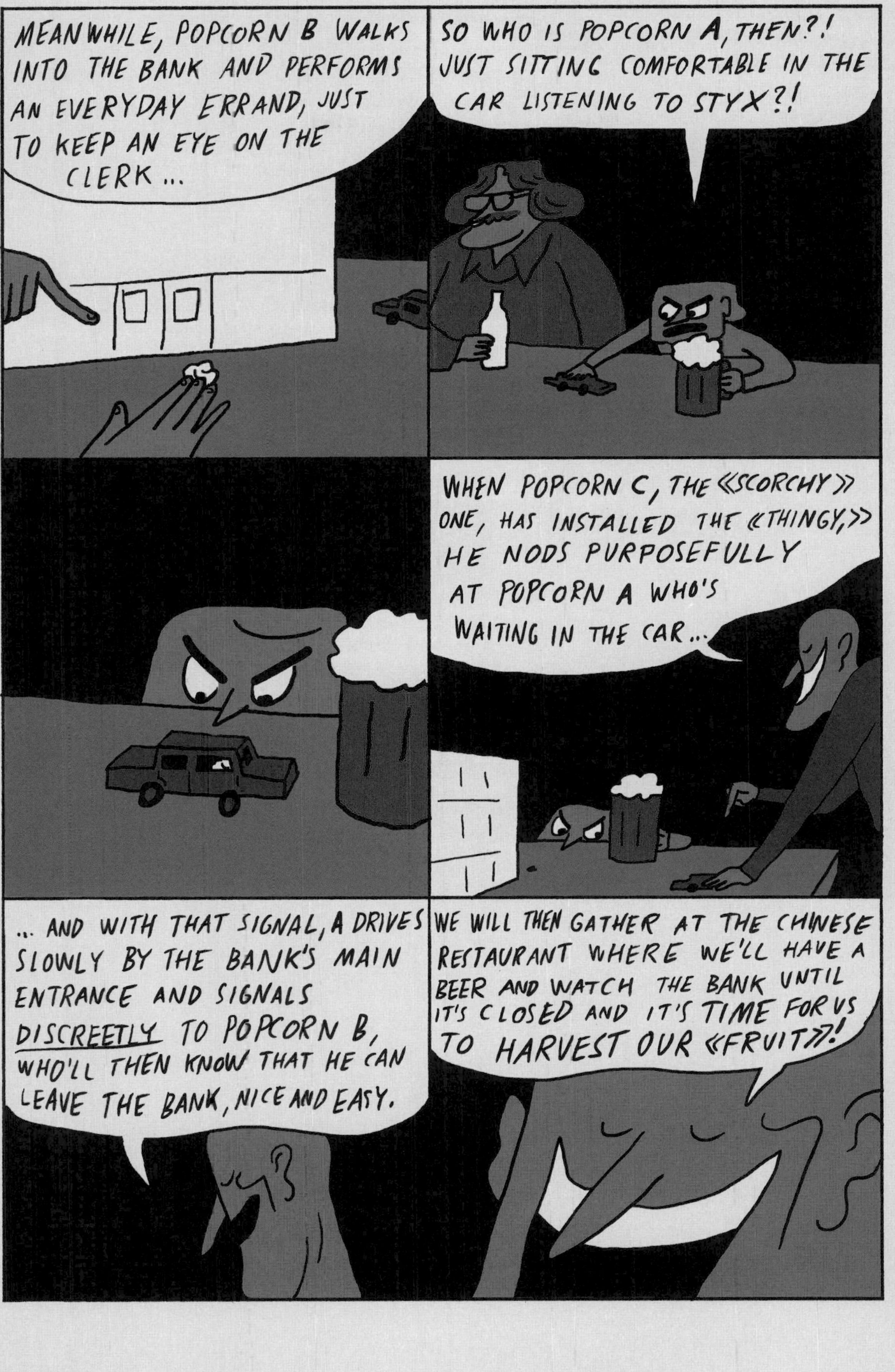
MEANWHILE, POPCORN B WALKS INTO THE BANK AND PERFORMS AN EVERYDAY ERRAND, JUST TO KEEP AN EYE ON THE CLERK ...
SO WHO IS POPCORN A, THEN?! JUST SITTING COMFORTABLE IN THE CAR LISTENING TO STYX?!
WHEN POPCORN C, THE «SCORCHY» ONE, HAS INSTALLED THE «THINGY,» HE NODS PURPOSEFULLY AT POPCORN A WHO'S WAITING IN THE CAR...
... AND WITH THAT SIGNAL, A DRIVES SLOWLY BY THE BANK'S MAIN ENTRANCE AND SIGNALS DISCREETLY TO POPCORN B, WHO'LL THEN KNOW THAT HE CAN LEAVE THE BANK, NICE AND EASY.
WE WILL THEN GATHER AT THE CHINESE RESTAURANT WHERE WE'LL HAVE A BEER AND WATCH THE BANK UNTIL IT'S CLOSED AND IT'S TIME FOR US TO HARVEST OUR «FRUIT»!

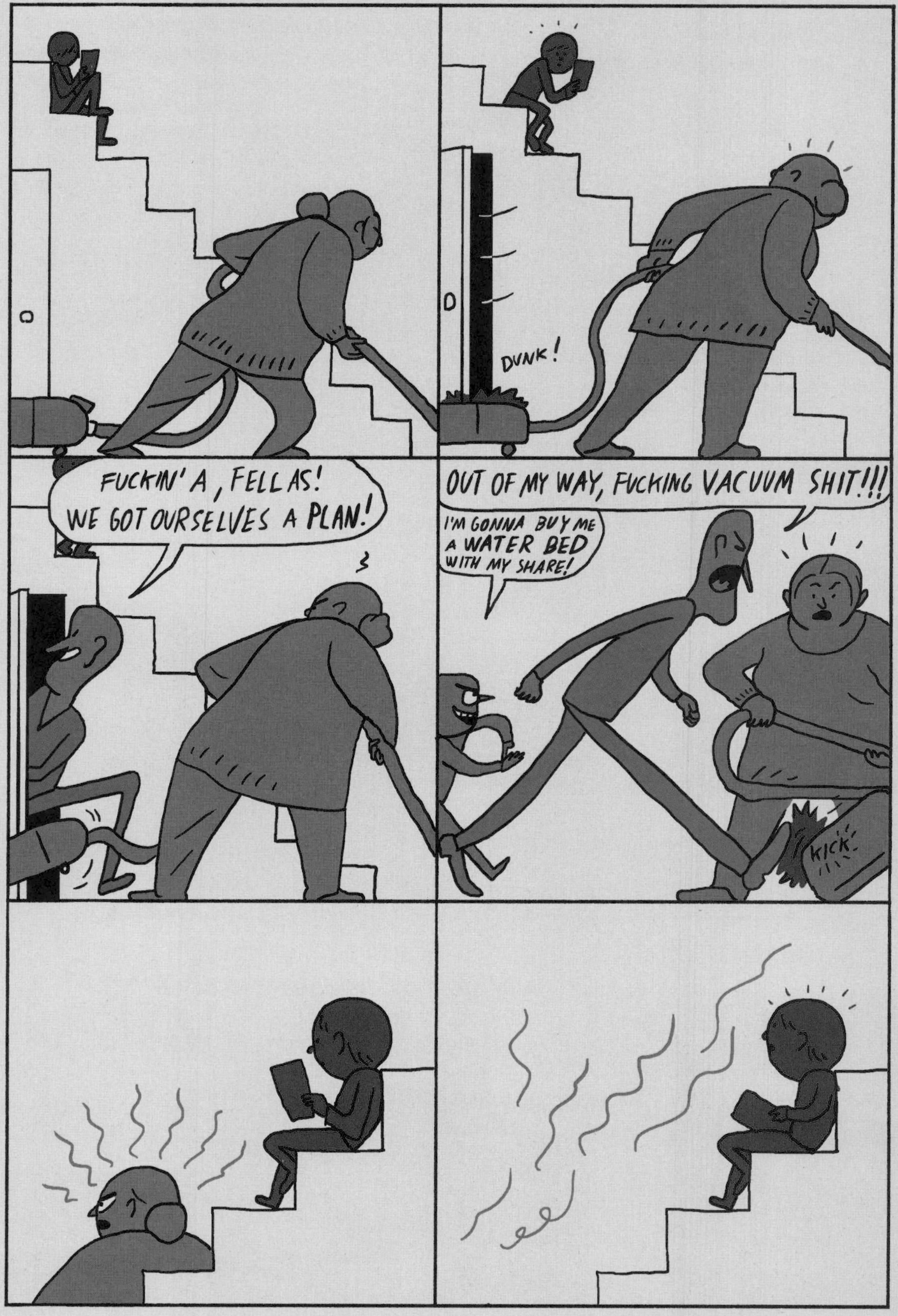
DUNK!
FUCKIN' A, FELLAS! WE GOT OURSELVES A PLAN!
OUT OF MY WAY, FUCKING VACUUM SHIT!!!
I'M GONNA BUY ME A WATER BED WITH MY SHARE!
KICK

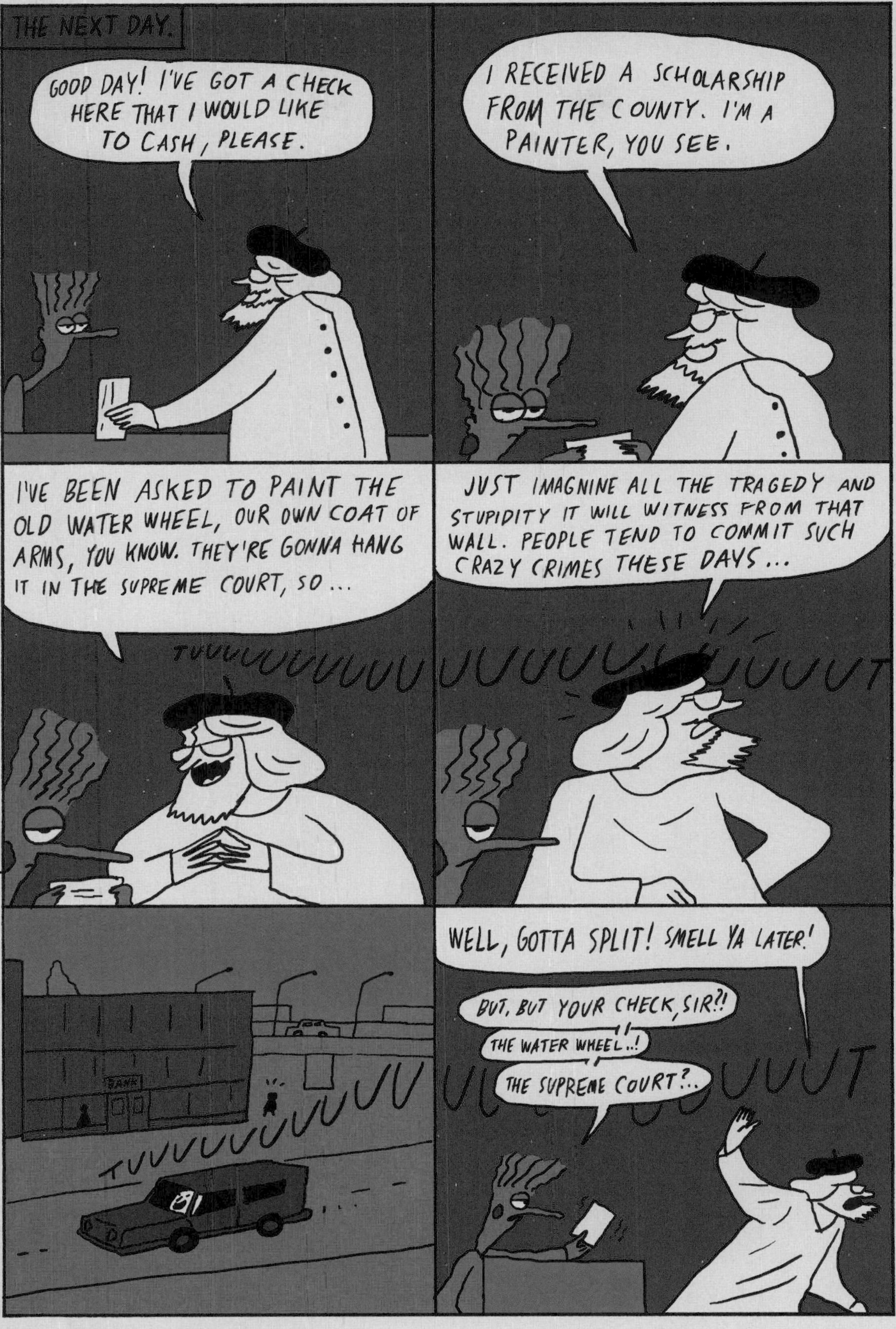
THE NEXT DAY.
GOOD DAY! I'VE GOT A CHECK HERE THAT I WOULD LIKE TO CASH, PLEASE.
I RECEIVED A SCHOLARSHIP FROM THE COUNTY. I'M A PAINTER, YOU SEE.
I'VE BEEN ASKED TO PAINT THE OLD WATER WHEEL, OUR OWN COAT OF ARMS, YOU KNOW. THEY'RE GONNA HANG IT IN THE SUPREME COURT, SO...
JUST IMAGNINE ALL THE TRAGEDY AND STUPIDITY IT WILL WITNESS FROM THAT WALL. PEOPLE TEND TO COMMIT SUCH CRAZY CRIMES THESE DAYS...
TUUUUUUUUUUUUUUUUUUUUUT
BANK
TUUUUUUUUUUUUU
WELL, GOTTA SPLIT! SMELL YA LATER!
BUT, BUT YOUR CHECK, SIR?!
THE WATER WHEEL..!
THE SUPREME COURT?..
UUUUUUT

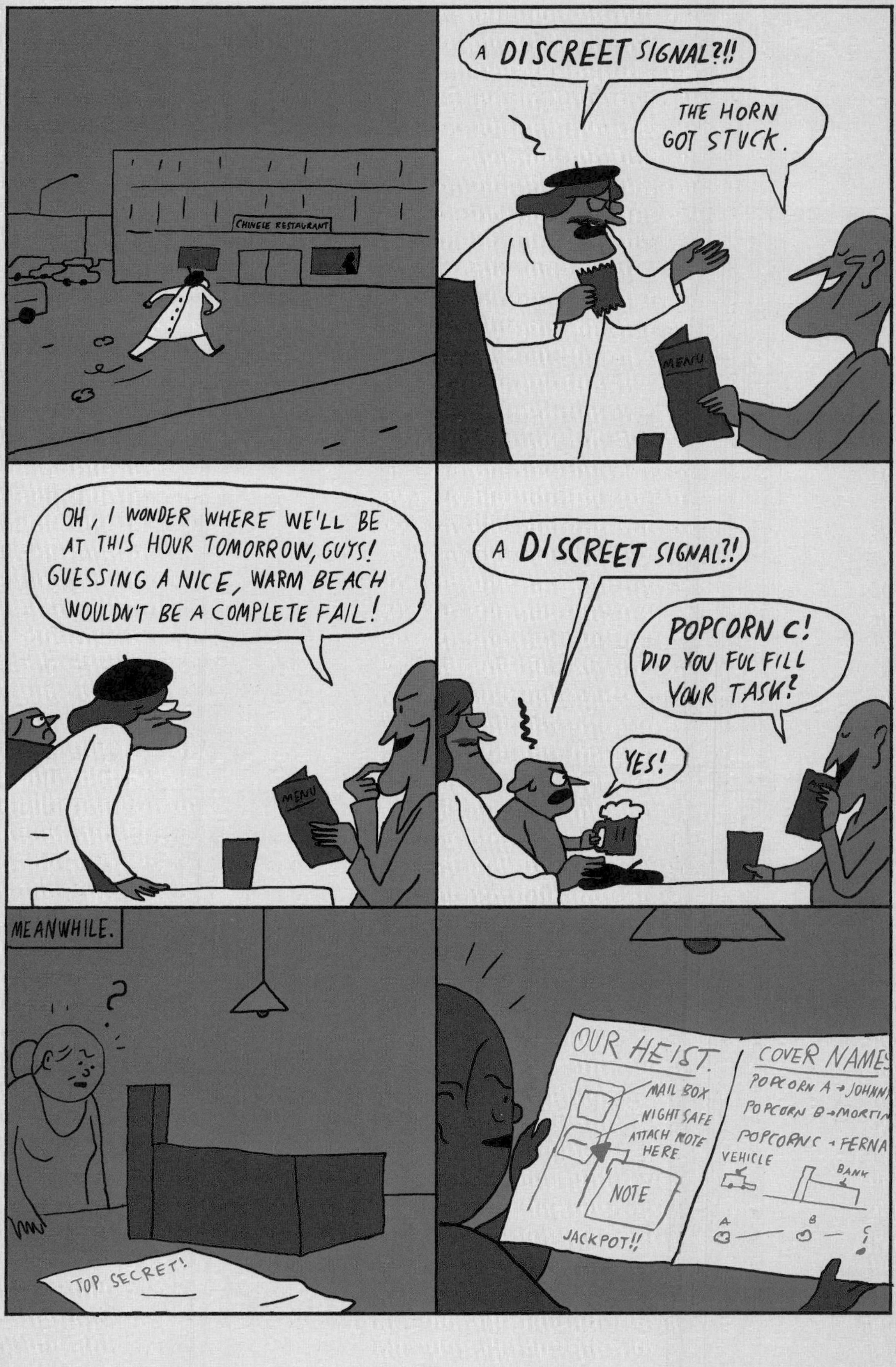
CHINESE RESTAURANT
A DISCREET SIGNAL?!!
THE HORN GOT STUCK.
MENU
OH, I WONDER WHERE WE'LL BE AT THIS HOUR TOMORROW, GUYS! GUESSING A NICE, WARM BEACH WOULDN'T BE A COMPLETE FAIL!
MENU
A DISCREET SIGNAL?!!
POPCORN C! DID YOU FULFILL YOUR TASK?
YES!
MEANWHILE.
TOP SECRET!
OUR HEIST.
MAIL BOX
NIGHT SAFE
ATTACH NOTE HERE
NOTE
JACKPOT!!
COVER NAMES
POPCORN A → JOHNN
POPCORN B → MORTIN
POPCORN C → FERNA
VEHICLE
BANK
A
B
C

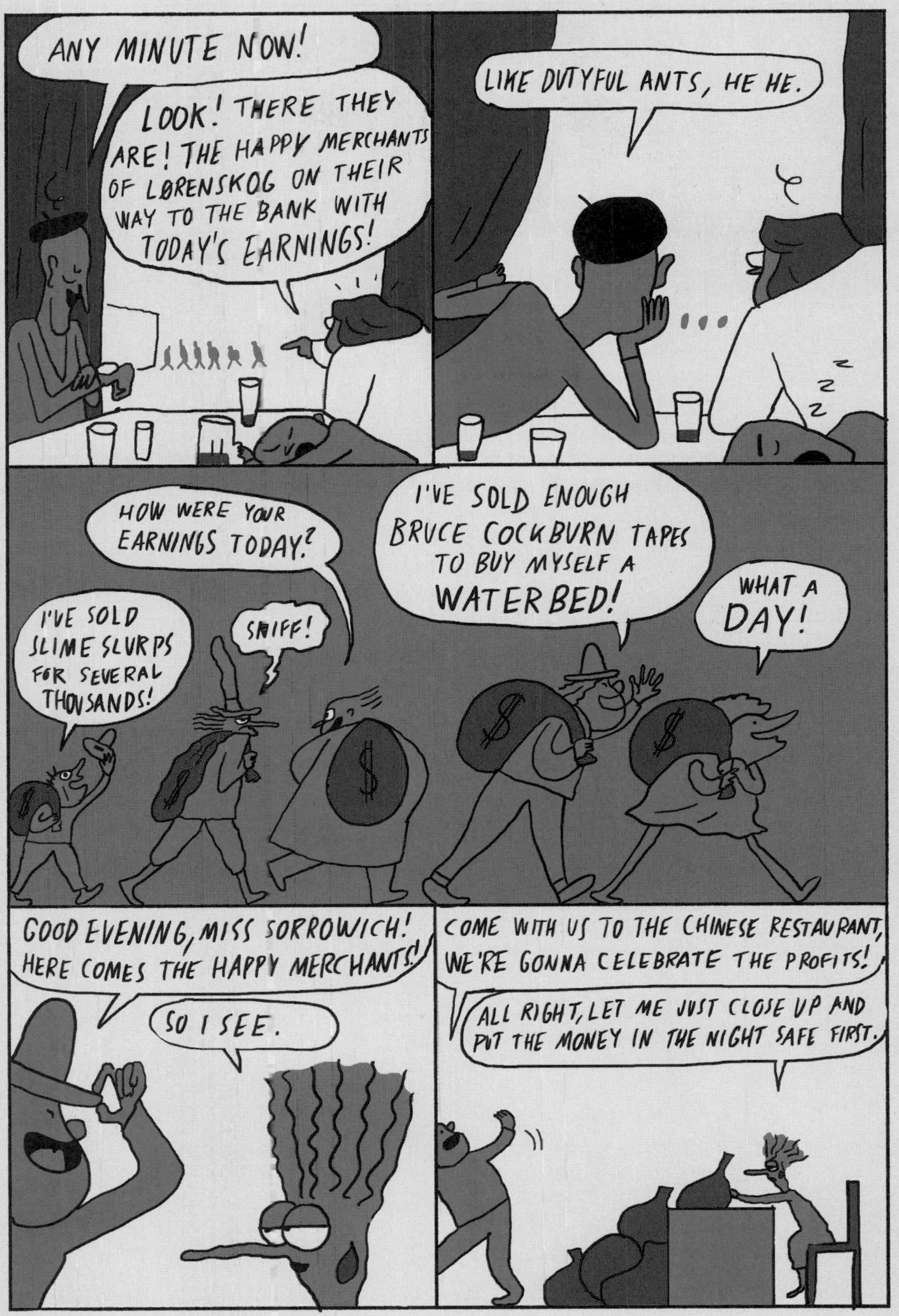
ANY MINUTE NOW!
LOOK! THERE THEY ARE! THE HAPPY MERCHANTS OF LØRENSKOG ON THEIR WAY TO THE BANK WITH TODAY'S EARNINGS!
LIKE DUTYFUL ANTS, HE HE.
...
HOW WERE YOUR EARNINGS TODAY?
I'VE SOLD SLIME SLURPS FOR SEVERAL THOUSANDS!
SNIFF!
I'VE SOLD ENOUGH BRUCE COCKBURN TAPES TO BUY MYSELF A WATERBED!
WHAT A DAY!
GOOD EVENING, MISS SORROWICH! HERE COMES THE HAPPY MERCHANTS!
SO I SEE.
COME WITH US TO THE CHINESE RESTAURANT, WE'RE GONNA CELEBRATE THE PROFITS!
ALL RIGHT, LET ME JUST CLOSE UP AND PUT THE MONEY IN THE NIGHT SAFE FIRST.

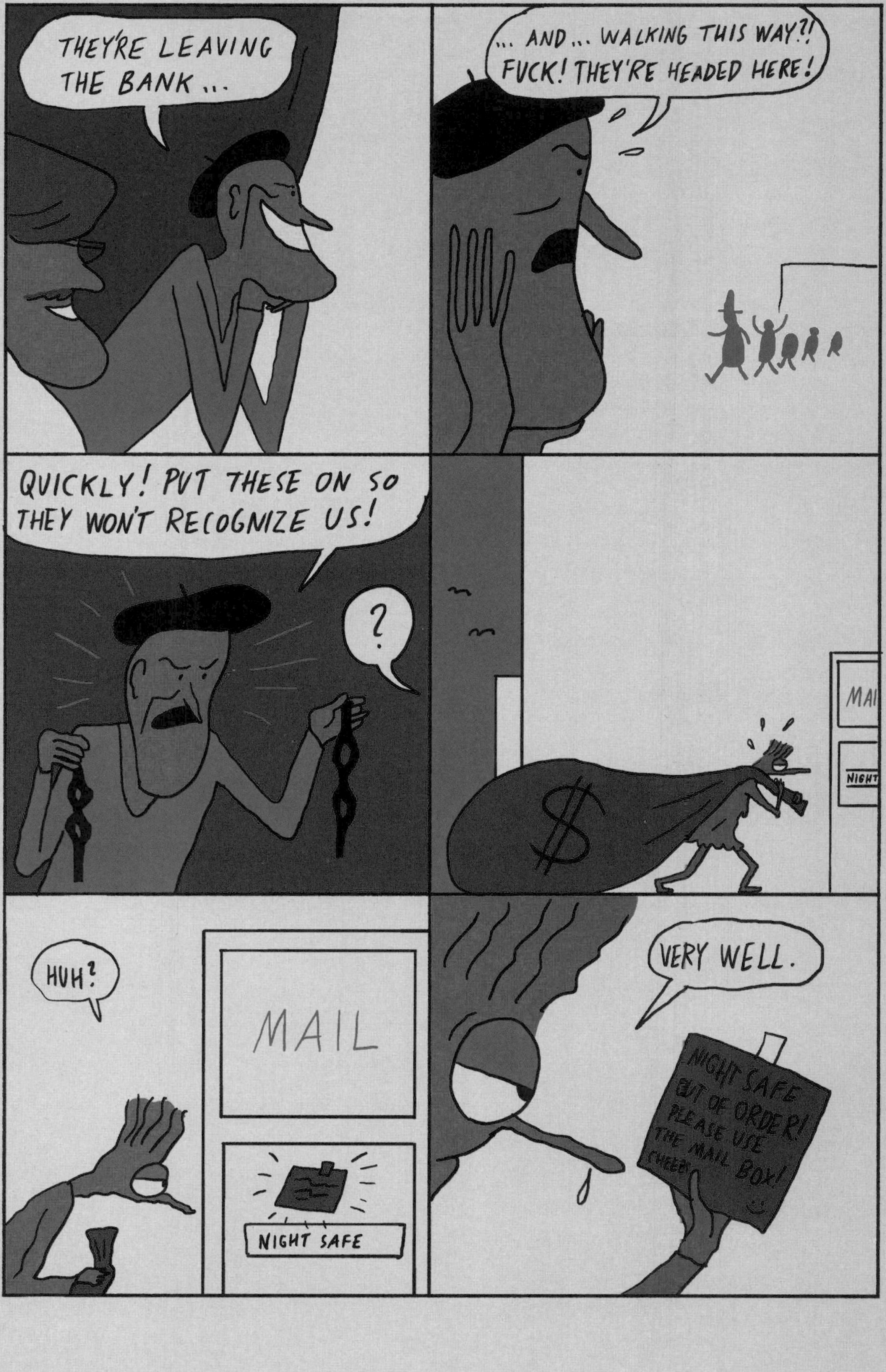
THEY'RE LEAVING THE BANK...
... AND... WALKING THIS WAY?!
FUCK! THEY'RE HEADED HERE!
QUICKLY! PUT THESE ON SO THEY WON'T RECOGNIZE US!
?
MAI
NIGHT
HUH?
MAIL
NIGHT SAFE
VERY WELL.
NIGHT SAFE OUT OF ORDER! PLEASE USE THE MAIL BOX!

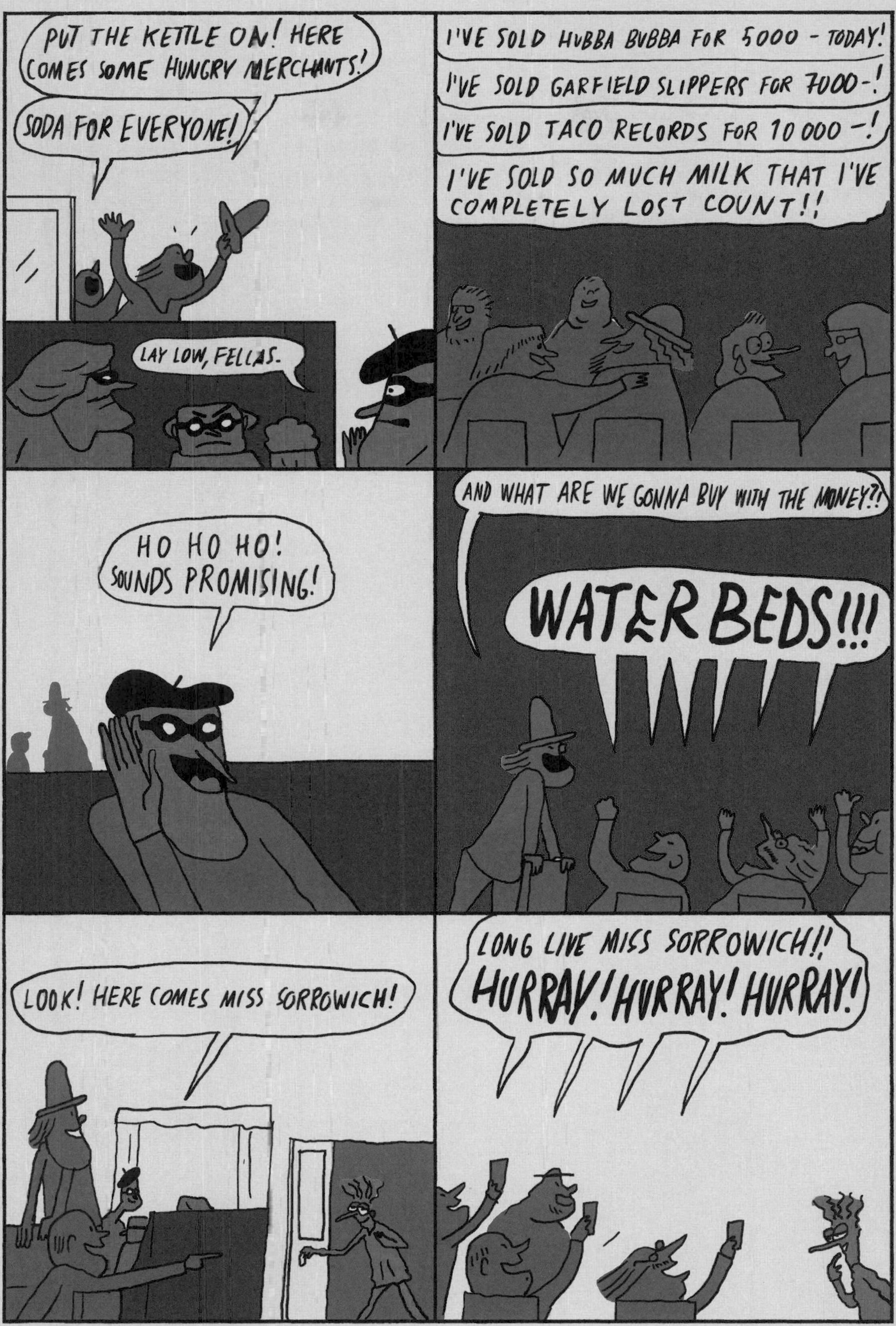
PUT THE KETTLE ON! HERE COMES SOME HUNGRY MERCHANTS!
SODA FOR EVERYONE!
I'VE SOLD HUBBA BUBBA FOR 5000 - TODAY!
I'VE SOLD GARFIELD SLIPPERS FOR 7000-!
I'VE SOLD TACO RECORDS FOR 10 000 -!
I'VE SOLD SO MUCH MILK THAT I'VE COMPLETELY LOST COUNT!!
LAY LOW, FELLAS.
HO HO HO! SOUNDS PROMISING!
AND WHAT ARE WE GONNA BUY WITH THE MONEY?!
WATERBEDS!!!
LOOK! HERE COMES MISS SORROWICH!
LONG LIVE MISS SORROWICH!!
HURRAY! HURRAY! HURRAY!

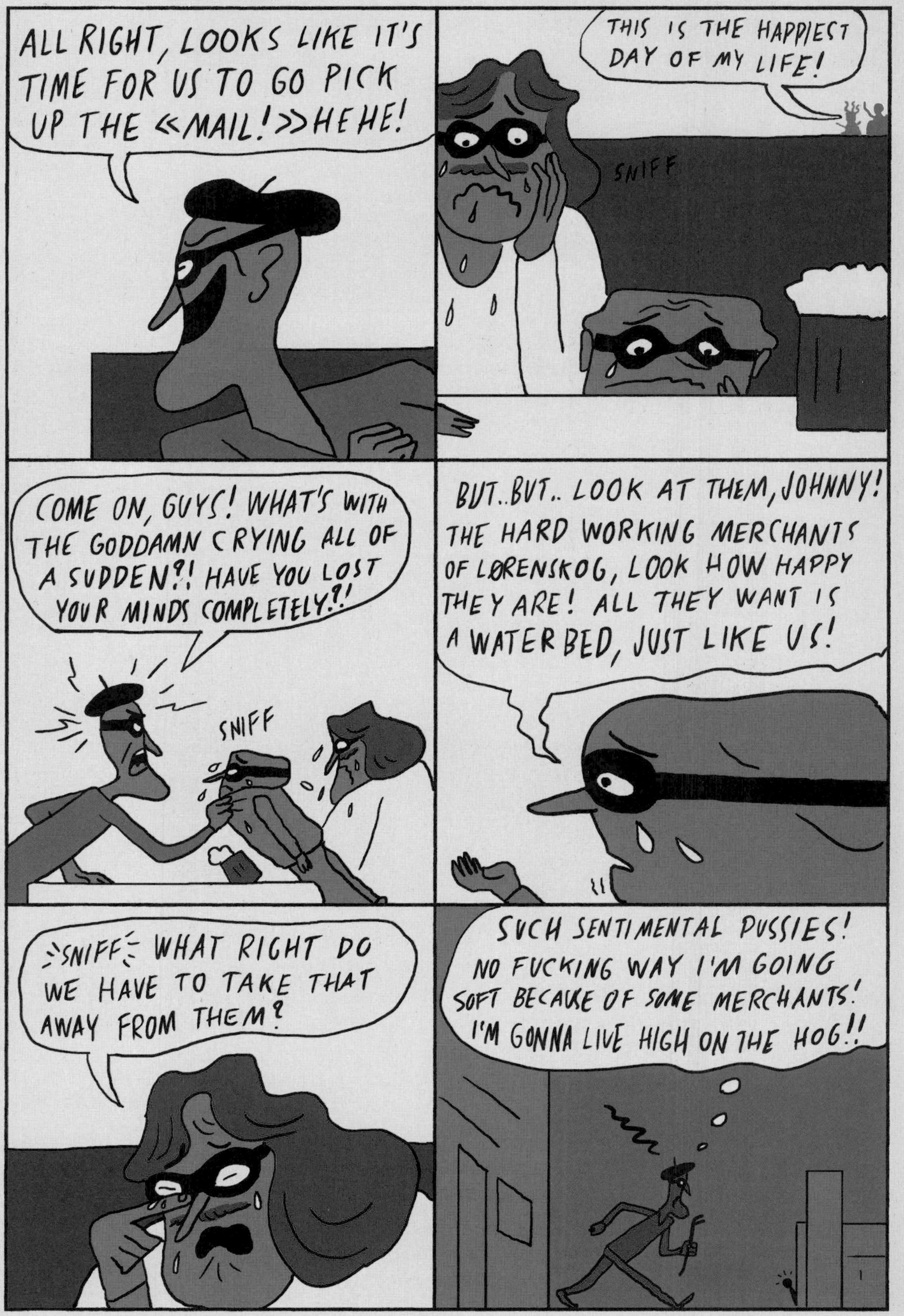
ALL RIGHT, LOOKS LIKE IT'S TIME FOR US TO GO PICK UP THE «MAIL!» HEHE!
THIS IS THE HAPPIEST DAY OF MY LIFE!
SNIFF
COME ON, GUYS! WHAT'S WITH THE GODDAMN CRYING ALL OF A SUDDEN?! HAVE YOU LOST YOUR MINDS COMPLETELY?!
SNIFF
BUT.. BUT.. LOOK AT THEM, JOHNNY! THE HARD WORKING MERCHANTS OF LØRENSKOG, LOOK HOW HAPPY THEY ARE! ALL THEY WANT IS A WATERBED, JUST LIKE US!
SNIFF WHAT RIGHT DO WE HAVE TO TAKE THAT AWAY FROM THEM?
SUCH SENTIMENTAL PUSSIES! NO FUCKING WAY I'M GOING SOFT BECAUSE OF SOME MERCHANTS! I'M GONNA LIVE HIGH ON THE HOG!!

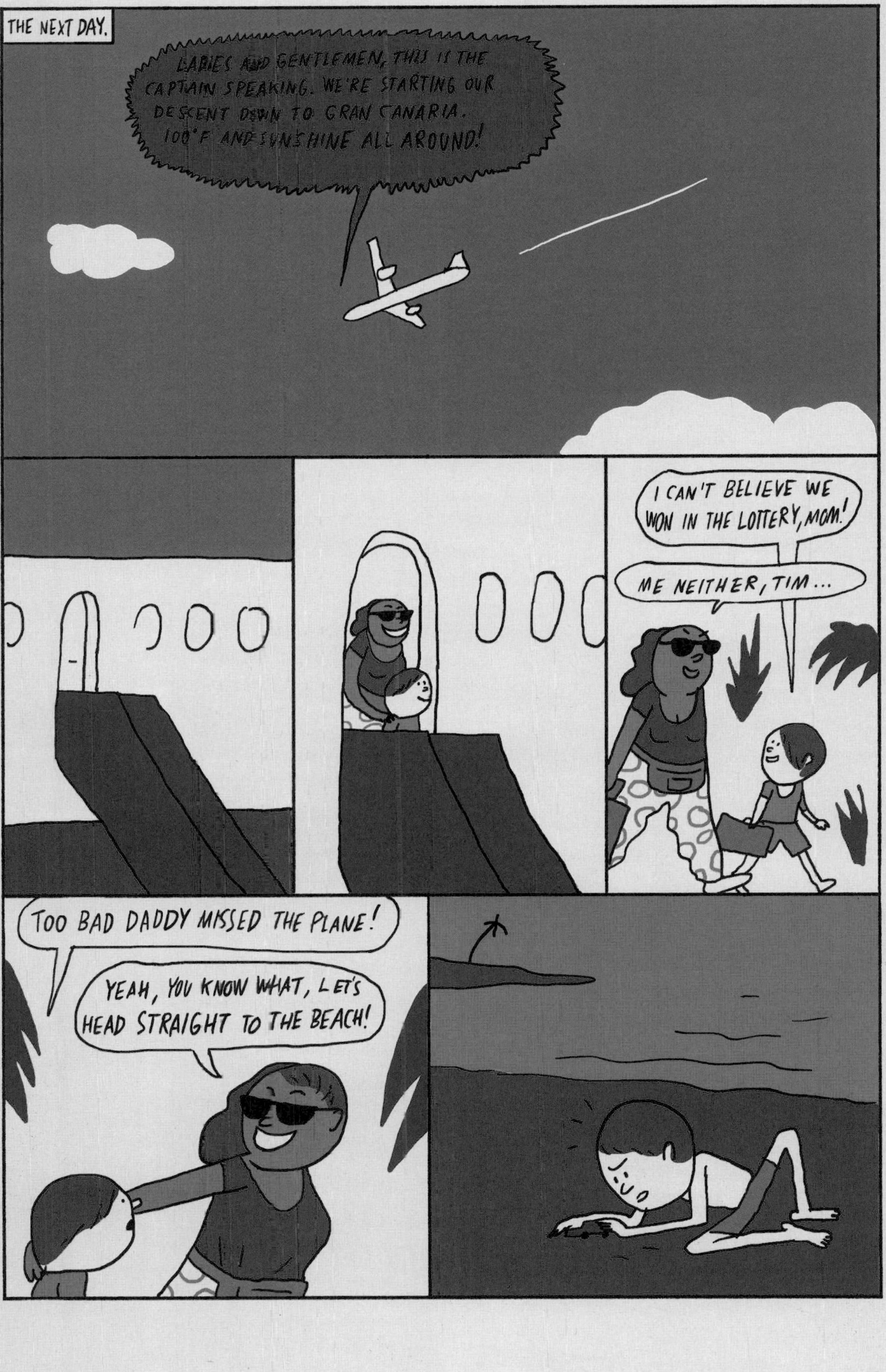
THE NEXT DAY.
LADIES AND GENTLEMEN, THIS IS THE CAPTAIN SPEAKING. WE'RE STARTING OUR DESCENT DOWN TO GRAN CANARIA. 100°F AND SUNSHINE ALL AROUND!
I CAN'T BELIEVE WE WON IN THE LOTTERY, MOM!
ME NEITHER, TIM...
TOO BAD DADDY MISSED THE PLANE!
YEAH, YOU KNOW WHAT, LET'S HEAD STRAIGHT TO THE BEACH!

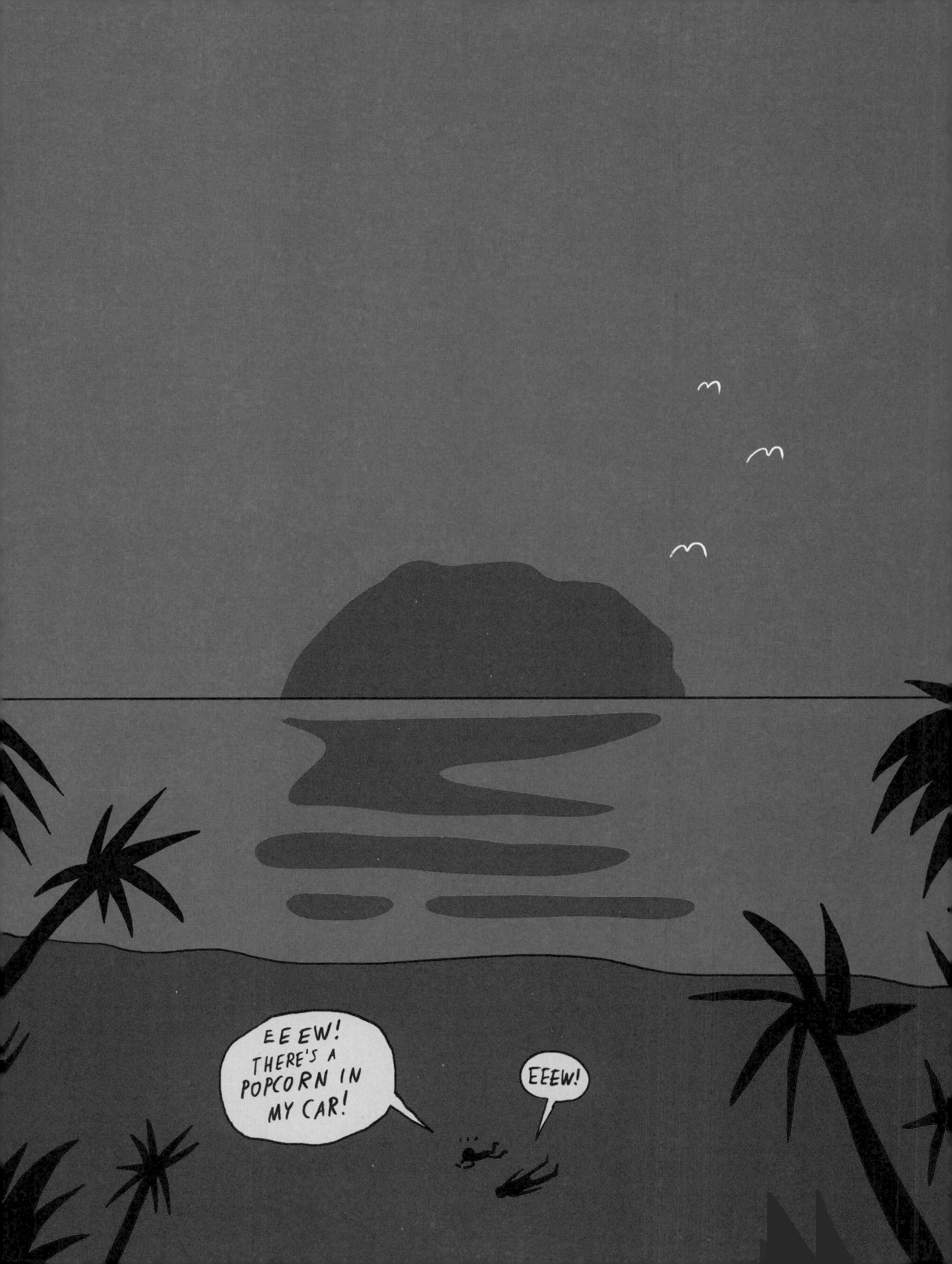
EEEW! THERE'S A POPCORN IN MY CAR!
EEEW!

– Jeg har aldri sett maken til frekkhet

Banksjef Kjell Sjulstok uttalte dette da bankens hovedkontor på Skårer ble utsatt for et usedvanlig utspekulert innbrudd i begynnelsen av oktober 1983. Denne gangen var det heldigvis ingen personer, men bankens postkasse, som ble robbet for penger. Lørdag formiddag, midt i butikkenes åpningstid, plasserte en person et oppslag på nattsafen der det ble opplyst at denne var ute av drift og at kundene i stedet måtte legge pengene i en postkasse som var bygget inn i veggen over selve safen. En rekke forretninger i Lørenskog legger dagens omsetning i bankens nattsafe og flere kunder fulgte de opplysningene som ble gitt på den falske plakaten. Tyvene fikk med seg omlag 200 000 kroner da de i løpet av kvelden eller natta kom tilbake til Skårer og greide å brekke opp postkassa.

En teori går ut på at tyvene har hatt B-gjengen i Donald Duck som forbilde ved dette innbruddet:

THEY GOT SOME NERVE

Bank manager Kjell Sjulstok spoke these words when his bank's main office was a victim of this devious robbery in early October 1983. Luckily, nobody was harmed, although the bank's mailbox was robbed of plenty of cash. It was during opening hours Saturday morning that someone attached a note on the night deposit box, claiming it was out of order and asking that the money be put in the mail slot above it instead. Many of Lørenskog's merchants use the night deposit and followed the instructions given on the false note. The thieves got away with around $33,000 when they returned to empty the mailbox that same night. One theory is that the thieves were inspired by the Beagle Boys from the *Donald Duck* comic for this break in.

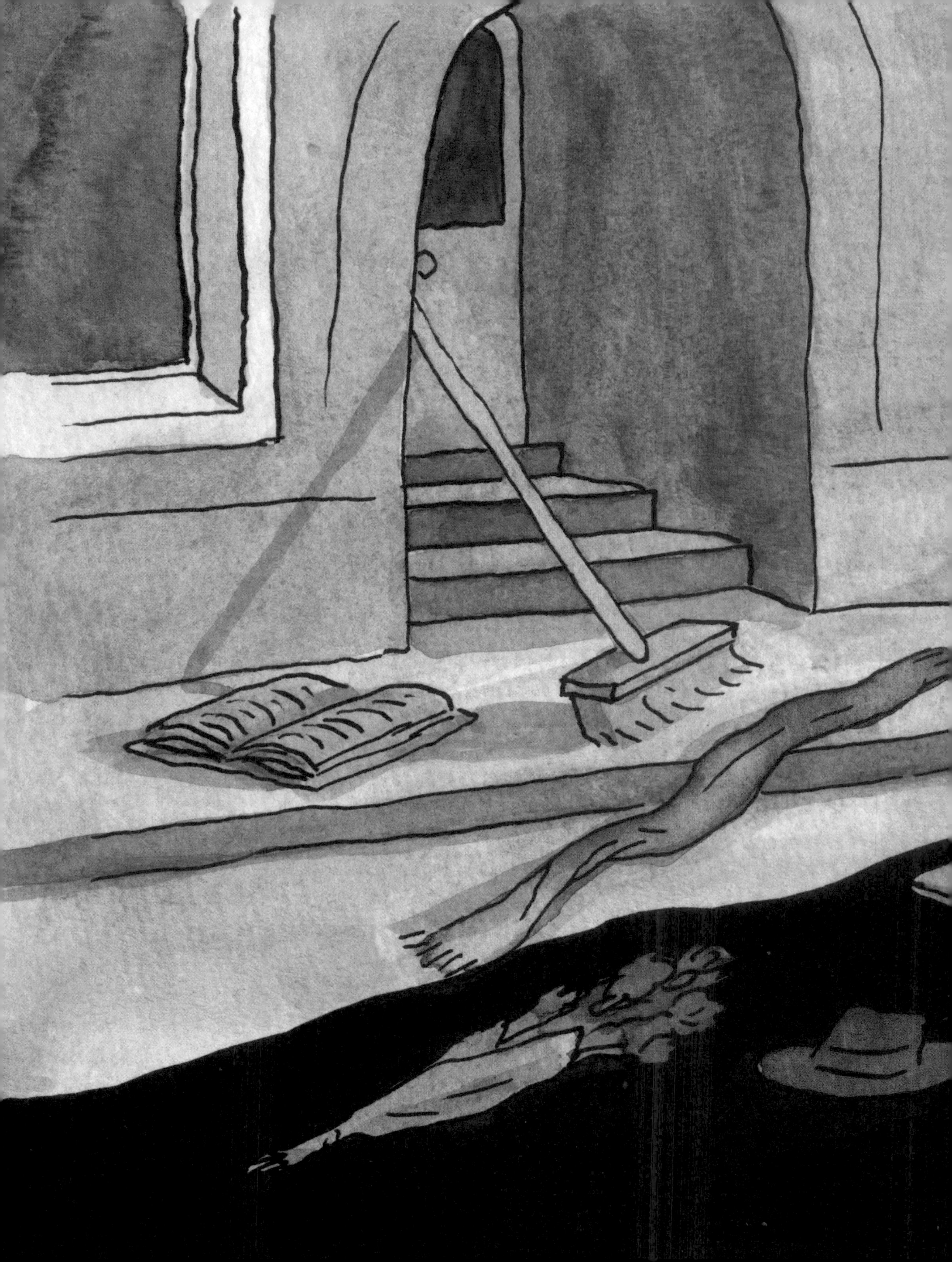

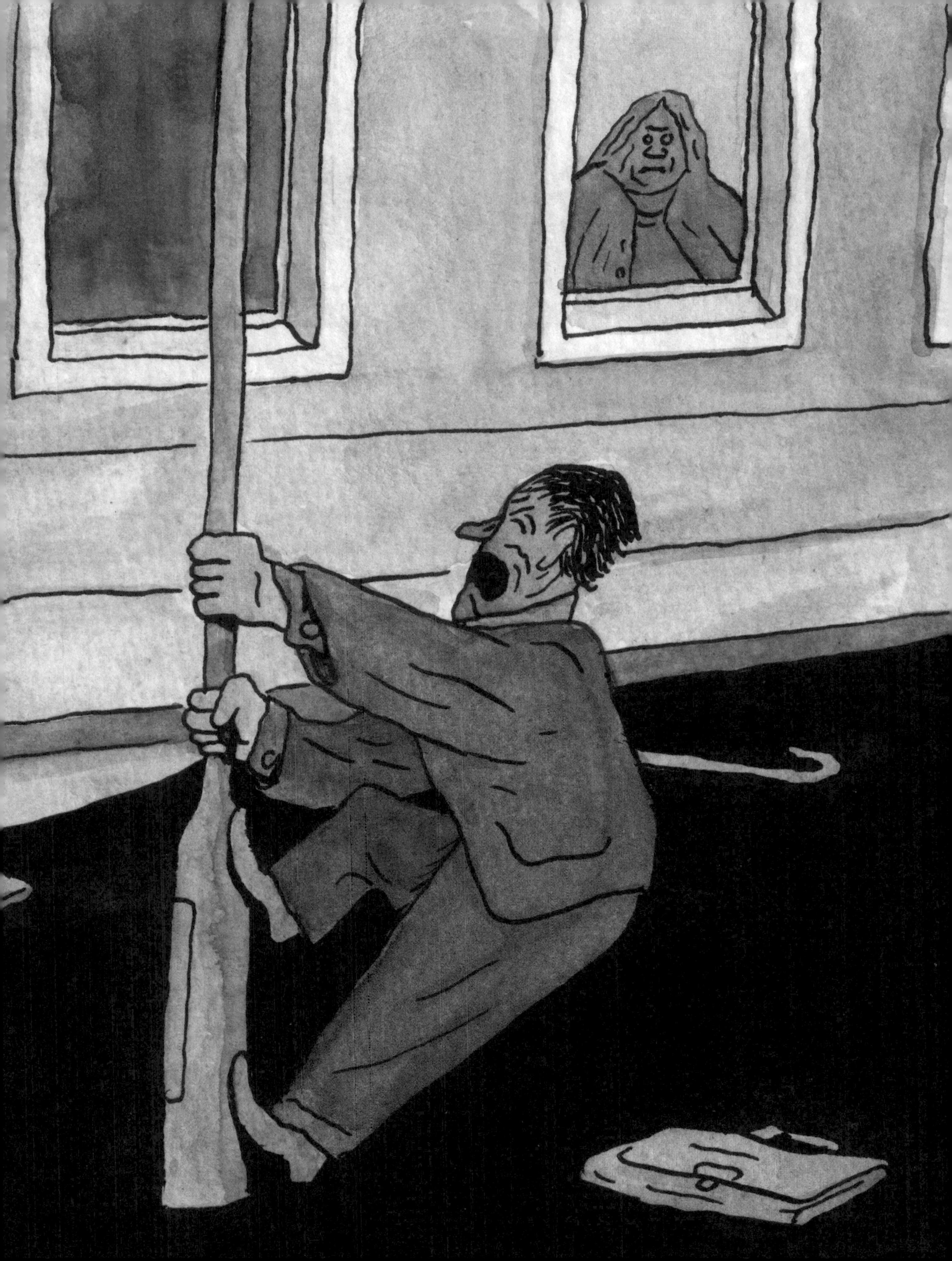

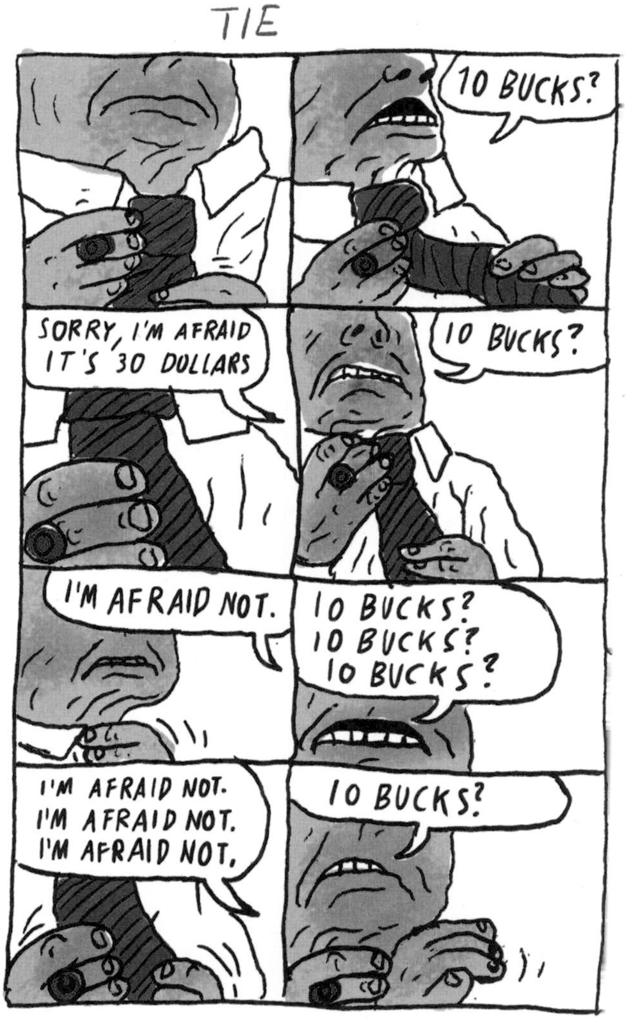
TIE
10 BUCKS?
SORRY, I'M AFRAID IT'S 30 DOLLARS
10 BUCKS?
I'M AFRAID NOT.
10 BUCKS? 10 BUCKS? 10 BUCKS?
I'M AFRAID NOT. I'M AFRAID NOT. I'M AFRAID NOT,
10 BUCKS?

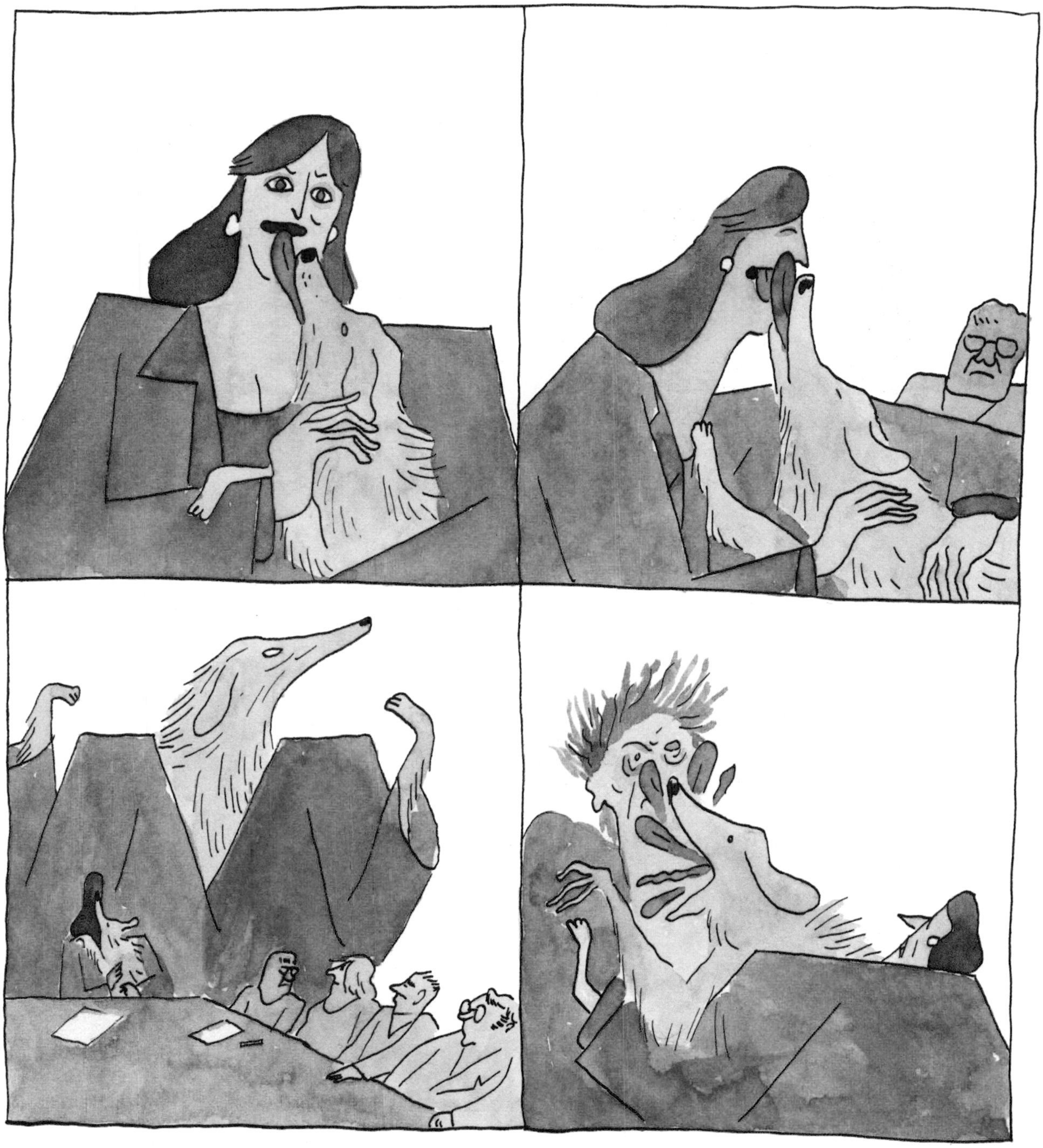

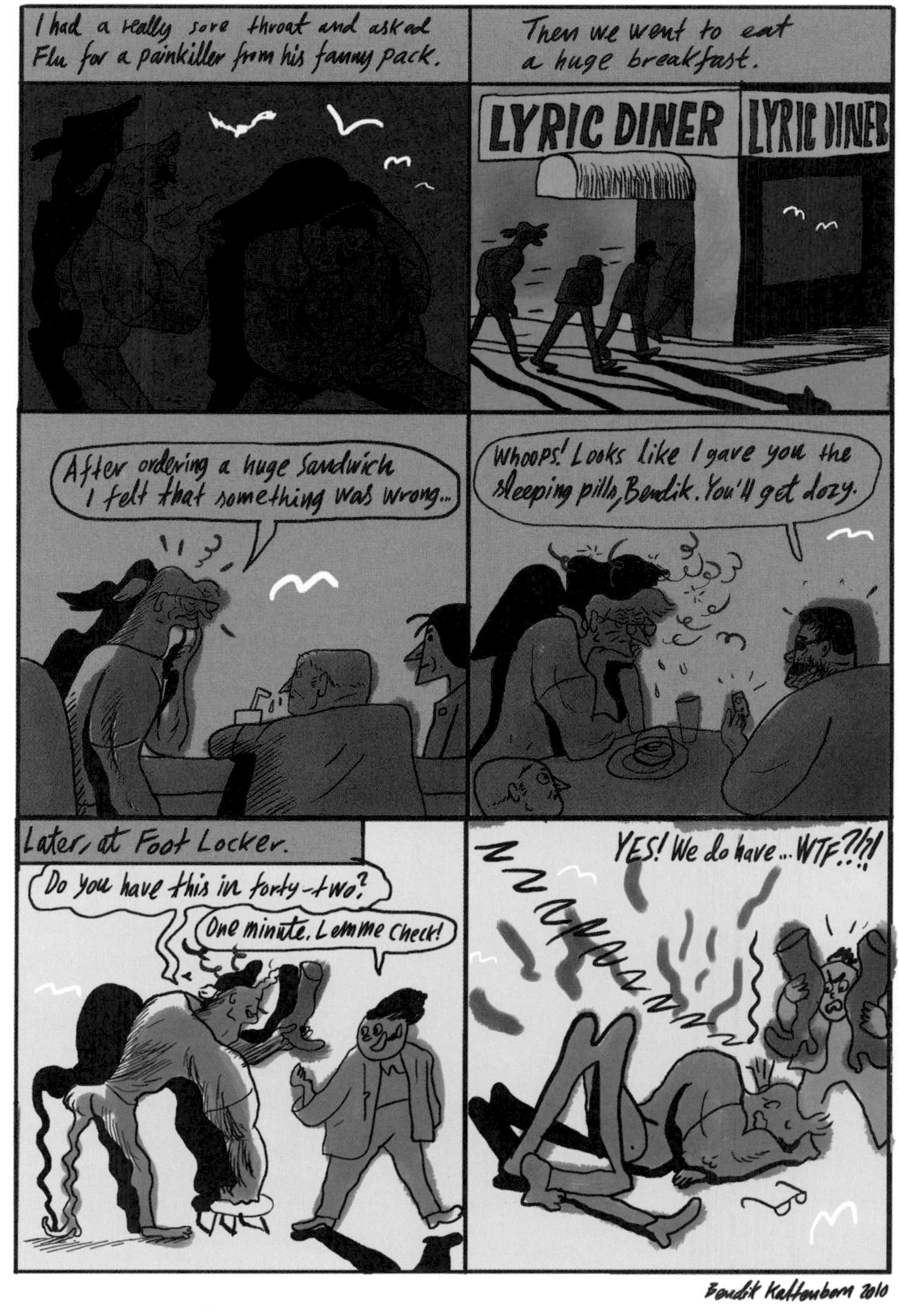
I had a really sore throat and asked Flu for a painkiller from his fanny pack.
Then we went to eat a huge breakfast.
LYRIC DINER
LYRIC DINER
After ordering a huge sandwich I felt that something was wrong...
Whoops! Looks like I gave you the sleeping pills, Bendik. You'll get dozy.
Later, at Foot Locker.
Do you have this in forty-two?
One minute. Lemme check!
YES! We do have... WTF?!?!
Bendik Kaltenborn 2010

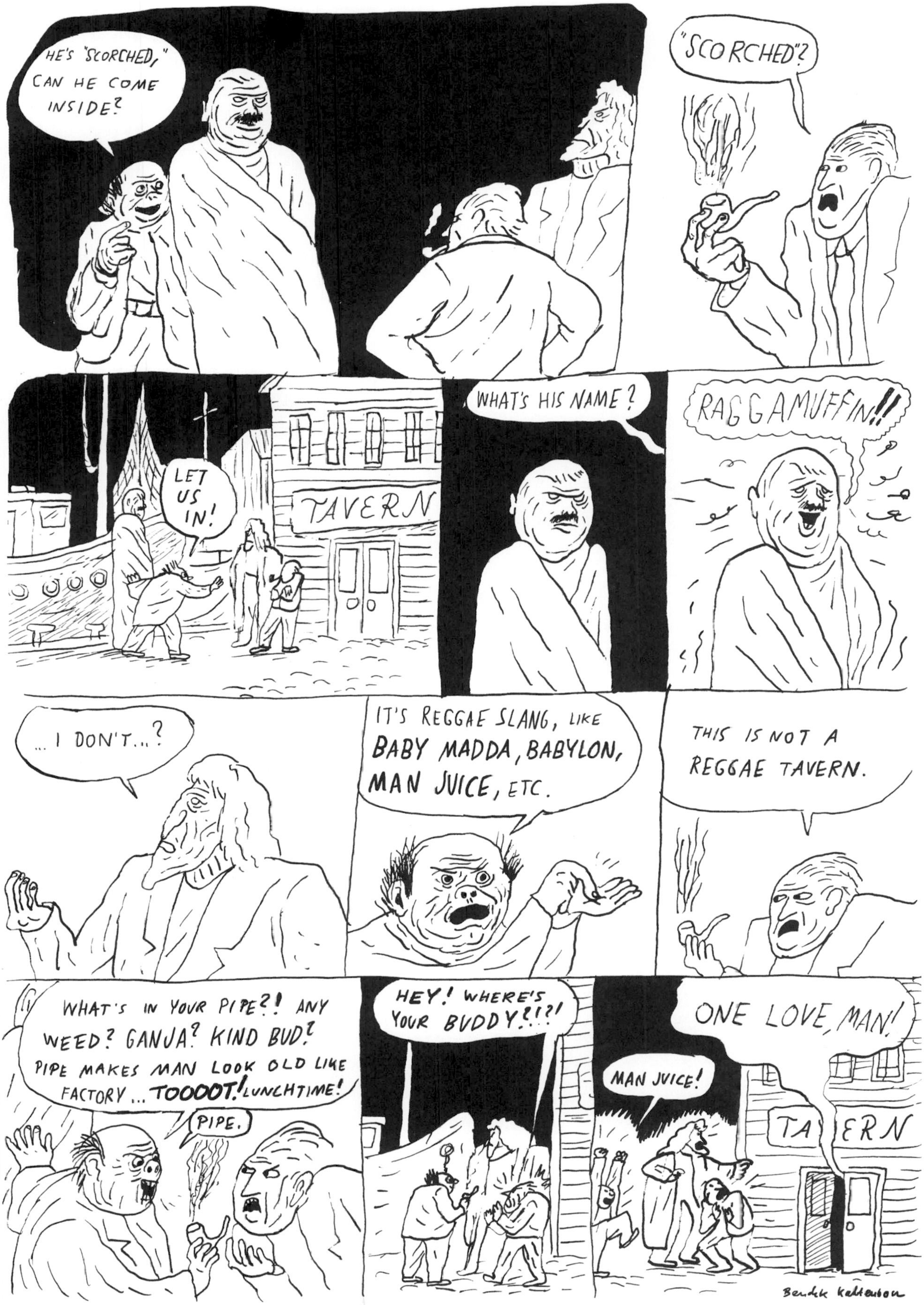

HE'S "SCORCHED," CAN HE COME INSIDE?
"SCORCHED"?
LET US IN!
TAVERN
WHAT'S HIS NAME?
RAGGAMUFFIN!!
... I DON'T...?
IT'S REGGAE SLANG, LIKE BABY MADDA, BABYLON, MAN JUICE, ETC.
THIS IS NOT A REGGAE TAVERN.
WHAT'S IN YOUR PIPE?! ANY WEED? GANJA? KIND BUD? PIPE MAKES MAN LOOK OLD LIKE FACTORY... TOOOOT! LUNCHTIME!
PIPE.
HEY! WHERE'S YOUR BUDDY?!?!
MAN JUICE!
ONE LOVE, MAN!
TAVERN

STOCKBROKER HANK

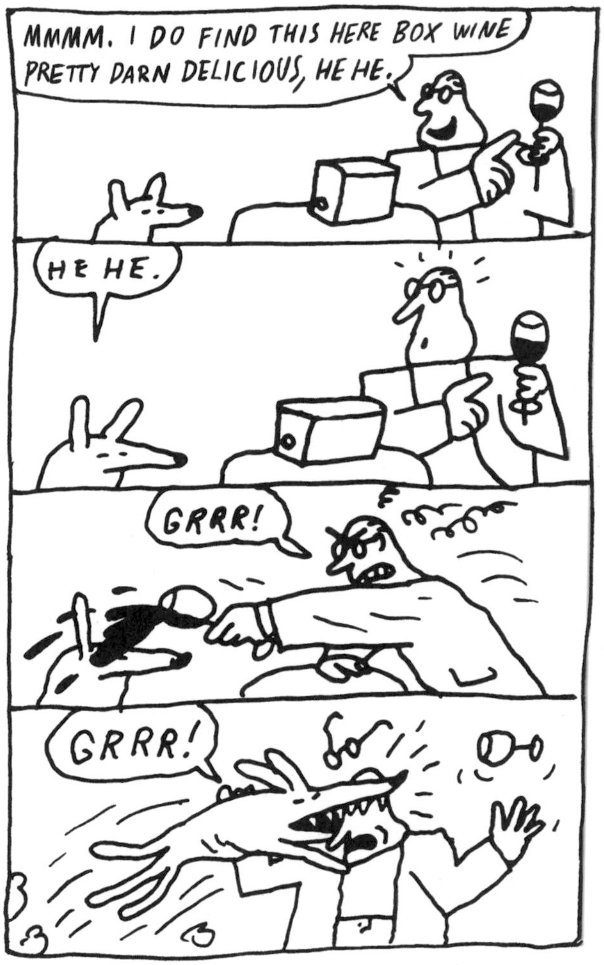
MMMM. I DO FIND THIS HERE BOX WINE PRETTY DARN DELICIOUS, HE HE.
HE HE.
GRRR!
GRRR!

STOCKBROKER HANK

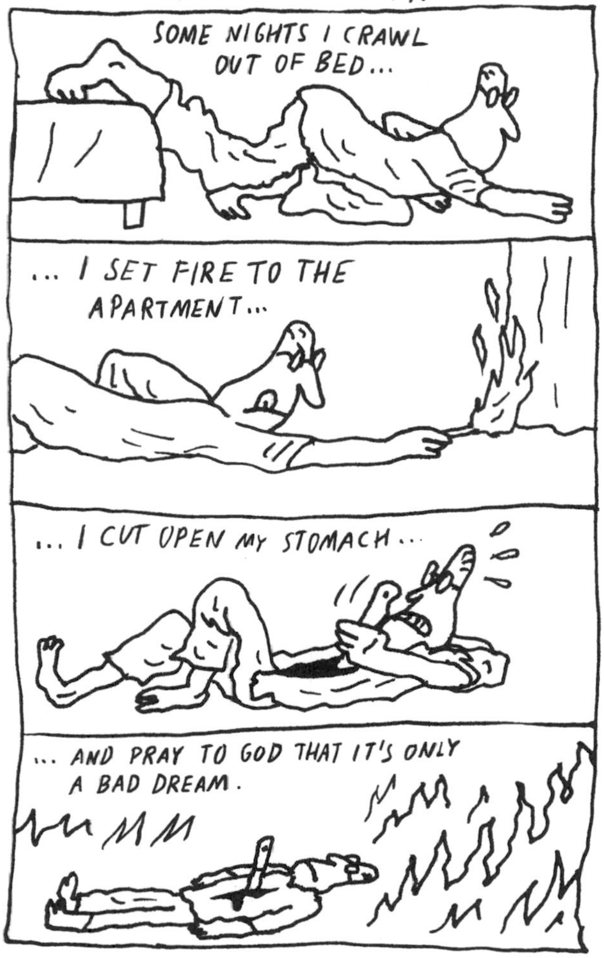
SOME NIGHTS I CRAWL OUT OF BED...
... I SET FIRE TO THE APARTMENT...
... I CUT OPEN MY STOMACH...
... AND PRAY TO GOD THAT IT'S ONLY A BAD DREAM.

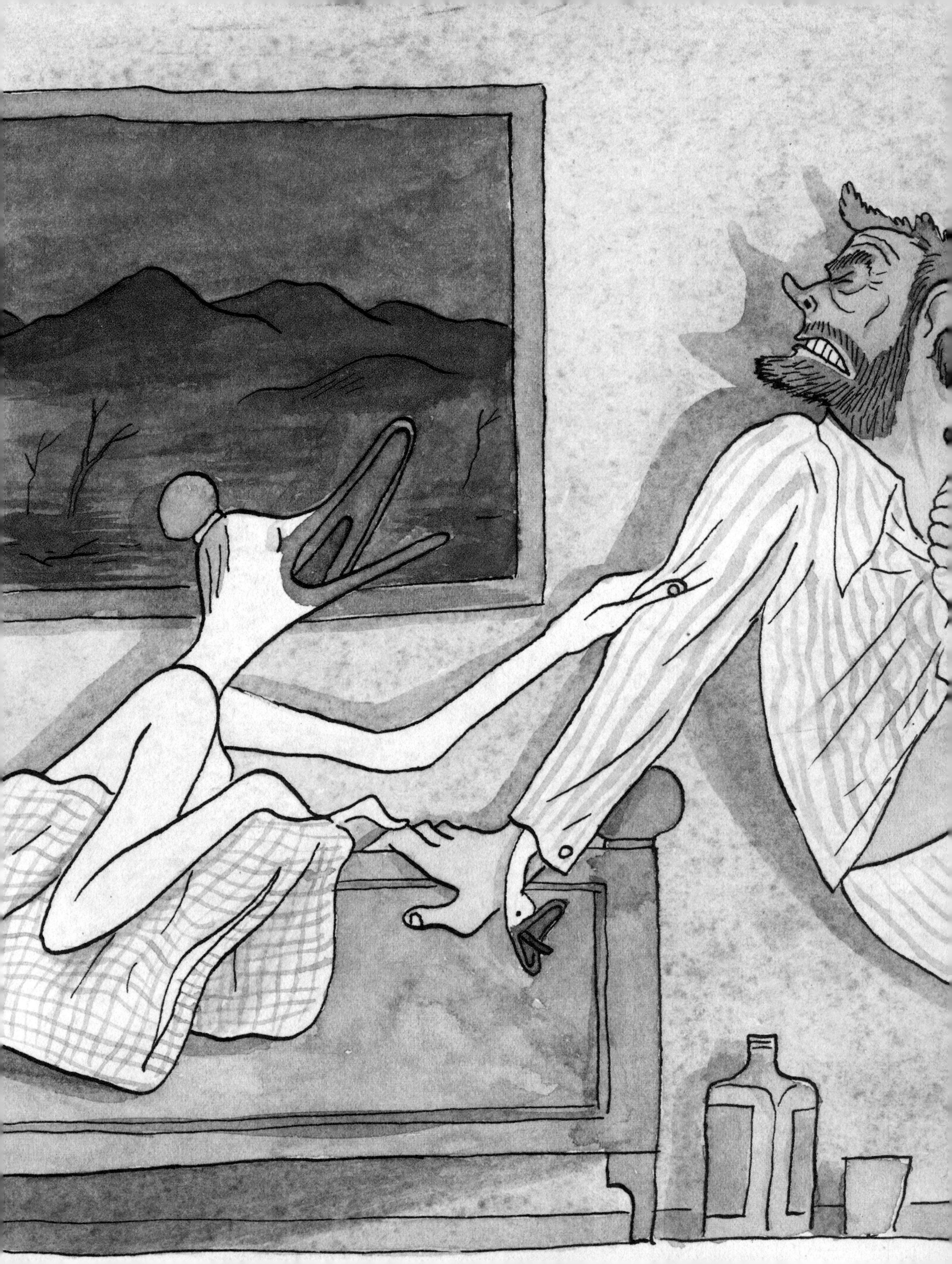

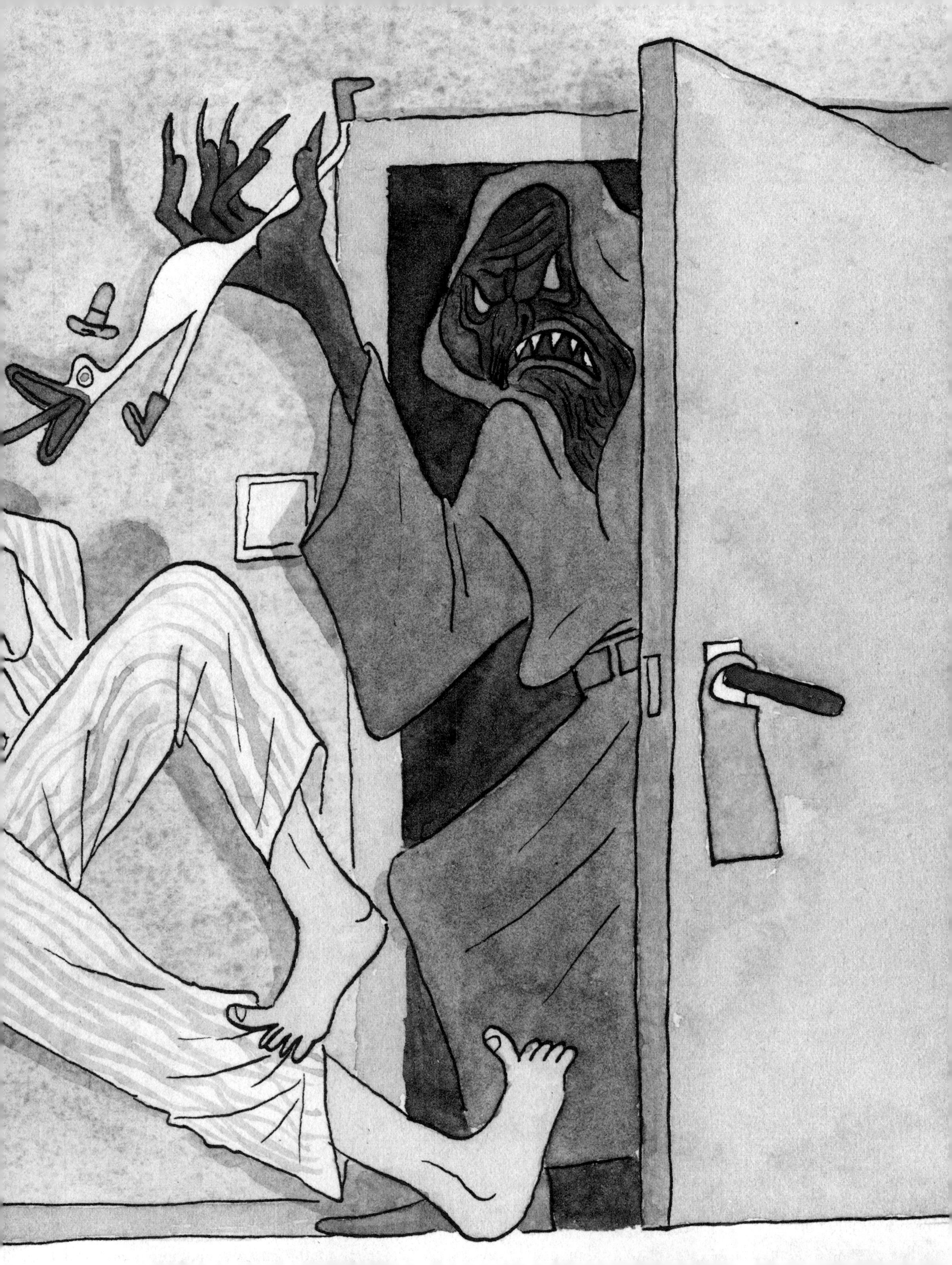

CALM CHAOS THIEF

The Oslo police came across a rather peculiar break-in at Grüner-løkka last night. A thief broke in to Café Chaos in Thorvald Meyers Street after closing hours, but when the police arrived he was just sitting there smoking a cigarette.

One bottle of beer was all the intruder managed to steal before he was arrested.

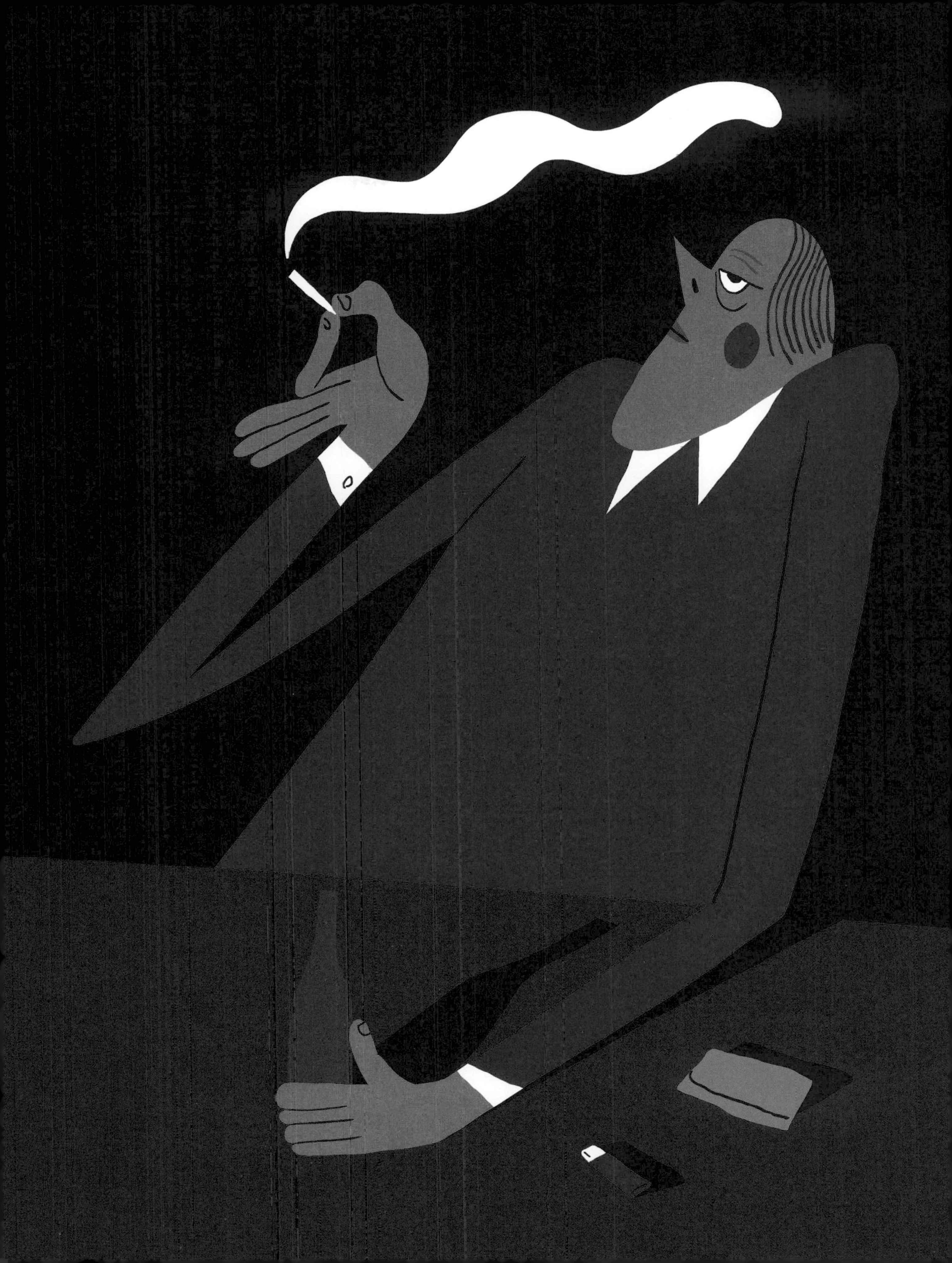

...seems to be unaware of this new addition to our neighbourhood.

WOMAN VISITED BY MYSTERIOUS MAN

A 25-year-old woman heard someone opening the mail slot in her apartment Wednesday. As she approached the door, she noticed that a man had put his fingers through the slot and was talking to her cats.

"Hello. Here I am again," he said. When the woman asked who it was, he told her to open the door. The woman believed it was the mailman and did open the door but was met by a complete stranger.

Startled, she slammed the door. The man then started shouting and banging on the door. Eventually, he gave up and left, says the Katarina Police.

folding.
t that?

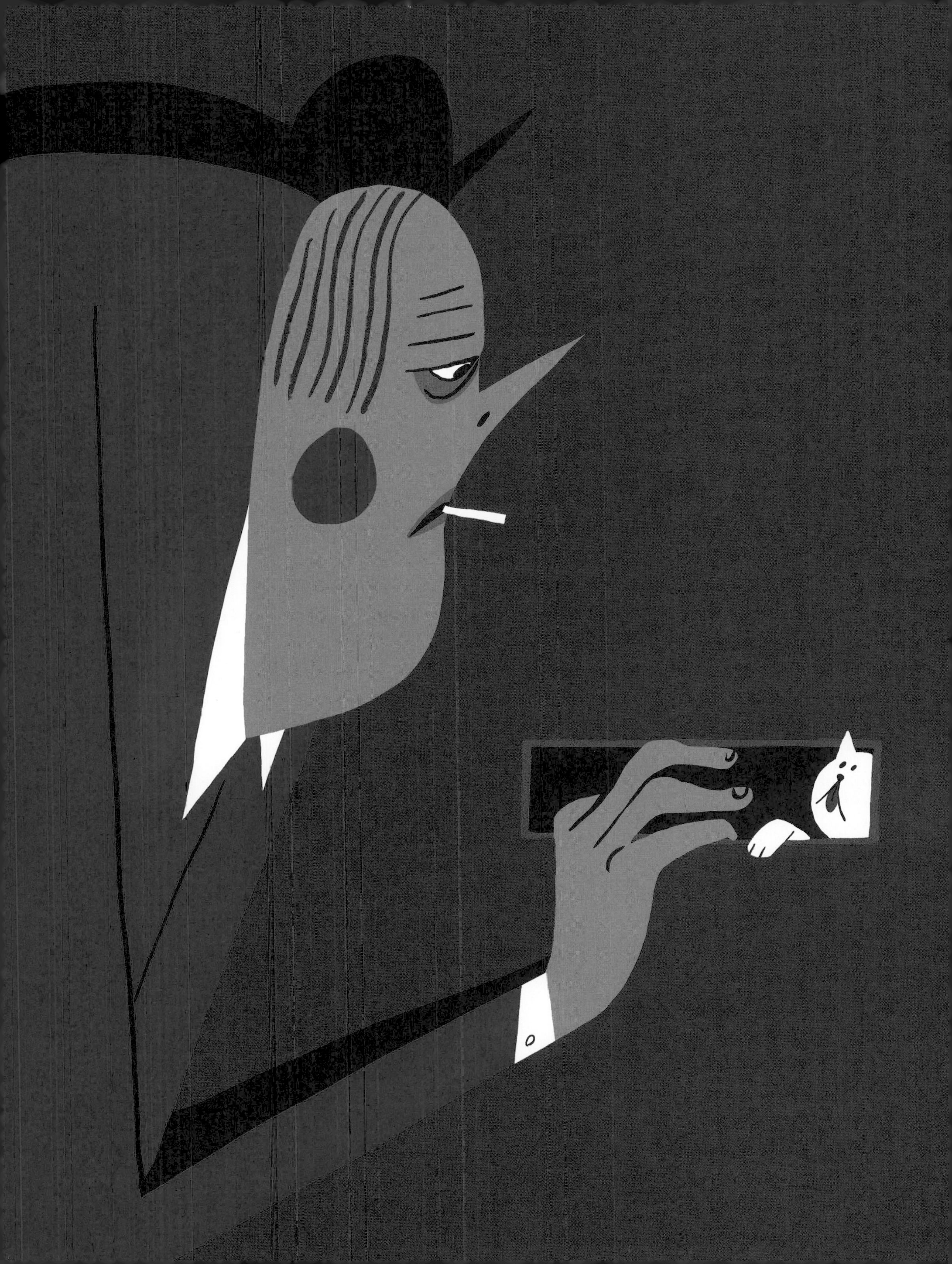

SWEET TOOTH RUNS AMOK

A man who wanted coffee and a danish created chaos at a 7-11 at Medborgarplatsen last Tuesday. The man bought a coffee and left, but returned a while later and wanted a free danish. When he didn't get one he became very angry and smashed a small cookie jar and splashed coffee on the staff and around the store. When the police arrived he was still outside the store. He was taken to the police station to sober up. He is now being charged with vandalism.

18

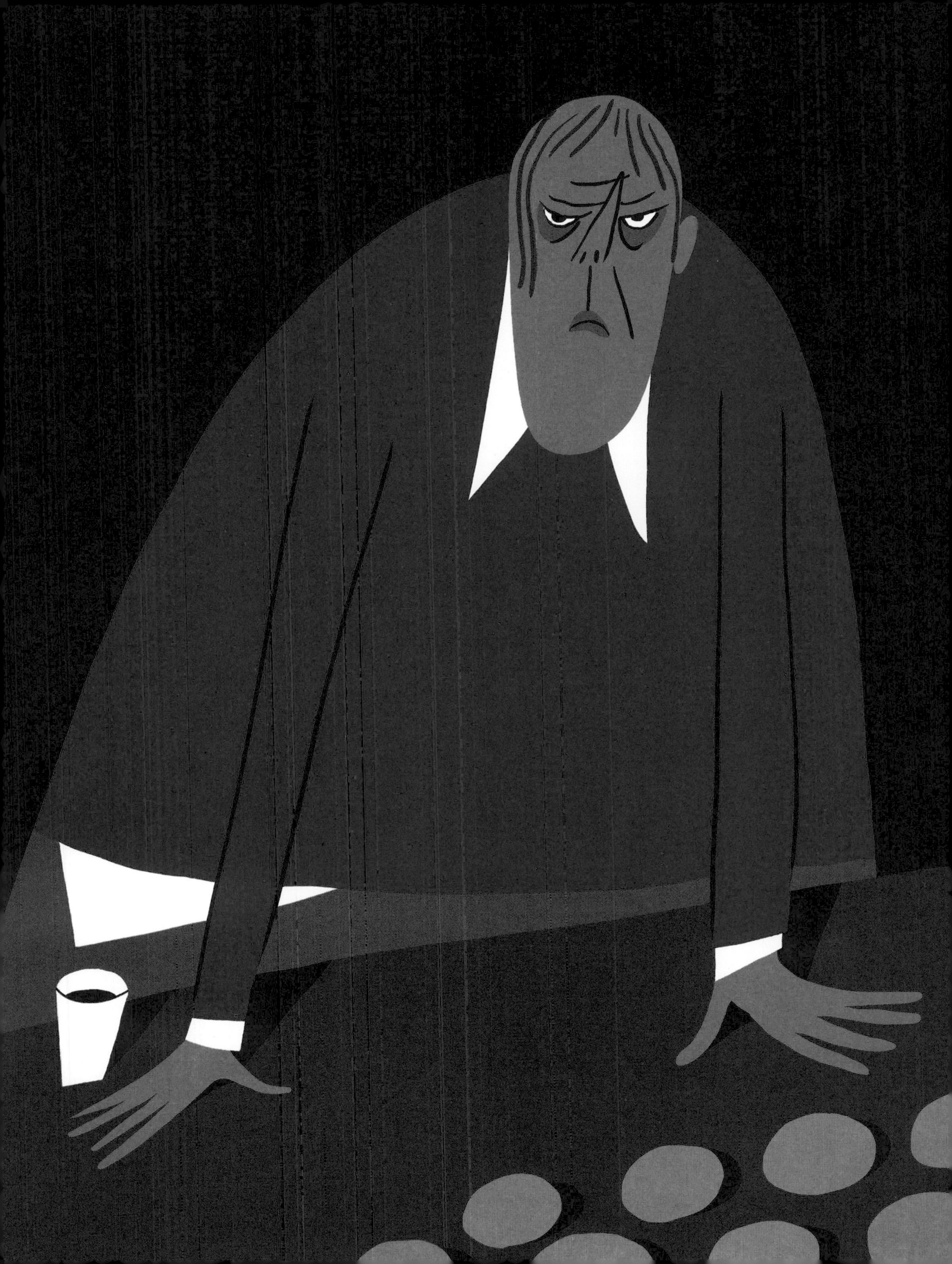

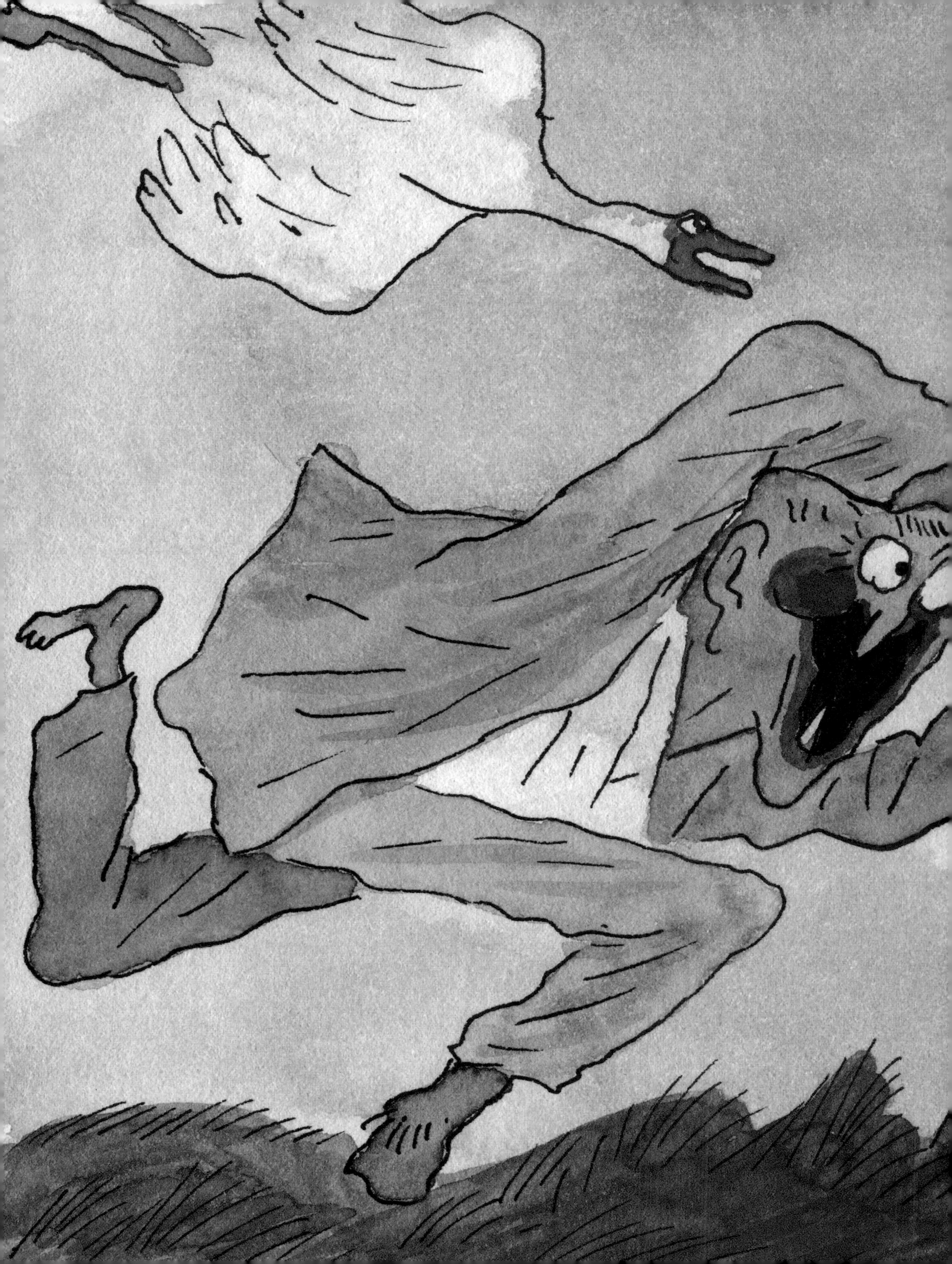

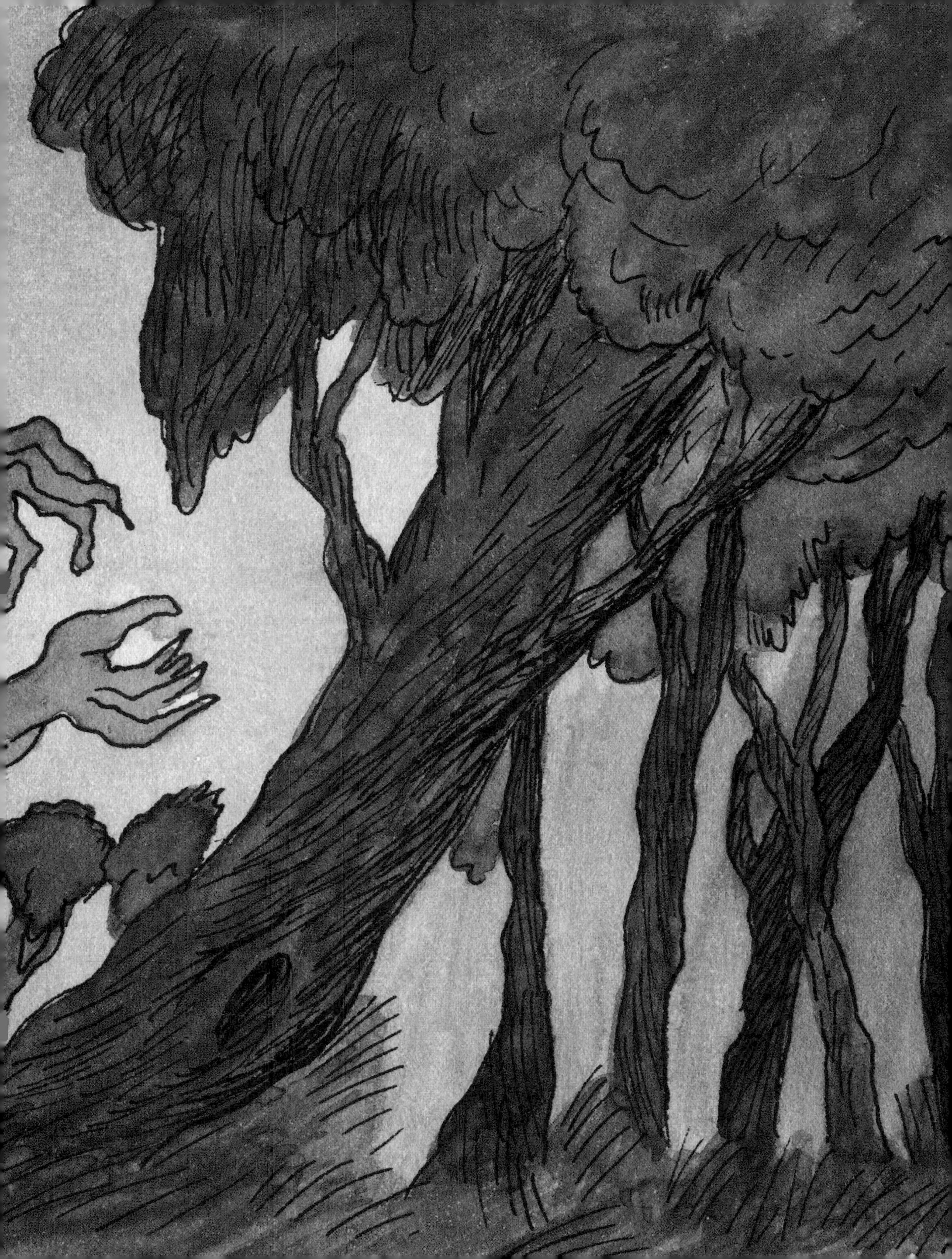

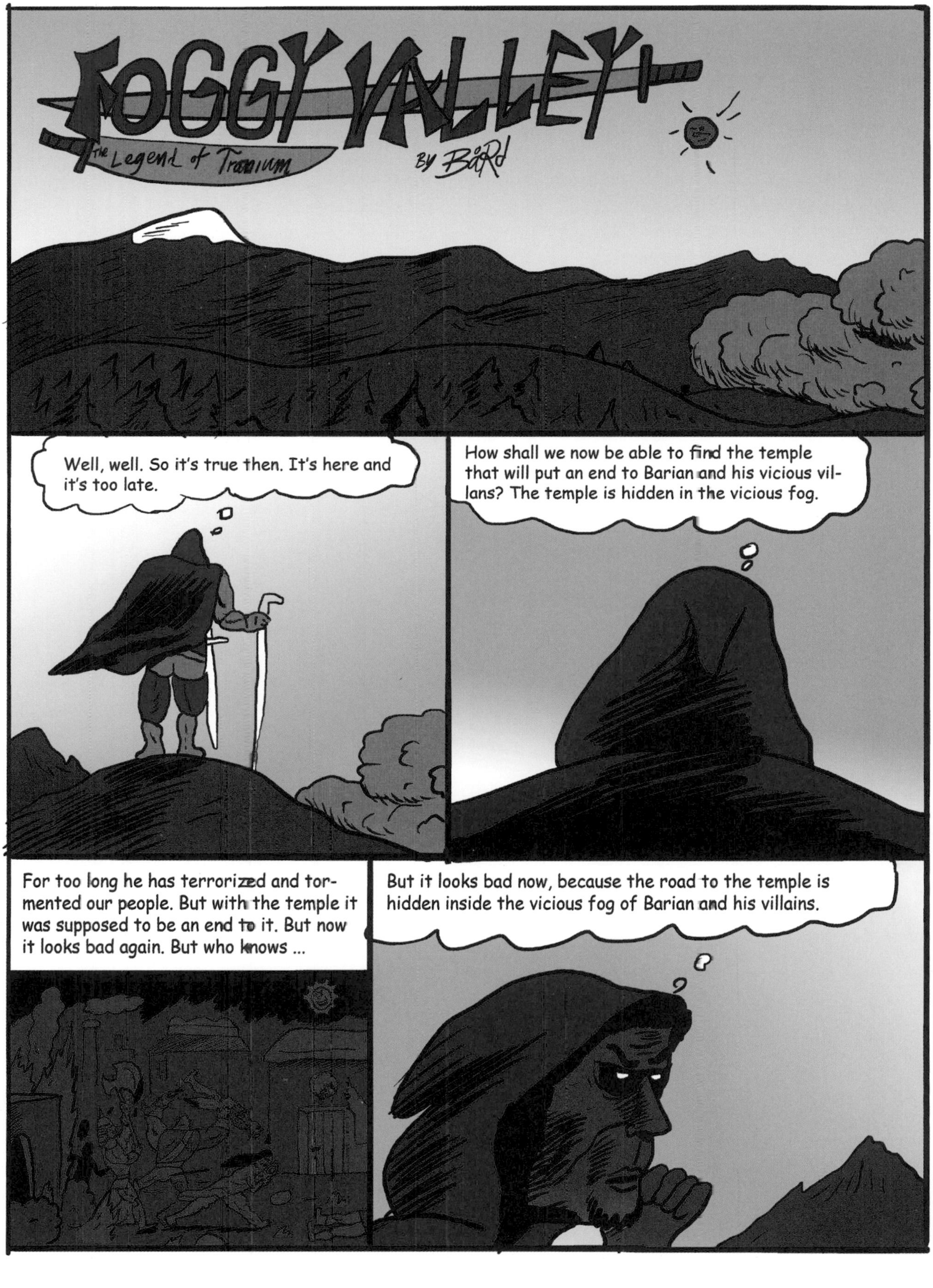
FOGGY VALLEY
the Legend of Tranium
BY BåRd
Well, well. So it's true then. It's here and it's too late.
How shall we now be able to find the temple that will put an end to Barian and his vicious villans? The temple is hidden in the vicious fog.
For too long he has terrorized and tormented our people. But with the temple it was supposed to be an end to it. But now it looks bad again. But who knows ...
But it looks bad now, because the road to the temple is hidden inside the vicious fog of Barian and his villains.

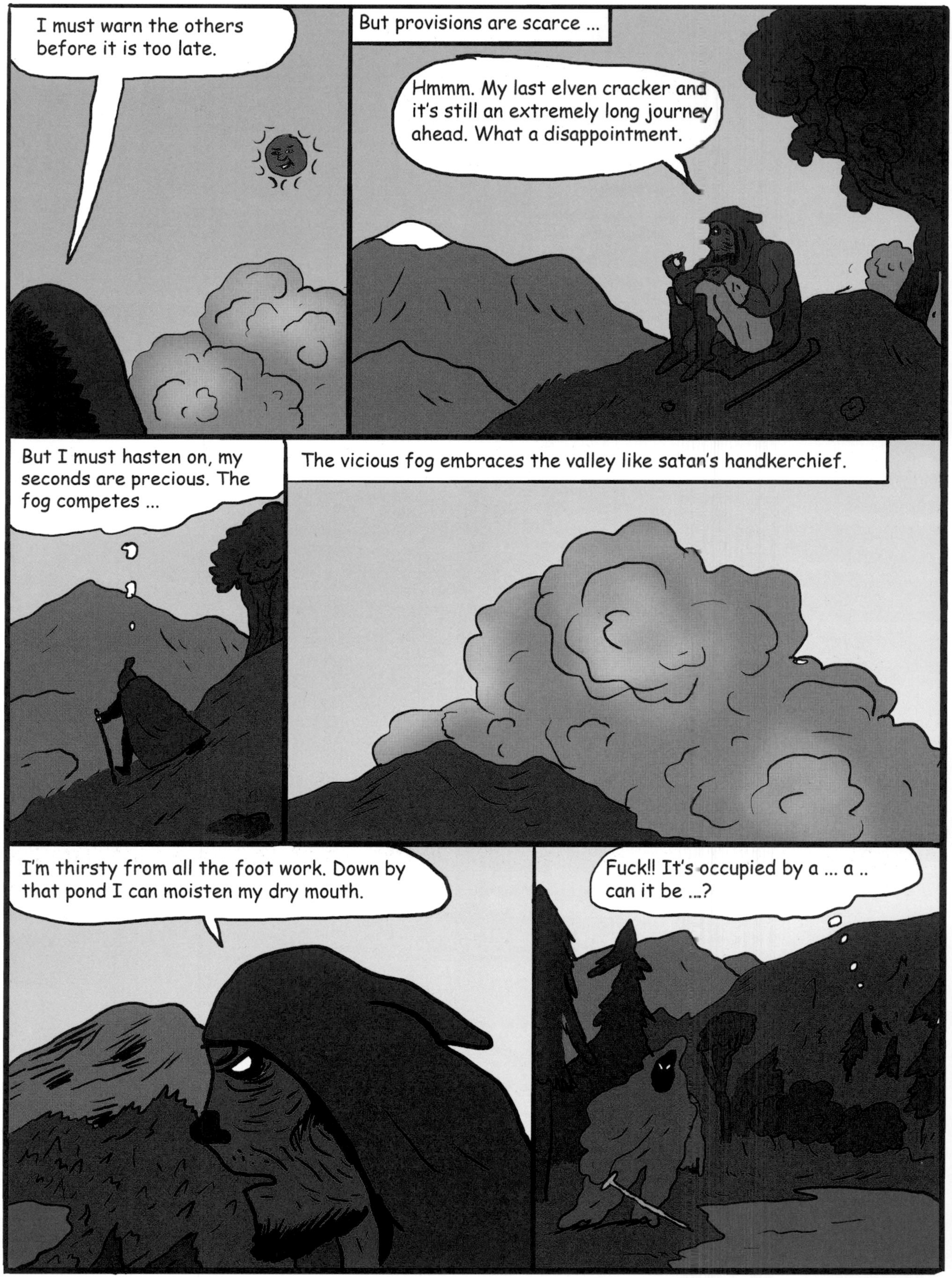
I must warn the others before it is too late.
But provisions are scarce ...
Hmmm. My last elven cracker and it's still an extremely long journey ahead. What a disappointment.
But I must hasten on, my seconds are precious. The fog competes ...
The vicious fog embraces the valley like satan's handkerchief.
I'm thirsty from all the foot work. Down by that pond I can moisten my dry mouth.
Fuck!! It's occupied by a ... a .. can it be ...?

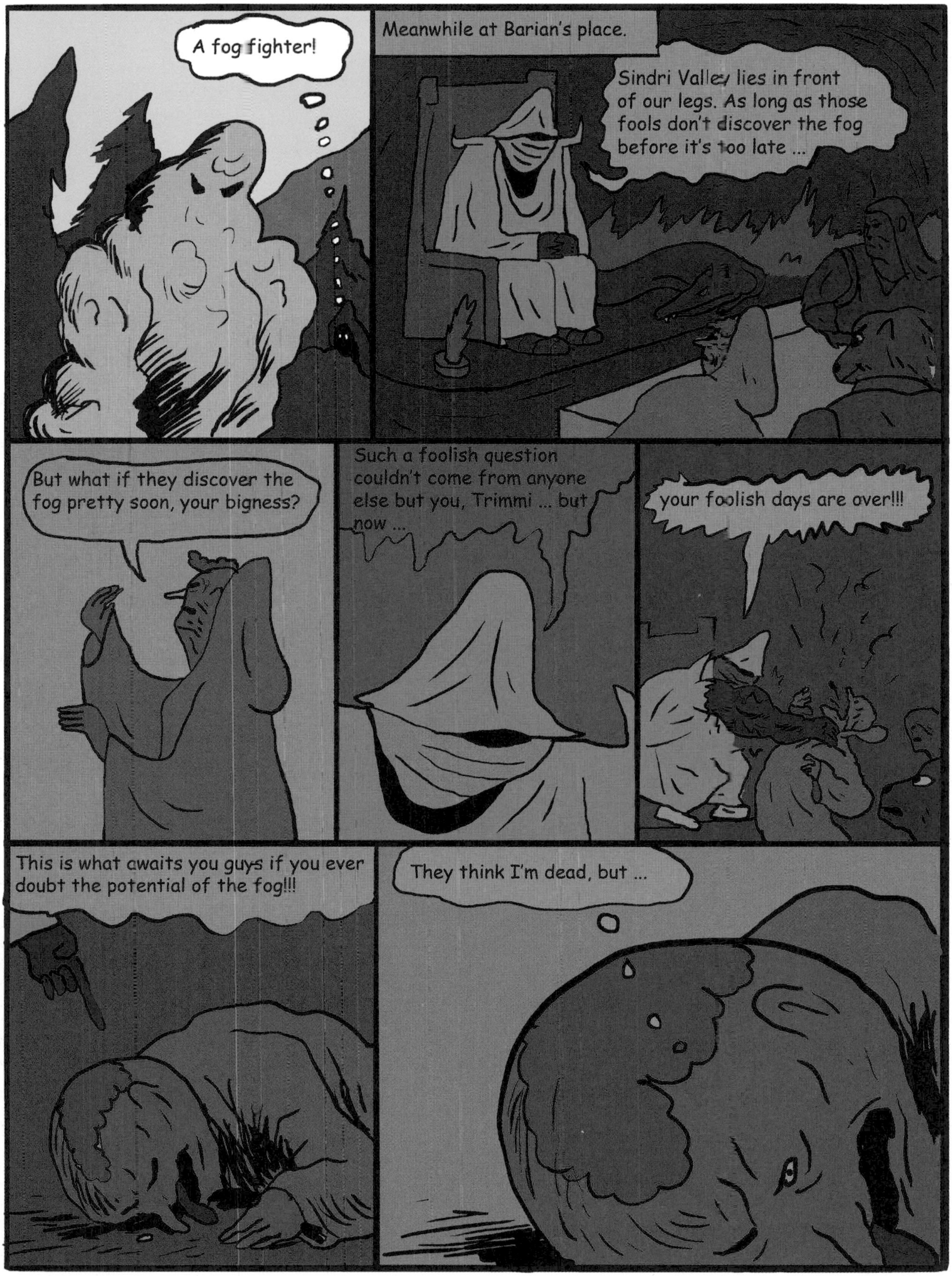
A fog fighter!
Meanwhile at Barian's place.
Sindri Valley lies in front of our legs. As long as those fools don't discover the fog before it's too late ...
But what if they discover the fog pretty soon, your bigness?
Such a foolish question couldn't come from anyone else but you, Trimmi ... but now ...
your foolish days are over!!!
This is what awaits you guys if you ever doubt the potential of the fog!!!
They think I'm dead, but ...

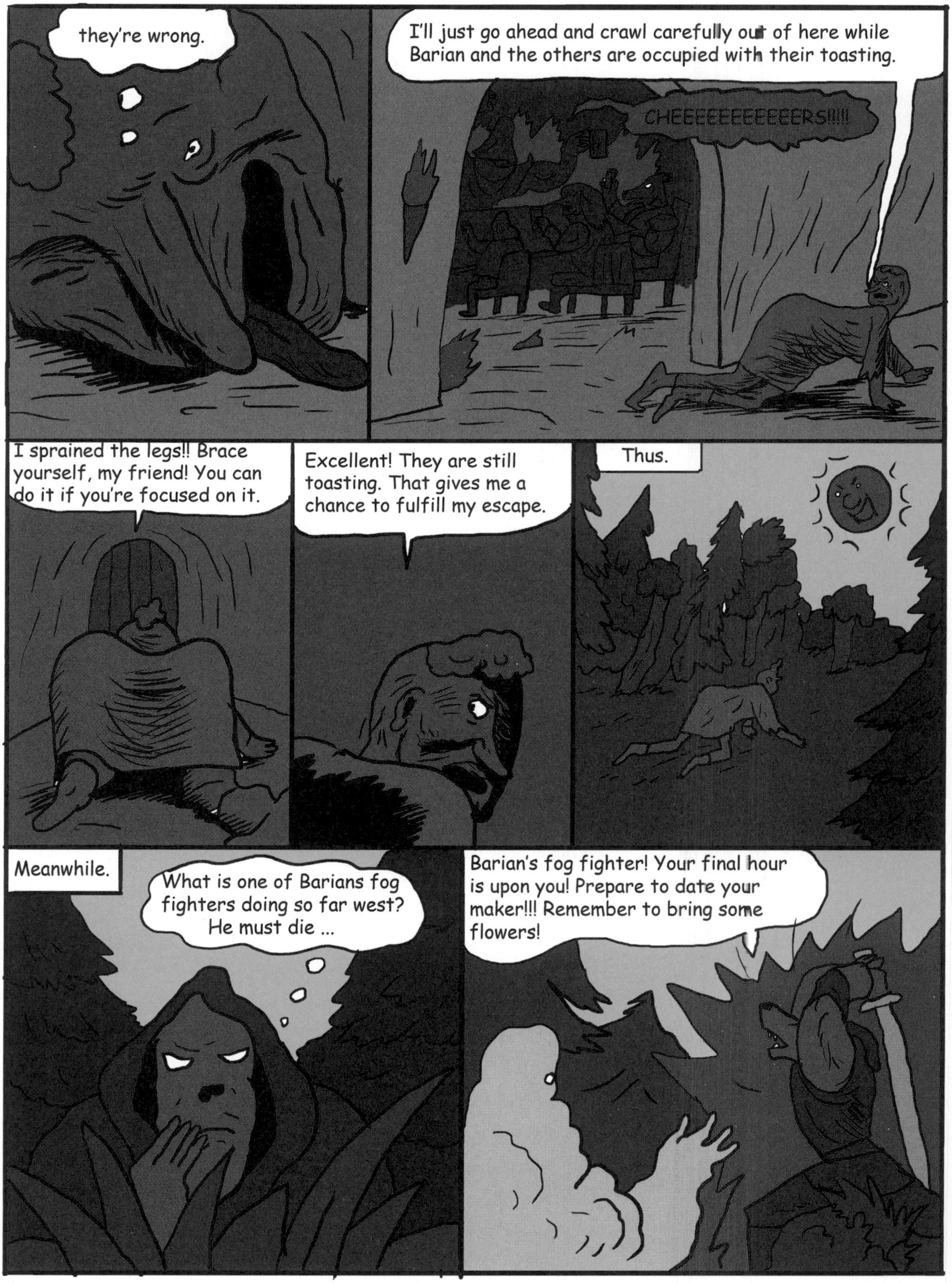
they're wrong.
I'll just go ahead and crawl carefully out of here while Barian and the others are occupied with their toasting.
CHEEEEEEEEEEEERS!!!!!
I sprained the legs!! Brace yourself, my friend! You can do it if you're focused on it.
Excellent! They are still toasting. That gives me a chance to fulfill my escape.
Thus.
Meanwhile.
What is one of Barians fog fighters doing so far west? He must die ...
Barian's fog fighter! Your final hour is upon you! Prepare to date your maker!!! Remember to bring some flowers!

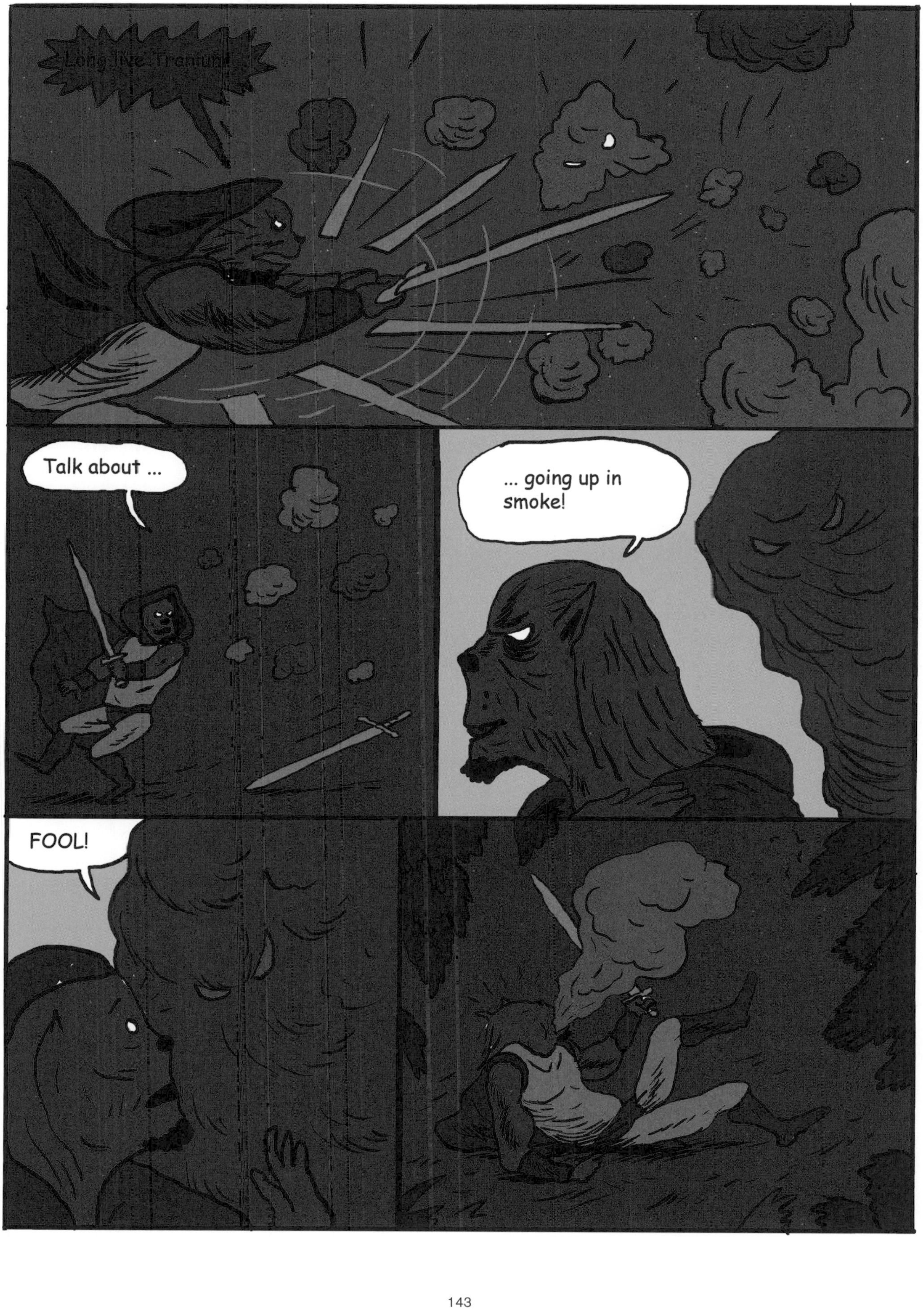
Long live Tranium!
Talk about ...
... going up in smoke!
FOOL!

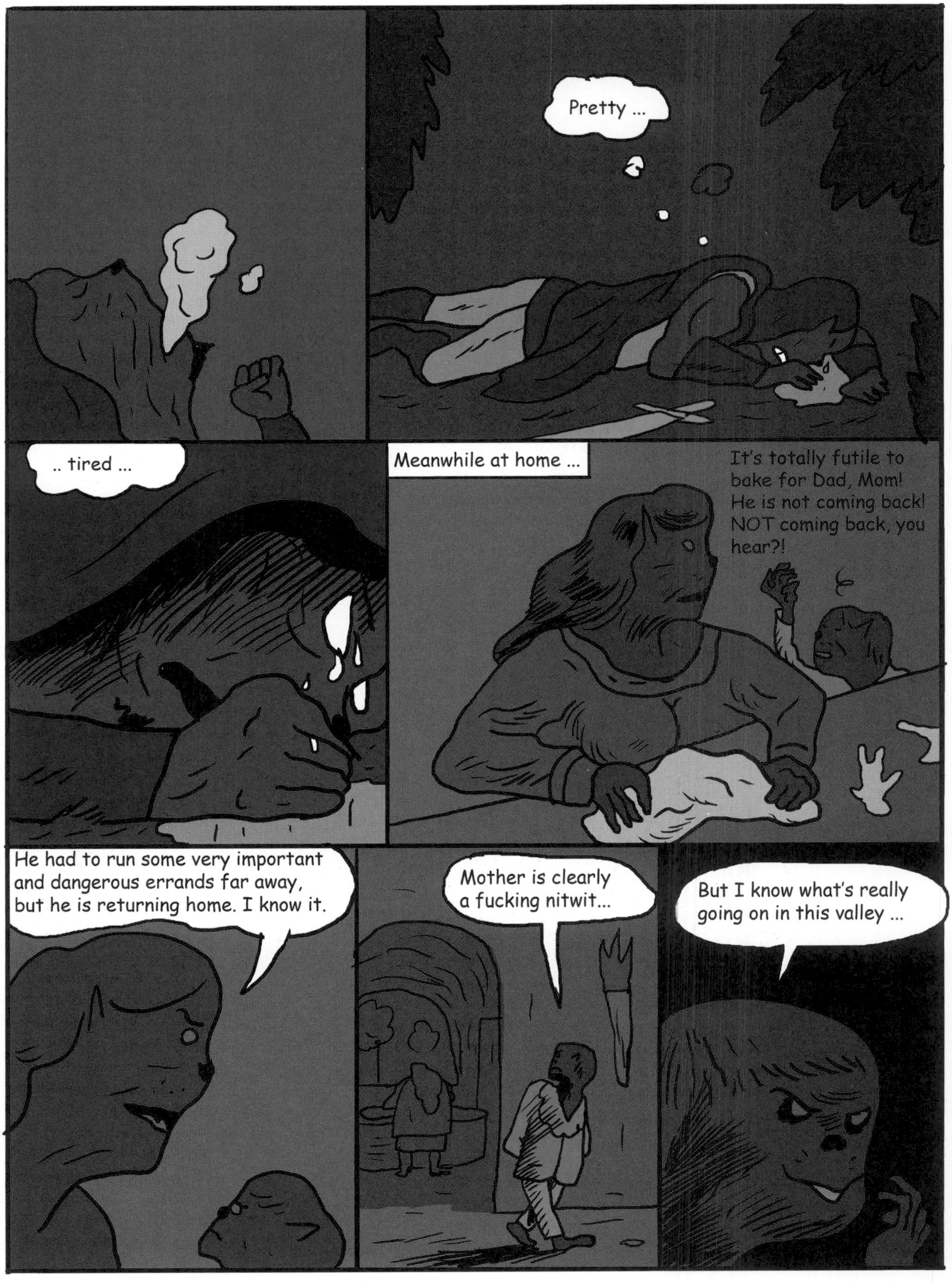
Pretty ...
.. tired ...
Meanwhile at home ...
It's totally futile to bake for Dad, Mom! He is not coming back! NOT coming back, you hear?!
He had to run some very important and dangerous errands far away, but he is returning home. I know it.
Mother is clearly a fucking nitwit...
But I know what's really going on in this valley ...

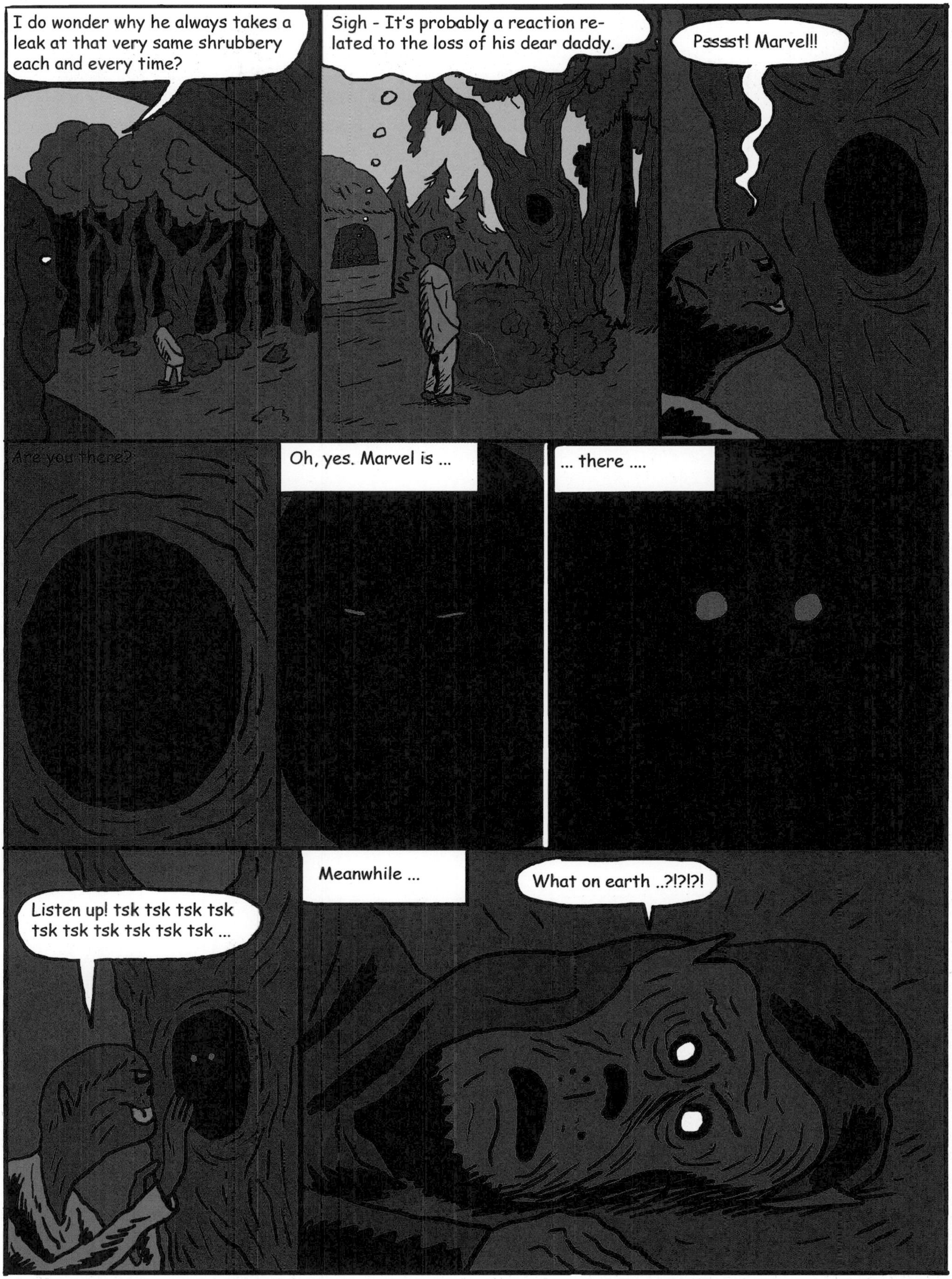
I do wonder why he always takes a leak at that very same shrubbery each and every time?
Sigh - It's probably a reaction related to the loss of his dear daddy.
Psssst! Marvel!!
Are you there?
Oh, yes. Marvel is ...
... there ....
Listen up! tsk tsk tsk tsk tsk tsk tsk tsk tsk tsk ...
Meanwhile ...
What on earth ..?!?!?!

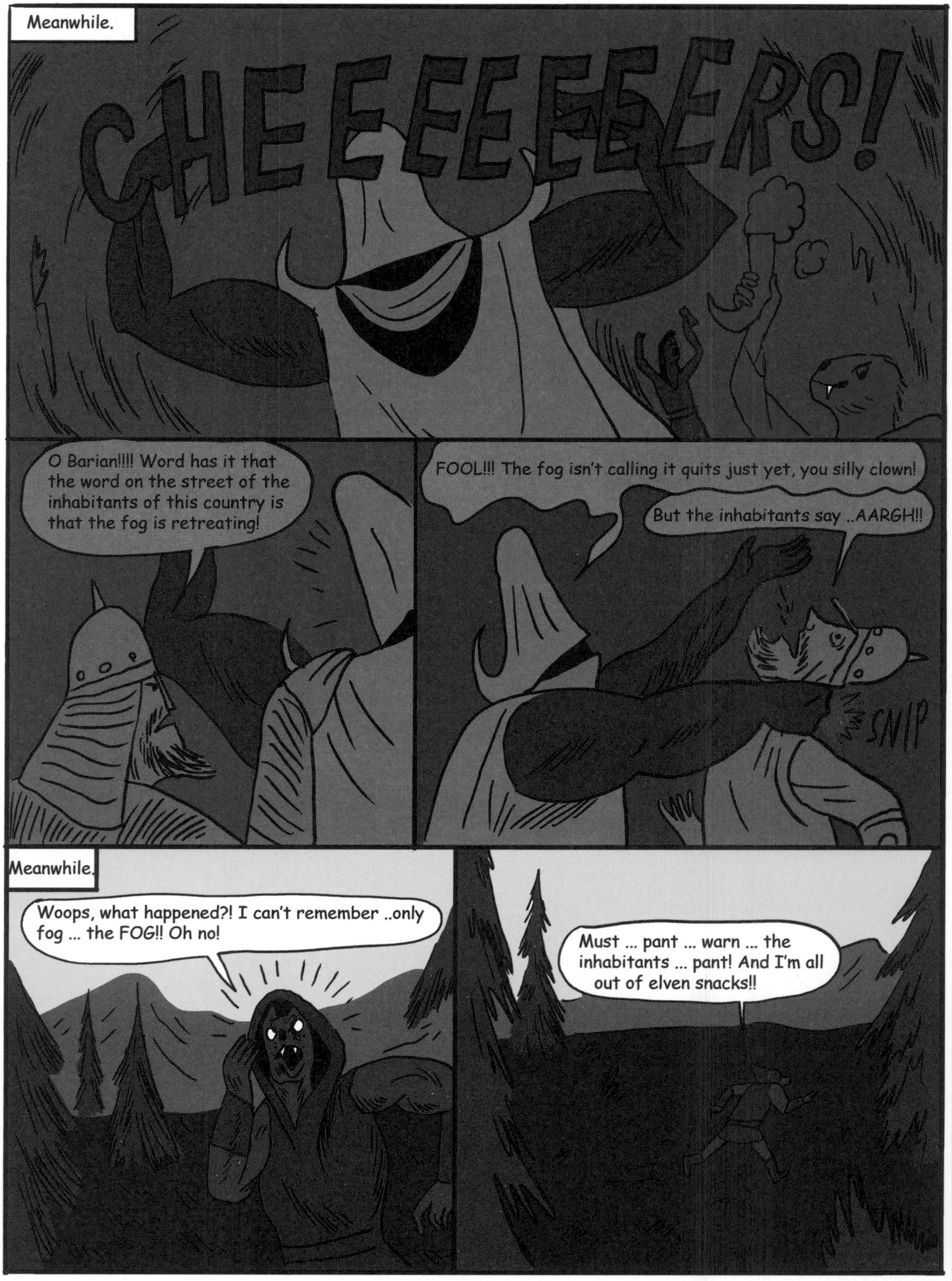
Meanwhile.
CHEEEEEERS!
O Barian!!!! Word has it that the word on the street of the inhabitants of this country is that the fog is retreating!
FOOL!!! The fog isn't calling it quits just yet, you silly clown!
But the inhabitants say ..AARGH!!
SNIP
Meanwhile.
Woops, what happened?! I can't remember ..only fog ... the FOG!! Oh no!
Must ... pant ... warn ... the inhabitants ... pant! And I'm all out of elven snacks!!

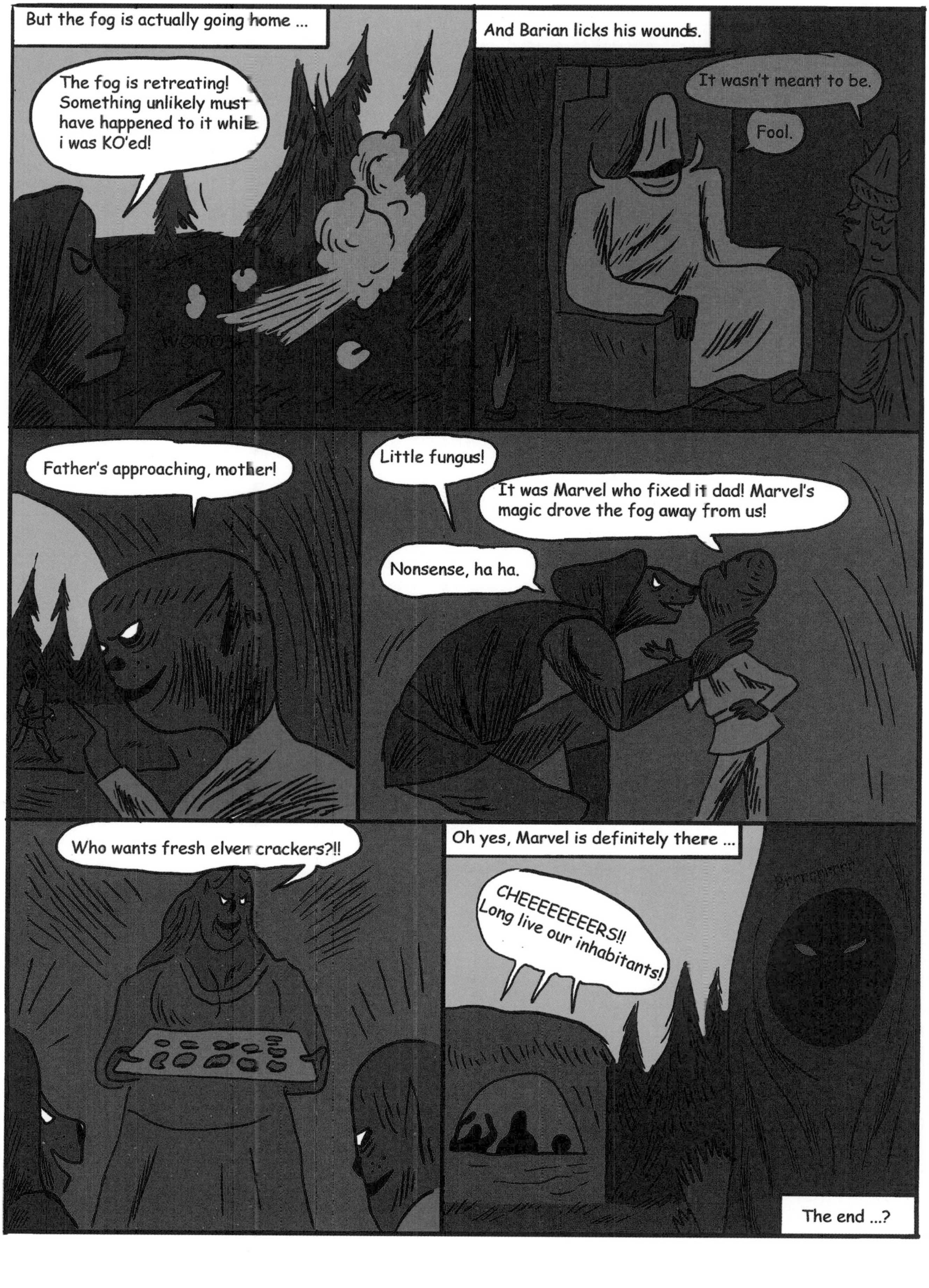
But the fog is actually going home ...
The fog is retreating! Something unlikely must have happened to it while i was KO'ed!
And Barian licks his wounds.
It wasn't meant to be.
Fool.
Father's approaching, mother!
Little fungus!
It was Marvel who fixed it dad! Marvel's magic drove the fog away from us!
Nonsense, ha ha.
Who wants fresh elven crackers?!!
Oh yes, Marvel is definitely there ...
CHEEEEEEEERS!! Long live our inhabitants!
The end ...?

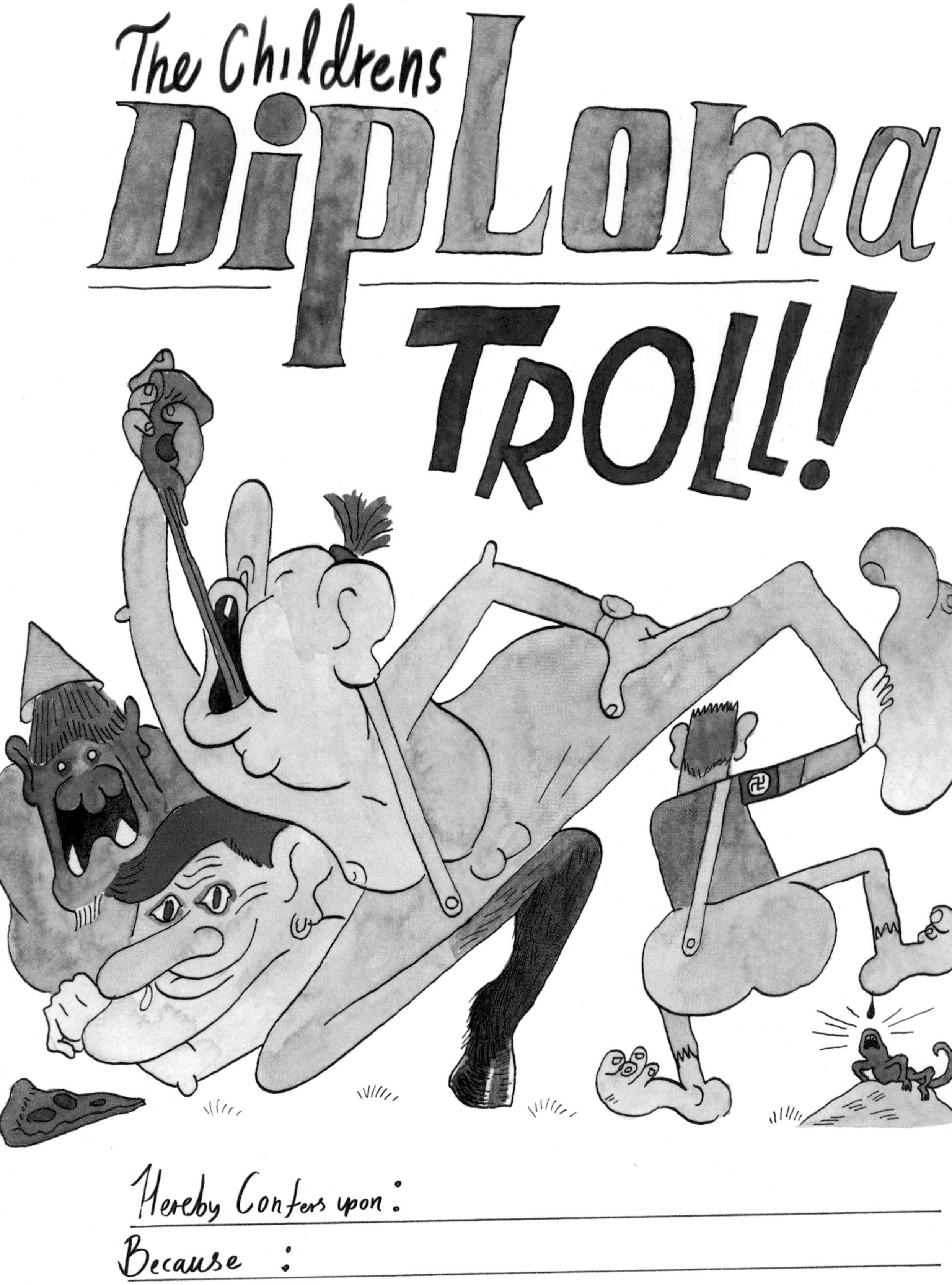
The Childrens
DipLoma
TROLL!
Hereby Confers upon:
Because :
Troll :
HAMAR

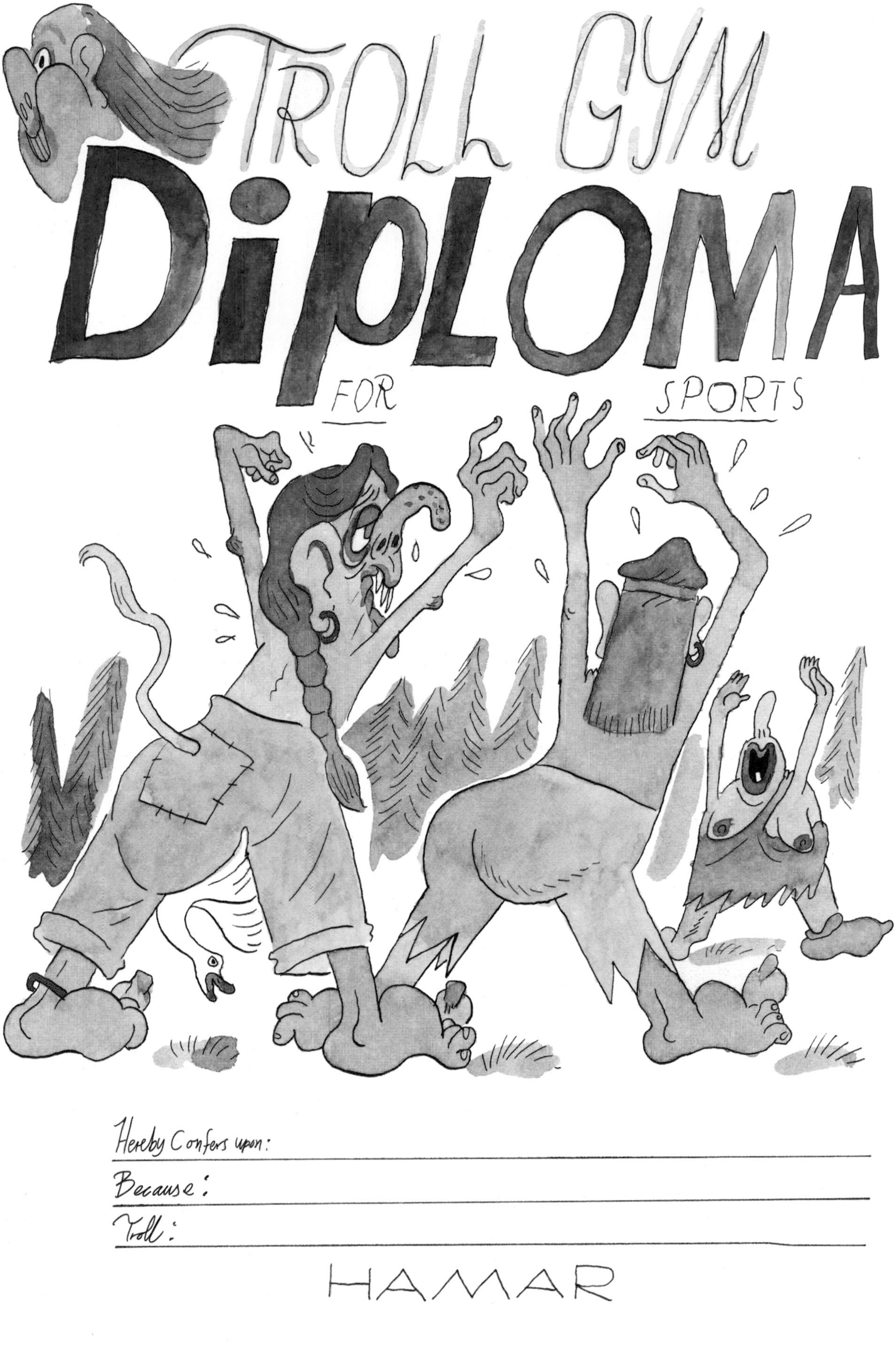
TROLL GYM
DIPLOMA
FOR SPORTS
Hereby Confers upon:
Because:
Troll:
HAMAR

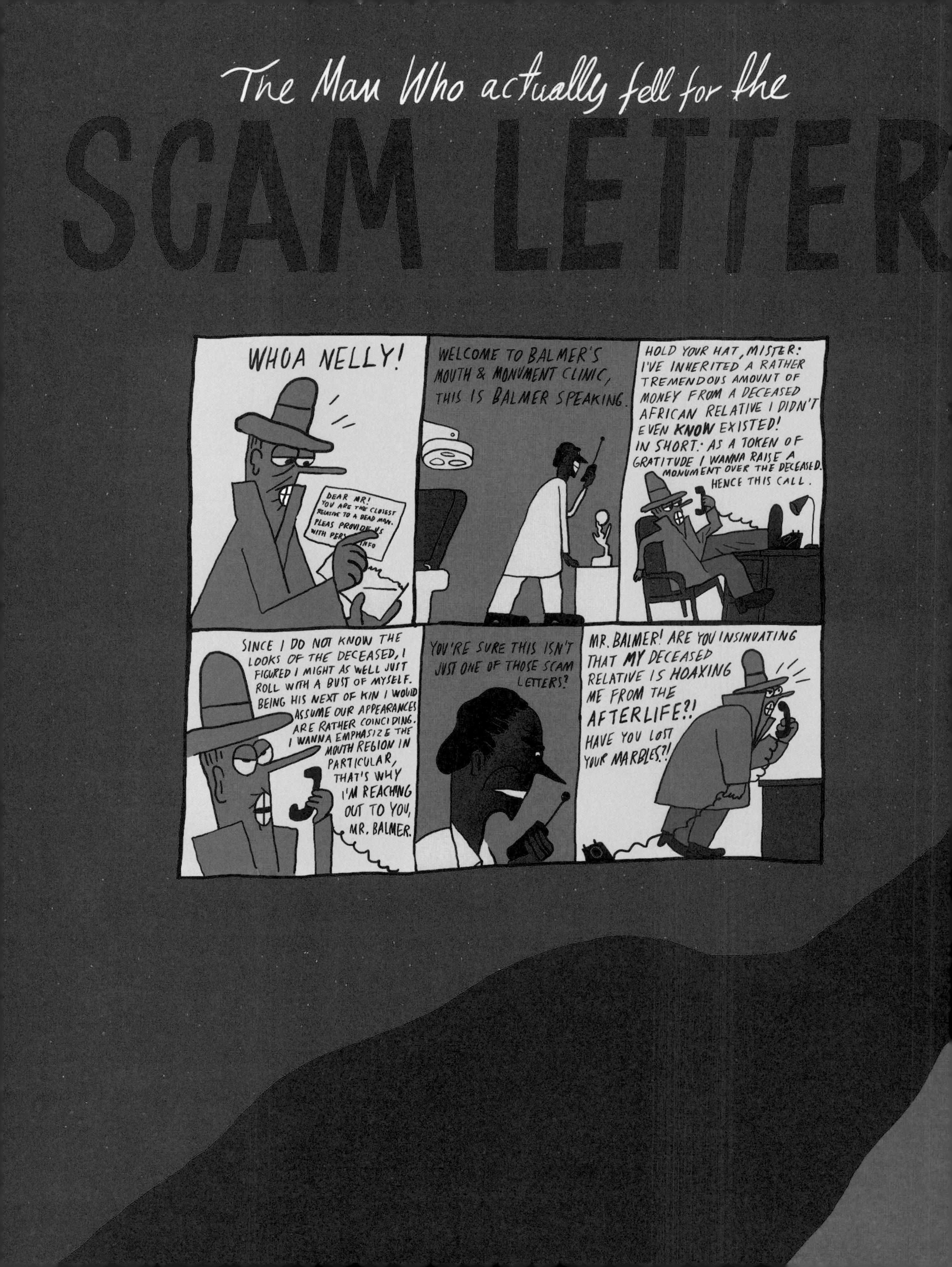
The Man Who actually fell for the
SCAM LETTER
WHOA NELLY!
DEAR MR! YOU ARE THE CLOSEST RELATIVE TO A DEAD MAN. PLEAS PROVIDE US WITH PERS INFO
WELCOME TO BALMER'S MOUTH & MONUMENT CLINIC, THIS IS BALMER SPEAKING.
HOLD YOUR HAT, MISTER: I'VE INHERITED A RATHER TREMENDOUS AMOUNT OF MONEY FROM A DECEASED AFRICAN RELATIVE I DIDN'T EVEN KNOW EXISTED! IN SHORT: AS A TOKEN OF GRATITUDE I WANNA RAISE A MONUMENT OVER THE DECEASED. HENCE THIS CALL.
SINCE I DO NOT KNOW THE LOOKS OF THE DECEASED, I FIGURED I MIGHT AS WELL JUST ROLL WITH A BUST OF MYSELF. BEING HIS NEXT OF KIN I WOULD ASSUME OUR APPEARANCES ARE RATHER COINCIDING. I WANNA EMPHASIZE THE MOUTH REGION IN PARTICULAR, THAT'S WHY I'M REACHING OUT TO YOU, MR. BALMER.
YOU'RE SURE THIS ISN'T JUST ONE OF THOSE SCAM LETTERS?
MR. BALMER! ARE YOU INSINUATING THAT MY DECEASED RELATIVE IS HOAXING ME FROM THE AFTERLIFE?! HAVE YOU LOST YOUR MARBLES?!

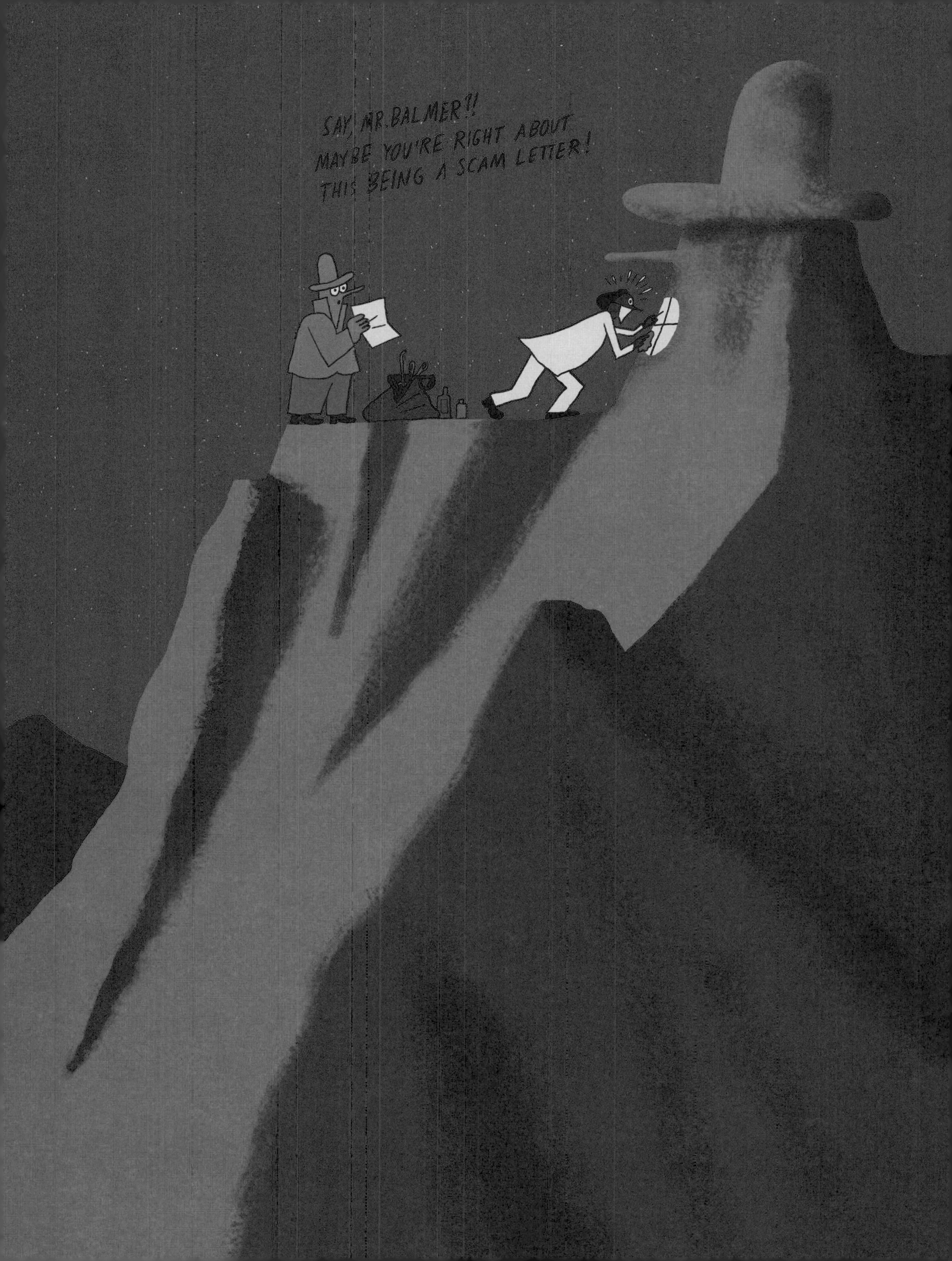
SAY, MR. BALMER?!
MAYBE YOU'RE RIGHT ABOUT
THIS BEING A SCAM LETTER!

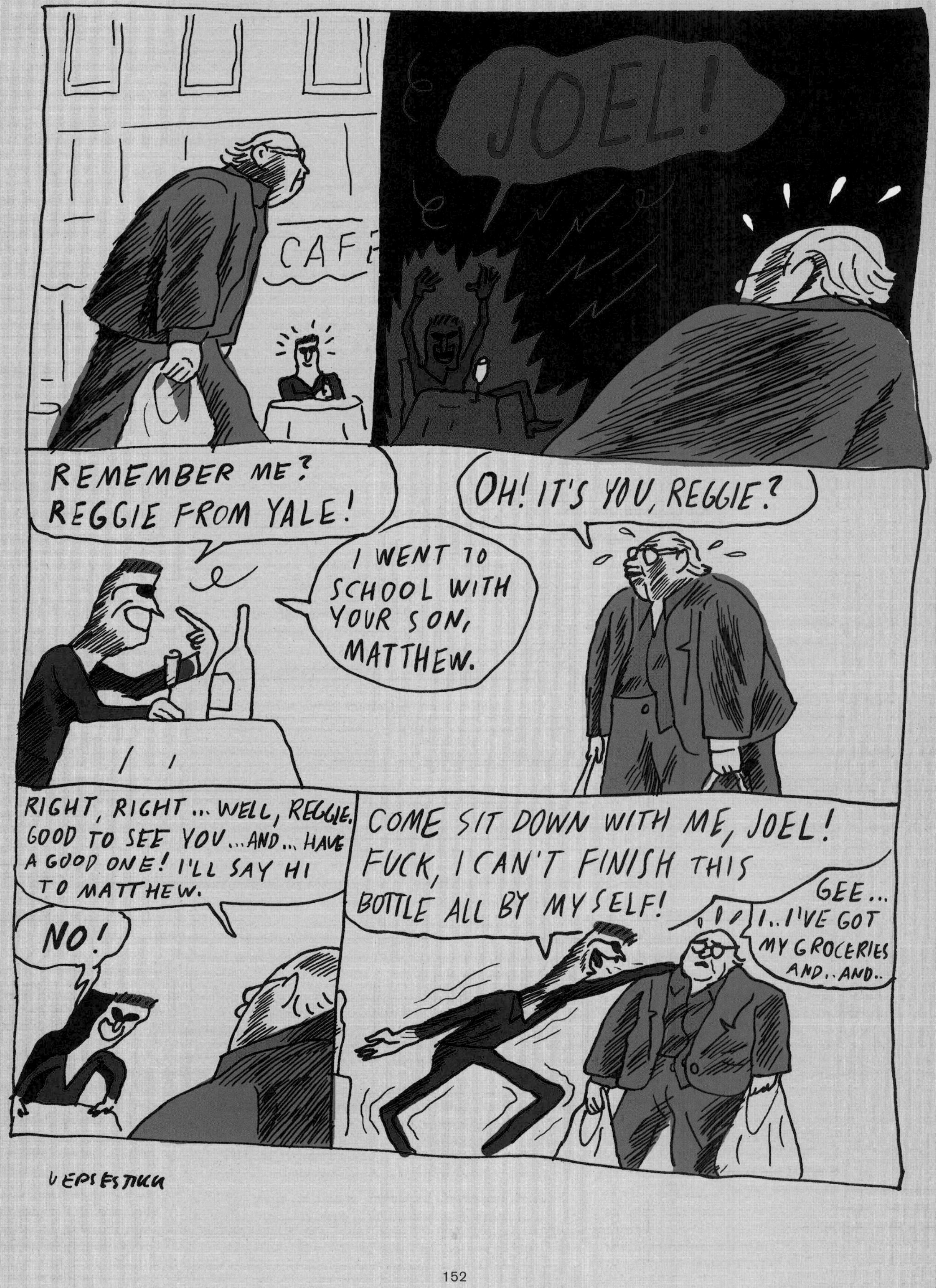

CAFE
JOEL!
REMEMBER ME? REGGIE FROM YALE!
I WENT TO SCHOOL WITH YOUR SON, MATTHEW.
OH! IT'S YOU, REGGIE?
RIGHT, RIGHT... WELL, REGGIE. GOOD TO SEE YOU... AND... HAVE A GOOD ONE! I'LL SAY HI TO MATTHEW.
NO!
COME SIT DOWN WITH ME, JOEL! FUCK, I CAN'T FINISH THIS BOTTLE ALL BY MYSELF!
GEE... I.. I'VE GOT MY GROCERIES AND.. AND..

VEPSESTUCU

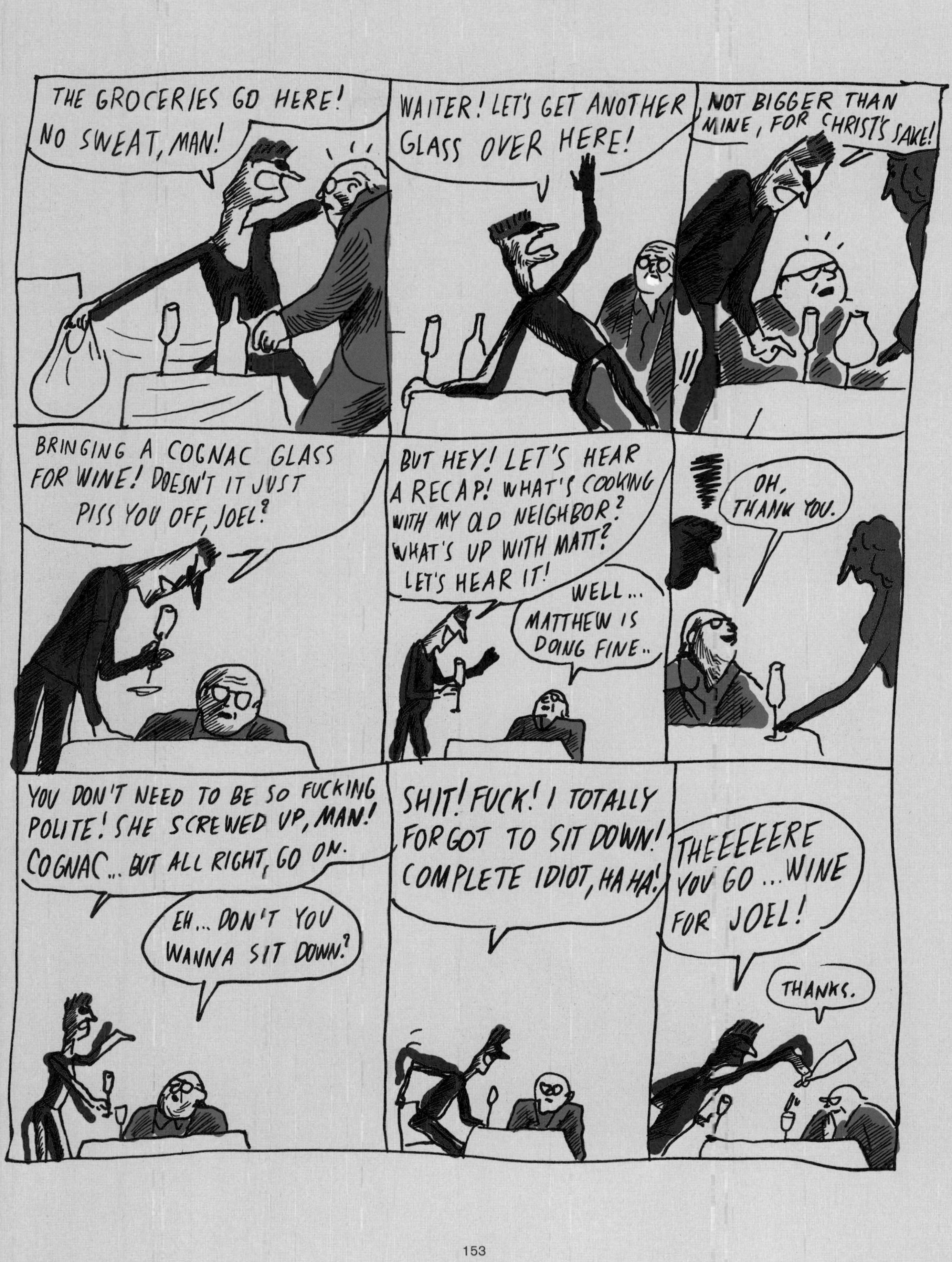

THE GROCERIES GO HERE! NO SWEAT, MAN!
WAITER! LET'S GET ANOTHER GLASS OVER HERE!
NOT BIGGER THAN MINE, FOR CHRIST'S SAKE!
BRINGING A COGNAC GLASS FOR WINE! DOESN'T IT JUST PISS YOU OFF, JOEL?
BUT HEY! LET'S HEAR A RECAP! WHAT'S COOKING WITH MY OLD NEIGHBOR? WHAT'S UP WITH MATT? LET'S HEAR IT!
WELL... MATTHEW IS DOING FINE..
OH, THANK YOU.
YOU DON'T NEED TO BE SO FUCKING POLITE! SHE SCREWED UP, MAN! COGNAC... BUT ALL RIGHT, GO ON.
EH... DON'T YOU WANNA SIT DOWN?
SHIT! FUCK! I TOTALLY FORGOT TO SIT DOWN! COMPLETE IDIOT, HA HA!
THEEEEERE YOU GO ...WINE FOR JOEL!
THANKS.

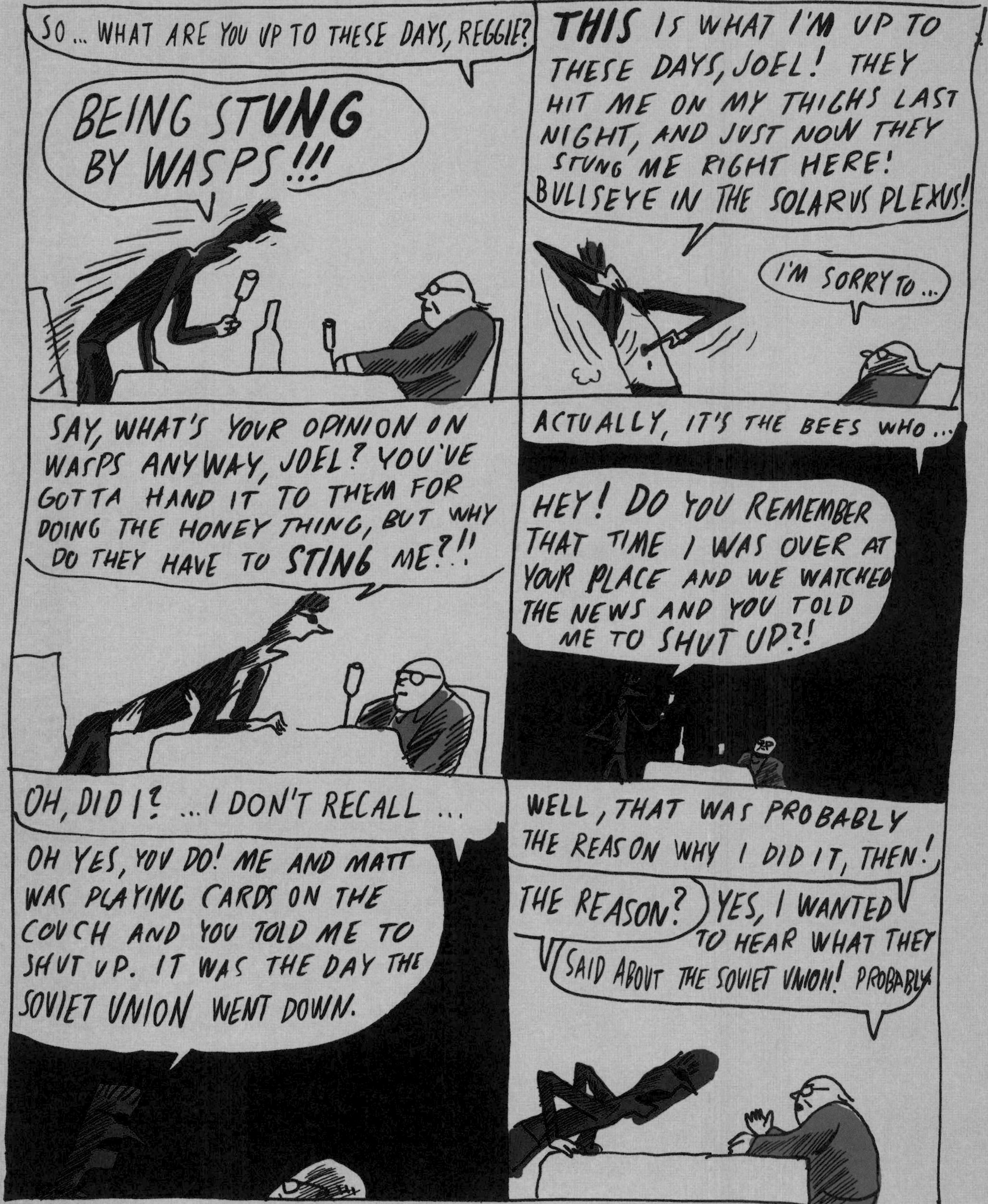
SO ... WHAT ARE YOU UP TO THESE DAYS, REGGIE?
BEING STUNG BY WASPS!!!
THIS IS WHAT I'M UP TO THESE DAYS, JOEL! THEY HIT ME ON MY THIGHS LAST NIGHT, AND JUST NOW THEY STUNG ME RIGHT HERE! BULLSEYE IN THE SOLARUS PLEXUS!
I'M SORRY TO ...
SAY, WHAT'S YOUR OPINION ON WASPS ANYWAY, JOEL? YOU'VE GOTTA HAND IT TO THEM FOR DOING THE HONEY THING, BUT WHY DO THEY HAVE TO STING ME?!!
ACTUALLY, IT'S THE BEES WHO ...
HEY! DO YOU REMEMBER THAT TIME I WAS OVER AT YOUR PLACE AND WE WATCHED THE NEWS AND YOU TOLD ME TO SHUT UP?!
OH, DID I? ... I DON'T RECALL ...
OH YES, YOU DO! ME AND MATT WAS PLAYING CARDS ON THE COUCH AND YOU TOLD ME TO SHUT UP. IT WAS THE DAY THE SOVIET UNION WENT DOWN.
WELL, THAT WAS PROBABLY THE REASON WHY I DID IT, THEN!
THE REASON?
YES, I WANTED TO HEAR WHAT THEY SAID ABOUT THE SOVIET UNION! PROBABLY.

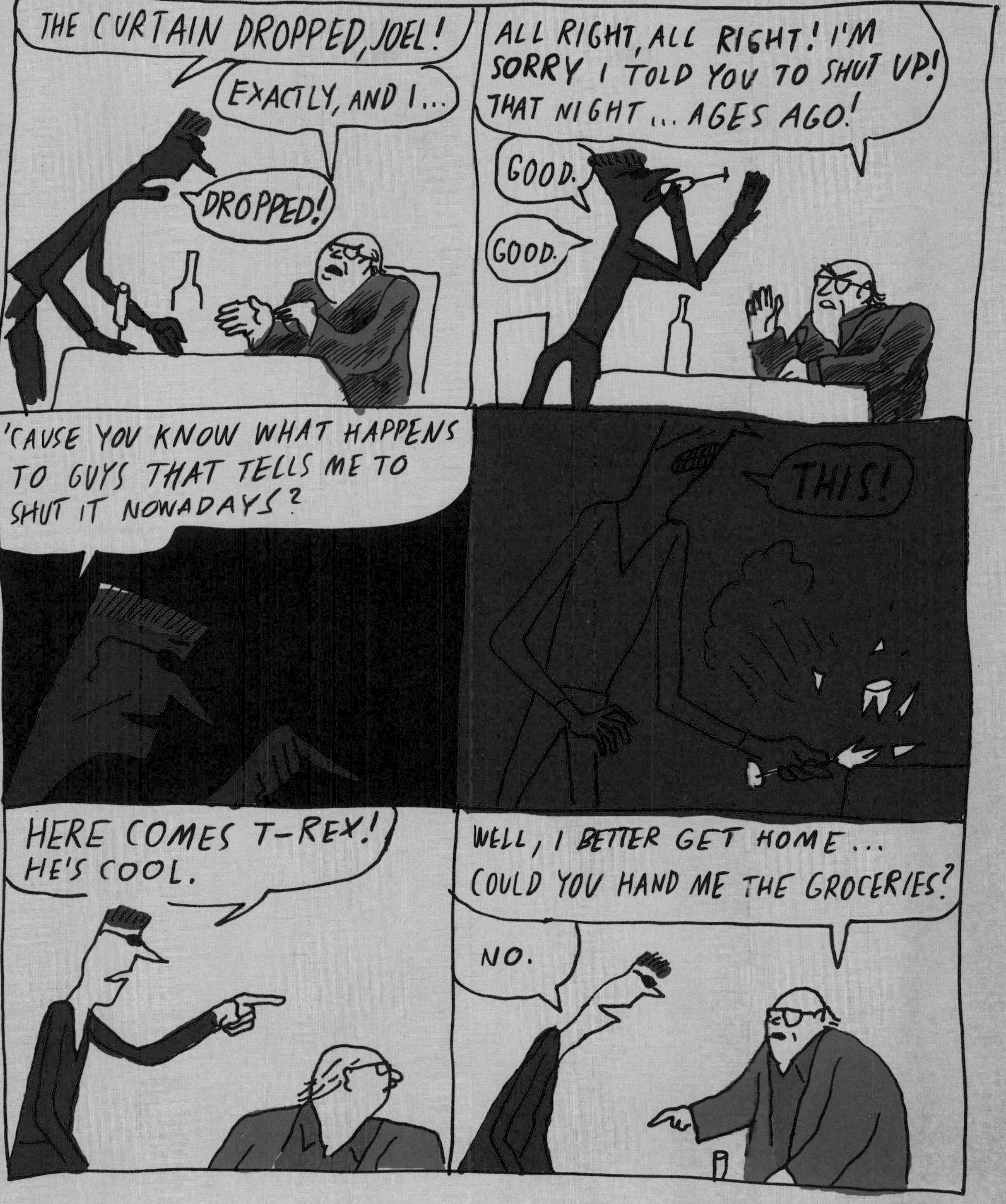
THE CURTAIN DROPPED, JOEL!
EXACTLY, AND I...
DROPPED!
ALL RIGHT, ALL RIGHT! I'M SORRY I TOLD YOU TO SHUT UP! THAT NIGHT... AGES AGO!
GOOD.
GOOD.
'CAUSE YOU KNOW WHAT HAPPENS TO GUYS THAT TELLS ME TO SHUT IT NOWADAYS?
THIS!
HERE COMES T-REX! HE'S COOL.
WELL, I BETTER GET HOME... COULD YOU HAND ME THE GROCERIES?
NO.

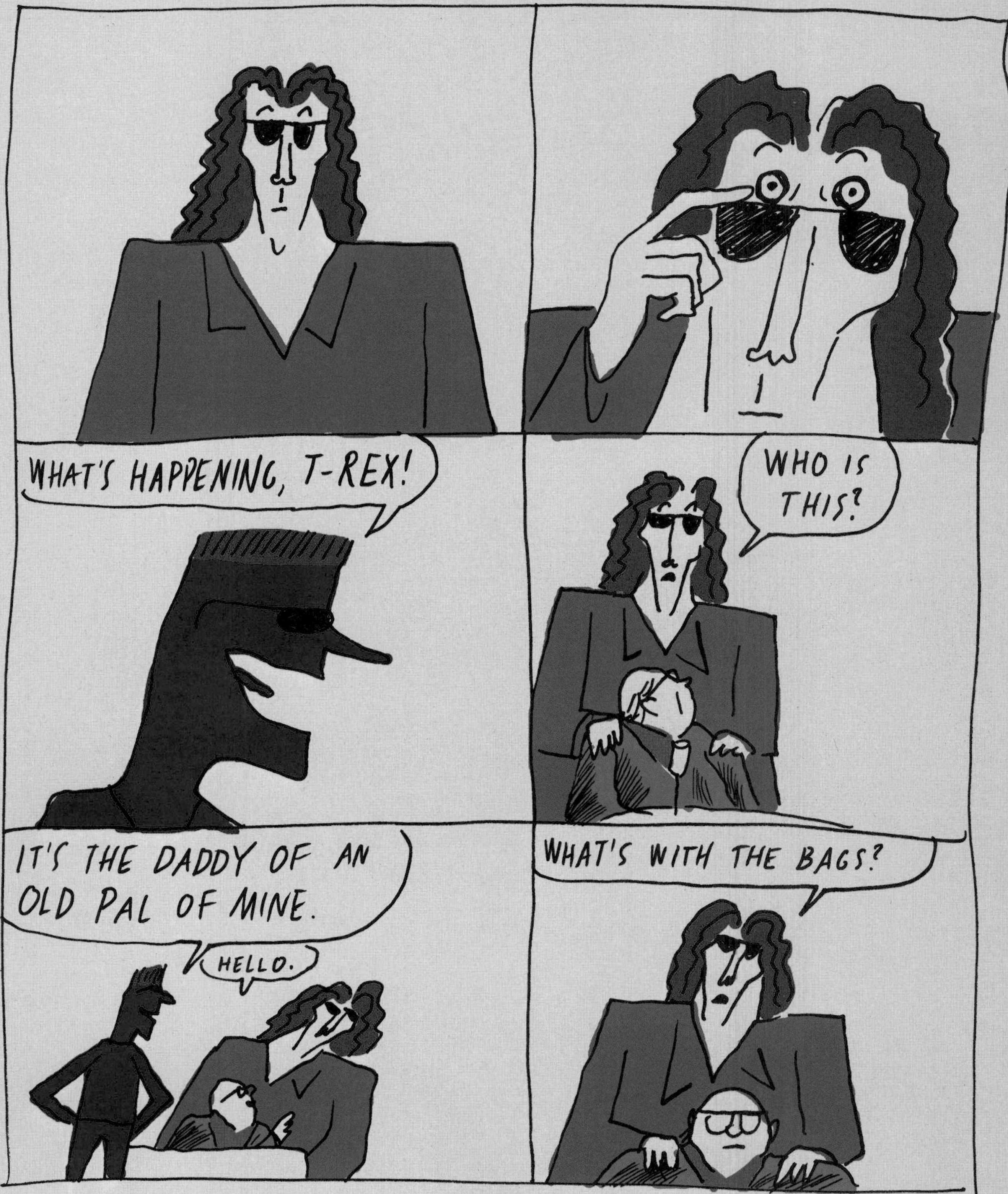
WHAT'S HAPPENING, T-REX!
WHO IS THIS?
IT'S THE DADDY OF AN OLD PAL OF MINE.
HELLO.
WHAT'S WITH THE BAGS?

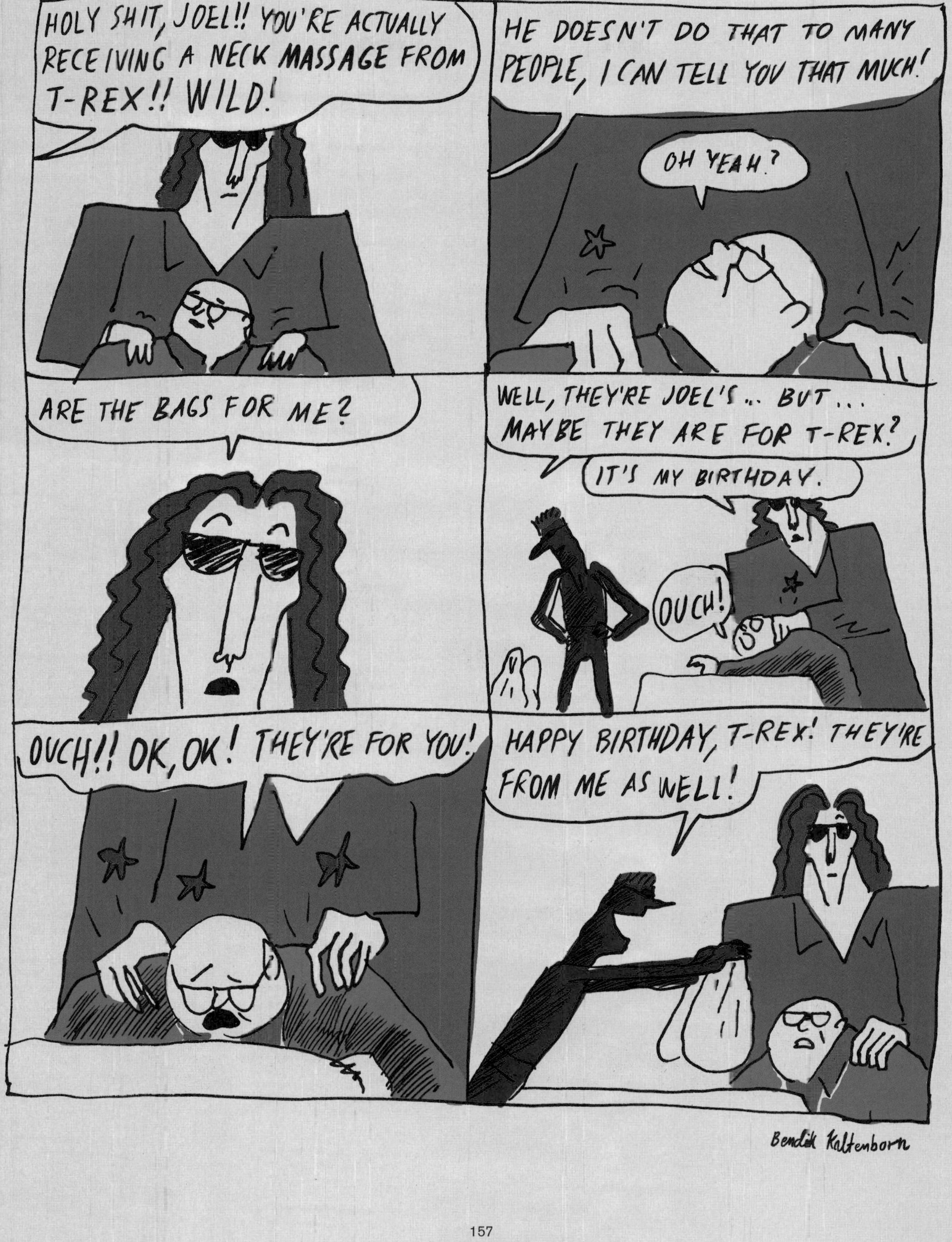
HOLY SHIT, JOEL!! YOU'RE ACTUALLY RECEIVING A NECK MASSAGE FROM T-REX!! WILD!
HE DOESN'T DO THAT TO MANY PEOPLE, I CAN TELL YOU THAT MUCH!
OH YEAH?
ARE THE BAGS FOR ME?
WELL, THEY'RE JOEL'S... BUT... MAYBE THEY ARE FOR T-REX?
IT'S MY BIRTHDAY.
OUCH!
OUCH!! OK, OK! THEY'RE FOR YOU!
HAPPY BIRTHDAY, T-REX! THEY'RE FROM ME AS WELL!
Bendik Kaltenborn

Consider it done;
WE'VE ALREADY WON

MARKED ASSOCIATON for FREE FLOW

We have a simple strategy;
IT'S ALL ABOUT EMPATHY

MARKED ASSOCIATON for FREE FLOW

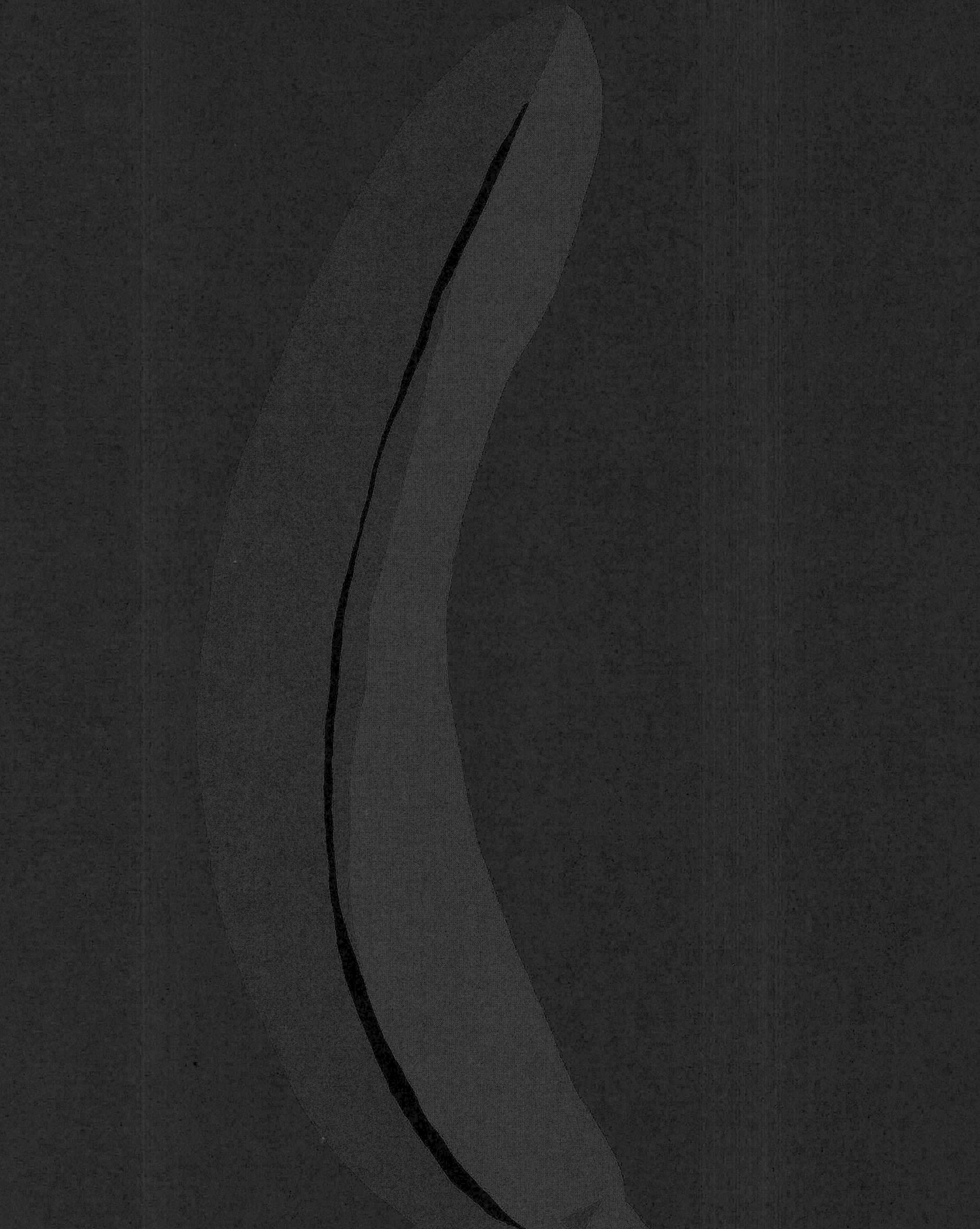
Keep your Wits about you

HEARD at CHARLES DE GAULLE

EAVESDROPPED BY BENDIK KALTENBORN 2010

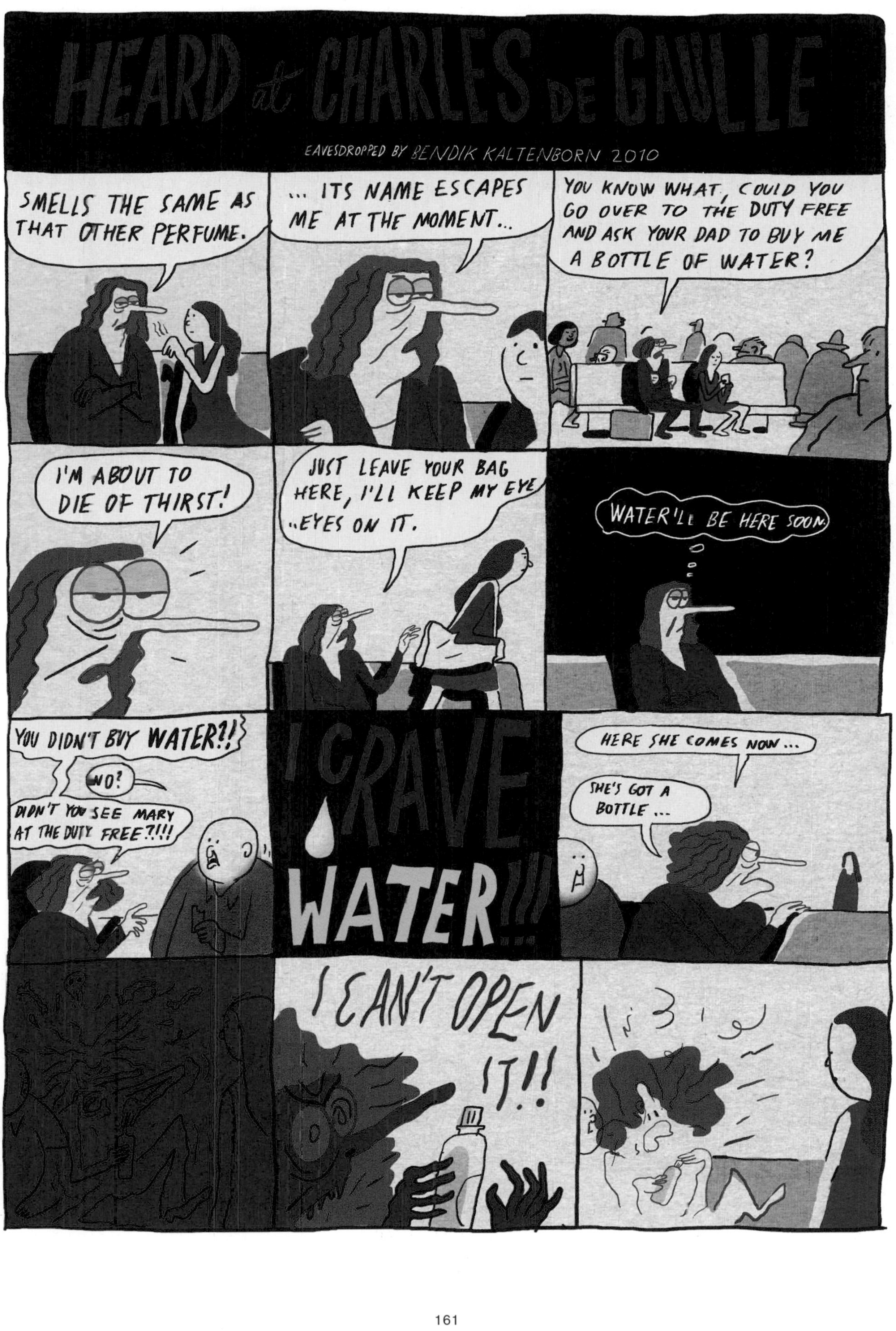
SMELLS THE SAME AS THAT OTHER PERFUME.
... ITS NAME ESCAPES ME AT THE MOMENT...
YOU KNOW WHAT, COULD YOU GO OVER TO THE DUTY FREE AND ASK YOUR DAD TO BUY ME A BOTTLE OF WATER?
I'M ABOUT TO DIE OF THIRST!
JUST LEAVE YOUR BAG HERE, I'LL KEEP MY EYE ..EYES ON IT.
WATER'LL BE HERE SOON.
YOU DIDN'T BUY WATER?!
NO?
DIDN'T YOU SEE MARY AT THE DUTY FREE?!!!
I CRAVE WATER!!!
HERE SHE COMES NOW...
SHE'S GOT A BOTTLE...
I CAN'T OPEN IT!!

LE MONDE DIPLOMATIQUE

IT MUST BE TERRIBLE TO BE SO NERVOUS

BENDIK KALTENBORN 2010

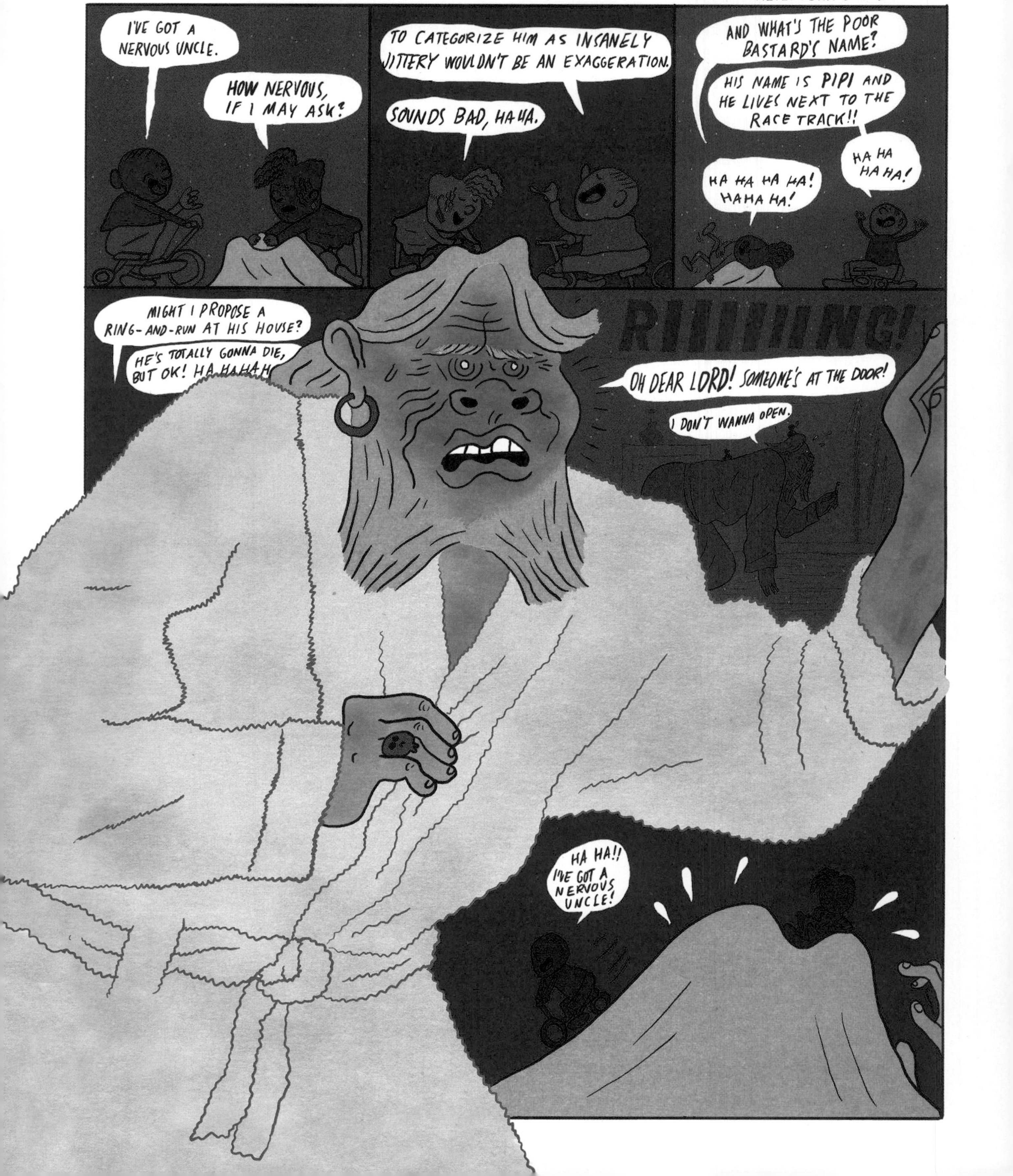
I'VE GOT A NERVOUS UNCLE.
HOW NERVOUS, IF I MAY ASK?
TO CATEGORIZE HIM AS INSANELY JITTERY WOULDN'T BE AN EXAGGERATION.
SOUNDS BAD, HA HA.
AND WHAT'S THE POOR BASTARD'S NAME?
HIS NAME IS PIPI AND HE LIVES NEXT TO THE RACE TRACK!!
HA HA HA HA! HAHA HA!
HA HA HAHA!
MIGHT I PROPOSE A RING-AND-RUN AT HIS HOUSE?
HE'S TOTALLY GONNA DIE, BUT OK! HA HAHAH
RIIIIIING!
OH DEAR LORD! SOMEONE'S AT THE DOOR!
I DON'T WANNA OPEN.
HA HA!! I'VE GOT A NERVOUS UNCLE!

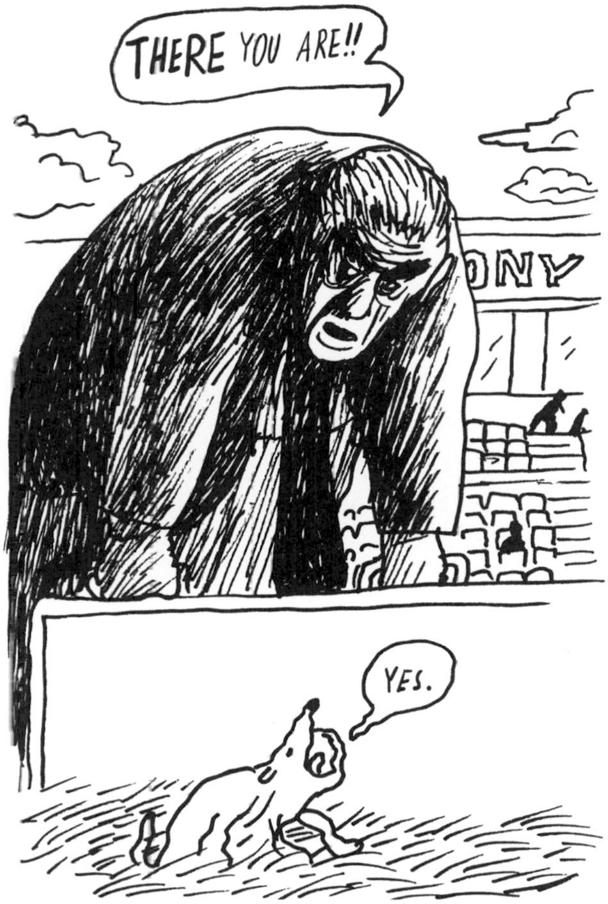
THERE YOU ARE!!
ONY
YES.

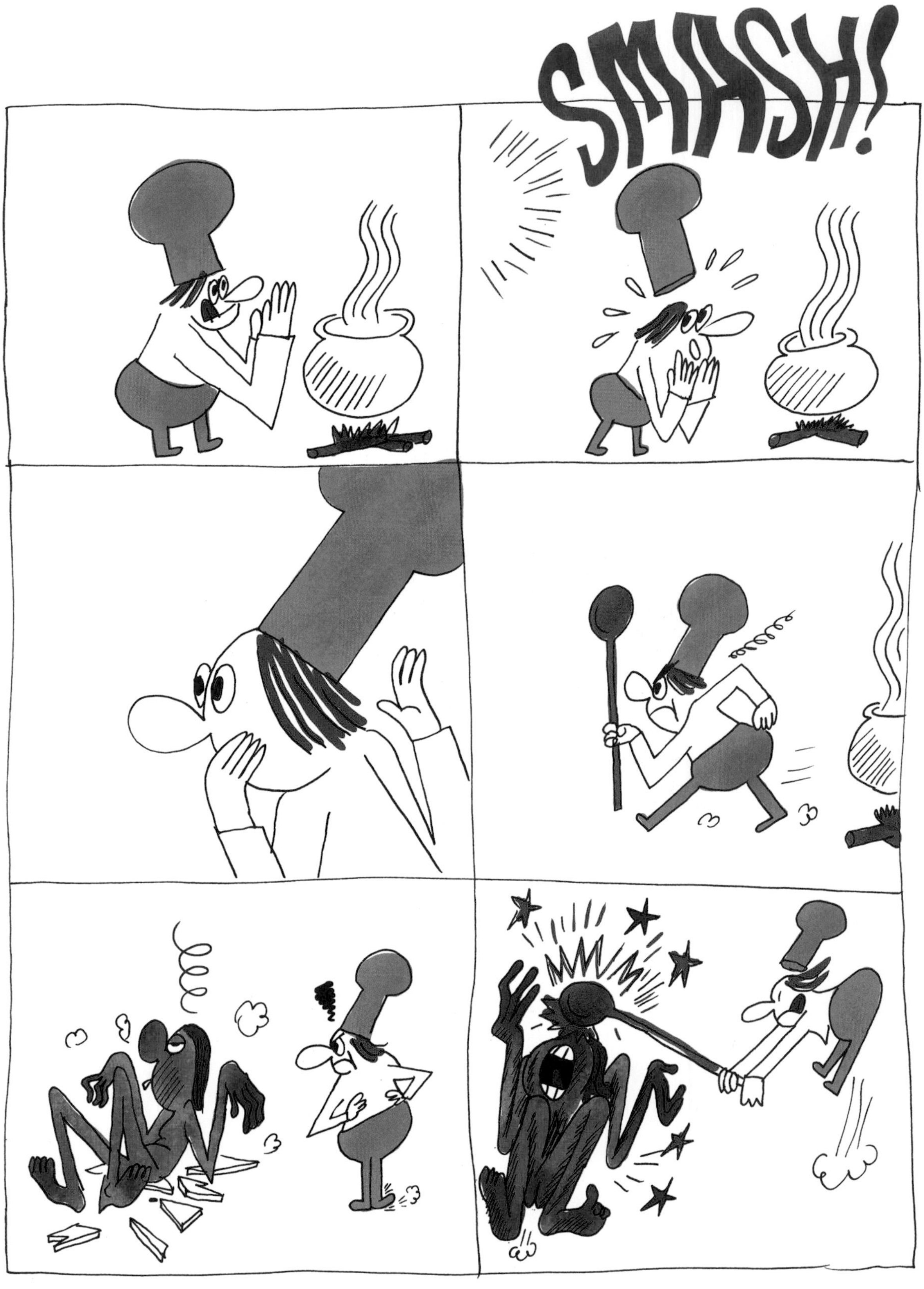
SMASH!

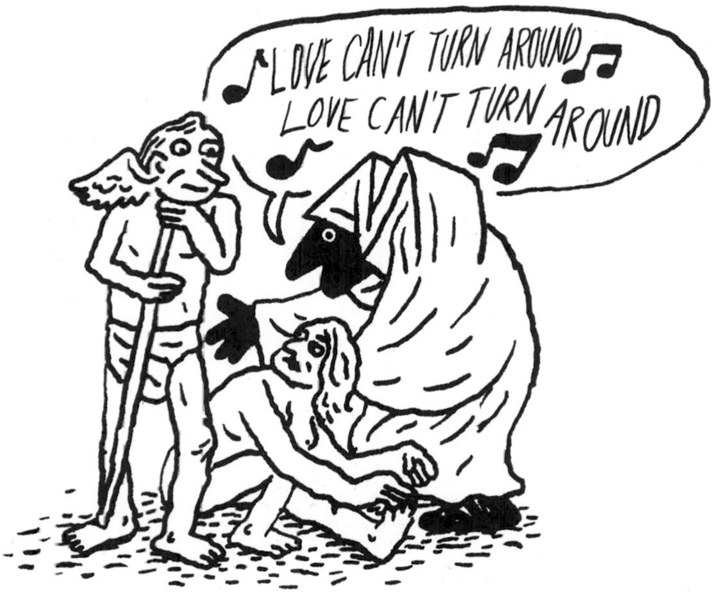
LOVE CAN'T TURN AROUND
LOVE CAN'T TURN AROUND

WHAT IS SHE DOING IN OUR GARDEN?

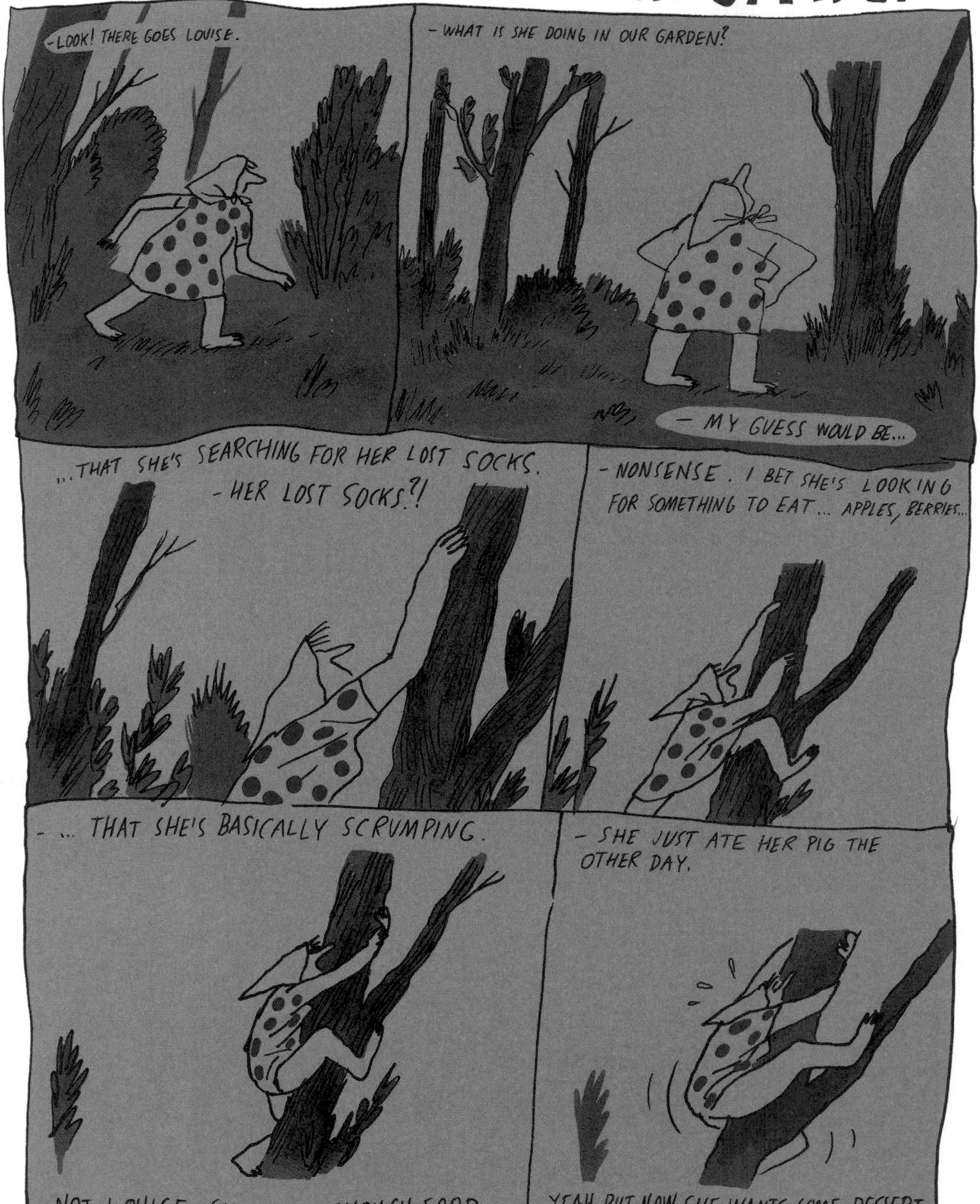

-LOOK! THERE GOES LOUISE.
- WHAT IS SHE DOING IN OUR GARDEN?
- MY GUESS WOULD BE...
...THAT SHE'S SEARCHING FOR HER LOST SOCKS.
- HER LOST SOCKS?!
- NONSENSE. I BET SHE'S LOOKING FOR SOMETHING TO EAT... APPLES, BERRIES...
- ... THAT SHE'S BASICALLY SCRUMPING.
- NOT LOUISE. SHE'S GOT ENOUGH FOOD.
- SHE JUST ATE HER PIG THE OTHER DAY.
-YEAH, BUT NOW SHE WANTS SOME DESSERT. SHE WANTS FRUIT.

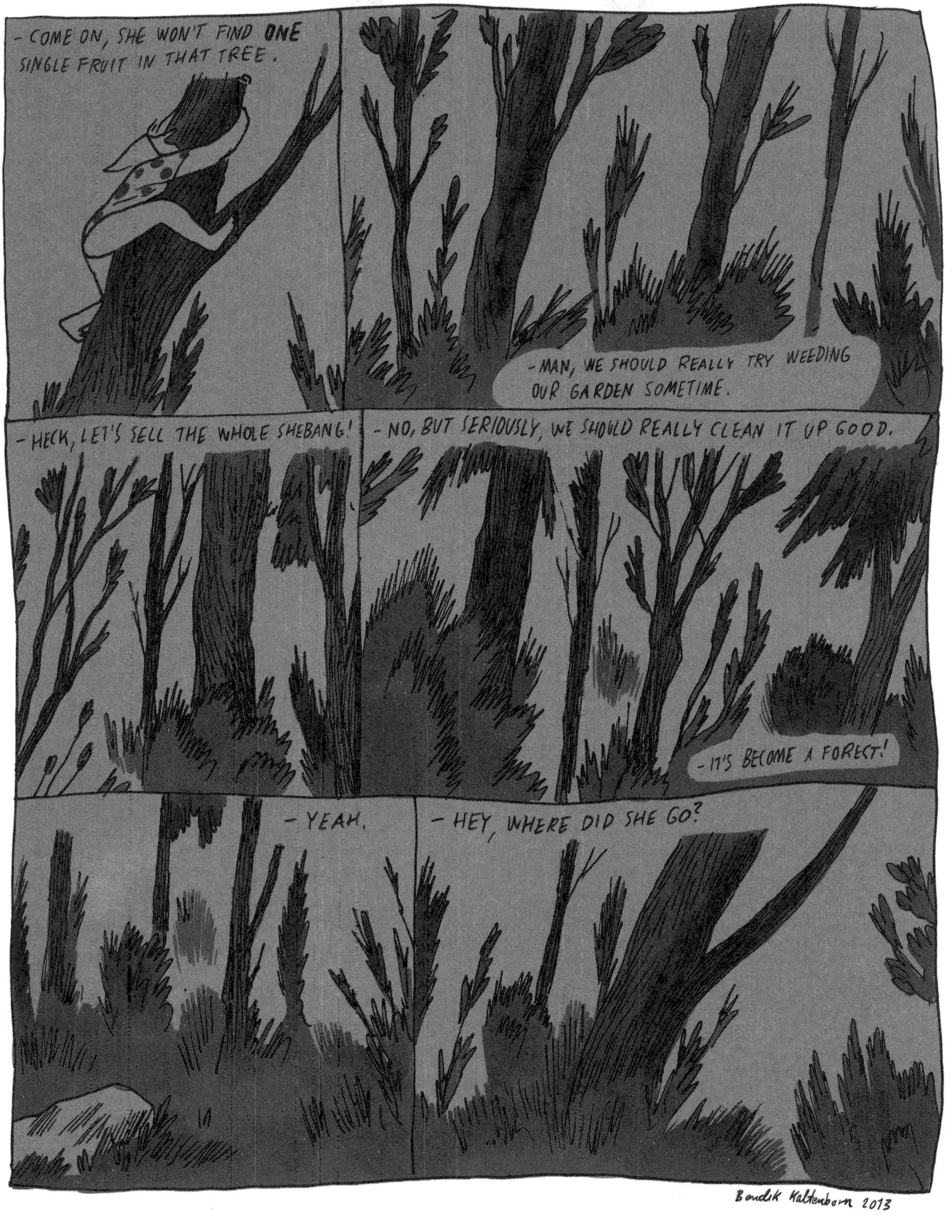
- COME ON, SHE WON'T FIND ONE SINGLE FRUIT IN THAT TREE.
- MAN, WE SHOULD REALLY TRY WEEDING OUR GARDEN SOMETIME.
- HECK, LET'S SELL THE WHOLE SHEBANG!
- NO, BUT SERIOUSLY, WE SHOULD REALLY CLEAN IT UP GOOD.
- IT'S BECOME A FOREST!
- YEAH.
- HEY, WHERE DID SHE GO?

Bendik Kaltenborn 2013

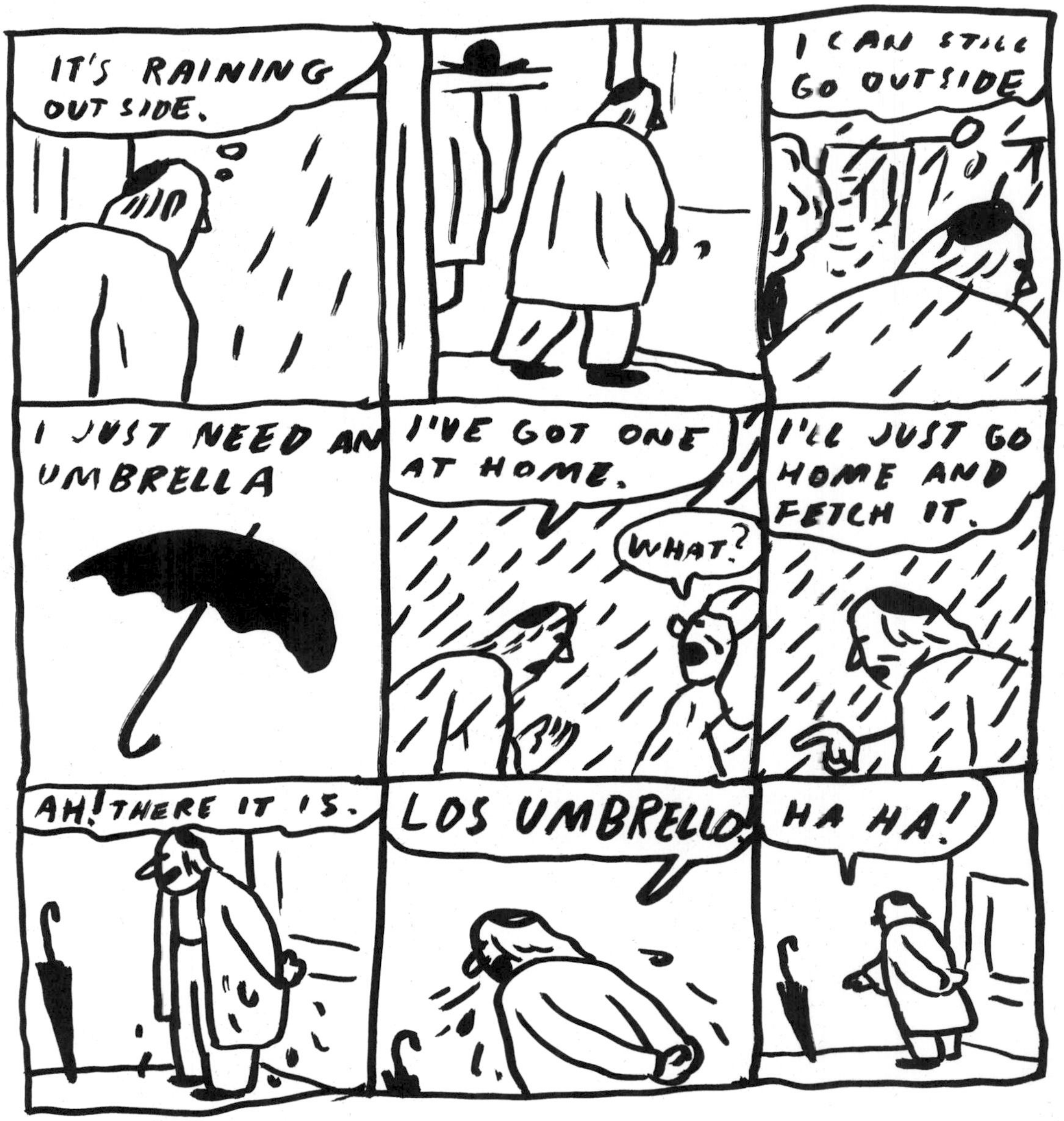
IT'S RAINING OUTSIDE.
I CAN STILL GO OUTSIDE
I JUST NEED AN UMBRELLA
I'VE GOT ONE AT HOME.
WHAT?
I'LL JUST GO HOME AND FETCH IT.
AH! THERE IT IS.
LOS UMBRELLO!
HA HA!

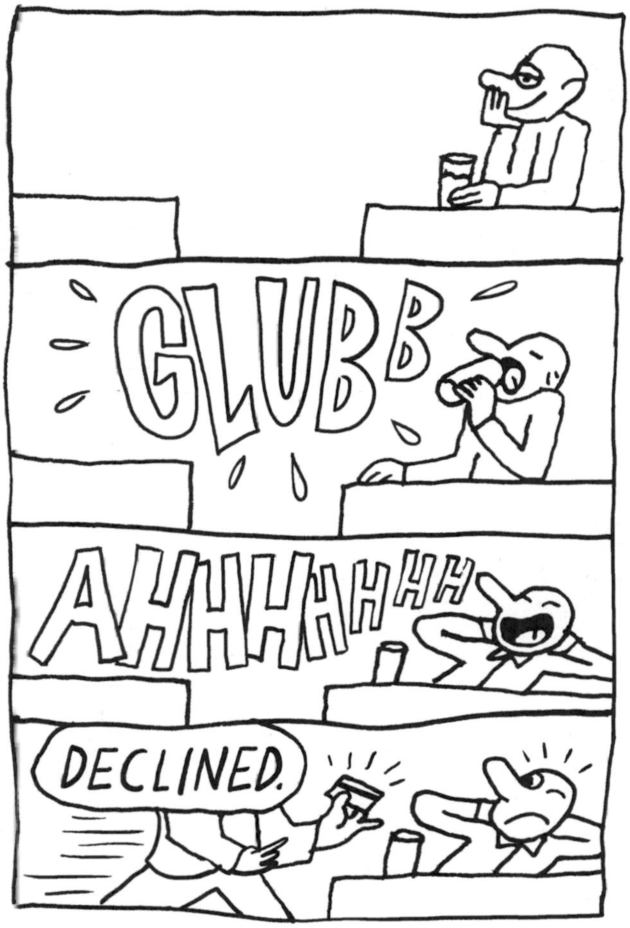
GLUBB
AHHHHHHHH
DECLINED.

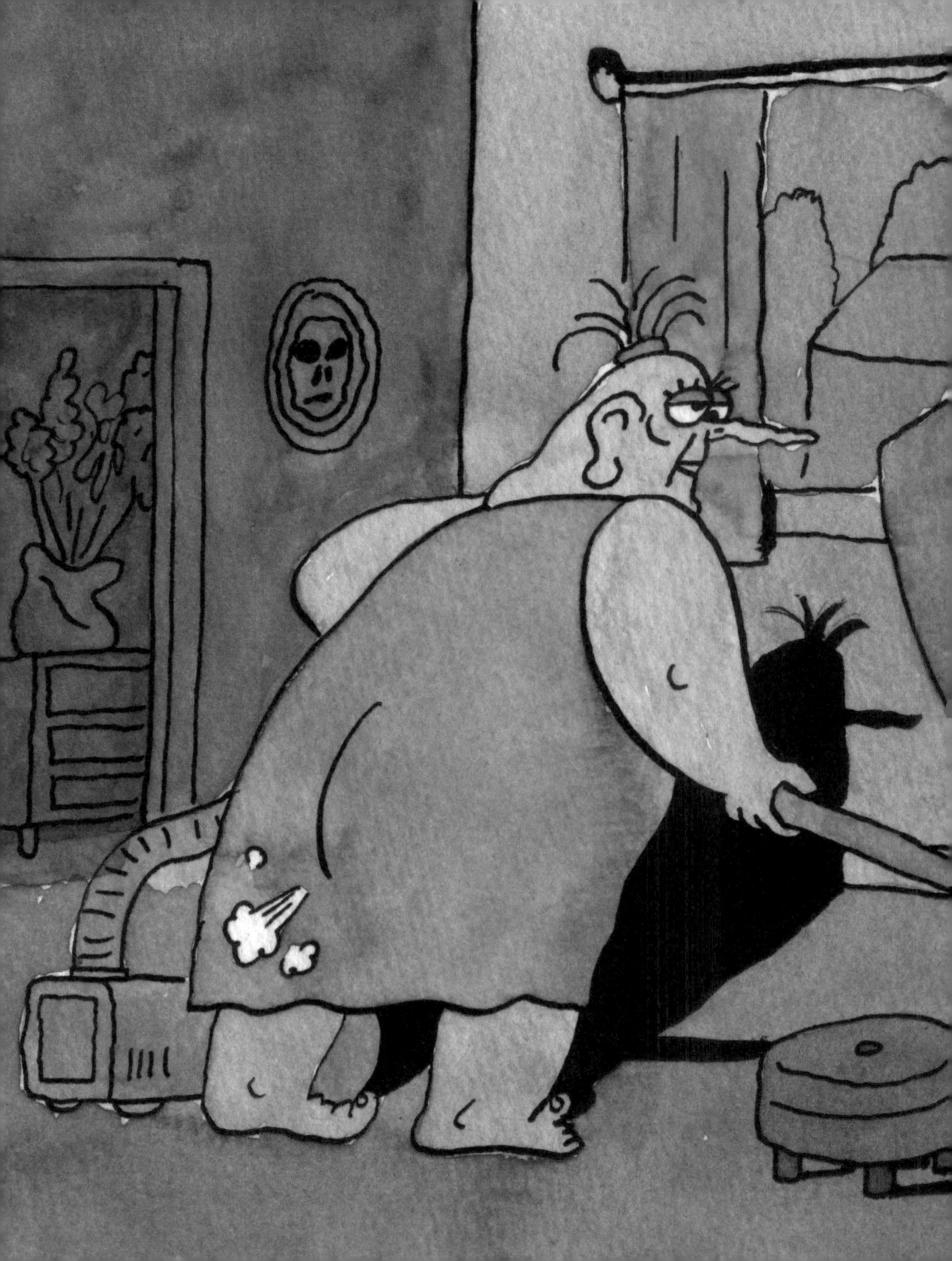

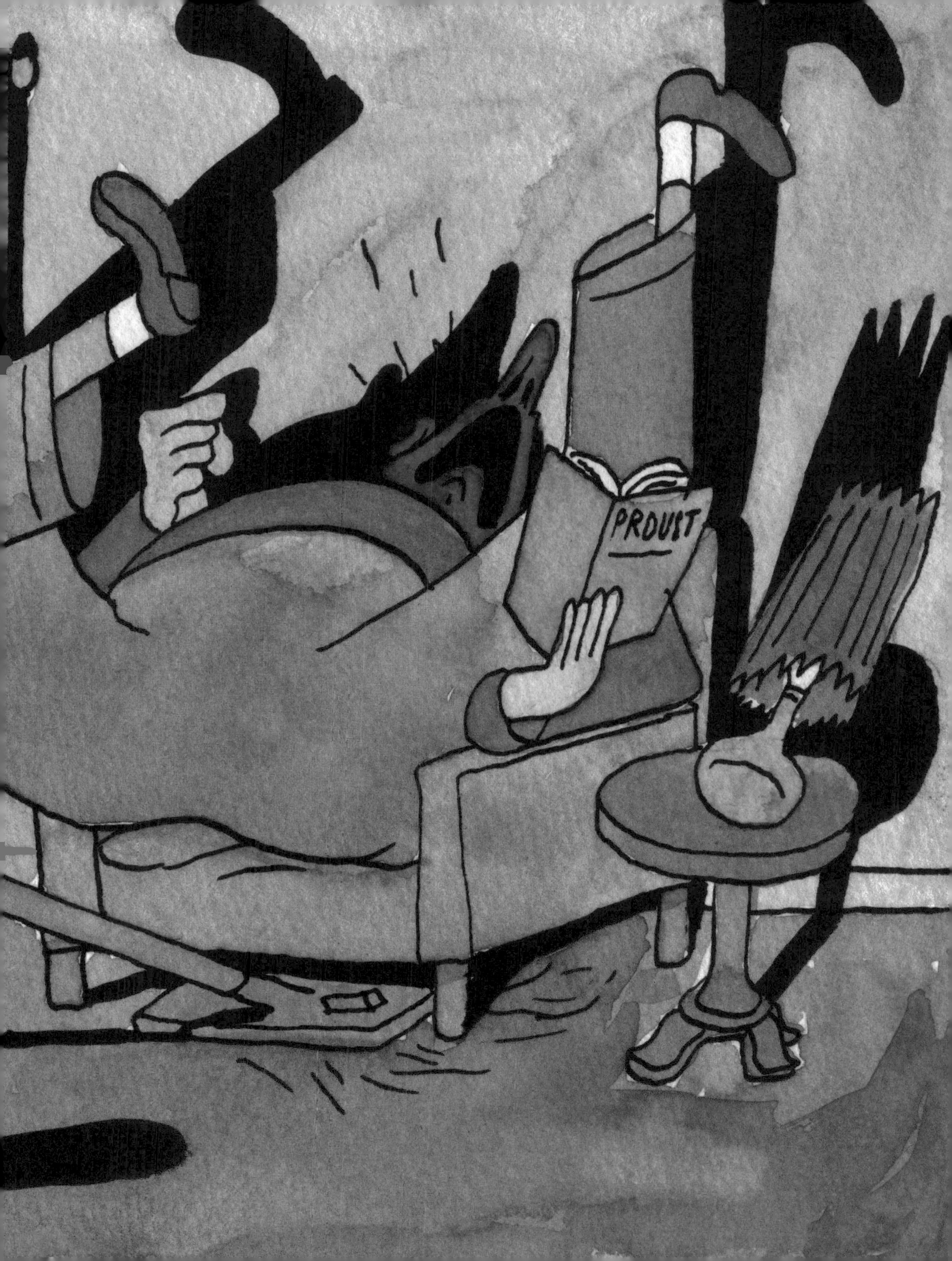
PROUST

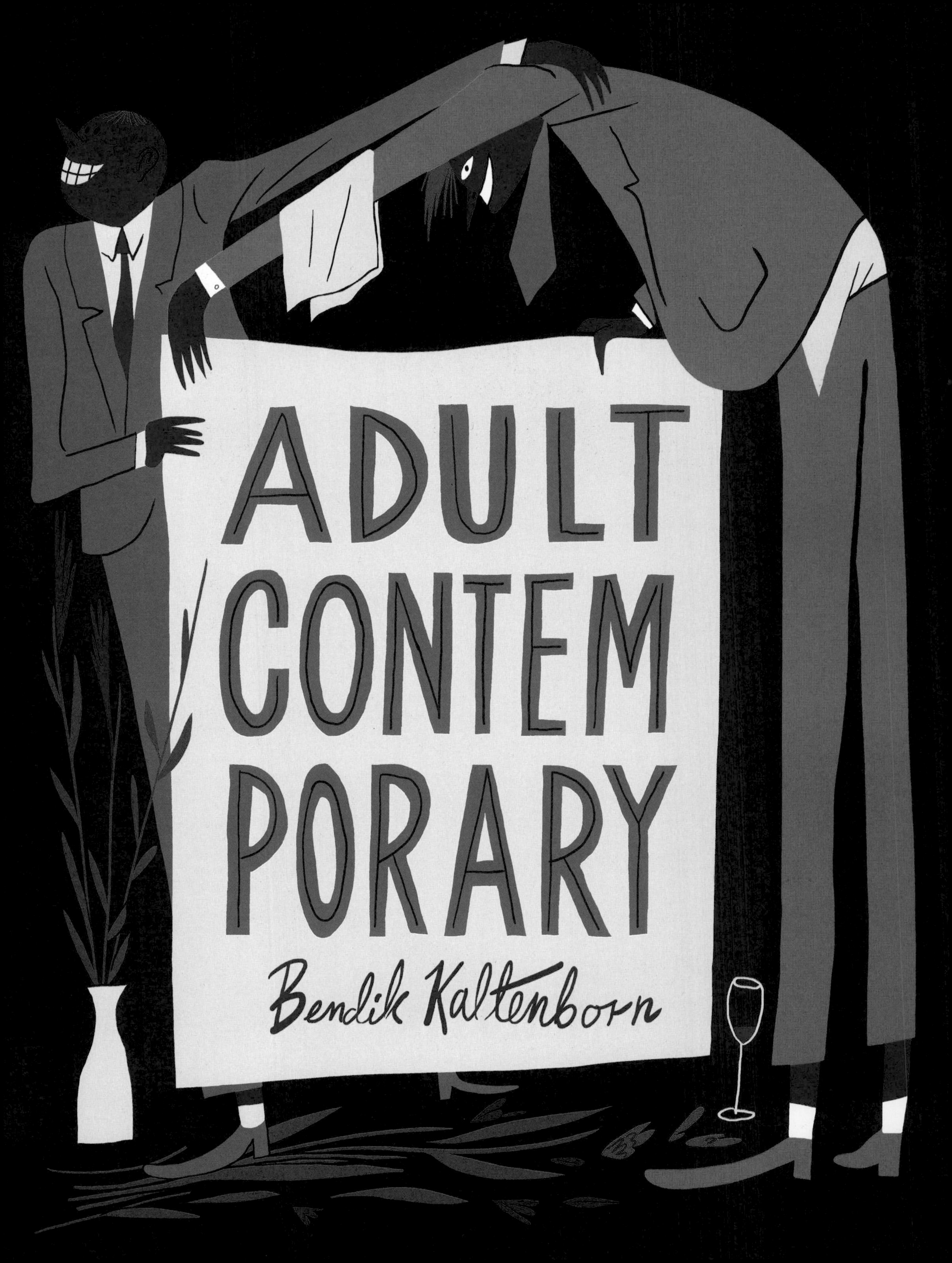
ADULT
CONTEM
PORARY
Bendik Kaltenborn

Did you know that...

Page 3–5: I drew this in my cabin while the German crime series *Derrick* was running on the TV in the background. Published in the French anthology *Blekk*, 2012.

Page 6–7: I drew this one late night in my cabin in the mountains. I work mostly digitally on a Cintiq screen these days, but when I'm alone in my cabin, I stay in touch with the paper, using nibs, ink, and watercolors. The cozier the setting the more brutal the drawings get. Unpublished.

Page 8: Drew this with a crushing hangover on the train from Angoulême. Published in *Dressed to Piss*, Dongery, 2011.

Page 9: Found in an old sketchbook. Based on a selection of different dads I've come across during the years. Unpublished, 2011.

Page 10: One thing most of my characters have in common is a total lack of social skill and understanding. Unpublished.

Page 11: Originally this was an old Norwegian saying but for this English version, Hemingway served the purpose. Published in the Norwegian illustration magazine *Numer*, 2010.

Page 12–15: Sometimes weird characters just appear on the paper and start rambling on about all kinds of crazy stuff. It can be difficult to keep pace and draw fast enough. This one was triggered by a friend who told me that he bought a bread knife as a Christmas gift for a carpenter working on his kitchen. Published in the Norwegian comic anthology *Forresten*.

Page 16–17: Drew this in the cabin. Again with the cabin! The cabin has a name, btw, it's called Blaffen, which means something like "Get Lost." All the watercolors in this book were made at Blaffen with no intention of being published or exhibited anywhere. I've been drawing at Blaffen since I was a little kid and there I can still experience the pure bliss of just drawing like I did when I was younger. This particular drawing is showing a hybrid of my two major fears: spiders and wolves. Unpublished.

Page 19–33: This short story appeared in the anthology *Kolor Klimax* (named after the old Danish porn movies). The anthology was intended to introduce Nordic comics to the US. The story is improvised, as usual—letting my gut feelings decide the direction. I somehow hear Dustin Hoffman's voice when Larry Gundersen speaks. His last sentence to Fanny is taken from Simply Red's "A New Flame Has Come," which was stuck in my head when I was drawing this comic. Published by Fantagraphics, 2010.

Page 34–35: I always listen to music or the radio while making these watercolors and the strange thing is that I can recall exactly what I listened to while drawing the specific lines, like I record what I hear into the drawing.

Page 36: Based on an overheard conversation. Unpublished, 2011.

Page 37: The Norwegian cartoonist Kjell Aukrust is one of my all time biggest inspirations—both his drawings and his writings—so his fictitious newspaper *Relsafus* in the first panel of this comic is an obscure homage. He's probably best known for his animated movie *The Pinchcliff Grand Prix* from 1975, animated by Ivo Caprino. Published in *Numer*, 2010.

Page 38: One cold day, I passed a man carrying cheap dog food while walking his dog. The rest is made up. Unpublished, 2011.

Page 39: Drawn during a lecture.

Page 40–41: Made for *Nobrow* no. 6. The theme was doppelgängers.

Page 42–43: This is the result when you draw inspiration from *Gyro Gearloose*, *Dark Souls*, *Monty Python's Flying Circus*, Theodor Kittelsen, and public baths.

Page 45: This is a comic I've been drawing regularly for the Norwegian lit mag *Bokvennen*. The basic premise of the drunken old men having a constant after-party is very much inspired by the great movie *Faces*, by John Cassavetes. Ran in *Bokvennen* from 2010–2015.

Page 50: A remix of a crucial scene in Cormac McCarthy's *Blood Meridian*.

Page 51: This was a commentary on the biggest Norwegian publishers' and bookstore chains' attempt to go digital with a very clumsy sort of "book cloud."

Page 53: Made during *carnaval* in Rio de Janeiro.

Page 54: "Christmas table" is a huge and intense tradition in Norway where every company from the biggest to the tiniest has an insane drunken party, often seasoned with lots of drama and violence. This one takes place at Olympen Restaurant in Olso.

Page 55: Sorry for this very in-joke comic. I made it when plans where announced to tear down Tronsmo bookstore and replace it and surrounding businesses with a ridiculous "knowledge street" with ugly skyscrapers. A very paradoxal thing to suggest. Tronsmo was once called "the coolest bookstore in the world" by Allen Ginsberg.

Page 57: I was laid-low with a fever when I made this one but I suppose you could believe the rest of the book was made while in the same state.

Page 58: The dialogue in the bottom strip is taken directly from a discussion I overheard at my local supermarket.

Page 60–61: I was raised in a part of Oslo with a lot of gardens. I guess that explains my garden hangup.

Page 62–69: These are posters made for my first solo exhibition that took place at Gallery Storck in Oslo in 2011. The show was called Sorry and I pursued my deep fascination with corporate life, Norwegian folklore, and poster design—mixing it all up. I even had my cousin and jazz musician Daniel Herskedal compose a soundtrack to tie it all together. Curated by Gerd Elise Mørland.

Page 70–71: I am part of the Norwegian comic collective Dongery, and every year we take turns hosting this earlier mentioned Christmas table at our homes. As usual, when we meet, we end up making comics together, and this time we wanted to make a sex fanzine. These two pages were my stupid contribution to the fanzine named something like "A horny, horny, vaginal greeting—an affordable wank for two bucks." It's probably the worst thing we've ever produced. Published 2008.

Page 72: Drew this on some paperwork during the day at a Dongery/No Comprendo Press stand at Helsinki Comics Festival, 2012. Unpublished.

Page 73: From a sketchbook, published in *Dressed to Piss*, Dongery, 2011.

Page 74–75: These two comics are obviously connected, although they're produced with a few years gap in between and for two separate occasions. I think putting references to things you like into comics can be quite tricky and very easily disturbing, but here I dared hang a poster of the '80s Australian band The Triffids on the kitchen wall, along with another poster of an obscure TV show about cars.

Page 76–77: Although many of my watercolors take place in nature, this is the only watercolor I've actually made outdoors, occasionally glancing at a branch or two. I usually never draw things I see, only relying on my (bad) memory for references.

Page 79–89: This is how I feel about most comic strips. One day, I got so fed up that I just started making this sort of parody, with the protagonist somewhat looking like the *Zits* guy. The strip was meant only for the earlier mentioned Sorry exhibition, not for one second did I have thoughts about actually having it run in a newspaper. Strangely, this was exactly what happened when *Dagbladet*, one of Norways biggest newspapers, asked if

I would be interested in making a guest strip for them. I told them I was too busy working on my exhibition when I realized that I actually had just made this strip! I sent over the strip, strongly presuming it was way too stupid and weird for publishing, but to my big surpise the editor loved it and had it running for two weeks prior my exhibition. The readers on the other hand, didn't love it one bit and went bonkers in the comments section, turning the whole thing into a social experiment. When I put together this book some years later, I was very happy that I'd saved all the comments so I could include them unedited as a crucial and entertaining part of the strip. Much more fun than the strip itself.

Page 91: Drawn in a sketchbook in Stockholm. Unpublished, 2007.

Page 92: I'll admit that this is loosely based on personal experience. Unpublished.

Page 93: My grandfather used to sing this song, long before Roberto Benigni. Published in *Forresten*.

Page 94: Scenario observed outside my window, dialogue and epilogue cooked up in my mind. Unpublished.

Page 95: Drawn on the train on the way to my cabin, inspired by *Professor Tought*–an old Norwegian comic from the '30s by Ivar Mauritz-Hansen. Unpublished.

Page 96: It was a rainy day in New York when my pal Kristoffer Kjolberg and I sought shelter in a dark old pub making this little fairy tale on a napkin, among other things. Unpublished.

Page 97: While making this book I found a piece of paper where I'd written down something my dad said when he visited my studio some years ago. I figured it was worth making a small comic about it. Unpublished.

Page 99–119: The Yokoland design studio, who also helped out with the layout of this book, commissioned me to make this story for a book about the Oslo suburbs that they were working on. As the newspaper clipping shows, the story is based on a real robbery back in the '80s. Since the thieves were never caught, I made up the events leading up to the actual robbery–which was executed exactly as described.

Page 120–121: From a group exhibition at the Nordic Watercolor Museum in Skärhamn, 2010.

Page 122: From a sketchbook, 2006. Unpublished.

Page 123: My uncle told me about a businesswoman who brought her dog to a meeting. That dog then continuously licked the woman's face during the entire meeting. Unpublished.

Page 124: This is a true story from New York. My colleague Flu Hartberg actually gave me sleeping pills instead of painkillers and I had to order a bucket of coffee not to fall asleep. On our way home we got stuck in the infamous volcano cloud that froze the air traffic for about a week.

Page 125: Improvised story drawn with a nib on copy paper. Published in *Dressed to Piss*.

Page 126–127: I made a lot of strips about this guy in my sketchbook for a while, but most of them are so weird and boring that I don't know what I was thinking when I made them. Published in *Dressed to Piss*.

Page 128–129: The man in the pajamas is loosely based on Johan from Ingmar Bergman's *Scenes from a Marriage*, which I was watching while drawing this. I grew increasingly angry with Johan and felt like giving him an unpleasant treatment. Great movie, though.

Page 130–135: Sometimes I rip out small articles from the newspaper with the idea that I could someday use them for something. I found these three clippings in a drawer while working on this book and suddenly this grumpy guy in the red sweater appeared, acting out all three scenarios.

Page 136–137: In old Norwegian folklore, you can always tell the devil by his leg.

Page 139–147: Another silly comic experiment, this time mocking fantasy comics. Using a pseudonym and pretending to be very pretentious, I published the comic on a daily basis on a Norwegian comic site. When people started commenting politely and helpfully on grammatical, anatomical, and other errors, my alter ego would condescendingly address them as "fans."

Page 148–149: Typical Norwegian kids' diplomas.

Page 150–151: Originally made for the French anthology *Nyctalope* but never printed. When I looked at it some years later, I realized it was just stupid and not very funny, so I called my "punch-up man" Kristoffer Kjølberg and got some advice.

Page 152–157: Another improvised story from the sketchbooks. T-Rex is modelled after the '90s Swiss eurodance king, DJ Bobo, and the Swedish equivalent, E-Type. His eyes, which are usually hidden by his sunglasses, were inspired by a far-out character, whose name I can't recall, in *Withnail and I*. Unpublished.

Page 158–159: More stuff from the Sorry exhibition. I love making posters for clients, but it was quite interesting making posters for no one as well.

Page 160: Also from Sorry. Bananas are a great remedy for anger and low blood sugar.

Page 161: I witnessed this episode at Charles de Gaulle airport, making a comic of it on location. Published in *Numer*.

Page 162: Commission work for the Norwegian edition of *Le Monde*.

Page 163: From a sketchbook. Unpublished.

Page 164: Made for Dongery's all Japanese fanzine that we brought to Tokyo Art Book Fair. I have no idea what that title says.

Page 165: If you haven't seen this music video, google "Darryl Pandy."

Page 166–167: Drew this in a hammock in the mountains. Later, colored in Photoshop, 2013.

Page 168: Another rainy day in New York. I drew this at a café in Manhattan.

Page 169: Drawn on a train.

Page 170: Wedding present for my cousin Daniel Herskedal and his lovely wife, Sigrun Ebbesvik.

Page 175: I drew this in my cabin while watching an old TV show about pillows. Jysk and Hansen & Dysvik are big pillow stores in Norway.

Page 176: This guy is loosely based on the Swedish botanist Carl Linnaeus.

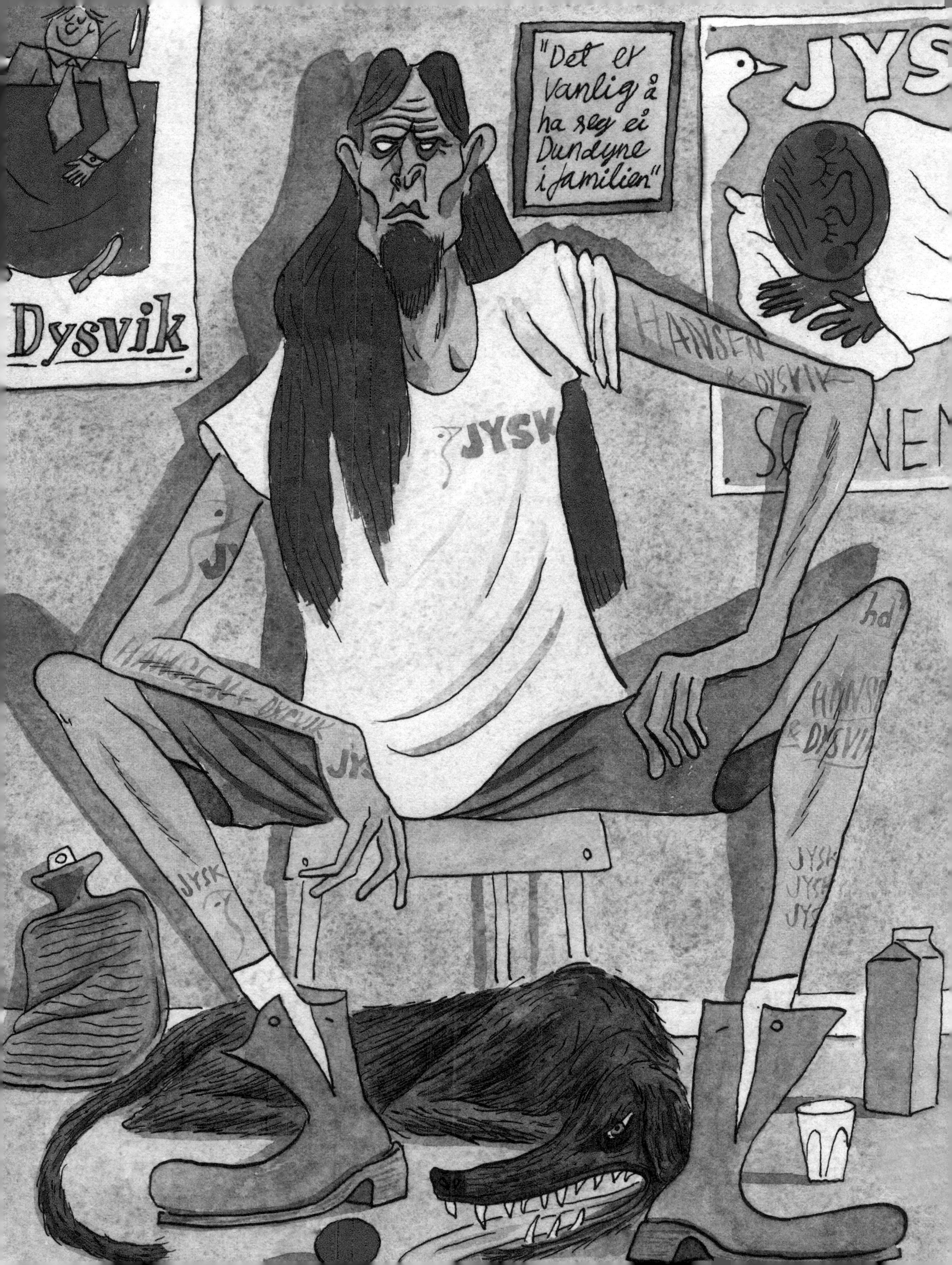
Dysvik
"Det er vanlig å ha seg ei Dundyne i familien"
JYS
SOVNEM
JYSK
HANSEN & DYSVIK
hd
JYSK
JYSK
JYSK

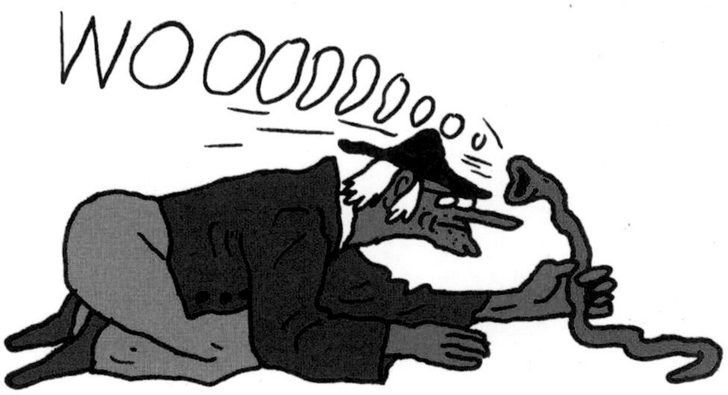
WOOOOOOOooo

« Howl Worm »

Discovered on a Saturday evening in my good friend John Fiddle's garden parcel. Lets out a long, shredded howl when provoked or interfered with.
About two feet long, pale yellow and robust skin. Has 2 small eyes. After the examination, John and yours truly tried to cook the worm, but it tasted of tar and was impossible to chew.
Nonetheless, a GREAT STUDY!

Hank Gorani